The Sages
Character, Context & Creativity
Volume I: The Second Temple Period

מגיד
MAGGID

Binyamin Lau

THE SAGES

CHARACTER, CONTEXT & CREATIVITY

VOLUME I: THE SECOND TEMPLE PERIOD

TRANSLATED BY

Michael Prawer

Maggid Books

The Sages: Character, Context & Creativity
Volume 1: The Second Temple Period

First Maggid English Edition, 2010
Second printing

Maggid Books
An imprint of Koren Publishers Jerusalem Ltd.

POB 8531, New Milford, CT 06676-8531, USA
POB 2455, London W1A 5WY, England
& POB 4044, Jerusalem 91040, Israel

www.korenpub.com

Published in cooperation with Beit Morasha

Cover artwork by Ora Ruven, oraruven@gmail.com

ISBN 978 159 264 245 8, *hardcover*

A CIP catalogue record for this title is available from the British Library

Typeset by Koren Publishing Services

The English translation of The Sages
was made possible by a generous grant from
the Jay and Hadasa Pomrenze Foundation

Contents

PART TWO:
THE PERIOD OF THE PAIRS – BETWEEN RELIGION AND THE STATE

PART THREE:
HILLEL AND SHAMMAI AND THEIR STUDENTS

PART FOUR:
WHEN DISPUTES PROLIFERATED IN ISRAEL

Author's Introduction

The synthesis of disparate worlds is the aspiration of many, the attempt of some, and the success of few. Since the dawn of the Oral Law, people have endeavored to imbibe the wisdom of the world in their Torah and in doing so broaden the scope of the teaching. In ancient times it was Hillel the Elder who surprised the Benei Beteira with innovative hermeneutical methods hitherto unaccepted in their study halls. In modern times, outstanding scholars such as Rabbi Dr. David Zevi Hoffmann and Rabbi Yeḥiel Yaakov Weinberg introduced academic research methods into the *beit midrash*.

These rabbis led the Orthodox world of Western Europe while blazing a trail that integrated Torah with academic learning, but they were also the exceptions. As a rule, rivalry prevails between the world of the yeshiva and the academic world. Even for the yeshiva world connected to modernity, the absorption of the academic world is not unequivocal. The exposure to the fruits of academia takes place at varying levels, oscillating between attraction and rejection. In recent years, we have seen the results of this oscillation: on one hand, there are more rabbis and yeshiva students interested in an academic education, for its own sake or otherwise, than ever before. On the other hand, suspicion of Jewish studies has increased and the yeshiva world frequently declares war on them. Their concerns are easily understood. The yeshiva world seeks to educate toward a life of belief without doubts, while the academic world educates toward skepticism and doubt. The yeshiva sees the entire corpus of the Oral Law as the complete and authentic crystallization of God's word as revealed by His sages, whereas the academic world deconstructs the word of God into particles of traditions, potentially positing a challenge to the sages' authority.

As a product of both worlds, I recognize the imperative of distinguishing between tools, frameworks, and content. The academic world should not presume to educate; its purpose is to equip its students with genuine and effective work tools. Philological methods should enable the student to encounter the sages' teachings in their purest, most refined form, which in turn confers great benefit on the *beit midrash*. Studying Talmudic sources with a critical apparatus has the potential to induce humility and consequently a more meticulous and cautious creativity, as well as greater attentiveness to God's word as transmitted through His sages. The results are reflected in the works of Torah scholars who have utilized all the research tools at their disposal to deepen and broaden their understanding of Torah and their awareness of its horizons. Their creations are likely to be more mature, more responsible, and hence of greater quality.

The question arises as to whether it is possible to introduce the fine tools of academia into the yeshiva world. According to Rabbi Avraham Yitzḥak Kook:

> We must establish a great yeshiva, in the center of the new *Yishuv*, that will benefit from all of the respectable sophistications of modern life, to the extent possible. The curriculum of such an institution should encompass the greater part of the Written and Oral Law in an organized fashion, and would also include the full scope of Jewish studies (*Ḥokhmat Yisrael/Wissenschaft des Judentums*) that has emerged in our generation.[1]

1. *Igrot HaRe'iya* 1 (Jerusalem: Mossad HaRav Kook, 1962), 118.

Rabbi Kook apparently aspired toward a fusion between the yeshiva and the academy in the fullest sense. Clearly, this represented a tremendous innovation when one considers what is accepted in the yeshiva world nearly a century later. The classical *shiur* in the yeshiva brings all generations together as partners in the creation of the Oral Law, as a Torah that has never and will never stop. Absorbing the academic approach into the yeshiva world's analytic approach would engender an awareness of the variety and differences between the many houses of study. It confers the ability to read a tannaitic dispute as it emerged from each house of study, without the mediation of the *amora'im* which is so important to us in halakhic and other contexts. It also enables us to reveal the roots of philosophical, ideological, and religious disputes among the Talmudic sages. Our assumption is that their disputes are not the product of formalistic problems of style and language, but rather that they have value-laden significance. They give expression to the foundations of Jewish philosophy and belief, social and family values, the tenets of nation building, and the laws for its administration.

In this book, I attempt to trace the development of Jewish thought as formulated by the sages of the Second Temple period. This necessitated a deep examination of the breadth of scholarly literature: philological, historical, Talmudic and philosophic. In the course of preparing the book, I became aware that the academic literature generally avoids any systematic study of the character of the sages:

> The problem of biography in Talmudic literature is one of the most complex problems that researchers have struggled with over the last generation. The unique character of this literature necessitates meticulous clarification of anything pertaining to the resolution of historical dilemmas in general, and the attempt to learn about the lives of specific people in particular. The reliability of the ascriptions and traditions, the identification of trends that characterize the writing and the editing of various sources, and the need to differentiate between earlier and later sources – these are just some of the problems encountered by writers of Talmudic biographies.[2]

2. Alon Goshen-Gottstein, "Rabbi Elazar ben Arakh: Symbol and Reality," [Hebrew]

In the yeshiva world, the tendency is to naively accept the testimonies appearing in Talmudic literature at face value. The best example of this trend is the important book of rabbinic biography by Rabbi Aharon Hyman, *Toldot Tanna'im VeAmora'im,*[3] which was open in front of me as I worked on this book. In his introduction, he surveys the biographies of the Jewish sages written until his time, analyzing them in the light of our basic historical knowledge. One of the interesting phenomena noted by Rabbi Hyman in his introduction, is the chasm between books that were the product of the old "traditional" *batei midrash* and those that originated in the *batei midrash* of *Wissenschaft des Judentums* (the movement of scientific or critical study of Jewish literature and history). In his view, the first group is plagued by gross errors both in questions of chronology and in biographical portraits, as the result of its intentionally non-critical approach. On the other hand, the second group is plagued by condescension regarding the sages under discussion. Rabbi Hyman felt that these scholars view the subjects of their research as equals, that "Rabbi Tzvi [Hirsch/Heinrich Graetz] in his generation, is as Rabbi Akiva in his generation." After compiling all that he was able from everything written about the Talmudic sages, he spent eight years delving into the depths of the Torah, his aim being to compose a work encompassing the entire history of the sages and their teachings as illuminated by the sources. His work is of immense importance and was invaluable to me in the course of my own research. There were numerous moments at which I sensed that the relationship between my work and his was like the relationship of the proverbial dwarf to the giant upon whose shoulders he stands. The century that has elapsed since Rabbi Hyman's day has seen the invention of computerized databases. With the assistance of the Bar Ilan Responsa Project, any student has

in Aharon Oppenheimer, Isaiah Gafni, Menaḥem Stern (eds.), *Jews and Judaism in the Second Temple, the Mishna and Talmud Period – Studies in Honor of Shmuel Safrai,* (Jerusalem: Yad Ben Zvi, 1993), p. 173.

3. Hereinafter: *History of the Tanna'im and Amora'im.* This book was first published pre–World War 1, in 1910–1911. It was written with the clear aim of endorsing the testimony of the Talmudic sages and rejecting the criticism of *Haskala* scholars (primarily its chief spokesmen in Germany). The Pri HaAretz Institute published a photocopied edition of the volume in Jerusalem, 1987.

easy and convenient access to the entire range of all the well-known and lesser-known sources. These databases give palpable expression to the well-known rabbinic saying, "An intelligent query is half the answer."

My purpose in this book is, however, different. My concern is not with rabbinic biography, but rather with their ideas against the background of their character and their historical context. The book is arranged in a chronological format: from the beginning of the Second Temple until its destruction.[4] I have arranged my treatment of the sages according to their eras and locales, and attempted to decipher their teachings and thought in the broader context of the spirit of their times, the historical events they lived through, and their overall character. My methodology was fixed: First, I gathered all of the available information from rabbinic literature regarding each particular sage. Second, with the sources at my disposal, I began to classify the sources according to their philological and literary quality, in accordance with the principles of Talmudic research. At the third stage, I analyzed the sources pertaining to each particular sage while examining the relevant historical research pertaining to the time and place of the personality under discussion. This process of going back and forth between the various sources yielded what should be viewed as neither historical nor Talmudic scholarship, but rather as lessons in Talmud with a historical background.[5]

In the process of my work, I endeavored to be guided by the teaching of Rabbi Elazar ben Azaria: "Make your ear like a hopper, and acquire a perceptive heart." The word *afarkeset* (= hopper) has its roots in Greek and connotes a funnel-shaped tool, one side narrow and one side broad. It serves for collecting grain prior to the sifting process. In this context, the funnel image evokes the notion of absorbing the multiplicity of audible voices, all of which are channeled into the funnel of the ear, into the receiver, from where they penetrate a person's consciousness. Rabbi Elazar instructs us to make our ear into a funnel; in

4. This is Volume I of the series. The second volume covers the period from Yavneh until after the Bar Kokhba rebellion, and the third will cover the period from the Hadrianic persecutions until the generation of the students of Rabbi Judah the Prince.
5. On the nature of this style of writing, see the Foreword by Professor Daniel Schwartz.

other words, to open ourselves up to expansive absorption of the many and varied voices coming from the world. The funnel neither selects nor censors; it absorbs all of the voices heard in the world of the sages. In the *beit midrash* there is no room for censorship. This is where a person becomes a receptacle for hearing the word of God. It is only then that the second stage arrives: "acquire a perceptive heart." The stages of classification, understanding, and internalization come after the absorption stage. Here too, man is charged with the responsibility of acquiring the heart, of being able to distinguish between the voices and to identify the voice that guides him to the path of God. Every voice has its place; a person must listen to them all. Any voice emanating from God's sanctuary is holy and has a place.

The examination of the teachings of the Second Temple sages is an attempt to listen to and contemplate world history and the teachings of the Jewish sages. I pray that as a result of this study we can draw closer to the world of the sages and, from our understanding of their world, gain a better understanding of our world and improve it for our own benefit and edification.

Binyamin Lau
Jerusalem, 2007

Foreword

The Book and Its Message

Jerusalem is graced with many talented orators and teachers of Torah. However, Rabbi Dr. Binyamin Lau, rabbi of the Ramban Synagogue in southern Jerusalem and director of the Beit Midrash at Beit Morasha, has established a unique and fascinating niche. This was attested to week after week by the hundreds of people who flocked to his synagogue every Shabbat afternoon in the spring and summer of 2004, to hear his lectures on the Ethics of the Fathers, *Pirkei Avot* – the lectures that constituted the basis for this book, first published in Hebrew in 2007.

Such eagerness to hear him is hardly surprising. It suffices to note the author's two titles, Rabbi and Doctor, the combination of which is hardly common in Israel today. Correspondingly, it is also clear, as emerges from a perusal of the present volume, that its author indeed presents a rare combination of interests and skills. If we ask whether the volume constitutes a work of history or, rather, a collection of sermons, the unequivocal answer is – both.

On one hand, the volume offers commentaries to the *mishnayot* of the first chapter of *Avot*. Writing a commentary on *mishnayot*, or sermonizing about them, is certainly a rabbi's forte. On the other hand, however, the tractate that was selected for this project is exceptional in comparison to the other tractates of the Mishna, just as the first chapter of *Avot* is exceptional in comparison with the others, insofar as its structure is clearly and avowedly historical. It opens with "Moses received the Torah at Sinai and transmitted it to Joshua, and Joshua to the Elders, etc.," and traces the transmission of the Torah chronologically over the entire Second Temple period, indicating how the sages of each generation added their own wisdom to the developing corpus before transmitting it to the next generation of disciples. A chapter of this kind demands historical treatment, and just as the ancient *tanna* who composed it was engaged in both Torah and history, so too the scholar expounding it in our time.

Rabbi Lau is certainly aware of the disparity between the two disciplines. Consider, for example, his treatment, in Part Five, of Rabban Shimon ben Gamliel's statement that "All my life I have grown up amongst sages and have found nothing better for a man's welfare than silence." Rabbi Lau interprets this as if it were an ironic observation by a person who lived at the time of the destruction of the Second Temple. According to this interpretation, Rabban Shimon is attacking the sages who remained silent, due to their dependence upon others or for other reasons, and who in doing so, allowed the Zealots and other evildoers to assume control of the entire people and drag them down into disaster. As Rabbi Lau shows, this commentary dovetails with the Talmudic critique (*Gittin* 55b–56a) of the sages who remained silent as their host (who was also their source of support!) humiliated Bar Kamtza and embarrassed him in public. The disastrous effects of silence are similarly evidenced in the story of Zekharia ben Avkulos (ibid.), who was, so the rabbis report, responsible for the conduct in the Temple. During the entire episode, Zekharia avoids making any kind of decision, and as a result, due to his "humility," he allowed a trivial embarrassment to escalate into a major crisis, war, and destruction of the Temple.

However, it is clear to all of us, Rabbi Lau included, that this interpretation of Rabban Shimon's statement is not what it means, in context, for it immediately continues with "Not study, but practice, is the most important thing." That clearly indicates that the first part of Rabban Shimon's words should be taken as *recommending* silence, not as condemning it; taken as a whole, his statement urges us to "speak little and do much" (as a nearby passage in *Avot* phrases it). Rabbi Lau recognizes this, and responds as follows:

> The sagacity of these words do credit to any sage, irrespective of his time and place, but I wish to add another explanation, echoing the voice (or the silence) of the period. We commented at length on the state of the society during the Temple's twilight days: the corruption of the priests, the Zealots' usurpation of the reins of power, and the debasement of the wealthy all demanded the clear voice of the Torah sages...The status quo in which the sages became part and parcel of the governing system, compelled them to remain silent, and thereby rendered them irrelevant.

Rabbi Lau's words are a commentary on an ancient text, but their target is contemporary, motivated by his concern for the ongoing relevance of the Torah and its spokesmen.

In the passage we discussed, Rabbi Lau directs his comments at his colleagues in the rabbinate, stridently protesting situations in which they become dependent upon various societal or political sources of power and therefore find themselves neutralized and muzzled. In other places, he addresses the community at large by invoking the *mishnayot* of *Avot*. Here too the simple meaning of the text is not necessarily his top priority. Rather, he expounds the text in order to make demands from his flock. Take, for example, his discussion of Rabban Gamliel's call for the exercise of authority, and its historical context in a world teetering on the brink of anarchy. Based on this perspective, he explained the three guidelines provided by Rabban Gamliel: (1) Acquire a teacher for yourself, (2) remove yourself from doubt, and (3) do not accustom yourself to tithing by estimate. Rabbi Lau explains that estimating of tithes was discouraged because almost invariably it leads to errors of excess leniency or excess stringency, both of which create halakhic quandaries. He concludes:

> Rabban Gamliel presented a solution to the problem of doubt... not by adopting the path of stringency, but rather by "acquiring a teacher for yourself."

Rabbi Lau is no doubt correct, but surprisingly one-sided, for as he himself explains, the mishna that criticizes "tithing by estimate" seeks to prevent unwarranted leniency no less than being overly strict. It seems, therefore, that if he selectively interpreted this mishna by stressing only its critique of stringency, we must again conclude that more than being a philologist or historian who deciphers the past, he is a rabbi who looks to the present and future of the path taken by his community. That is, his discussion of this mishna is a critique of the tendency to stringency that is so ubiquitous today as well as a declaration that regular consultation with rabbis, at least with the more courageous among them who are prepared to swim against the current, would mitigate the tendency toward stringency. This is not because, God forbid, they view the Torah and the halakha flippantly, but because they know that excess stringency, which blurs the boundaries between the sacred and the profane, may lead to pitfalls. Just as she who was convinced that she would die merely by touching the Tree of Knowledge (which was in fact not forbidden), ultimately not only touched it but also ate of its fruit (see Rashi on Genesis 3:3), so too, more generally, will one who prohibits the permitted end up by permitting the prohibited.

This does not mean that there are no grounds for innovation in the world of Torah. For example, when discussing Hillel and the enactment of *prozbul* (the mechanism for circumventing the annulment of debts in the *Shemitta* year, and thereby encouraging loans to the needy even immediately before the *Shemitta* year), Rabbi Lau offers an interesting formulation:

> Hillel, combining social sensitivity with his own doctrine, created a set of enactments that preserved the Torah's eternal relevance.

There is a paradox here: Hillel "created" and the result was that he succeeded in "preserving the Torah's eternal relevance." This is a paradox: How can an innovative creation preserve that which already exists? Spokesmen of various other camps would have avoided this kind of formulation, or perhaps even condemned it. Those of one camp would prefer to say that Hillel innovated and the Torah changed, while those of another camp would insist that all he did was define debts in a way that the Torah did not address, so that his enactment did not affect the Torah itself. Rabbi Lau, however, embraces the paradox:

> *Prozbul* was not Hillel's own invention, but was actually an application of an existing rule derived from biblical exegesis, whereby "He who transfers his bills to the *Beit Din*, [his debts] are not annulled" (*Shevi'it* 10:2). Hillel's "exploitation" of this halakha rescued the Torah. This is one of the greatest examples of the Torah's inherent capacity to address changing times and of the power of halakhic authorities to discover its hidden potential.

Similar to his comments on "Acquire a teacher for yourself," and on the sages who buried their heads in the sand on the eve of the Destruction, here too we see the assumption that rabbis have something to say, and that their role is to lead. Moreover, Rabbi Lau adds that they are *required* to innovate and that their innovative creations are nothing less than the realization of the potential embedded in the Torah.[6] This balance between innovation and tradition expresses a conceptual-ideological approach that is particularly appropriate for a book on the first chapter of *Avot*, which presents the Torah's chain of tradition. For were it the case, on the one hand, that all of those who transmitted the Torah gave their disciples only and precisely what they had received from their own masters, their actions would have been purely mechanical. On the other hand, if they were innovators and creators it would seem that there is no tradition to speak of. Rabbi Lau's formulation provides a solution to this dilemma: innovations and creations can be regarded as the realization of the Torah's inherent potential and the preservation of its eternal relevance.

Rabbi Lau addresses his community repeatedly throughout the book – just as he addresses his fellow rabbis. We have already noted his use of the admonition against mixing *ḥullin* (non-sacred foods) with tithes as a metaphor for the dangers of excessive stringency. A similar approach characterizes his perceptive discussion of the dispute between

6. As evidenced, for example, by the story of Moses who did not understand the meaning of the decorations on the letters of the Torah – from which Rabbi Akiva deduced "laws given to Moses at Sinai" (see *Menaḥot* 29b).

Beit Hillel and Beit Shammai over the correct posture for reciting the *Shema*: Beit Hillel maintains that a person should read the *Shema* "as it suits him," and not literally "when you lie down and when you stand up" as prescribed by Beit Shammai (*Berakhot* 1:3) – a position which is to be understood, in light of recent research concerning the formalistic customs related to the acclamation of kings in antiquity, as a demand for a formal ceremony. Rabbi Lau explains Beit Hillel's position as follows:

> God has no need for us to honor Him with extravagant ceremonies – rather, "when you sit down in your house and when you walk by the way." Reciting the *Shema* and accepting the yoke of heaven must be integrated into the daily routine, as a part of everyday life.

That is, Rabbi Lau calls upon his readers not only to avoid mixing *ḥullin* and tithes, and to respect rabbinic authority, but also to allow their acceptance of the yoke of heaven to infuse their daily routine, rather than limiting it to defined ceremonial moments. The difficulty involved in this balance is formidable – a glance at the various groups that make up Jewish society today shows that it is far easier to treat everything as holy, or everything as profane. The present volume, in contrast, is the work of a rabbi-educator who has not despaired of imparting complex and demanding messages.

At the same time, however, the book is also the work of a historian, and the importance and uniqueness of this fact should not be ignored. Generally speaking, the relationship between history and rabbinic literature, or for that matter, between rabbis and historians, has not been characterized by cooperation; at its best it is usually one of mutual disregard. Just as the Talmudic rabbis were likely to express their disdain for one who would waste their time with matters exclusively of historical significance, saying "whatever happened – happened" (and is therefore unworthy of further attention),[7] so too historians generally eschew any concern for

7. For example, see *Ketubot* 3a. See also M.D. Herr, "The Sages' Conception of History," in *Proceedings of the Sixth World Congress on Jewish Studies* III [Hebrew], (1975), pp. 129–142.

the normative significance of the matters they study. Moreover, in the particular case at hand, historians of the Second Temple era almost totally ignore rabbinic traditions about this period, presuming that collections such as the Mishna, compiled more than a century after the Destruction, cannot be relied upon to shed any real historical light on the era of the Temple. In fact, since the seminal work of Joseph Derenbourg, *Essai sur l'histoire et la géographie de la Palestine* (*An Essay on the History and Geography of Palestine*, 1867, also published in Hebrew in 1896/7), which strove to integrate rabbinic literature into the corpus of historical data concerning the Second Temple period,[8] there has been little real progress in this field. Most of what has been done relates to specific details, and no serious attempt has been made to enlist Talmudic literature to enrich our understanding of an extended period, nor to enlist knowledge from other sources on the period to enrich our understanding of rabbinic dicta about it. There are indeed good reasons for this situation, and caution is required, but even so, it is clear that rabbinic literature has preserved authentic memories from the Second Temple period,[9] and in certain cases the most obvious and reasonable course is indeed the one that allows rabbinic tradition to take its place alongside our other sources in our analysis and reconstruction of the earlier period.

In the present volume, Rabbi Lau traces the various periods within the Second Temple era, from the days of Ezra and Nehemiah, through the Hasmonean period and Herod, and terminating with the Destruction, locating rabbinic statements in their various contexts. In that sense, it is an effort to deal with this neglected sphere and renew the work in the historical realm. The footnotes of this volume attest to the author's extensive use of recent scholarly literature in his attempt to make his picture of the period, presented in this book, as well founded as possible.

In short, the author is a rabbi and spiritual leader who is also fully at home with the historian's craft[10] and in scholarship concerning early

8. Its subtitle: *d'après les Thalmuds et les autres sources rabbiniques* ("according to the Talmuds and the other rabbinic sources").
9. See, for example: Richard Kalmin, "Jewish Sources of the Second Temple Period in Rabbinic Compilations of Late Antiquity," in P. Schäfer (ed.), *The Talmud Yerushalmi and Graeco-Roman Culture*, vol. 3, (Tübingen: Paul Mohr Verlag, 2002), pp. 17–53.
10. See for example, his doctoral dissertation: "Restoring the Crown to its Former Glory:

Judaism – a combination that is as rare as it is welcome in our polarized world. His book is meant to enable us to fulfill an important component of the commandment to "remember the days of old, consider the years of generations past" (Deuteronomy 32:7), exposing his readers to a critical period in Jewish history, during which, for the last time until 1948, there was a Jewish state, but during which that state was lost and destroyed. He supplements his observations and analysis of the period with the reflections and guidelines of a wise, conscientious person, who, like other rabbis, bears heavy responsibility as we attempt to find our way in the restored Jewish state.

It is often said that "Zionism brought the Jews back into history." The truth is, however, that there are many good Jews who cleave to Judaism but have no interest in Zionism or in history, and many other good people whose world has a place for Zionism and history, but none for Judaism.[11] Occasionally it even seems that this polarity is natural and to be expected. But it is also quite perturbing. The message of this refreshing book is that Judaism and history do have important things to say to each other. This call, coming from the author's heart, may well resonate in the hearts of many readers – who will, accordingly, join me in applauding the initiative of publishing this book and, now, making it available to English readers as well, in the hope that they too, just as the crowds that filled our synagogue to hear these lectures, will enjoy the unique Torah that emerges from this book and succeed in confronting the challenges that it poses.

Daniel R. Schwartz
Professor of Jewish History, The Hebrew University of Jerusalem,
Gabbai at the Ramban Synagogue, Jerusalem
Jerusalem, 2007

Studies on Rabbi Ovadia Yosef's Halakhic Oeuvre" [Hebrew], (Bar Ilan University, 2002), published as *MiMaran ad Maran: Mishnato HaHilkhatit shel HaRabbi Ovadia Yosef* (Tel Aviv: Yedioth Ahranoth/Hemed, 2005).

11. See D. Schwartz, "From Alexandria to Rabbinic Literature to Zion: The Jews' Departure from History, and Who Is It Who Returns to It?" in S.N. Eisenstadt & M. Lissak (eds.), *Zionism and the Return to History: A Reappraisal* [Hebrew] (Jerusalem: Yad Ben Zvi, 1999), pp. 40–55.

Part One

From Prophecy to Halakha

The Men of the Great Assembly	The Pairs	Shammai, Hillel and Their Students	Rabban Gamliel the Elder	The Destruction

-450	-300	-200	-50	30	60	70

Cyrus to Alexander of Macedonia	The Hasmoneans	Herod	The Governors	The War with Rome

Preface

Standing at the foot of Mount Sinai ready to receive the Torah, the Jewish people experienced a moment of revelation beyond human comprehension, in which, as the Bible describes it: "They saw the voices." Awed by the harrowing intensity of the experience, the children of Israel pleaded with Moses:

> You speak to us, and we will obey; but let God not speak to us, lest we die ... So the people remained at a distance while Moses approached the thick cloud where God was. (Exodus 20:15, 17)

However we understand the experience of "seeing the voices," it is clear that the people found this moment of revelation terrifying and bewildering. Their response was to forgo the direct visual experience of the Divine, and even its direct voice. Rather, they entreated Moses to intercede: "You speak to us and we will obey." From this moment on, communication between God and the Jewish people would be mediated through the hearing ear. Moses would receive the Torah and transmit it to Joshua, who would pass it on – from one person to another – through an ongoing process of listening.

Alongside this transmission of the Torah by word of mouth, throughout the entire period of the First Temple, the prophets added their voices, sketching visions of God's will and His message. Though this message was not always heeded, the prophets were recognized by all to be the direct recipients of God's revelation.

During the period of the Second Temple, the era of prophecy came to an end and a new era, the era of the sages, began. It was in this period, when the voice of prophecy became silent, that it became crucial to attune one's ear carefully and to listen meticulously to the voices of wisdom that were connected to the voice of God. Undeniably, in the absence of prophetic vision, there arose a fear of inaccuracy, of confusion among a multiplicity of voices of unknown sources. Life lived in a fog of divergent and sometimes contradictory voices inevitably led to uncertainty and doubt.

The chapters which follow introduce us to this dynamic period. In particular, they chart the arrival of Ezra and the establishment of the Great Assembly, the era of the *Zugot* (pairs of sages) and their activities, the establishment of the Hasmonean State, and the age of Hillel and Shammai. All of these events took place in parallel with the ascent of Rome and the decline and ultimate elimination of Jewish political independence. As we follow these momentous historic events, we will trace the spiritual progression of the Jewish people through the lives and characters of its sages.

Chapter One

The Men of the Great Assembly

Moses received the Torah at Sinai and transmitted it to Joshua. Joshua transmitted it to the Elders, the Elders to the Prophets, and the Prophets transmitted it to the Men of the Great Assembly. They said three things: Be cautious in judgment, raise many students, and make a protective fence for the Torah. (Avot 1:1)

Tractate *Avot* introduces us to the world of the Oral Law. It begins with a description of the Torah's transmission: Sinai, Moses, the Great Assembly. There is much to be learned about the method of transmitting the Oral Law, but our focus is on the final stage, which is also the first stage of the world of the sages – the transition from the prophets to the members of the Great Assembly.

HISTORICAL AND POLITICAL BACKGROUND[1]

In 539 BCE, Cyrus, Emperor of Persia, conquered Babylonia: a conquest which began the Persian Age, ended the Jewish Exile, and initiated the period of *Shivat Tziyon* – the Return to Zion. Cyrus made a proclamation bringing seventy years of Jewish Exile to an end and heralding the beginning of the return to *Eretz Yisrael*, the land of Israel. The Persian policy of restoring peoples to their homelands was not directed exclusively at the Jews, but rather at all subjects of the Persian Empire, and was based on the principle of granting religious freedom and administrative autonomy to all subjects of the Empire. The restoration of the Jewish people to their homeland in Zion was financed by the treasury of the Persian State, which considered it important to settle its subjects at the western borders of the Persian Kingdom. The return to *Eretz Yisrael* occurred in several waves:

The first wave, shortly after Cyrus' proclamation, was accompanied by an abundance of frustrated hopes. This was the period of which Zechariah had prophesied, "Sing and rejoice, O daughter of Zion! For lo, I will come and dwell in your midst, says the Lord" (Zechariah 2:10). The words "I will come" are God's promise to return home with His people. If the people would only gather themselves and return to Zion, God would come back with them. It seems that, after years of crisis and the destruction of the Temple, there was a tremendous religious revival, accompanied by a great optimism. But great expectations led to great disappointment. The immigrants comprised a number of groups, including many of unclear family background. Another significant group was composed of Jews who had assimilated through intermarriage. In all, some tens of thousands moved back to *Eretz Yisrael* in this first wave, while the majority of Jews remained in Babylonia. A wonderful but tragic description of the consequences of this failed *aliya* is provided by Rabbi Yehuda HaLevi, in the *Kuzari*, responding to the Khazar king's query

1. Historians are divided regarding the historicity of the Men of the Great Assembly in Jewish History (see H.D. Mantel, *The Men of the Great Synagogue* [Tel Aviv: Devir, 1983], pt. 2, pp. 63–88). In the current framework however we will rely exclusively on the works of the rabbis, taken from all realms of the Torah.

regarding the phenomenon of Jews who, while praying for the return to Zion, actually fail to return there:

> It is the sin which prevented the divine promise with regard to the Second Temple: viz. "Sing and rejoice, O daughter of Zion" [Zechariah 2:10], from being fulfilled. Divine Providence was ready to restore everything as it had been at first, if they had all willingly consented to return. But only a part was ready to do so, whilst the majority and the aristocracy remained in Babylon, preferring dependence and slavery, and unwilling to leave their houses and their affairs. An allusion to them might be found in the enigmatic words of Solomon, "I was asleep, but my heart was wakeful" [Song of Songs 5:2–4]. He designates the exile as sleep, and the continuance of prophecy among them by the wakefulness of the heart. "Hark, my beloved knocks" [ibid.] means God's call to return; "My head is drenched with dew" [ibid.] alludes to the Divine Presence which emerged from the shadow of the Temple. The words: "I had taken off my robe" [ibid. 5:3] refer to the people's slothfulness in consenting to return. The sentence: "My beloved took his hand through the latch" [ibid. 5:4] may be interpreted as the urgent call of Ezra, Nehemiah, and the Prophets, until a portion of the people grudgingly responded to their invitation. (*Kuzari* II:24)

Led by Zerubbabel and Joshua the High Priest, these returnees to the land of Israel laid the foundations for the Temple but did not rebuild Jerusalem. For lack of sources, we have only vague knowledge of the sixty-year period between Cyrus' proclamation and the arrival of Ezra. The book of Ezra jumps from the days of the first returnees (Zerubbabel and Joshua) to the arrival of Ezra himself, in the mid-fifth century BCE. Ezra's governorship and that of Nehemiah which followed soon after, mark the beginning of what we know as the period of the "Men of the Great Assembly." The last of the prophets – Haggai, Zechariah and Malachi – all belong to this period of the Return to Zion. Ezra himself, though a member of a distinguished priestly family, is referred to as "scribe," a term whose meaning we shall consider below. This group of people came in the wake of the prophets, but lacked the force of prophetic revelation. In brief, the period of the Great Assembly can be viewed as extending from the days of Ezra to the time that the Greeks entered upon the stage of our history, around 400–350 BCE.

Among this entire group, the only sage known to us by name is Shimon HaTzaddik, Simeon the Just, the last surviving member of the Great Assembly. The group as a whole is anonymous, and we will have to explore its nature and its teachings without becoming familiar with individual personalities.

THE ABSENCE OF THE PRIESTS IN MISHNA AVOT

In the description of the chain of tradition which opens Mishna *Avot*, the absence of the priests is striking: "... from the Elders to the Prophets, and the Prophets transmitted it to the Men of the Great Assembly."[2] This absence cries out for an explanation, especially in light of the Bible's description of the tribe of Levi in general, and the priests in particular, as being responsible for receiving and transmitting the Torah. The verses on this point in Deuteronomy are explicit: "And Moses wrote this Teaching, and gave it to the priests, sons of Levi, who carried the Ark of the Lord's Covenant, and to all the elders of Israel" (31:9). The priests were chosen as the teachers of Torah, and it was for this reason that they were exempt from all the other burdens borne by the rest of the nation and did not inherit portions in the land itself. Throughout the biblical period, it was the priests who were charged with the transmission of the Torah and its instruction, as the Bible notes: "They shall teach Your laws to Jacob and Your instructions to Israel" (Deuteronomy 33:10).

The priests were evidently a disappointment in that they failed to transmit the Torah as expected of them. This expectation is reiterated on a number of occasions by the First Temple prophets. For example, the prophet Jeremiah presents the ideal division of leadership roles:

2. On the exclusion of the priests from the chain of transmission of the Torah, see article of M.D. Herr, "Continuity in the Chain of Transmission of Torah," *Zion* 44 (5739) pp. 43–56. He attempts to determine the editing date of these sources and to prove that the exclusion of the priests began toward the end of the Hasmonean era, but, as mentioned, my intention is to listen to the sources themselves and not to the dates of their redaction.

> For instruction shall not fail from the priest, nor counsel from the wise, nor the word from the prophet. (Jeremiah 18:18)

And likewise in the book of Ezekiel:

> And they shall seek a vision of the prophet in vain, instruction shall perish from the priest, and counsel from the elders. (Ezekiel 7:26)

At the time of the Return to Zion, the expectation remained that the priests would bear the mantle of instruction, but their failure apparently matched the level of expectation:

> For the lips of the priest shall guard knowledge, and men seek rulings from his mouth; for he is the messenger of the Lord of hosts. But you have turned away from that course: You have made the many stumble through your rulings; you have corrupted the covenant of Levites, said the Lord of hosts. (Malachi 2:7–8)

The books of Ezra and Nehemiah abound with criticism of a corrupt priesthood, which had intermarried with foreign women and was alienated from the people. Hence, the Mishna (*Avot*) chose to skip over the priests and to convey the torch of the Torah directly from the prophets to the sages of the Second Temple: Ezra, Nehemiah and the Men of the Great Assembly.

THE CHANGES INTRODUCED BY THE MEN OF THE GREAT ASSEMBLY

The dramatic transition from a world characterized by Divine Revelation to one governed by acquired knowledge, meant that the Men of the Great Assembly had to bring about far-reaching changes in the way the people interacted with the Torah. In particular, their twofold challenge was to change (1) the *context* of this interaction – bringing the Torah out of the Temple into the world of the people; and (2) the *nature* of this interaction – moving from a world of prophets and visions to one of tradition and learning.

We shall examine these changes as they found expression in the enactments of the sages of the period.

1. Bringing the Torah out of the Temple into the public realm

The greatest innovation of the leaders in this period was transferring the center of divine service from the Temple into the home and community. Ezra and Nehemiah generated a religious reform that emphasized reaching out to broad sectors of the people and calling for their active participation in all aspects of religious life. The tenth chapter of the book of Nehemiah describes the making of a covenant between Nehemiah, the leader, and all the residents of the land. Looking at the names of the signatories, we can see that all sectors of society were involved. This covenant represented a direct continuation of the approach of the prophets. Every prophet, from first to last, warned against ritual practice disconnected from a focus on the relationship between man and God: "Surely obedience is better than sacrifice" (1 Samuel 15:22); "What need have I of the multitude of your sacrifices" (Isaiah 1:11); and, the most sublime hope, that "the land shall be filled with the knowledge of the Lord, as waters cover the sea" (Isaiah 11:9). In the spirit of these teachings, the first action of the Men of the Great Assembly was to bring the Torah into the public realm, bequeathing it to the entire nation without making any distinction based on tribe or status.

The enactment of prayers and blessings

The renewal of life in the land of Israel spurred the leadership to actualize the teachings of the prophets as part of the religious reform. This required the enactment of edicts, decrees, and customs. The most well-known of these dealt with the institutionalization of religious life:

> The Men of the Great Assembly enacted blessings and prayers, sanctifications and *Havdalot*, for Israel. (*Berakhot* 33a)

This sentence from the Talmud embodies a wealth of material concerning the activities of the Men of the Great Assembly. The single phrase "blessings and prayers" encompasses almost the entirety of our religious world. Can a person be religious without reciting blessings and prayers?

Our daily routine is almost inconceivable in their absence, since one's entire daily connection to God is summed up in these two words, "blessings" and "prayers." Without a blessing or a prayer we have no stable meeting point with God, and are left only with spontaneous overtures at times of grace, of joy or, heaven forbid, of crisis. The Men of the Great Assembly understood that the life of simple people far from the Temple – a rural farmer perhaps – had no spiritual dimension or possibility of touching the holy. They saw that only by formalizing the relationship between the individual and his Creator would all people have access to their inner spiritual lives. Prayer and blessings introduced a framework of basic religious consciousness into the religious world of the layman. This was a revolution that called upon every Jew to participate actively in the service of God, rather than simply to rely on the knowledge that sacrifices were being offered in the Temple on his behalf.

The enactment of reading the Torah

The Talmud recounts that ten enactments were introduced by Ezra the Scribe:

> Ezra enacted ten enactments: That the Torah be read [publicly] in the Afternoon Service on the Sabbath; that the law be read [publicly] on Mondays and Thursdays... (*Bava Kamma* 82b)

Ezra's first enactment was the public reading of the Torah. Astonishingly, throughout almost the entire period of the First Temple there was hardly any study of Torah even at the most basic level. There are many who love to romanticize this era, claiming that during the First Temple period all the people were suffused with Torah. A frequently quoted passage of this kind appears in Tractate *Sanhedrin*, praising the generation of Hezekiah:

> The yoke of Sennacherib shall be destroyed on account of the oil of Hezekiah, which burned in the synagogues and houses of study. What did he do? He planted a sword by the door of the house of study and proclaimed, "Whoever does not study the Torah will be pierced with the sword." They searched from Dan until Beer Sheba, and no ignoramus was found; from Gabbath unto

> Antipatris, nor did they find a single boy or girl, man or woman, who was not thoroughly familiar with the laws of purity and impurity. (*Sanhedrin* 94b)[3]

Yet, notwithstanding the greatness of Hezekiah's generation, this was the exception among all the generations of the First Temple. A more typical situation is described by Ezra, Jeremiah and the other prophets, in which the people were estranged from the Torah.[4] Conceivably, this alienation may have had its source in the priests' distinct status and their guarding of the Torah in inner sanctums, remote from the nation. However, this was not born of malevolence. Rather it was the result of an overzealous sense of their responsibility for preserving the Torah and ensuring its transmission, intact and complete, to the coming generations. This protectiveness led the priests to conceal the Torah from the masses, just as one hides a valuable vessel. But as the priests guarded the secrets of Torah, they slowly and unintentionally caused the nation's spirit to wither, severed from its life source. Ezra came to redress this

3. This passage is usually cited when depicting the decline of the generations. See, for example, the letter of rebuke written by the Ḥatam Sofer to the Trieste community in Italy, addressing the issue of small children baking *matzot* (*Responsa Ḥatam Sofer*, ch. 5, "Omissions," 196): "It appears that the source of this stumbling block is in the decline of the generations. In the days of our ancestors, the youth were proficient in the halakha, as our sages said, 'In the days of Hezekiah the King of Judah they searched from Dan until Beer Sheba and even the children were thoroughly familiar with the laws of impurity and purity.' Such was the situation in days of old, when the young boys were learned in Torah and were God-fearing, and so the judges and scholars were also prepared to rely on them. However, since then, due to our copious sins the generation is no longer qualified, and the Torah has been forgotten by the laymen and neither are they God-fearing, and so take courage and be strengthened you nobles of Israel and continue to do as we are doing here today…"
4. According to Talmudic tradition it was Moses who enacted the custom of reading the Torah on the Sabbaths and Festivals (see Tractate *Soferim*, ch. 10), but it is doubtful whether this enactment endured during the First Temple period, bearing in mind the total surprise at the discovery of the Torah in the days of King Josiah. While the forgetting of Torah can be ascribed to the period of Josiah's grandfather, Menasseh (whose reign the sages describe as so wicked that it engendered the hiding of the Torah by the righteous priests), our concern is still with the common people and not its leadership, and evidently the people had no knowledge of the Torah.

situation. The Talmud teaches that Ezra's enactments were inspired by the biblical verse describing the Israelites walking in the desert for three days until they found water to quench their thirst. By comparing the Torah to water ("there is no water other than Torah"), Ezra ensured that three days would never pass without the reading of Torah: Monday, Thursday and Shabbat.

Changing the script of the Torah

The Talmud also states that Ezra was not satisfied with establishing a framework for the reading of the Torah, but even changed its script.[5]

> Originally, the Torah was given to Israel in Hebrew characters and in the sacred [Hebrew] language; in the time of Ezra, the Torah was given again in Assyrian script and the Aramaic language. Finally, they chose the Assyrian characters and Hebrew language for Israel, leaving the Hebrew characters and Aramaic language for the *hedyotot* [usually: "laymen"].
>
> To whom does *hedyotot* refer? Rabbi Ḥisda said: The Cutheans.
>
> And what is meant by Hebrew characters? Rabbi Ḥisda said: The *libuna'ah* [i.e., ancient Hebrew] script.
>
> It was taught: Rabbi Yose said: Had Moses not preceded him, Ezra would have merited receiving the Torah for Israel. Of Moses it is written, "And Moses went up to God" [Exodus 19:3], and of Ezra it is written, "He, Ezra, went up from Babylon" [Ezra 7:5]. Just as the going up of the former refers to the [receiving of the] Law, so too the going up of the latter. Of Moses it says: "And at that time the Lord commanded me to teach you statutes and laws" [Deuteronomy 4:14]; and of Ezra it says: "For Ezra prepared his heart to expound the law of the Lord [his God] to do it and to teach Israel statutes and laws" [Ezra 7:10]. Even though the

5. The subject of the script in which the Torah was given and its transformation during time of Ezra, raises profound questions that have engaged Jewish scholars from the tannaitic period and throughout the generations. See a partial summary of the topic in Rabbi Kasher, *Torah Shelema, Yitro* (Supplements, letter *yod*).

> Torah was not given through him, its script was changed through him. (*Sanhedrin* 21b)

This homily links the character of Ezra to that of Moses. While Moses was chosen to give the Torah to Israel, it was Ezra who merited the renewal of its script and, by extension, the creation of a framework linking the Torah to the people. The Babylonian exile had not only severed the Jewish people from its land, but from its language as well. Seventy years of exile sufficed to replace the Hebrew vernacular with Aramaic. Over the vast expanses of the Persian Empire, Aramaic was the "official state language"; indeed we have found letters and bills written entirely in Aramaic. The book of Ezra describes how Ezra, meeting with the returnees in Jerusalem, discovered that the Hebrew Torah was incomprehensible for many of them:

> Ezra the priest brought the Torah before the congregation consisting of men and women, and all those old enough to understand, on the first day of the seventh month. And he read from it, facing the square...to the men and the women and those who could understand; the ears of all the people were given to the scroll of the Torah.... And they read from the scroll, in the Torah of God, translating it and giving the sense, so that they understood the reading. (Nehemiah 8:2–8)

Without Ezra's mediation ("translating it and giving the sense"), there was no chance of understanding the text.

The ancient Hebrew script of the monarchical period was that used by the educated classes, the Torah's professional spokesmen. We see a similar phenomenon today in the professional writing of various disciplines, such as law, medicine, and science, which leave laymen totally dependent upon the mediation of the professionals. Evidently, the Torah was preserved by the priests in its ancient language, and none of the laymen (*amei ha'aretz*) had any possibility of understanding or reading it. The educated strata were loath to have the masses of ordinary folk participate in their lofty deliberations. Concealment served the interest of guarding a body of knowledge that was regarded as infinitely precious.

This code was violated by Ezra, a member of the professional guild of the priests. Ezra thus rendered the Torah comprehensible and accessible to the masses. Now that the script had been changed, Ezra could demand that the people begin to avail themselves of this user-friendly Torah, which had until then been a closed book.

Ensuring payment for the scribes

The Talmud, in Tractate *Pesaḥim,* describes a number of fasts that were observed by the Men of the Great Assembly:

> Rabbi Yehoshua ben Levi said: The Men of the Great Assembly observed twenty-four fasts so that those who write [Torah] scrolls, *tefillin,* and *mezuzot* would not become wealthy, for if they became wealthy they would not write. (*Pesaḥim* 50b)

Unless we recalled the prior enactments of the Men of the Great Assembly, this passage makes no sense. Why was it specifically the Men of the Great Assembly who had to fast and to ensure the livelihood of the scribes? Evidently, introducing the Torah to the entire people through public readings, and writing it in comprehensible Assyrian script, resulted in an increased demand for the scrolls, and naturally prices rose. The Men of the Great Assembly wanted Torah scrolls to be in every household, and it was for this reason that they prayed for the scribes not to become too rich, to make sure they would continue their work.

Restoring Torah observance

Alongside renewing the study of the Torah by all sectors of the nation, the Men of the Great Assembly attempted to restore the former stature of the observance of the Torah. The spiritual condition of the returnees to Zion was abysmal. Assimilation, estrangement from the Torah, and the banality of everyday existence all combined to create an alienated Jewish society with an amorphous religious identity. At this point the Men of the Great Assembly acted to "make a protective fence around the Torah." The need to introduce edicts so as to prevent people from sinning resulted from the loss of standing of the halakha among the people. The clearest example of this is the decree of the Men of the Great Assembly regarding the laws of *muktzeh*:

> Our rabbis taught: At first they [the sages] ruled that three utensils may be handled on the Sabbath: a fig-cake knife, a soup-pot ladle and a small table-knife. Then they permitted [other articles], and they permitted again [still more], and they permitted yet further, until they ruled: All utensils may be handled on the Sabbath except a large saw and the pin of a plough [...] Rabbi Ḥanina said: This mishna was taught in the days of Nehemiah son of Ḥakhalia, as is written [Nehemiah 13:15], "In those days I saw in Judah some treading winepresses on the Sabbath, and bringing in sheaves." (*Shabbat* 123b)

The oral tradition recorded in this *baraita* describes the development of the laws of *muktzeh*. According to this tradition, Nehemiah witnessed wholesale desecration of Shabbat in Jerusalem, as evidenced by people treading winepresses and gathering sheaves. Shabbat had become totally profane, its observance at an all-time low. Not only was it not observed, its very existence had been forgotten. Perhaps it was the returnees' struggle for survival that had thrown them into such an intense whirlwind of work – seven days a week, three hundred and sixty-five days a year – but this was the sad situation in Jerusalem in the days of the Great Assembly. The people's alienation from Torah was so deep that it could not be remedied simply by the cosmetic fix of instituting public readings of the Torah. A major upheaval was needed to bring the people back to its roots.

Nehemiah was no democrat and made no pretension of consulting with others. To make the Shabbat part of the world and the mentality of the Jews once again, he decided to introduce a dramatic change. The Shabbat was desecrated primarily by the wine-treaders and wine merchants; in other words, in the context of trade and employment. Accordingly, Nehemiah prohibited the use of all tools on Shabbat, only permitting the three tools that were used by the people for their Shabbat meals. Over the years, as general awareness of Shabbat observance increased, it became possible to become gradually more lenient, so "they permitted again [still more]," until they arrived at the Mishnaic formulation: "All utensils may be handled on the Sabbath except a large saw and the pin of a plough" – classic utensils for performing professional work on Shabbat. This was part of the concept, "place a protective fence around the Torah."[6]

2. From the world of the prophets to the world of the sages: From prophetic vision to auditory transmission

As the Men of the Great Assembly were instituting these changes, they also had to confront a major shift in the manner in which the Torah was transmitted. It was toward the end of their era, during the days of Shimon HaTzaddik, or Simeon the Just (discussed in detail in the following chapter), that the phenomenon of prophecy disappeared, to be replaced by the transmission of wisdom and knowledge.

Prophecy had instilled tremendous religious trust among the people, so much so that its disappearance created a crisis that almost defies description. When the prophet "who beheld the likeness of God" (Numbers 12:8) stood by the leaders who bestowed the Torah, everyone knew that God's word was present in the world, even if in practice they did not listen to it. But the Second Temple period heralded a new era.

The Tosefta records a tradition that "Upon the death of the last prophets, Haggai, Zechariah and Malachi, the Holy Spirit [i.e., prophetic inspiration] departed from Israel" (*Sota* 13:3). These three were the last link in the chain of prophets who transmitted the Torah to the Men of the Great Assembly. This occurred at the dawn of the return from Babylonia, the beginning of the rebuilding of the Second Temple, and the Jewish people's renewed attempt to consolidate itself in the land. The cessation of prophecy actually facilitated the growth of the Oral Law during the Second Temple, a process for which the scribes were responsible. The scribes were called *sofrim* (the Hebrew root *s-f-r* means "to count") because they counted the letters of the Torah, and by dint of their learning succeeded in arriving at the required halakhic conclusion. This group, apparently led by Ezra, is generally regarded as consisting of scholars who sat in the study houses, where they engaged in the transcribing of the

6. See Y.Z. Gilat, "*Isurei Shevut Aḥadim*," *Meḥakrei Talmud*, 2 (5753), pp. 197–219.

holy Scriptures and the teaching of halakha based on the Written Torah.[7] We do not have an exact date for the beginning of the Oral Law, nor for the work of the scribes; it seems that the beginning of this period must be placed somewhere between the time of Ezra and Nehemiah (about 450 BCE) and the ascent of Alexander of Macedonia (333 BCE). It was this stretch of one hundred and twenty years that saw the development of the learning format of the sages-scribes, who replaced the prophets. This is the dating which is clearly described in *Seder Olam Raba*:

> "And the rough he-goat is the king of Greece [...] he is the first king" [Daniel 8:21]. "And a mighty king shall stand up [...] And when he shall stand up his kingdom shall be broken" (Daniel 11:3–4). This is Alexander of Macedonia, who reigned for twelve years. Until then the prophets prophesied with the divine spirit; from this time onward "incline your ear and hear the words of the wise" [Proverbs 22:17]. (*Seder Olam Raba* 30)

The disappearance of prophecy during the Second Temple is similarly attested to by Rabbi Aḥa in the Jerusalem Talmud:

> In the name of Rabbi Aḥa: Five things existed in the First Temple, but were missing from the Second Temple: Divine Fire, the Holy Ark, the Urim and Thummim, the anointing oil and the Holy Spirit [of prophetic inspiration]. (Talmud Yerushalmi, *Ta'anit* 2:10 [5a])

The same tradition is repeated in the Babylonian Talmud:

> Our rabbis taught: Since the death of the last prophets, Haggai, Zechariah and Malachi, the Holy Spirit has departed from Israel. (*Sanhedrin* 11a)

The tension between the clear vision of the world of prophecy and the

7. E.E. Urbach, *The Halakha – Its Sources and Its Development* (Ramat Gan: 1984), pp. 71–72.

understanding of the world of wisdom generated a wealth of dicta, generally extolling the superiority of wisdom. For example:

> The words of scribes are more beloved than the words of Torah... to what can they be compared? To a king who sent two emissaries to a certain province. Concerning one of them he wrote, "If he does not show you my seal and signet, do not believe him." But concerning the other he wrote, "Even though he does not show you my seal and signet, believe him." Thus, in the case of a prophet it is written, "and he gives you a sign or wonder" (Deuteronomy 13:1), but here [regarding a scribe] it says, "according to the instructions they give you." (Talmud Yerushalmi, *Avoda Zara* 2:4[41c])

In his introduction to the Mishna, Maimonides recognizes that prophecy may reflect a higher spiritual level than wisdom, but insists that wisdom takes precedence:[8]

> And you should know that prophecy has no advantage over explanation of the Torah and the derivation of its laws on the basis of the thirteen hermeneutical principles, for the inferences and logical deductions derived by Joshua and Pinehas are of the same standing as those of Rabina and Rabbi Ashi.

This leads us from the prophetic era to the era of wisdom, with its advantages and disadvantages.

SUMMARY OF THE LEGACY OF THE MEN OF THE GREAT ASSEMBLY

We have seen how the Men of the Great Assembly, feeling a responsibility to transmit the Torah to all walks of society, worked to ensure that the renewed Jewish state would be grounded on the foundations of Torah and that its people would reestablish their connection with God. On the

8. See the words of Rabbi Kook in his article, "The Sage Is More Important than the Prophet" [Hebrew], *Zera'im, Orot* (Jerusalem: 1963).

one hand, they actively established themselves as the connecting force that linked the Jewish people to the Torah by the process of translating and mediating the Torah. On the other hand, they ensured that the life cycle of every Jew would involve the service of God and study of Torah, "so that it not be forgotten from the mouths of their seed." This is the meaning of the teaching of the Men of the Great Assembly as taught to us by the following mishna in *Avot*:

> Be prudent in judgment, raise up many students, and make a fence for the Torah. (*Avot* 1:1)

This mishna provides a succinct description of their activity. They understood that prudence in law, sensitive and cautious adjudication, is the key to connecting with all levels of the people. They understood that the Torah could only thrive among the people and be experienced in a heartfelt way if it was present everywhere, through the spread of its students. They also understood the need for legislation and protective measures in those fields which were characterized by defiance and forgetfulness.

THE MEN OF THE GREAT ASSEMBLY – THE MEANING OF THE NAME

What is the meaning of the unique name conferred upon this new and revitalizing group that paved the way to the world of the Oral Law: namely, "The Men of the Great Assembly"? The Talmud provides the following answer:

> Rabbi Simon said in the name of Rabbi Yehoshua ben Levi: Why were they called the Men of the Great Assembly? Because they restored the "crown" to its former status. Rabbi Pineḥas said: Moses fixed the formula of benediction: "The great, the mighty, and the awesome God" [Deuteronomy 10:17].
>
> Jeremiah said [Jeremiah 32:18], "the great and the mighty God," but he omitted "the awesome." Why did he say "the mighty"? He may properly be called "mighty," for He witnesses the destruction and is silent. And why did he not say "the awe-

some"? Awesome only applies regarding the Temple, as it is said, "You are awesome, O God, in Your holy place" [Psalms 68:36].

Daniel said [Daniel 9:4], "The great and the awesome God," but did not say "the mighty." His sons are put in neck irons, where then is His might? Why then did he say "the awesome"? He may well be called awesome, for the wonders He did for us in the fiery oven.

But when the Men of the Great Assembly came, they restored the crown to its former place: "The great, the mighty and the awesome God." Does flesh and blood have power to set limits in these matters? Rabbi Yitzḥak ben Elazar said, "The prophets know that their God is Truth and they will not fawn before Him." (Talmud Yerushalmi, *Berakhot* 7:3 [11c])

The Talmud contrasts the prayer of the Men of the Great Assembly with the prayers of great figures from previous generations: Moses, Jeremiah and Daniel. Moses established the formula for describing God's virtues: "great, mighty, and awesome." The prophets, who saw God through His actions, praised Him according to His works. For Jeremiah, God's might is seen when He remains silent as He watches His House burning, but when His Temple is no longer, He is awesome no more; the fear of God exists only in the context of His Sanctuary: "You shall be in awe of My Sanctuary" (Leviticus 19:30). This indeed is the basis of Jeremiah's devastating challenge to Heaven: without the Sanctuary, there can be no fear of God in our religious life. God's presence in the world finds expression only in the holy place. According to Daniel, by contrast, it is God's acts which attest to His awesomeness, such as the fearsome deeds He performed in the fiery furnace. For Daniel, the powerful experience of entering the jaws of death and emerging alive opened his eyes to the awesomeness of God, though not His greatness. For when the King's sons are led in shackles as humiliated prisoners, the King Himself is humiliated. Accordingly, Daniel omitted the adjective "mighty" when addressing God.

According to the Talmudic passage, the prophets recognize God's reality. They do not seek to flatter Him, but rather they tell Him what they think. But ours is the world of the Men of the Great Assembly, a world in which there is no longer any prophecy. We have made the transition from the world of vision to the world of hearing and listening to God's voice. At times He displays His greatness, at others His might, and on still other occasions – His awesomeness. Sometimes we see all them all and sometimes we see none of them.

In a lecture on prayer, Elie Wiesel argued that the existing prayers appear to us as either incongruous or irrelevant. "How can a person praise and extol divine justice and divine mercy in the generation of Majdanek and Treblinka? 'Great love' and Auschwitz? 'Great and exceeding compassion' and Belsen? How can a person utter these words without turning them into lies and a desecration of God?!"[9]

This was the great innovation of the Men of the Great Assembly. They, like us, were not prophets. We too are not privy to visions. Rather, we hear and we listen. Our responsibility for the transmission and bequeathal of the Torah to the next generations requires us to pray, to communicate with God, and not to allow the Temple service to be the focus of religious ritual. This was the starting point of the activity of the Great Assembly. A man's prayer is not the result of his understanding or knowledge of the ways of God, for he knows that he does not know. When we stand in prayer on Holocaust Remembrance Day, uttering the words "the great, the mighty and the awesome," as we are instructed to do by the Men of the Great Assembly, we are not lying, neither are we praising God in vain. Rather, we are approaching God with a demand, as if to say: We received the Torah from Moses, who received it at Sinai. It was he who taught us that You are a great and mighty and awesome God. Now we turn to You, with a prayer that You reveal Yourself to us in all of Your attributes, in all of Your greatness and glory. There are times when this prayer can only be said with gritted teeth, but still it must be said, because it links us to the prayers of all those generations who preserved the tradition of the Torah in its transmission from Sinai, to Moses, and on to themselves, through the Men of the Great Assembly.

9. E. Wiesel, "Prayer and Contemporary Man" [Hebrew], in G. Cohen (ed.), *Jewish Prayer: Continuity and Innovation* (Ramat Gan: 1978), pp. 13–26.

Chapter Two

Simeon the Just – "Great Among His Brothers and the Glory of His People"

Simeon the Just was one of the last survivors of the Great Assembly. He would say: The world is sustained by three things: The Torah, the [Temple] service and deeds of loving-kindness. (Avot 1:2)

HISTORICAL AND POLITICAL BACKGROUND

In the previous chapter we looked at the era and the activity of the Men of the Great Assembly (circa 450–300 BCE). In terms of dates, the only thing we know about Simeon the Just, the first sage mentioned in Mishna *Avot,* is that he lived at the end of the period of the Men of the Great Assembly.

The end of the fourth century BCE saw the ascent of Hellenism. The eastern conquests of Alexander of Macedonia had brought about the collapse of the Persian Empire. Alexander then united the Persian, Macedonian, and Greek kingdoms, heralding an entirely new era in the region. The change found expression in all realms: in the structure of government, and in religious and cultural influences. But the unified empire would not survive long and it soon splintered into a number of separate kingdoms. Syria and the surrounding areas came to be dominated by the Seleucids, who are credited with one of the most interesting innovations of this period: the calendar based on *shetarot*, bills of indebtedness, according to which the first year of the calendar was the first year of Seleucid rule: 312 BCE. This innovation is reflected in the Talmud:

> Rabbi Naḥman said: In the Diaspora we only count according to the Greek kings. (*Avoda Zara* 10a) [1]

During this period, *Eretz Yisrael* was part of the empire and was not considered an independent state. Throughout the period, the land was the subject of competing claims to sovereignty between the regional powers. Indeed the wars between the Ptolemaic and Seleucid dynasties centered on control over the land of Israel, which served as a buffer between the two kingdoms. But at any given moment the land was part of one of these kingdoms, and its administration, its currency, its language and its culture developed in accordance with the surrounding host culture. In the urban centers the Hellenistic influence was seen in the *polis*, which was accepted throughout the cities of the kingdom. The Jewish upper classes assimilated into the society of the ruling Hellenist settlers, and so a new class of Jewish Hellenists developed, trying to imitate all aspects of their Hellenist rulers' lifestyle. It was during this period that the Greek language took hold in the educational and cultural institutions, accompanied by a great awakening in literature, poetry, philosophy and research. Simeon the Just is the representative of this period in Tractate *Avot*.

1. The Babylonian Jews continued dating according to the calendar of *shetarot* for the duration of the Geonic period and even for a certain period thereafter. The *Letter of Sherira Gaon* is dated according to the calendar of *shetarot*, and many notes were found in the Cairo Geniza attesting to the same dating. Maimonides too used this system of dating, along with that based upon the Creation.

THE CONNECTION BETWEEN THE RISE OF ALEXANDER OF MACEDONIA AND THE DISAPPEARANCE OF PROPHECY

We have already seen in the previous chapter the connection between the disappearance of prophecy and Alexander's rise to power:

> "And the rough he-goat is the king of Greece [...] he is the first king" [Daniel 8:21]. "And a mighty king shall stand up [...] And when he shall stand up his kingdom shall be broken" (Daniel 11:3–4). This is Alexander of Macedonia, who reigned for twelve years. Until then the prophets prophesied with the divine spirit; from this time onward "incline your ear and hear the words of the wise" [Proverbs 22:17]. (*Seder Olam Raba* 30)

This tradition links the entrance of Greek culture into the region at the end of the fourth century BCE, with the disappearance of the Holy Spirit and the new emphasis on studying the Torah by listening to the sages. The rule of Alexander of Macedonia and his successors was of no longer duration than that of the Persians who preceded them or of the Roman Empire that followed them, but its influence on the area was profound. Greek language penetrated society at all levels and, above all, Greek wisdom – science, philosophy, poetry and art – left a permanent imprint on life in *Eretz Yisrael.* Jewish society, and especially its upper strata, would never be the same again.

THE CHARACTER OF SIMEON THE JUST

The most prominent figure of this period was Simeon the Just, who was, our Mishna tells us, "one of the last survivors of the Great Assembly." His personality still straddles the world of the priesthood and the world of the political and spiritual leadership which replaced it. After Simeon the Just, this connection was severed and a chasm emerged between the Temple and the world of the sages. But during this period – the end of the Persian era and the beginning of the Greek period – the High Priest still enjoyed the status of head of the Jewish community.[2] In all the

2. D. Schwartz, "Priesthood and Monarchy during the Hasmonean Period" [Hebrew], in Y. Gafni (ed.), *Kahal Yisrael*, vol. 1 (Jerusalem: 2002), pp. 13–26.

sources, Simeon the Just appears as such a leader, in charge of all aspects of the Jewish community, both religious and political. His character is engraved upon the national memory and was anchored in the pantheon of the Jewish people, meriting the following description in the Talmud:

> "I have not rejected them" – in the days of the Chaldeans, when I raised up for them Daniel, Ḥanania, Mishael and Azaria; "neither did I abhor them" – in the days of the Greeks when I raised up for them Simeon the Just and the Hasmonean and his sons and Mattathias, the High Priest.... (*Megilla* 11a)

Simeon will forever be remembered as the "last of the Mohicans," as one who terminated an age. In the Book of Ben Sira (second century BCE) he is described thus:

> The leader of his brothers and the pride of his people was the high priest Simeon son of Yoḥanan the Priest, who in his life repaired the house and in his time fortified the Temple. (*Ben Sira* 50:1–4)

A closer understanding of his midrashic and historical character will shed light on this period, in which the mantle of leadership moved from the world of the end of prophecy to the world of the beginning of wisdom.

SIMEON THE JUST MEETS ALEXANDER OF MACEDONIA

An interesting tradition that has survived through a number of channels reconstructs an encounter between Alexander of Macedonia and Simeon the Just. This tradition appears in *Megillat Ta'anit* (Scroll of Fast Days)[3] in relation to the 25th of Tevet, a minor holiday known as "the

3. *Megillat Ta'anit*: a short treatise in Aramaic composed toward the end of the Second Temple period. It enumerates about thirty-five days on which joyous events happened to the Jewish people, as a result of which fasting therein is proscribed, and in some cases it is even forbidden to eulogize the dead. The joyous events dealt with in the scroll are spread over period of about five hundred years – from the time of Ezra and Nehemiah in the fifth century BCE, until the annulment of Caligula's edicts, around the Destruction of the Second Temple. The prohibitions against fasting found in *Megillat Ta'anit* were practiced until the end of the tannaitic period; their

Day of Mount Gerizim." Tannaitic tradition describes the background of that day's events:

> The twenty-fifth [day of Tevet] is the day of Mount Gerizim, on which no mourning is permitted. This is the day on which the Cutheans requested permission from Alexander of Macedonia to destroy the House of our God, and he gave them permission, whereupon some people came and informed Simeon the Just. What did the latter do? He donned his priestly garments, and some of the noblemen of Israel escorted him carrying fire torches in their hands. They walked all night, some walking on one side and others on the other side, until dawn broke. When dawn broke, he [Alexander] said to them [the Samaritans]: Who are these? They answered: the Jews who rebelled against you. Upon reaching Antipatris, the sun having risen, they met. When he saw Simeon the Just, he descended from his carriage and bowed down to him. They said to him: Should a great king like yourself prostrate himself before this Jew? He answered: It is his image which leads me in victory in all my battles. He said to them: What have you come for? They said: Is it possible that star-worshipers should mislead you into destroying the House in which prayers are said for you and your kingdom! He said to them: Who are these people? They said to him: These are Cutheans who stand before you. He said: They are delivered into your hand. At once they perforated their heels, tied them to the tails of their horses and dragged them over thorns and thistles until they came to Mount Gerizim, which they plowed and planted with vetch, just as they had planned to do with the House of God. And that day they made a festive day. (*Yoma* 69a)[4]

observance ceased in the third century. A scientific edition of the Megilla with a commentary was compiled by Vered Noam (Jerusalem: 2004).

4. I am using the standard Talmudic version. There are parallels to this story (with both minor and major variations) both in *Megillat Ta'anit* (on the 21st of Kislev, the day of Mount Gerizim), and in halakhic midrashim (*Vayikra Raba* 13:5, and others). Obviously, such a meeting could not have taken place historically (see V. Noam's notes, *Megillat Ta'anit*, pp. 262–265), but our interest is in the sages' tradition which

Let us try to understand the political background alluded to in this passage:

THE STRUGGLE OF THE SAMARITANS

During the course of the seventy years of Babylonian exile, the majority of the Jews were separated from the land, enabling the Samaritans, or Cutheans, who were imported as part of the Assyrian policy of population transfer, to claim primacy over the land, challenging the Jewish claim. Following the Greek conquest of the land, the Samaritans attempted to consolidate their hold on the land by accusing the Jews of rebelling against the kingdom. Josephus (see *Antiquities of the Jews* XI, 321)[5] describes how the Samaritan leader Sanballat appeared before Alexander, leading thousands of his people, to proclaim his fealty to the king. Alexander permitted Sanballat to build a Temple for the Samaritans, to be headed by Sanballat's son-in-law, Menasseh. It is against this tense background that Simeon the Just is depicted as a savior. The force of his personality enables him to receive Alexander of Macedonia with dignity and pride. And indeed the tradition of "the Mountain of Gerizim" reflects Simeon the Just's genuinely impressive diplomatic activity, which succeeded in diverting Alexander's sympathy away from the Samaritans in favor of the Jews. The aggada ends with the destruction of the Temple in Mount Gerizim, attesting to the termination of the Samaritans' role as a threatening and incendiary force in the region.[6]

sought to have the two of them meet, as the representatives of a confrontation and the transition from one period to the next.

5. Josephus, *Antiquities of the Jews* (Jerusalem: 1983). (Hereinafter: *Antiquities.*)
6. Most historical sources refer to the reign of John Hyrcanus as the period of uprooting of the Temple at Mount Gerizim. Archeologists are skeptical as to the very existence of a Samaritan Temple at Mount Gerizim during the Persian period. However, recently, Y. Magen wrote that there was already a Temple there in the fifth century BCE. See Y. Magen, "Mount Gerizim – Temple-City" [Hebrew], *Kadmoniot* 33 (2001), pp. 74–118.

The connection between Simeon the Just and Alexander of Macedonia

Even if the historical probability of a meeting between Simeon the Just and Alexander of Macedonia is unlikely, it is important to appreciate the interest of the rabbinic tradition in describing such an encounter. This would have been a meeting of cultures, not dictated by coercion or religious edict. The Jewish people had experienced many cultural encounters, all of which forced a confrontation between their Jewish inner world and the dominant surrounding culture. When the dominant culture worshiped alien gods, the lines of confrontation were clearly drawn: "Whoever is for the Lord – come to me." To be sure, the charm and power of idol worship allured many into its net. The Talmud describes an exchange between Rabbi Ashi and King Menasseh, a king more responsible for the spread of idol worship than any of his predecessors. In response to Rabbi Ashi's question as to why he engaged in idol worship, Menasseh replies:

> Had you been there, you would have caught the skirt of my garment and run after me [to worship idols]. (*Sanhedrin* 102b)

This description seeks to convey the intense attraction of idol worship. This power increases sevenfold when dealing with Greek culture, which did not worship fetishes of wood and stone, but rather man and his intellect, together with the power and centrality of the natural world. A Jew, believing himself to be created in "God's image," might also easily be tempted to believe in the centrality of man, to the extent of forgetting God. An encounter between these two giants – Simeon and Alexander – would be the equivalent of a meeting between the two leading ideologies of mankind: the man-centered approach of Greece and the God-centered approach of Israel.

The character of Simeon the Just in the Aggada

Simeon the Just was a classic figure in the Aggada. Like the description of his encounter with Alexander of Macedonia, he also appears in other danger-fraught confrontations. For example, tradition relates that during the period of Caligula (about 40 CE, approximately four hundred and fifty years after the death of Alexander) a delegation was sent to frustrate Caligula's sinister plan to place an idol in the Sanctuary. According to this tradition, Simeon the Just led the delegation, ensuring its safety from evil.[7] This is a non-historical, mythic image of Simeon the Just, who leads Alexander in all of his battles and leads the Jewish forces in their confrontations with all-powerful rulers. What does all this tell us? My understanding is that the character of Simeon the Just is an attempt to depict the "watershed" between the old world and the new, between the divine spirit and the spirit of man. Simeon the Just still harbors memories of prophetic revelation, and this is the source of his strength. He is the only one capable of advocating the people's cause. It is he who is always at the forefront, be it for the establishment of the Temple, the prevention of the Hellenist conquest, or leading the nation in its struggle against the Cutheans. This is not violation of the separation of powers (as we shall see in the Hasmonean period) because as yet, there is no state. Simeon the Just was not spearheading a nationalist trend, because the Jewish community was not demanding political independence, but rather religious freedom. It was attempting to preserve the supremacy of the Temple in Jerusalem, and the governing authorities were perceived, not as an enemy, but rather as a patron. Simeon's victory was a victory of the God of the Hebrews over the foreign gods of the local nations, the Cutheans. Accordingly, the identity of the political ruler was irrelevant, as long as he recognized Jerusalem as the place of the Temple in which Jewish religious life could be conducted in absolute freedom.

Simeon's promises to Alexander of Macedonia

According to early traditions, Alexander's agreement with Simeon the Just regarding freedom of worship was subject to a number of conditions:

> And the King made a condition with Simeon the Just that every son born to the priests during that year would be called Alexander in his name, and that Israel would count their calendrical year from that year onward. (From Rabbi Abraham ibn Daud's *Sefer HaKabbala*, p. 51)

7. See scholia on *Megillat Ta'anit*, 22 Shevat; *Sota* 33a.

Had Simeon's world been defined by a clear Jewish national consciousness, these conditions would have been unacceptable. Alexander aspired to rule over the entire region and knew that his influence would be guaranteed by determining the prevailing culture. His name was established as a living symbol, and not just as a monument. He embedded his memory in the structure of the annual calendar. Nothing else was necessary. But for Simeon the Just none of this really mattered. He simply wanted the freedom to serve God. National-political ambitions were for those who would follow him.

Simeon the Just meets the Nazirite Shepherd

The Midrash describes the meeting between Simeon the Just and a product of the new culture:

> Simeon the Just said: "In my entire life only once did I eat the guilt-offering of a Nazirite. A man from the south once came to me and I saw that he had beautiful eyes, a handsome face, and curly locks. I said to him, "My son, why do you wish to destroy that glorious growth of hair?" He replied to me, "I used to be a shepherd in my village, and one day while I was drawing water from the river I beheld my reflection in the water and I was tempted to give way to the sinful inclination and be lost. I said to myself, 'Evil one! Will you take pride of that which does not belong to you, in that which is but dust, worms, and corruption?!' I therefore took upon myself to shave these locks for the glory of Heaven." I lowered his head and kissed him and said to him, "My son, may people like you, who do the will of the Almighty, multiply in Israel. Through you is fulfilled this Scripture, as it is said, 'A man or a woman, when he will express a vow to be a Nazirite, to abstain for the sake of the Lord' [Numbers 6:2]." (Tosefta, *Nazir* 4:7 [*Nedarim* 9b])

The shepherd's encounter with beauty reflects the genesis of human self-contemplation. He is fascinated by beauty, confronting its power for the first time. The shepherd passes the test of Jewishness, and relates to his body as something which is destined to "turn into dust, worms, and corruption." By doing so he merits a kiss from Simeon the Just, the champion of God's battle against Grecian culture. Simeon himself is enthralled by the shepherd's beauty and asks: "Why would you shave off that glorious growth of hair?" We should remember that during his years of his service as High Priest, Simeon the Just had often encountered Nazirites coming to the Temple with their offerings. Most of these wanted to escape from the world, seeking to build an insulated spiritual alternative. Simeon the Just's critique, however, is more complex. He does not recoil from beauty, but he nonetheless remains keenly aware of the distinction between that beauty which adds splendor to the "image of God" in man, and that beauty which can turn a person into a god in his own eyes. It is for this reason that Simeon agrees to accept the shepherd's guilt-offering, and even more so, rewards him with his blessing.

THE WORLD AFTER SIMEON THE JUST: THE DEPARTURE FROM THE TEMPLE

The Tosefta records a tradition describing the world after Simeon the Just:

> So long as Simeon the Just was alive the Western Lamp remained permanently lit. When he died, they went and found it extinguished. From that time onward, sometimes they found it extinguished and sometimes lit.
>
> So long as Simeon the Just was alive, the altar fire was perpetual. When they arranged it in the morning it would gain in intensity throughout the day and they were able to offer the daily burnt-offerings and additional offerings, with their libations. And they did not add to it more than two loads of wood with the daily burnt-offering of twilight so as to fulfill the commandment of adding wood, as it is said: "The fire on the altar shall be kept burning on it, it shall not go out; the priest shall burn wood on it every morning" [Leviticus 6:5]. After Simeon the Just died, the power of the altar fire diminished. For even after they had laid it out in the morning, they still needed to add wood to it all day long.
>
> So long as Simeon the Just was alive, the Two Loaves and the Showbread were blessed. The Two Loaves were divided on *Atzeret* [Pentecost] among the priests and the Showbread on each

> festival to all the watches. Some of them ate and were sated, while others ate and left bread over. And no one received more than an olive's bulk. But when Simeon the Just died, the Two Loaves and the Showbread were no longer blessed. The modest priests kept their hands off the bread, and while the gluttons divided it up among themselves, none of them received more than the size of a bean. (Tosefta, *Sota* 13:7)

The Tosefta describes the twilight of a vanishing world. The Western lamp has begun to flicker, the power of the altar wood is steadily diminishing, and the two loaves have lost their vitality and are beginning to shrivel up. Nothing will be as it was.[8]

The allusion here is to the ascent of Greece and the intrusion of man into the kingdom of God. Divine power is being replaced by mortal power. Together these descriptions convey a sense of the world that was, with the Temple at the heart of Jewish life, the ancient expression of the Divine Presence in Israel. The world in which prophecy disappeared was also the world that lost the Divine Presence and in which the connection between the people of Israel and their Father in heaven began to fade. Many sources place Simeon the Just at the center of all that was holy. According to one prevalent Talmudic tradition, Simeon the Just served as High Priest for forty years (*Yoma* 9a) while, according to the Jerusalem Talmud, his departure from the Temple portended the events of the next generation:

> There was a case of a high priest who prolonged his prayer, so

8. There is an interesting parallel between this tradition and that of Rebecca, who replaces Sarah in the matriarchal tent (*Bereshit Raba*, 60): "And Isaac brought her into his mother Sarah's tent." As long as Sarah lived, a cloud hung over her tent; when she died, the cloud disappeared but returned with the arrival of Rebecca. As long as Sarah lived, her doors were wide open; at her death that hospitality ceased; but with Rebecca that hospitality returned. As long as Sarah lived there was a blessing on her dough, and a lamp would burn continuously from one Sabbath eve till the next; when she died, these ceased, but when Rebecca arrived, they returned. The cosmic calamity of the disappearance of prophecy in the time of Simeon the Just is depicted in similar terms.

> they decided to go in after him. They said it was Simeon the Just. They said to him, "Why did you take so long?" He said to them, "I was praying for the Sanctuary of your God so that it should not be destroyed." They said to him, "Even so, you should not have prolonged your prayer."
>
> For forty years Simeon the Just served as High Priest. In the final year he said to them, "This year I am going to die." They said to him, "How do you know?" He said to them, "Every year when I entered the house of the Holy of Holies, an old man dressed in white went in with me and came out with me. This year he went in with me but did not come out with me. (Talmud Yerushalmi, *Yoma* 5:2 [42c])

Alongside the rise of Alexander of Macedonia and Greek culture, Simeon the Just stands out as the man of the Temple and of holiness. He serves as the bastion of sanctity, and as a spiritual barrier against the powerful winds of progress that were blowing in full force around the camp.

THE LEGACY OF SIMEON THE JUST

This background sheds light on the teaching of Simeon the Just in the first mishna of *Avot*, with which we began.

> Simeon the Just was one of the last survivors of the Great Assembly. He would say: The world is sustained by three things: The Torah, the [Temple] service, and deeds of loving-kindness. (*Avot* 1:2)

Simeon the Just confronted the cultural torrents threatening to submerge the land of Israel. Like the Dutch boy who used his finger to prevent the flooding of the dam, he too attempted to forcefully maintain the old world: the Torah that he, together with the other men of the Great Assembly, had received from the prophets; the Temple service that connects Israel to their Father in heaven; and the acts of loving-kindness which liberate man from idolizing himself and compel him to acknowledge his true essence.

Chapter Three

Antigonus of Sokho: His World of Spiritual Elitism

Antigonus of Sokho received [the Torah] from Simeon the Just. He would say: Be not like servants that minister to their master for the sake of receiving a reward, but rather be like servants who minister to their master not for the sake of receiving a reward; and let the fear of Heaven be upon you. (Avot 1:3)

Antigonus, the first of the *tanna'im*, takes us from the time of the Great Assembly to the era of the Pairs (*Zugot*). His very name indicates the Hellenistic influence in *Eretz Yisrael*. "Antigonus" is a purely Greek name, indicating the extent to which his parents identified with the prevailing culture. The Hellenizing process in Judea took place in parallel with the consolidation of Seleucid hegemony over the country. During this period (the early second century BCE), one already finds prominent Jews with Greek names such as Jason the Priest, Eupolemus and Antigonus.[1] But the adoption of Greek culture by Jews was not limited to names, and included the assimilation of Greek concepts and ideas.[2] The confrontation with the spirit of Greece compelled the sages of that time to confront such fundamental questions as Providence and the nature of religious service. It was in this atmosphere that Antigonus articulated his philosophy.

Just as we cannot be certain regarding dates, so ought we to be wary in our assumptions about the philosophical identity of those surrounding Antigonus. Still, however we look at it, it is clear that the environment in which he found himself was in philosophical turmoil over questions of Providence, the service of God, and reward and punishment. There are good grounds for Rabbi Zacharias Frankel to maintain that the period was characterized by the spread of a variety of philosophical opinions throughout Israel regarding the essence of man and his role in the world. The views of the philosopher Epicurus, who claimed that "there is no good but for a man to rejoice," attracted particular support. As Rabbi Frankel describes it:

> ...In fact most of his students and followers chose the path of bodily pleasures, arguing that there is no good but for a person to eat and drink and indulge his flesh. Epicurus also advanced another principle, even more corrupt than the first: Given that happiness is the purpose of all man's actions, and the objective expression of happiness is rest and relaxation, the most exalted honor that man can confer on the kingdom of heaven is to say that God on high is sitting relaxing and pays no attention to the travails of man; He has no feelings of mercy, nor does He pun-

1. M. Stern, "Judaism and Hellenism in the Land of Israel in the Third and Second Centuries BCE" [Hebrew], *Studies in Jewish History in the Second Temple* (Jerusalem: 1991), pp. 3–21 (especially pp. 14–15); see also T. Ilan, "Names of the Hasmoneans during the Second Temple" [Hebrew], *Eretz Yisrael* 19 (1987), 238–241.
2. There is extensive literature concerning the influence of Hellenism on the Jews in the land of Israel. The central pioneer in this field was S. Lieberman, *Greek in Jewish Palestine* (New York: 1965) and *Hellenism in Jewish Palestine* (New York: 1962). The subject is summed up (provisionally) in Lee I. Levine, *Judaism and Hellenism in Antiquity – Conflict or Confluence?* (Seattle and London: 1998).

> ish sin or reward virtue, for any such action would disturb his tranquility and peace... Indeed there is no view more worthless than this, which is equivalent to absolute denial of divinity, yet Epicurus himself tended to this opinion.[3]

According to this explanation, Antigonus' teaching was directed against Epicurus.

> In fact, the best thing is for a man to do good for the sake of choosing good, and not by reason of the obligation imposed upon him and the anticipated reward for fulfilling the commandment, but rather of his own free intention and will. For man's soul is a part of God on high, and nothing can be more pleasurable for it than doing good. But should you be misled into seeking a different type of pleasure, and saying that I will do that which is good in my own judgment and that which I judge as pleasurable, he [Antigonus] added, "Let the fear of Heaven be on you" – to emphasize, in contrast to the view of Epicurus, that there is indeed a God who judges on earth, who oversees all men and their actions. (Frankel, ibid.)

ANTIGONUS' TEACHING: SERVE NOT FOR THE SAKE OF RECEIVING A REWARD

This mishna confronts us with one of the greatest dilemmas facing the believing Jew. From start to finish, the Bible expresses an approach that is the antithesis of Antigonus', namely, that there is a direct relationship between man's actions and divine reward: "If then you obey My commandments.... I will grant the rain on your land in its time" (Deuteronomy 11:11–14; see also, Leviticus 26:4).

At the beginning of the Second Temple period, the prophet Malachi challenges the people:

> Bring all the tithes into the storehouse, and let there be food in My house, and put Me to the test with that, says the Lord of hosts:

3. Z. Frankel, *Darkhei HaMishna* (Tel Aviv: 1959), pp. 8–9.

> if I will not open for you the windows of heaven and pour out for you blessings immeasurable. (Malachi 3:10)

These are clear statements establishing a direct connection between the religious act and the result which follows. Antigonus' teaching directly contradicts this view, seeking to disconnect the religious act from any reward. There is, he argues, a kind of servitude which involves a framework and a discipline which are an end in themselves. The servant does and will do whatever is demanded of him, irrespective of the master's response to his acts. The awareness of slavery that lies at the basis of Antigonus' teaching can only have originated in a crisis in the self-confidence of those who worshiped God.

ANTIGONUS' DISCIPLES AND THE ORIGIN OF THE BOETHUSIANS

A rabbinic tradition informs us that Antigonus' teaching was in fact one of the sources of sectarianism among the people:

> Antigonus of Sokho had two disciples who used to study his teachings. They taught them to their disciples, and their disciples to their disciples. These disciples began analyzing the words closely and asked: "Why did our ancestors see fit to say this thing? Is it possible that a laborer should work all day and not take his reward in the evening? To the contrary, if our ancestors had believed in another world and in the resurrection of the dead, they would not have spoken in this manner."
>
> So they arose and withdrew from the Torah and split into two sects, the Sadducees and the Boethusians:[4] The Sadducees were named after Tzaddok, and the Boethusians after Boethus. And they used silver vessels and gold vessels all their lives – not

4. *Avot deRabbi Natan* (recension B), relates the emergence of "two families." By way of conjecture, this formulation may be a more moderate one, because it omits the expression "sects," using the term "families" (= streams). See the discussion of M. Kister, "Studies in *Avot deRabbi Natan* – Text, Redaction and Interpretation," Doctoral Thesis [Hebrew], (Jerusalem: 1994) 152–153.

because they were ostentatious, but because the Sadducees said, "It is a tradition amongst the Pharisees to afflict themselves in this world; yet in the World to Come they will have nothing." (*Avot deRabbi Natan,* recension A, ch. 5)

According to *Avot deRabbi Natan,* Antigonus' teaching was studied in depth ("closely analyzing") in an attempt to understand the possibility of unrewarded service. The entire basis of religious service had always been "according to the effort – so shall be the reward," predicated on the belief that at the end of the day there will be an accounting and a reward. The disciples believed that Antigonus' teaching concerning unrewarded service of God alluded to a more esoteric doctrine; and as a result they "withdrew from the Torah." The entire principle of reward and punishment having been undermined, it disappeared from the thinking of these disciples. And if there is no World to Come, it follows that there is no reason to expend efforts in this world. So "they used silver vessels and gold vessels all their lives" – a simple and direct expression of a mentality that focuses on maximizing pleasure in the "here and now," unconcerned by thoughts of a reckoning in the remote future.

It seems that the mistake of these students stemmed from a misunderstanding of their teacher's words. Antigonus spoke about *service* which should not be motivated by expectations of reward; he was not dealing with the question of the reward itself. The students, however, took their master's teaching a step further, concluding that there was no reward at all – no World to Come and no Resurrection of the Dead – thereby denying two fundamental tenets of Judaism. Cynically and contemptuously, they taunted the Pharisees who "afflict themselves in this world; although in the World to Come they will have nothing." In other words, no one can guarantee that there will be any future recompense for putting effort into a life of Torah and its commandments and complying with all the restrictions and prohibitions. Attitudes of rejection or skepticism with regard to the belief in a future reward, paved the way to a total breakdown in commitment to the service of God.[5]

5. On the origins of the Sadducees and the Boethusians (and the connection, or lack thereof, between them) see E. Regev, *The Sadducees and Their Laws, Religion and*

THE FEAR OF HEAVEN IN THE TEACHING OF ANTIGONUS

The heresy that resulted from the mistaken understanding of Antigonus' approach was only one of the pitfalls of Antigonus' doctrine. According to the *baraita* in *Avot deRabbi Natan,* Antigonus himself was aware of the danger of his teaching and this is the reason that he concludes his dictum with the words, "and let the fear of Heaven be upon you":

> ["And let the fear of Heaven be upon you."] This may be compared to a man who does his master's will, while his mind rebels against his master's will, [or who does his father's will] while his mind rebels against his father's will. One who acts out of love is not comparable to one who acts out of awe and fear. One who acts out of love inherits the life of this world and does not inherit the life of the World to Come. One who acts out of awe and fear inherits the life of this world and the life of the World to Come. For we find that such was the case among the forefathers, who served in awe and fear and who inherited the life of this world and of the World to Come. What does Scripture say about Abraham? "For now I know that you fear God" [Genesis 22:12]. What does Scripture say about Joseph? "For I fear God" [Genesis 42:18]. What does Scripture say about Jonah? "And I fear God" [Jonah 1:9]. (*Avot deRabbi Natan,* recension B, ch. 10)[6]

The great danger inherent in boundless love is that it invites arrogance. If one reaches a level of total identification with one's master, one loses the fear of what the master might say, how he might react, what he might decide, etc. At this stage the servant is in danger of overstepping his boundaries and treating his master with contempt. This phenomenon is familiar to us from our world of employees and employers. Familiarity can often breed contempt, when loss of distance leads to a loss of respect.

Society in the Second Temple Period, ch. 1, "The Relationship between the Sadducees and the Boethusians," (Jerusalem: 2005), mainly pp. 44–50.

6. The wording of this recension appears to have been totally distorted, and this point was raised in Schechter's edition. In this text I have used the wording that appears in the original manuscripts. See E.E. Urbach, *The Sages – Their Concepts and Beliefs* (Jerusalem: 1979), pp. 402ff.

For this reason Antigonus felt the need to introduce another component: "the fear of God should be upon you" (notwithstanding the fact that you are not motivated by fear of punishment or anticipation of reward in your fulfillment of His commandments). This was a tremendous innovation. We are accustomed to assuming that service based on love is preferable to service based on fear. In fact, later generations were unable to accept the view espoused in *Avot deRabbi Natan,* which derived the principle of fear from Abraham. Rabbi Meir (of the generation of Usha, after the Bar Kokhba rebellion) categorically rejected this view:

> It has been taught: Rabbi Meir says: It says "one that feared God" of Job and it says "you feared God" of Abraham. Just as with Abraham "fearing God" indicates that it is done from love, so does "fearing God" with Job indicate that it is from love. From whence do we know this in connection with Abraham? For it is written: "The seed of Abraham who loved Me" [Isaiah 41:8]. (*Sota* 31a)

PHARISAISM OF FEAR

Nonetheless, reversing the pyramid and elevating fear over love also creates problems of "*yira tata'a*" ("lower fear"), fear based not on awe of Heaven, but simply on fear of sin. An example of this kind of fear is provided by the following *baraita* in Tractate *Sota*:

> Our rabbis have taught: There are seven types of Pharisee: The *shikhmi* [Shechemite] Pharisee; the *nikfi* [knocking] Pharisee; the *kizai* [bloodletting] Pharisee; the "pestle" Pharisee; the "what-is-my-duty-and-I-will-fulfill-it" Pharisee; the Pharisee out of love; and the Pharisee out of fear. The *shikmi* [*shikhmi*] Pharisee is one who acts in the manner of Shechem; the *nikpi* [*nikfi*] Pharisee is the one who knocks his feet together. The *kizai* Pharisee: Rabbi Naḥman bar Yitzḥak said: he is one who lets his blood flow against walls. The "pestle" Pharisee: Rabba bar Shila said: [his head] is bent like a pestle when he walks. The Pharisee who constantly exclaims, "What is my duty and I will fulfill it." But is this not a virtue?! No, [what he means is]: "What further duty is there for me to fulfill." The Pharisee from love and the

> Pharisee from fear: Abaye and Rabba said to the *tanna*: Do not teach "the Pharisee from love" and "the Pharisee from fear," for Rabbi Yehuda said in the name of Rav: A man should always occupy himself in Torah and the commandments even if not for their own sake, because through [occupying himself in them] not for their own sake, he will come to [occupy himself in them] for their own sake. (*Sota* 22b)

The Talmud describes several different types of obsessive religious behavior. We are all too familiar with these kinds of "Pharisees" in our everyday religious experience:

The Shikhmi Pharisee: one who acts in the manner of Shechem, that is, the person whose actions are motivated entirely by his own benefit, such as the circumcision of the men of Shechem. There is hardly need to even mention this type, because all of his acts are purely for his own sake, and not for the sake of Heaven. He may fulfill commandments with the very best Pharisees, but his motivations are entirely self-centered, without any trace of Godliness.

The Nikfi Pharisee: one who knocks his feet on the ground. This is the person who walks heal after toe, who avoids lifting his foot for fear of not finding where to tread, and so he drags one foot after the other, ruining his feet and going nowhere. This is a foot-dragging religiosity based on fear, which brings a person (and those around him) to spiritual paralysis. Any innovation, any untrodden territory, seems to him to be an impassable minefield. This kind of fear paralyzes.

The Kizai Pharisee: one whose blood spurts out on the walls. He averts his eyes from seeing evil. When he thinks he might see a woman in the street he closes his eyes so that he bumps into walls, injuring his head. The description of the bleeding wound here is significant. In his attempt to avoid what he sees as a sin, this person is capable of shedding his own blood. Such a Jew ends up bruised and wounded, and his fearful approach is condemned.

The Pestle Pharisee: one whose head is bent in humility when he walks. This is the person whose sense of fear makes him want to simply disappear. The sheer weight of his overwhelming fear of Heaven crushes any possible expression of his own personality. This kind of Pharisee reflects the type of excessive humility which leads to total self-negation.

The "What-else-should-I-do-and-I-will-do-it" Pharisee: one who is obsessed with fear, constantly looking for more strictures to obey. He can never relax, because he is convinced that there must always be some additional obligation, some new stricture, some new task. There must be something more he can do to improve his worship. He wants to achieve religious perfection but only feels a sense of his own imperfection. This kind of obsession can create tremendous tension and social pressure.

The common factor in all of these is a nervous, neurotic kind of religiosity grounded in the basest type of fear, and which fails to help a person attain any spiritual elevation at all.

PHARISAISM OF LOVE

The *baraita* describes two additional categories of Pharisee: the "Pharisee of love" and the "Pharisee of fear." These two are the subject of a dispute between the Babylonian and Jerusalem Talmuds. The Babylonian Talmud is critical of both the Pharisee of love and the Pharisee of fear. According to Rashi (*Sota* 22b), the reason for this criticism is the fact that their love is love of the commandments' reward, and their fear is fear of punishment; neither is rooted in a genuine sense of God's majesty. Nonetheless, the commentary of the Tosafot refers us to the Jerusalem Talmud, which teaches that love and fear are qualities that must complement each other:

> One verse of Scripture says, "And you shall love the Lord your God" (Deuteronomy 6:5) and another verse of Scripture says, "You shall fear the Lord your God; and you shall serve Him" (Deuteronomy 10:20). [From this we learn:] Do His will out of love, do His will out of fear. "Do His will out of love" so that should

> you come to hate, you will know that you love Him, and one who loves cannot hate. "Do His will out of fear," so that if you come to rebel against Him, you will know that one who fears does not rebel." (Talmud Yerushalmi, *Sota* 5:5 [20c])

In the Jerusalem Talmud, this passage is immediately followed by the *baraita* of the Seven Pharisees, and an example is given of the Pharisee of fear and of love:

> The Pharisee of fear is Job, and the Pharisee of love is Abraham, and the most beloved of them all is Abraham, the Pharisee of love.

The Jerusalem Talmud clearly prefers Abraham to Job, but the mishna in *Sota* questions the status of Job as servant of God:

> On that day Rabbi Yehoshua ben Hyrcanus expounded: Job only served the Holy One, blessed be He, from love. As it is said: "Though He slay me yet will I wait for Him" [Job 13:15]. And if there is doubt whether the meaning is "I will wait for Him" or "I will not wait for Him," there is another text which states: "Until I die I will not put away my integrity from me" [ibid., 27:5]. This teaches that he acted out of love. Rabbi Yehoshua [ben Ḥanania] teaches: Who will remove the dust from your eyes, Rabban Yoḥanan ben Zakkai, since you have expounded all your life that Job only served the Omnipresent from fear, as it is said: "That man was perfect and upright, and one that feared God, and eschewed evil!" (ibid. 1:8). Did not Yehoshua, your disciple's disciple, teach that what he did was from love? (Mishna, *Sota* 5:5)

Until the homily of Rabbi Yehoshua ben Hyrcanus, the tendency was to make a clear distinction between "fear-based service" and "love-based service." One who loves asks no questions, and one who fears does not approach God. In the homily of Rabban Yoḥanan ben Zakkai, Job is perceived as one who was motivated by fear, because his recoiling from evil was rooted in fear ("and eschewed evil"). Rabban Yoḥanan ben Zakkai valued this kind of fear ("lower fear") and even instructed his students,

"Would that you should fear Heaven as you fear men" (*Berakhot* 28b). Nonetheless, there is a higher level: unconditional love. After the Bar Kokhba rebellion and the Hadrianic decrees, in the generation of the "aftermath of persecution,"[7] there was a tendency to try to move Job from the world of fear to the world of love, though clearly his love of God cannot be compared to Abraham's. Job's words are ambiguous. We read his words according to an oral tradition: "Though He slay me yet will I wait for Him," but the written tradition does not have לו, but rather לא – that is, not "I will wait *for Him,*" but rather "I will *not* wait"). The received text and the oral tradition, the *ketiv* and the *keri,* are diametrically opposed. In a test similar to Abraham's at the *Akeda* (the Binding of Isaac), did Job's faith crack, or did he summon the faith to declare: "I came upon trouble and sorrow, yet I invoked the name of the Lord"?

Apparently, in this era of the aftermath of the persecution, following the death of Rabbi Akiva, a new form of belief emerged, consisting of the knowledge that even fear which involves borderline components such as these can also be interpreted as a form of love. This was an approach which tended to give legitimacy to questioning, doubting and challenging God, as long as they were also characterized by the dictum: "I will maintain my integrity."

We will now make a brief digression from our main focus, to consider the impact of Antigonus' doctrine in the Jewish tradition over the generations.

AN ASIDE: SOME THOUGHTS ABOUT THE ELITIST TENDENCY IN JEWISH TRADITION

The simple meaning of Antigonus' teaching is that a Jew's religious service should not be motivated by the desire for recompense. In other words, there should be no calculation of reward and punishment. This was indeed the understanding of Rabbi Shimon ben Tzemaḥ Duran:[8]

7. According to many sources, over half a million Jews were killed during the post–Bar Kokhba period, thousands were imprisoned, and many more perished from starvation; this period is traditionally referred to as "the aftermath of the persecution."
8. Rabbi Shimon ben Tzemaḥ Duran (= Rashbetz) was born in 1361 in Barcelona and was the leading rabbi in Algiers at the beginning of the fifteenth century.

> [Antigonus] always warned his students that their service of God must not resemble that of the servant who administers to his master for the sake of reward, for service of this kind is deficient because the receiving of the reward is of greater importance than the service of the master, and were he not to receive the prize he would abandon the work. The servant's service of his master is at its highest level when motivated by love for his master, irrespective of the reward, and this kind of worshiper is referred to as one who worships out of love. (*Magen Avot* 1:3)

1. Interpretations of Antigonus' teaching: Rabbi Yosef Alashkar

Antigonus' teaching stands in contrast to passages in the Torah which promise rewards to those who walk in God's path. But even leaving aside this issue, there is another, equally disturbing aspect to his approach. Is he advocating a normative position, or a higher standard for the select few, above and beyond the demands of the Torah? Rabbi Yosef Alashkar[9] takes the latter approach in explaining the Mishna:

> This *tanna* said: "Do not be like the slaves who serve their master for the sake of reward." The intention is that they receive a meal from their master in return for their labor. But let it flow from His kindness to you, for He brought you into being from nothing. And you should not see yourself as the slave who receives his daily or yearly wage and when his tenure is completed leaves his master's service. Rather be like the slaves who serve the master not for the sake of remuneration,[10] such as the slave born in his master's house, who is obligated to serve him even if the man does not give him breakfast, on the basis of his previous kindnesses, that he raised him in his home, and so he never moves and will never leave him. For he does not resemble the employed or the purchased slave, who upon finding an opportunity to escape will immediately flee – for one finds that most of the slaves who

9. The author of *Merkevet HaMishna* lived about one hundred years after Rashbetz.
10. This is the wording according to the manuscripts of Mishna *Avot* (for example, in the Kaufman manuscript). See Urbach, *The Sages* (see footnote 6 above), p. 351, n. 21.

> are purchased by their masters have a tendency to flee from the master. Rather, one should regard himself as a slave who is the son of a handmaid who grew up in the master's house, as it says: "I am Your servant, the son of Your handmaid" (Psalms 116:16), for even though "You have loosed my bonds" and do not guard me, I still seek to work for You, as it states: "I will offer to You the sacrifice of thanksgiving" (ibid., 17) and my love for You is undying, whether because of Your love or Your sublimity. Accordingly, the *tanna* warned that your service of God, may He be blessed, should be of that kind. And having warned that the worship of God should be based on this manner of love, he reiterated the importance of fear, as it states, "And let the fear of Heaven be upon you." In the manner of the celestial bodies which eternally worship God, so too should be your worship of God, may He be blessed. (*Merkevet HaMishna, Avot* 1:3)

The message conveyed here is one of service based on a sense of continuity: "Your servant the son of Your maidservant." We have nowhere to flee to, and in any case we have no interest in fleeing. This approach sees us as if we have been raised in a place where no importance is attached to private, personal interests, and where our very essence consists of being in the master's service. With such an outlook, there is no longer any place for the question of reward and punishment. A comparison could be made to a nation of slaves that has been weaned of its yearning for freedom and its desire for liberty. Their dreams are not of freedom, nor can they even imagine the idea of receiving reward for their service. Their entire existence is geared toward serving the master to his satisfaction, for this is the very reason for their existence.[11] Rabbi Alashkar adds that the concluding phrase in our mishna, "Let the fear of Heaven be upon you," is intended to invoke a comparison between us and the celestial bodies which function ceaselessly. This is a maximalist

11. The literature on slaves in the U.S.A. abounds with examples of slaves who lost their yearning for freedom, and the difficulty of rekindling it. The Jewish people too were hardly eager to leave Egypt after 210 years of slavery and the redemption was forced upon them.

understanding of the subservience involved in the service of God. Man is in no way superior to God's other servants; the angels, the sun, the moon, the stars and man are all focused on the service of God. This call for servile devotion, devoid of any anticipation of reward and without hope of a divine response to man's actions, represents a major challenge to any feeling that man is special and unique having been created in God's image, or that the Jew is, as he has been called, a "child" of the Almighty. Comparing man's service of God to that of the sun and the other celestial beings is a harsh, almost ruthless comparison. Although in the Shabbat morning prayers we wax poetic about the heavenly hosts that "rejoice and are glad to perform their Creator's will" – in fact their service has no element of free will.

This also provides a key to understanding the blessings preceding the reading of *Shema* in the morning, which prepare a Jew to accept the yoke of heaven. The first blessing describes the heavenly luminaries, and links acceptance of the divine yoke with an awareness of the heavenly hosts. A person awakens in the morning to the service of God together with all of God's creatures who awaken to the service of their Creator; in that sense there is no difference between the sun, an angel or a man. The second blessing is *Ahava Raba*, "Great love," referring specifically to the chosenness of the Jewish people and God's intimate connection to His people. This chosenness places the person accepting the heavenly yoke in a special position not shared by other created beings. Nonetheless, the blessings are immutably linked, and may be viewed as two levels of divine service of God: fear (shared by all of God's servants), and love (as sons of God). According to this division, Antigonus conferred a more profound dimension to the sense of fear, raising it to the level of love, albeit not to the level of a father's love for his son (or a son for his father), but rather to that of the servant who proclaims, "I love my master [...] I will not go out free...." This is a radically different form of love, based on effacing oneself, rather than uniting with another.

2. Maimonides' interpretation of Antigonus' teaching

In his introduction to the tenth chapter of Tractate *Sanhedrin*, known as *Perek Ḥelek*, Maimonides gives us a complete and detailed account of his understanding of the teaching of Antigonus of Sokho. Due to their importance and eloquence, I will cite his words almost in full:

> Imagine a small child who has been brought to his teacher so that he may be taught the Torah, which is his ultimate good because it will bring him to perfection. However, because he is only a child and because his understanding is deficient, he does not grasp the true value of that good, nor does he understand the perfection which he can achieve by means of Torah. Of necessity, therefore, his teacher, who has acquired greater perfection than the child, must bribe him to study by means of things which the child loves in a childish way. Thus, the teacher may say, "Read and I will give you some nuts or figs; I will give you a bit of honey." With this stimulation the child tries to read. He does not work hard for the sake of reading itself, since he does not understand its value. He reads in order to obtain the food. Eating these delicacies seems far more important and beneficial to him than reading. Therefore, although he thinks of study as work and effort, he is willing to do it in order to get what he wants, a nut or a piece of candy....
>
> When his understanding has so improved that even this reward has ceased to be valuable to him, he will desire something more honorable. His teacher may say to him then, "Study so that you may become president of a court of three judges so that people will honor you and rise before you as they honor So-and-So. He will then try hard to read in order to attain his new goal. His incentive then will be to achieve honor, the admiration and praise which others might confer upon him. Now, these are base goals. Yet, this approach is unavoidable because of man's limited insight, as a result of which he makes the goal of wisdom something other than wisdom itself, and assumes that the purpose of study is the acquisition of honor, which makes a mockery of truth. Our sages called this "learning not-for-its-own-sake." They had in mind the kind of person who performs the commandments and energetically studies Torah, not for their own intrinsic worth, but with some other purpose in view. Our sages warned against this,

> saying, "Do not make the Torah a crown for self-glorification or a spade with which to dig" [*Avot* 4:7]. They hinted at what I have just explained to you, that the end of wisdom is neither to acquire honor from other men nor to earn more money. One ought not to busy oneself with God's Torah in order to earn one's living by it, nor should the end of studying wisdom be anything but knowing it as the truth and that the Law is the truth, and that the goal of its study is its fulfillment....
>
> Antigonus of Sokho, a man who had achieved perfection and grasped the truth of things, meant precisely this when he said: "Do not be like servants who serve their master for the sake of receiving a reward, but be like servants who serve their master without expecting a reward" [*Avot* 1:3]. He meant by this that one should believe the truth for the sake of the truth. We say of such a man that he serves out of love.... Only a disturbed fool whose mind is deranged by folly and by fantasy will refuse to recognize this truth. Abraham our father achieved this level; he served God out of love [*Sota* 31a]. (Maimonides, Introduction to *Perek Ḥelek*)[12]

In simple, straightforward language, Maimonides here describes the virtue of divine service not predicated on receiving a reward, as the mark of the man who has achieved perfection. Antigonus is the "man who had achieved perfection and grasped the truth of things," and he taught us to be servants who serve their master for the sake of service itself. The question is: how does Maimonides reconcile this with the biblical and rabbinical conceptions, whereby the study and observance of Torah not for their own sake are commendable and desirable? Maimonides' answer to this question appears further on in the same passage:

> However, our sages knew that this is a very difficult goal to achieve and that not every man could achieve it. One may understand the goal and still reject it, failing to apprehend that it is a principle

12. Translation taken from I. Twersky, *A Maimonides Reader* (New York: Behrman, 1972), pp. 404–406.

> of faith. Men do not do anything except to achieve profit or to avoid loss. Most men would regard any other action as useless and meaningless.
>
> Under these circumstances it is hard to say to one who is studying Torah, "Do certain things and refrain from doing certain other things, but not out of fear of divine punishment and not in order to acquire a reward." This is an exceedingly difficult thing to do, because most men have not achieved such truth that they are able to be like Abraham our father. Therefore, in order that the masses stay faithful and do the commandments, it was permitted to tell them that they might hope for a reward and to warn them against transgressions out of fear of punishment.... It is good for them insofar as it strengthens and habituates them in loyalty to what the Torah requires. Out of this effort they may be awakened to the knowledge of the truth and serve God out of love. This is what the sages meant when they said, "A man ought always to labor in the Torah, even not for its own sake! For by doing it not for its own sake, he may yet come to do it for its own sake" [*Pesaḥim* 50b]. (Ibid.)

The Torah takes human weaknesses into account. Service for the sake of reward is in fact a lower level, far less honorable than worship for its own sake. Maimonides further notes that the dichotomy of service based on love (the servant's love for his master) as opposed to service based on fear, is reflected in the tension between the first paragraph of the *Shema* ("And you shall love") and the second paragraph ("And if you listen"). The first paragraph is based entirely on love, whereas the second is based entirely upon the fear of punishment and yearning for reward. In accordance with this view, Maimonides (*Guide for the Perplexed* 3:28) notes that the second paragraph, based on fear, is designated for people on a lower level. Those on a higher level attempt to be on the level of "And you shall love," such as Rabbi Akiva, who waited all of his life to be able to actualize the commandment of love.

3. Critiques of Antigonus' teaching: the position of Tosafot

Antigonus' doctrine posed a daunting threshold for his disciples. Even if one accepts the yoke of servitude, can one actually serve without reward? So much of the world of religious practice is founded on a system of reward-based service, that the doctrine espoused in this mishna seems alien to the normative Jewish tradition. For example, Tractate *Ta'anit*, which deals with the prayer for rain, begins with a tannaitic dispute regarding the time from which this prayer begins to be said. The Jerusalem Talmud explains the dispute as follows:

> Rabbi Eliezer said: When the slave has completed the service of his master, that is when he seeks his reward from him.
>
> Rabbi Yehoshua said to him: "And is it not when the slave has completed serving his master and the master is pleased with him, that the slave seeks his reward from him? (Talmud Yerushalmi, *Ta'anit* 1:1 [3c])

Even without fully delving into the complexities of this passage, we can immediately sense that it stands in clear contrast to the teaching of Antigonus. The argument presented here is over the question: when is it most appropriate to request reward for one's service? The question as to whether reward is actually due is not even raised. Reward may be delayed, and may not even come, but there is not the slightest doubt that service is performed in anticipation of reward.

In a number of places the Talmud states that "He who says 'I give this *sela* [coin] as charity so that my children will live' is considered to be absolutely righteous." Clearly, this statement chooses the most blatant and extreme case to exemplify service based on the anticipation of personal and immediate reward. The request for healthy children as recompense for giving charity recalls the following statement by Raba:

> Raba said: [Length of] Life, children and sustenance depend not on merit, but [rather] on *mazal* [fortune]. Raba and Rabbi Ḥisda were both saintly rabbis; one master prayed for rain and it came, the other master prayed for rain and it came. Rabbi Ḥisda lived to the age of ninety-two; Raba [only] lived to the age of forty. In

> Rabbi Ḥisda's house sixty marriage feasts were held; at Raba's house there were sixty bereavements. At Rabbi Ḥisda's house there was the purest wheat bread for dogs, and even that went to waste; at Raba's house there was barely bread for human beings, and that not to be had. (*Mo'ed Katan* 28a)

"Children, life and sustenance," represent the individual's prayer for his own personal needs. Indeed, health, offspring, and livelihood are the three most immediate requests for the individual himself, before any loftier (or altruistic) value. Serving God for these three things cannot be considered "service for its own sake," and Raba asserts that the fulfillment of these requests is dependent neither on a person's deeds nor on his merits, but rather on good fortune. Either way, it is clear that there is no implied criticism of asking God to grant one's personal needs, in stark contrast with the teaching of Antigonus.

In Tractate *Rosh HaShana* 4a, Tosafot actually contrasts this statement with Antigonus' teaching. The context is the Talmud's inquiry (ibid.) into whether Cyrus was a righteous king or not. The Talmud cites a verse from Ezra (chapter 6) describing the sacrifices that Cyrus sent to the Temple, as proof of his righteousness. Rabbi Yitzḥak dismisses this proof, claiming that the sacrifices were not offered in the service of God, but rather so that the priests would pray for the welfare of Cyrus' kingdom and his descendants. The Talmud questions the logic of the question, saying: "And what is wrong with that? Have we not learned: He who says 'I give this *sela* as charity so that my children will live,' is considered to be absolutely righteous." And the Talmud replies: "There is no difficulty: one case refers to Jews and the other to non-Jews."

The Talmud suggests that a Jew who gives a *sela* to charity so that his children will live is to be considered a righteous person, but a non-Jew is not permitted to do so. Tosafot (*Rosh HaShana* 4a, s.v. *bishvil sheyiḥyu banai*) asks how this can be reconciled with the teaching of Antigonus:

> …and that which we taught in the first chapter of Tractate *Avot*: do not be like the servants who serve the master for the sake of receiving a reward?

His answer is concise:

> This refers to the nations of the world who question divine justice. (Ibid.)

Tosafot's response is radical, effectively excluding Antigonus' teaching from Jewish tradition. According to Tosafot, the normative Jewish teaching is: "so that my children will live," while Antigonus' doctrine is not directed to Jews, but rather to idol worshipers "who question divine justice." As Tosafot understands it, the Jew who gives charity does not premise his connection to God on his acts of charity; rather, his prayer stems from his hope for the best. The phrase, "so that my children will live" is not a condition in the sense that were his child to die, Heaven forbid, he would lose his faith. The Jew would continue to believe, even under those circumstances.[13]

4. The position of Yeshayahu Leibowitz

In his discussions on *Pirkei Avot,* Yeshayahu Leibowitz devotes considerable attention to the teaching of Antigonus. Like Tosafot, he contrasts Antigonus' approach with the statement of the Talmud: "He who says 'I will give this *sela* to charity so that my children will live, etc." But in contrast to Tosafot's rejection of Antigonus' teaching in favor of the Talmudic statement, Leibowitz writes the following:[14]

> There is no doubt that service of God which is not for its own sake is unacceptable from a religious viewpoint. According to one Talmudic teaching, "He who says 'This *sela* is for charity'" – that is, he who fulfills the commandment of charity – "is considered to be absolutely righteous." Let us leave aside the possibility that this statement is intended sarcastically (which is not uncommon in Rabbinic dicta) and accept it at face value: that even one who treats the commandment as a means for attaining something

13. A similar response appears in Tosafot, *Pesaḥim* 8b.
14. Y. Leibowitz, *Discussions on Ethics of the Fathers and on Maimonides* [Hebrew], (Jerusalem: Schocken, 1979).

> that he desires and does it specifically for that purpose, is nonetheless regarded as having fulfilled the commandment, and it is counted to his credit…The performance of the commandments as the service of God is man's objective, and this is the meaning of the statement of Antigonus of Sokho… [Antigonus] does not prohibit service of God motivated by the expectation of reward, but he asks that we refrain from it, and this may indeed be his intention in the supplementary statement to his dicta: if you are incapable of serving God out of love, then in any event, the fear of Heaven should be upon you.

Leibowitz's talks were originally broadcast on the radio and elicited many responses from listeners, to which Leibowitz replies later in his book:

> Some of those who wrote to me recoil from the notion of belief that requires no reward other than itself. They seek their refuge in the distinction between this world and the World to Come. Service of God for which the reward is in the World to Come is, in their view, service for-its-own-sake, and the study of Torah in order to merit a portion in the World to Come is Torah for-its-own-sake. But this approach is absurd… such a belief empties the concept of "for-its-own-sake" of any real meaning. If the person engaged in the service of God expects reward or fears punishment in any place at all, or at any time at all, whether in concrete reality, in a bodily context or in a spiritual context, then his service is for the sake of receiving a reward and intended for his own benefit. In this sense there is no difference between "life, children and sustenance" and the pleasures of the World to Come, or the "Garden of Eden"… (pp. 80–81)

These comments are a direct continuation of Maimonides' approach, without any allowance for human frailty. Leibowitz is well aware of the difficulty of living a religious life in accordance with this mishna, but he is not prepared to give up on it as a truth of the Torah. In support of his view he also cites the words of Rabbi Ḥayim of Volozhin in his commentary on Mishna *Avot,* who interprets Antigonus' words precisely in accordance with Maimonides. However, he deliberately hides the fact that this mishna was by no means the only voice of Jewish tradition and avoids mentioning its comparative insignificance in the philosophies identified with the ideological circle of Rabbi Yehuda HaLevi, the Maharal of Prague, or Rabbi Kook. In fact, there were many who warned of the dangers lurking in the path of Antigonus.

Leibowitz, following Maimonides, bases his compartmentalization of "fear" and "love" on the first two sections of the *Shema*. The first, *Shema Yisrael*, is a pure reflection of love of God with no expectation of hope for reward, while the second, *Vehaya im shamoa* is a pure reflection of fear of God and calculations of reward and punishment. The two paragraphs thus represent two fundamentally different worlds. Like Maimonides, Leibowitz views the section of *Shema Yisrael* as the highest ideal, while *Vehaya im shamoa* represents a compromise with human reality. Leibowitz's approach to the teaching of Antigonus is evident in all his writings[15] to various degrees. I would not presume to challenge the legitimacy of his approach, which accurately reflects Maimonides' position on the issue.[16] Nevertheless, we cannot totally ignore the classical Jewish position found in the Talmud and expounded in the Tosafot, whereby the mishna of Antigonus does not represent a Jewish doctrine, but rather a doctrine of the Gentile nations.

15. See his 1943 article, "Education toward *Mitzvot*" [Hebrew], in *Torah U'Mitzvot BeZeman Hazeh* (Tel Aviv: 1954), 27 (reprinted in his book, *Judaism, the Jewish People and the State of Israel* [Tel Aviv: 1975]). It would not be an exaggeration to state that the subject of "for-the-sake-of-Heaven" in the service of God is considered the central theme in Leibowitz's religious philosophy.
16. In contrast to the position of H. Kolitz, "In the Speculum of Faith," in H. ben Yerucham and H. Kolitz (eds.), *Negation for the Sake of Heaven* (Jerusalem: 1983). Even the title of the book attests to the editors' understanding of the centrality of the concept of "for the sake of Heaven" (= *lishma*) in Leibowitz's philosophy.

Chapter Four

Servants and Sons: Ḥoni the Circle Maker and the World of God's Servants[1]

The search for the connection between man and God, along with a sense of alienation from the strange new culture that had spread throughout the country, gave rise to a variety of new groups and ideologies. In a world without prophecy everyone seemed to be looking for the magic key that from the world below could bring about changes in the world above. Prayer began to become more formalized, and private and public fasts were institutionalized, with the sages guiding the public

1. Historically, this section on Ḥoni belongs with that on the third of the *Zugot* (Shimon ben Shetaḥ and Yehuda ben Tabbai), and that on Ḥanina ben Dosa with Rabban Yoḥanan ben Zakkai (the generation of the Destruction). I have advanced this discussion to this point so as to consider their characters in the same context as that of Antigonus of Sokho regarding the "servants and sons" dichotomy.

and showing them the proper path. But this institutionalized service of God was also a source of intense frustration, for after completing his prayer the individual had no inkling as to whether or not it had had any impact upon the celestial world. The ethos of "And it shall be if you listen… and I will give rains in their time…" made it clear that there was a nexus between our deeds and His deeds, even in a world bereft of prophecy. Yet the seeds of doubt crept through, and people were left searching for something more definite. Our encounter with Ḥoni the Circle Maker and his actions introduces us to the world of religious yearning, in which man stands in prayer and wonders whether he can indeed influence his Creator.

ḤONI THE CIRCLE-MAKER: A CHILD CLINGING TO HIS FATHER

One of the best-known sources highlighting the tension between the laborious and routine service of God on the one hand, and the desire for immediate and direct contact with Him on the other, is the story of Ḥoni the Circle-Maker and Shimon ben Shetaḥ (Mishna, *Ta'anit* 3:8). Ḥoni was widely known as a pious miracle worker, in the mold of the ancient prophets. He was capable of confronting the divine decree of drought and bringing about a miraculous rainfall, in total defiance of the Talmudic statement that the keys for rain were not given to man, but were kept exclusively by God:

> Rabbi Yoḥanan said: The Holy One, blessed be He, has retained three keys in His own hands and not entrusted them to the hand of any messenger: namely, the key of rain, the key of childbirth, and the key of Resurrection of the Dead; as it is written: "The Lord will open for you His good treasure, the heavens to give the rain of the land in its season" [Deuteronomy 28:12]. (*Ta'anit* 2a)

The theological point of departure here is that certain matters are not given to men, or even to God's messengers. Rather they are entirely a matter of divine providence, sealed in a divine treasury to which God alone has the keys: rain, childbirth, and the Resurrection of the Dead. The story of Ḥoni – who draws a circle, stands inside it, and declares "I will not move from here until You have mercy on Your children" – undermines the categorical nature of the above statement, for it implies that there is someone capable of forcing God to use the key to give plenitude to the world. Ḥoni is somewhat reminiscent of Elijah the prophet, who likewise held the key to rainfall; indeed, the *baraita* in *Ta'anit* does in fact compare Ḥoni to Elijah. But as we shall soon observe, a close reading of Tractate *Ta'anit* reveals that, in fact, Ḥoni is the subject of serious criticism.

It is against this background that we now turn to the story of Ḥoni the Circle-Maker.

DESCRIPTION OF THE EVENT: THE MISHNA IN TA'ANIT

> It happened that the people said to Ḥoni the Circle-Maker: "Pray for rain to fall." He replied: "Go and bring in the [earthenware] ovens [used to roast] the Paschal offerings so that they do not dissolve." He prayed, and no rain fell.
>
> What did he do? He drew a circle and stood within it and exclaimed: "Master of the Universe, Your children have turned to me because they believe me to be as a member of Your household. I swear by Your great name that I will not move from here until You have mercy on Your children."
>
> The rain then began to drizzle.
>
> He thereupon exclaimed: "It is not for this that I prayed, but for abundant rain to fill the cisterns, the ditches and the caves."
>
> The rain then began to come down with great force, whereupon he exclaimed: "It is not for this that I prayed, but for rain of benevolence, blessing and bounty."
>
> The rain then fell in the normal way.
>
> Shimon ben Shetaḥ sent him [this message]: "Were you not Ḥoni, I would have pronounced a ban against you. But what can I do? You act like a spoiled child before God and yet He accedes to your request, just as a father accedes to the request of his spoiled son. It is of you that Scripture says, 'Let your father and your mother be glad, and let her that bore you rejoice' [Proverbs 23:25]." (Mishna, *Ta'anit* 3:8)

Later we will consider more closely Shimon ben Shetaḥ's understanding of Ḥoni's character.[2] But both from Ḥoni's own words and from those of Shimon ben Shetaḥ, it is clear that Ḥoni's uniqueness lies in his special relationship with God: "like a spoiled son." Indeed, throughout the entire episode Ḥoni refers to himself as "son" and to God as "father." No other relationship is mentioned: Ḥoni is not a servant, and God is not his king. Apparently the description of the relationship as one of son in the presence of his father is particularly apposite, and perhaps it sums up the entire story, providing a striking contrast with the figure of Shimon ben Shetaḥ, the paragon of legal procedure who exemplifies the servant in his master's presence. A son can approach his father without fear of rejection, he can get on his father's nerves and while his father may rebuke him, and even be angry at him, he will ultimately grant his request. This is the ultimate message of the story. Shimon ben Shetaḥ appreciates Ḥoni's unique power as a son spoiled by his father, but he also expresses his reservations about him. This particular son may dismantle the entire institutionalized network of connections between the people and God.

THE PEOPLE'S YEARNING FOR ḤONI AND HIS LIKE

Shimon ben Shetaḥ's misgivings regarding Ḥoni derived first and foremost from his awareness that such a character held immense and seductive power. In the Oral Tradition, Ḥoni's character parallels that of Elijah, a sorely-missed personality in the era of the sages. Indeed, the sages liken Ḥoni to Elijah in a number of places. For example, in a *baraita* in the Babylonian Talmud parallel to the aforementioned mishna (*Ta'anit* 24b), and also in the Midrash:

> "There was not a man to till [*la'avod*] the soil" [Genesis 2:5]: there is no man to make men serve [*leha'avid*] the Holy One, blessed be He, as Elijah and Ḥoni the Circle Maker. (*Bereshit Raba* 13)

There will always be a certain nostalgia for the world of the prophet who could give clear expression to a sense of nearness to God. The voice that

2. See the course of the Open University, *The World of the Sages* [Hebrew] (Tel Aviv: 1977), unit 2, which is devoted entirely to Ḥoni the Circle Maker.

yearns for Elijah and Ḥoni is the same voice that cries "We want to see our king" – but the price of such longings may be heavy, in that they are likely to be accompanied by a closed-mindedness to new experience and a dependence on momentous vision that once was, but is no longer

In parallel sources we see how Ḥoni's character was seen as a carryover from the Temple period. In this sense he is similar to Simeon the Just. He exemplifies a pristine, untainted world, in whose presence one can attain a kind of pure, unadulterated vision. The peak of Honi's spiritual elevation is expressed in the description of his seventy-year slumber, as it appears in the Jerusalem Talmud:

> This is Ḥoni, the Circle Maker, the grandson of Ḥoni, the Circle Maker. Near the time of the destruction of the Temple, he went out to a mountain to see his workers. Before he got there, it rained. He went into a cave and, once he sat down, he became tired and fell asleep. He slept for seventy years, during which the Temple was destroyed and was rebuilt a second time. At the end of seventy years he awoke from his sleep, left his cave, and saw a world completely changed. Areas that had been planted with vineyards now produced olives, and areas planted with olives now produced grain. He asked the people of the district, "What is happening in the world?" They said to him, "Don't you know what the news is?" He said to them, "No." They said to him, "Who are you?" He said to them, "Ḥoni the Circle Maker." They said to him, "We heard that when he used to enter the Temple courtyard it would light up the surroundings." He went in to the courtyard and indeed it lit up. He recited, in relation to himself, the verse of Scripture: "When the Lord restored the fortune of Zion, we were like those who dream" [Psalms 126:1]. (Talmud Yerushalmi, *Ta'anit* 3:9 [66d])

Ḥoni is here presented as the source of the light of the Temple. He is the manifestation of the return of the Divine Presence to Zion and its shining upon the Jewish people. The world longed for the revelation of Ḥoni's power. Indeed, it was precisely for that reason that he incurred the wrath of Shimon ben Shetaḥ.

THE SPOILED SON

The world of the sages, based as it is on an ethos of effort and hard work, is in danger of being blown to pieces by this phenomenon of a son who bursts his way directly into the Father's house without any objection. The teaching of Antigonus of Sokho, the student of Simeon the Just, was founded in an awareness of our position as servants of God. Antigonus' innovation was simply that our servitude should not be motivated by an expectation of reward, but should be without any desire for recompense. This is indeed a unique approach to servitude, since the reward is normally regarded as providing the legitimacy for one's status as slave. Ḥoni, however, took a different path. His conduct was not that of a servant but rather that of a son – indeed, that of a spoiled son.[3] This trait is eloquently expressed in the *baraita* cited in the Babylonian Talmud, which is a parallel, albeit expanded version of the mishna in Tractate *Ta'anit*:

> It once happened that most of Adar had passed and rain had not yet fallen. The people sent a message to Ḥoni the Circle Maker: "Pray that rain may fall." He prayed and no rain fell. He thereupon drew a circle and stood within it in the same way as the prophet Habakkuk had done, as it is said, "I will stand my watch, take up my station at the post" [Habakkuk 2:1].
>
> They then said to him: "Master, in the same way that you prayed for the rain to fall, pray for the rain to cease." He replied: "I have it as a tradition that we may not pray on account of an excess of good. Despite this bring unto me a bullock for a thanksgiving-offering." [...]
>
> Thereupon Shimon ben Shetaḥ sent him this message: "Were it not that you are Ḥoni I would have placed you under a ban; for were it like the years [of famine in the time] of Elijah [in whose hands were the keys of rain], would not the name of Heaven be profaned through you? But what can I do to you, who act petulantly before the Omnipresent and He grants your desire,

3. It bears mention that as early as *The Vitry Maḥzor* (§424) we find comment on the gap between the conduct of Ḥoni and that which is required in accordance with the teachings of Antigonus of Sokho.

> like a son who acts petulantly before his father and he grants his desires. Thus he says to him: Father, take me to bathe in warm water, wash me in cold water, give me nuts, almonds, peaches, and pomegranates; and he gives them to him. Of you Scripture says, 'Let your father and your mother be glad, and let her that bore you rejoice' [Proverbs 23:25]." (*Ta'anit* 23a)

This *baraita* adds two striking nuances. The first is the clear comparison of Ḥoni with the prophets Habakkuk and Elijah. Like them, he too "stands on the watch," and is capable of establishing a unique and direct connection with the heavenly powers. In this aspect of Ḥoni's description we can sense a desire to preserve the power of the prophet even after the spirit of prophecy has departed from Israel.

The second point is the severity of Shimon ben Shetaḥ's response. Ḥoni is the spoiled child who must always have his way. He will perennially ask, and his father, who is so proud of his son, will always give. This is the root of Shimon ben Shetaḥ's deep concern. He cannot tolerate the notion that Ḥoni's unorthodox conduct might become the accepted norm. The one-time success in bringing rain could radically reduce the emotional pitch of prayer. Why bother to persist with all the efforts of prayers and fasts for rain, when just down the road there lives a man who has the keys to Heaven!

THE DECLINE IN THE GENERATION AFTER ḤONI

Shimon ben Shetaḥ's reservations were not unfounded. The knowledge that there was a person who held the key to rainfall and was capable of assuaging his Father's anger led to an attitude of religious laxity among the people. During the generation following Ḥoni, the people had become accustomed to directly turning to Ḥoni's grandson. The Talmud (*Ta'anit* 23a) relates that whenever famine beset the world, the people would send emissaries to Ḥoni's grandson, Aba Ḥilkia, entreating him to pray for rain. But there is something amiss when one lives in an atmosphere of immediate divine gratification, like a father pleasing his son. One loses the awesome sense of mystery, the inclining of the ear, the attentive heart; eventually, over-familiarity with the source of one's awe is likely to engender an attitude of contempt. The rabbis understood all this and more when they said that Ḥoni "behaved in an overly familiar fashion with Heaven" (*Berakhot* 19a). This grave statement likens Ḥoni to the seventy elders who went up to see God in a state where "they ate and they drank" (Exodus 24:11). "Over familiarity" refers to that state of presumptuousness which dulls the senses, and fosters an attitude of conceit toward oneself, one's surroundings and God. Parents, who are naturally proud of their children, are not always sensitive to their children's vanities. Shimon ben Shetaḥ reflects this in his admonition to Ḥoni: "It is of you that Scripture says, 'Let your father and your mother be glad, and let her that bore you rejoice.'" The parents may not notice the child's flaws, but the bystander can well see that overconfidence will lead to a presumptuous arrogance which does not bode well.

ḤONI'S END ACCORDING TO JOSEPHUS FLAVIUS

Our discussion of the dangers involved in adopting Ḥoni as a model miracle-worker, leads us to the story of his death, as recorded by Josephus Flavius.

> There was a certain Ḥonio, who was a righteous man and dear to God. Once in a time of drought he prayed to God to end the drought, and God had heard his prayer and sent rain. This man hid himself when he saw that the civil war continued to rage, but he was taken to the camp of the Jews, and was asked to place a curse on Aristobulus and his fellow rebels, just as he had by his prayers put an end to the drought. But when, in spite of his refusals and his excuses he was forced to speak by the mob, he stood up in their midst and said, "O God, King of the Universe, since these men standing beside me are Your people and those who are besieged are Your priests, I beseech You not to hearken to them against these men nor to bring to pass what these men ask You to do to those others." And when he had prayed in this manner the villains among the Jews who stood round him stoned him to death. (*Antiquities* XIV, 22–24)

Josephus speaks of a period during which two Hasmonean sons, Hyrcanus and Aristobulus, were struggling over the monarchy in Jerusalem. We will address the particulars of their struggle in their proper place in Part II, but for our purposes we should note what happened to the nation that relied on a miracle worker such as Ḥoni. He was brought into the camp of one part of the people to offer his prayers against the other part of the same people. When Ḥoni refuses to pray for one camp against the other, he is attacked by the masses who stone him to death. In the absence of miracles he has no life. It was not him they wanted, but his wondrous powers.

ḤONI'S END ACCORDING TO THE BABYLONIAN TALMUD

The Babylonian Talmud preserves a different tradition regarding Ḥoni's end, in a source parallel to that cited above from the Jerusalem Talmud regarding his sleeping for seventy years:

> Rabbi Yoḥanan said: Throughout his life that righteous man [Ḥoni] was troubled about the meaning of the verse: "A Song of Ascents, When the Lord brought back those that returned to Zion, we were like dreamers" [Psalms 126:1]. He said: Is it possible for a man to dream continuously for seventy years? (*Ta'anit* 23a)

Rabbi Yoḥanan's point of departure is that the righteous man (Ḥoni) was always perturbed by the verse, "When the Lord brought back those that returned to Zion, we were like dreamers." He understood that a dream expresses tense anticipation. He also knew that the Return to Zion of Ezra and Nehemiah occurred seventy years after the Temple's destruction. For seventy years the light of the dream had been hidden. For Ḥoni, who stands before God in the here and now and dictates his wishes to his Heavenly Father with immediacy, there can be no such thing as yearning for seventy years:

> One day he was journeying on the road and saw a man planting a carob tree. He asked him: "How long does it take [for this tree] to bear fruit?" The man replied: "Seventy years." He then further asked him: "Are you certain that you will live another seventy years?" The man replied: "I found [ready grown] carob trees in the world; as my forefathers planted these for me, so too do I plant these for my children."

> Ḥoni sat down to have a meal and was overcome by sleep. As he slept a rocky formation enclosed upon him, hiding him from sight, and he continued to sleep for seventy years.

One could hardly imagine a greater meeting of opposites than the meeting of Ḥoni and the carob-tree planter. There is probably no task with less chance of immediate gratification than that of the planter. The fruit of the carob tree will not come forth for many years. The seventy years described here may be an exaggeration, but the point is to present Ḥoni with the notion of a life of work and effort, in which one may not even see the fruits of one's labor. Someone labored here before me and I eat the fruits of their efforts; so will those who come after me benefit from mine. Ḥoni, his entire life one of being pampered and satisfied, cannot fathom such an approach. He eats his bread and retreats into sleep for seventy years – the passage of time required for him to reappear with a belated maturity:

When he awoke he saw a man gathering the fruit of the carob tree and he asked him: "Are you the man who planted the tree?" The man replied: "I am his grandson." Thereupon he exclaimed: "It is clear that I have slept for seventy years." He then caught sight of his ass which had given birth to several generations of mules.

> He returned home, where he inquired: "Is the son of Ḥoni the Circle Maker still alive?" The people answered him: "His son is no more, but his grandson is still living." Thereupon he said to them: "I am Ḥoni the Circle Maker," but no one believed him.
>
> He then retired to the study house. There he overheard the scholars say, "The law is as clear to us as in the days of Ḥoni the Circle Maker, for whenever he came to the study house he would resolve any difficulties that the scholars had." Whereupon he called out, "I am he"; but the scholars would not believe him nor did they give him the honor due to him. This hurt him greatly and he prayed [for death] and he died. Raba said: "Hence the saying, 'Either companionship or death.'"

Rabbi Yoḥanan, the very sage who asserted that the keys to rain were not given to emissaries, relates that Ḥoni was perturbed by the problem of whether one could live for seventy years in a dream. The verse expounded for the purpose of Ḥoni's question was the same as that used to describe the Babylonian exiles, who were destined to live seventy years in the dream of "when the Lord brought back those that returned to Zion." Ḥoni was unable to come to terms with the notion that one may not see the fulfillment of one's expectations. Seventy years is the human lifespan ("The days of our years are seventy; or if by reason of special strength, eighty years" – Psalms 90:10). The person who dreams for seventy years will not live to see the fulfillment of his dreams. For Ḥoni the Rain Maker, this was intolerable, and he was forced to experience it himself.

According to this Babylonian tradition, Ḥoni was a man of the study house, and upon not being recognized there, he loses his senses. In his original path, he had found a person planting a carob, which only yields its fruit after seventy years. Ḥoni was curious as to the purpose of such planting: "Are you certain that you will live another seventy years to enjoy its fruit?" The planter reassures Ḥoni with his simple reply: "I found [ready grown] carob trees in the world; as my forefathers planted these for me, so too do I plant these for the next generations." At this stage Ḥoni goes into a prolonged slumber; for seventy years he is absent from the world. Upon awakening, he encounters the new world. Everything has continued from the point at which Ḥoni's old life stopped, only the characters have been replaced. The donkey has already given birth to several generations of offspring, the carob produces fruit for the old man's grandchildren, Ḥoni's children are no longer alive and the grandchildren are unwilling to accept his presence. The gravest thing of all, however, is that in the one place Ḥoni calls home, the place where he is in his element, the study house, he is not even recognized. He hears his own name on the lips of others: How much light there was in the times of Ḥoni, when everything was lucid and all problems were solvable, when there was life without doubt and without questions. From the students' benches he hears the yearning for the days of old, yet at the very moment that he identifies himself as Ḥoni he finds himself rejected: "They didn't believe him." The world has progressed another seventy years forward and distanced itself from the world of miracles. In a world accustomed to living in doubt, there is no longer any room for

Ḥoni and his unique powers. He is forced to leave the study house and, consequently, to leave the world itself, to which he no longer belongs. Ḥoni's world has died.

BEHOLDING GOD:

"It Begins With Labor and Ends in Reward"

Beholding the face of God, as described by Rabbi Moshe Ḥayim Luzzatto in his book *Mesilat Yesharim* (*The Path of the Just*), is located at the top of the scale of achieving holiness, at the level of sanctity. According to Luzzatto, there are two aspects to holiness: "It begins with labor and ends in reward." There are no shortcuts. In the approach of Shimon ben Shetaḥ, service of God does not promise an open door or a direct response. The world of the sages dictated a different routine for communication between man and God: a routine of discipline, a measured rhythm, a regular timetable.

Nonetheless, there is a hierarchy in the world of servants too, and servants can find themselves on different levels. At the highest level are those who serve as the king's advisers and ministers. They may not belong to the royal family, but they enjoy high standing and a central role. It is their job to consult with the king, to present him with the needs of their ministries, to ensure the best interests of the office with which they are charged and to assist the king in ruling his kingdom. But there is another type of servant, who behaves neither as son nor as minister, but rather as the king's personal valet, who is with him at his most intimate moments. While the ministers are described as being those "who see the king's face, who sit first in the kingdom," the personal assistants, even though they may not "sit first in the kingdom," also see the king's face, by simply being in the king's presence. In the world of the sages the exemplar of these servants, whose fear and awe precede their wisdom, is Rabbi Ḥanina ben Dosa.

Chapter Five

His Fear Precedes His Wisdom: Ḥanina ben Dosa

Rabbi Ḥanina ben Dosa said: "He whose fear of sin precedes his wisdom, his wisdom shall endure; but he whose wisdom precedes his fear of sin, his wisdom shall not endure." He used to say: "He whose deeds exceed his wisdom, his wisdom shall endure; but he whose wisdom exceeds his deeds, his wisdom shall not endure. (Mishna, Avot 3:11)

Alongside the sages, there were always significant secondary figures who, though not partners in the creation of the halakha, nonetheless influenced in their own way the shaping of their spiritual world. These are generally identified with the group known as "Hasidim," characterized by saintly piety. As distinct from the sages, the Hasidim were distinguished for their virtues, their devotion and their humility. The central characters in this world are Ḥoni the Circle Maker and Ḥanina ben Dosa. As we turn to the character of Ḥanina ben Dosa, we should recognize that, like Ḥoni, his character is not presented chronologically (he belongs with Rabban Yoḥanan ben Zakkai in the generation following the Destruction), but I would like to compare and contrast him with Ḥoni the Circle Maker.

RABBI ḤANINA: SERVING GOD WITHOUT REQUESTING MIRACLES

The following story appears in the Midrash:

> Once, Rabbi Ḥanina ben Dosa saw the inhabitants of his city taking offerings [*nedarim* and *nedavot*: avowed- and voluntary-offerings] up to Jerusalem. He exclaimed, "They are all taking offerings up to Jerusalem, but I am taking nothing!" What did he do? He went out to the waste land of his city and found there a stone which he chipped, chiseled, and polished. He then said, "Behold, I take it upon myself to convey it to Jerusalem." He sought to hire workmen, and five men chanced to come his way. He asked them, "Will you carry this stone up to Jerusalem for me?" They answered, "Give us five selas and we will carry it up to Jerusalem." He wanted to give them the money, but he had none with him at the time; so they left him and departed.
>
> The Holy One, blessed be He, arranged for five angels to appear to him in the likeness of men. He asked them, "Will you carry this stone up for me?" They answered, "Give us five selas and we will carry your stone up for you to Jerusalem, but on condition that you place your hand and finger with ours." He placed his hand and finger with theirs and they found themselves standing in Jerusalem. He wanted to pay them their hire but could not find them. He entered the Chamber of Hewn Stone and inquired about them. [The men in the Chamber] said to him, "They were probably Ministering Angels who carried your stone up to Jerusalem."
>
> They applied to him this text: "Do you see a man diligent in his business? He shall stand before kings" [Proverbs 22:29]. They read the phrase as "He shall stand before angels" [i.e., as *malakhim* rather than *melakhim*]. (*Kohelet Raba* 1)

Rabbi Ḥanina did not request miracles. He was overwhelmed with sadness for not being able to bring a gift of vows and voluntary sacrifices up to Jerusalem. He wished to be connected to the Almighty through prayer and sacrifice. The world of vows and voluntary offerings provided the ideal format for a Jew wishing to connect to God above and beyond the call of his duties. He wanted more. Making a vow to God is an expression of good will, but for the wealthy man the gesture involves no more than the minor effort of buying a sacrifice and sending it to the Temple. Rabbi Ḥanina did not enjoy that privilege, so all that he could do was to chisel a simple stone. The miracle of the stone being conveyed to Jerusalem occurred by reason of Ḥanina's devotion and the effort invested in expressing his desire to come close to God. By extending his finger to the angels he was rewarded with the blessing of being miraculously transported to Jerusalem.

In this sense, he differs from Ḥoni the Circle Maker, who draws a circle and challenges God with "I will not move from here until You have mercy on Your children." Rabbi Ḥanina has no desire to alter the natural order. He is a simple, unpretentious person whose sole desire is to partake in a religious act, and it is precisely this simplicity that makes him deserving of reward. He is never referred to as a "son," but only as a "man." He does not stand before a kind and merciful father, rather "he stands before kings." He is rooted in the world of servants, but he has the simple soul of a servant of God, "and he alone is free," which brings him to the level of the miracle of standing "before kings."

The Talmud in Tractate *Ta'anit* devotes an entire page to the character of Rabbi Ḥanina, from which we can learn much. We will follow the stories in order.

RABBI ḤANINA'S WIFE AND THE NEIGHBOR:

> Rabbi Yehuda said in the name of Rav: Every day a heavenly voice is heard declaring, "The whole world draws its sustenance because [of the merit] of Ḥanina my son, and Ḥanina my son suffices with a *kab* of carobs from one Sabbath eve to another [...].
>
> Every Friday his wife would light the oven and throw twigs

> into it so as not to be put to shame. She had a bad neighbor who said, "I know that these people have nothing; what then is the meaning of all this [smoke]?" She went and knocked at the door. [The wife of Rabbi Ḥanina], feeling humiliated [at this], retired into an inner room.
>
> A miracle happened and [her neighbor] saw the oven filled with loaves of bread and the kneading trough full of dough.
>
> She called out to her: "You, you, bring your shovel, for your bread is getting charred." And she replied, "That is why I went into the inner room, to fetch the shovel." (*Ta'anit* 24b–25a)

Like Rabbi Ḥanina, his wife does not ask for miracles. She is simply embarrassed in front of her neighbor. Her life is based not on miracles but on humility; a humility that leads the couple to conceal their impoverishment with the smoke that hides the emptiness of their oven. They suffice with a small repast of carobs from one Shabbat eve to the next, but so as not to become common paupers, they conceal their poverty. The neighbor's knock invades the privacy of Mrs. Ben Dosa, who is struck by panic mixed with shame. At this point the miracle occurs. Here too, it is not the result of a demand presented to Heaven; she does not impose her poverty on the Holy One, blessed be He; rather, it is He who intervenes and saves her from embarrassment.

An addition that downplays the character of Ḥanina's wife

Our analysis of this story was evidently not accepted by the Talmudic editor. Hence his intervention, so that at the end of this wonderful story the following line appears:

> It was taught: Indeed she did go inside the inner room to bring a shovel, for she was accustomed to miracles.

The concluding statement "it was taught" is not part of the story and in fact it diminishes its force. The story's power derives from the fact that Ḥanina's wife enters the inner room, not because she expects a miracle, but quite the opposite: she was fleeing from shame. But the Talmud does not wish to leave her such words as: "I just went inside to fetch the shovel," and prefers to place her in the category of those righteous people that are "accustomed to miracles," and who in fact expect them. This is a Talmudic development of the story that is not necessarily connected, at its source, to the initial characterization of Rabbi Ḥanina ben Dosa.

RABBI ḤANINA AND HIS WIFE ARE LIBERATED FROM REWARD IN THIS WORLD

> His wife said to him: "How long will we go on suffering in such great poverty?" He replied: "What shall we do?" She said to him: "Pray for mercy, so that something might be given to you." He prayed, and there emerged the figure of a hand giving him one leg of a golden table. He then saw in a dream that the pious would one day eat at a three-legged golden table, but he would eat at a two-legged table. Her husband said to her: "Are you content that everybody shall eat at a perfect table and we at an imperfect table?" She replied: "What then shall we do? Pray for mercy that the leg be taken away." He prayed and it was taken away. (*Ta'anit* 25a)

This story stretches to the very limit of tolerance for a life of abject poverty, with no hint of material reward in this world. The tension between the absence of temporal reward and the sturdy table of the World to Come is more evocative of the world of the sages during the post-Destruction period than it is of the Mishnaic sages who lived during Temple times. The entire story bears the stamp of the miraculous: Rabbi Ḥanina's abilities are unlimited. He can instigate a miracle whenever he chooses, but considerations related to the advantages of reward in the World to Come prevent him from doing so. He educates his wife, who seeks to escape from poverty, and shows her what the valuable table looks like when one of its legs has already been consumed in this world.

An addition that enhances Rabbi Ḥanina's miraculous powers

As in the previous story, here too there is a *tanna* – an editor who is not prepared to let the story end without highlighting the miraculous powers of Rabbi Ḥanina:

> A *tanna* taught: The latter miracle was greater than the former.

As before, the *tanna*'s addition urges us to view Rabbi Ḥanina as a "miracle worker," who belongs to more elevated worlds, is aware of his special powers and utilizes them. The message of the original story is quite the opposite. Rabbi Ḥanina does not presume to create havoc in the supernal worlds by using his powers, and he actually attempts to conceal them.

LIGHTING THE SHABBAT CANDLES FROM VINEGAR

> It was sunset on Erev Shabbat and he [Ḥanina] noticed that his daughter was sad. He said to her, "My daughter, why are you sad?" She replied: "A jar of oil got mixed up with my vinegar jar and I used it for the Sabbath light." He said to her: "My daughter, why should this trouble you? He who commanded the oil to burn will also command the vinegar to burn." (*Ta'anit* 25a)

As in the previous stories, no miracle has been promised to Ḥanina or his family. The daughter cries because vinegar does not burn. She doesn't entreat her father to effect a miracle, nor does she expect one. She acts with honesty, even if the result may be unfavorable. Rabbi Ḥanina's response also promises no miracle, but educates toward the fear of Heaven and trust in God. He is unperturbed by the combustibility of the material; if God so desires, the vinegar will burn just as well as oil, or even better.

An addition that magnifies the miracle

Here too, the story has no conclusion: the candle may or may not burn, but the Talmud concludes by magnifying the miracle beyond all possible boundaries:

> It was taught: it kept burning the entire day until it was used for the *havdala* lamp.

RABBI ḤANINA BEN DOSA BECOMES A MIRACLE WORKER

The final two stories in the series are related from a perspective that views Rabbi Ḥanina as a miracle worker:

> Rabbi Ḥanina ben Dosa kept goats. He was told [by neighbors]: "They are causing us damage." He exclaimed: "If they are indeed causing damage, may bears devour them; but if they are not, may they each of them bring home at evening time a bear on their horns." At evening time each of them brought home a bear on their horns.
>
> Rabbi Ḥanina had a woman neighbor who was building a house, but the beams did not reach the walls. She came to him for help. He asked her: "What is your name?" She replied: "Iku." He thereupon exclaimed: "Iku, may your beams be lengthened." (*Ta'anit* 25a)

These are already stories of a miracle worker, of the genre that was prevalent among the *Ba'alei Shem*, "Masters of the Name," of a later period. Rabbi Ḥanina is no longer anonymous, a private individual. He has neighbors who are aware of his unique powers and who seek to avail themselves of them. This is a development that does not preserve the original and unique nature of this character, as he is presented by the *tanna'im*.

> From where did Rabbi Ḥanina ben Dosa have goats, seeing that he was poor? And furthermore, did the sages not teach that we may not rear small cattle in the land of Israel? Rabbi Pineḥas said: Once it happened that a man passed by his house and left some hens there and the wife of Rabbi Ḥanina ben Dosa found them. Her husband said to her: "Do not eat their eggs." And the eggs and chickens increased in number and they were extremely troubled by them and so sold them and with the proceeds he purchased goats. One day the man who lost the hens passed by [the house] again and said to his companion: "This was where I left my hens." Rabbi Ḥanina overheard him and said: "Have you

> any sign [by which to identify them]?" He replied: "Yes." He gave him the sign and took away the goats. These were the same goats that brought bears on their horns. (*Ta'anit* 25a)

It seems almost certain that this story consists of two layers. The earlier layer is the story told by Rabbi Pineḥas (which is brought in the Talmud entirely in Hebrew). In that story Rabbi Ḥanina is not trained in miracles; he conducts himself with honesty to the furthest extreme, becoming an exemplar for the commandment of returning and guarding of lost property. The Talmud, however, pins the story of returning lost property to the story of the goats bringing the bears on their horns. This is an attempt to transform Rabbi Ḥanina from a simple righteous man to a miracle worker. I think that this layer of his personality was added after he had already acquired a name as someone whose virtues generated a divine response.

A FURTHER STAGE IN ḤANINA BEN DOSA'S TRANSFORMATION INTO A MIRACLE WORKER

The final stage in the "development" of Rabbi Ḥanina ben Dosa's character from pious individual to miracle worker appears in *Avot deRabbi Natan*, which tells the story of Rabbi Ḥanina's animal, which was careful not to eat with thieves. Here too the account is not aimed at conveying a sense of the miraculous, but rather at broadening Rabbi Ḥanina's sphere of righteous influence – from his wife, to his daughter, and even to his donkey.

> Just as the righteous of old were pious, so, too, were their beasts pious. They said: The camels of our father Abraham would not enter a house in which there was an idol, as it is said: "For I have cleared the house and made room for the camels" (Genesis 24:31), [meaning,] I have cleared the house of teraphim. And why does the verse say, "And he made room for the camels"? This teaches that they would not enter into the house of Laban the Aramean until all the idols were removed from their sight.
>
> Once, the ass of Rabbi Ḥanina ben Dosa was stolen by thieves. The thieves tied the ass up in the yard and gave it straw

> and barley and water, but it would neither eat nor drink. They said: "Why should we let it die and befoul our yard?" So forthwith they opened the gate and drove it away. It walked along braying until it reached the house of Rabbi Ḥanina ben Dosa. When it reached the house, Rabbi Ḥanina's son heard its voice. "Father," he said, "that sounds like our beast." Rabbi Ḥanina ben Dosa replied to him: "My son, open the door for it, for it has almost died of hunger." He arose and opened the door, and put before it straw, barley and water, and it ate and drank. Hence it was said that: "Just as the righteous of old were saintly, so too were their beasts saintly like their masters." (*Avot deRabbi Natan*, recension A, ch. 8)

This story about the "righteous donkey" appears in earlier midrashim attributed to Rabbi Pineḥas ben Yair, but in the current context the story is told of Ḥanina ben Dosa, who is also presented as a miracle worker. In fact, the Talmud refers to both characters together:

> Rabbi Zeira said in Raba bar Zimuna's name: If the early ones were sons of angels, we are sons of men; and if the early ones were sons of men, we are like asses – and not like the asses of Rabbi Ḥanina ben Dosa and Rabbi Pineḥas ben Yair, but like ordinary asses. (*Shabbat* 112b)[1]

RETURNING TO THE ORIGINAL CHARACTER OF ḤANINA BEN DOSA – SERVICE IN SIMPLICITY

The character of Rabbi Ḥanina ben Dosa was, as we know, a model of behavior elevated far above regular people. But as I have noted, I do not think that this was his original character. Indeed, in my view the secret

1. The reference to Rabbi Ḥanina ben Dosa's donkey raises a number of questions. It is clear that according to the wording of the Gemara as received by Rabbi Nissim Gaon and by Rashi, the story refers to Rabbi Ḥanina. Rabbi Nissim elaborates upon the story based on *Avot deRabbi Natan*, and Rashi refers to *Ta'anit* 24a. The difficulty is that the story in *Ta'anit* refers to the donkey of Rabbi Yose of Yokrat. This point was already observed by the commentators (see the Vilna edition) but the matter requires further examination.

of his power and influence lay precisely in the simplicity of his character, in his honesty and his refusal to seek refuge in miracles. Another story, which further highlights the gap between the original sources and the later ones, is the story of the scorpion. According to the Mishna in *Berakhot*, when a person is standing in prayer it is forbidden for him to interrupt his prayer even if a snake is coiled at his heel. This is the background for the Tosefta's account of how Rabbi Ḥanina passed this test:

> They related of Rabbi Ḥanina ben Dosa, that once while he was standing in prayer, a poisonous lizard bit him but he did not interrupt [his prayer]. His students came and found it [the lizard] dead at the entrance to its hole. They said, "Woe to the man who is bitten by a lizard. Woe to the lizard that bites Ben Dosa." (Tosefta, *Berakhot* 3:20)

In the Jerusalem Talmud, this citation is followed by the following paragraph:

> His students said to him: "Rabbi, were you not afraid?" He said to them, "He to whom I direct my heart in prayer will attest whether I was afraid." (Talmud Yerushalmi, *Berakhot* 5:1 [9a])

Before turning to the formulation of this story in the Babylonian Talmud, we should take note of the details. Rabbi Ḥanina is standing in prayer. He has no intention of hurting a snake or any other beast. This is the source of his power, that he always behaves naturally and with simplicity.[2]

2. Rabbi Ḥanina's confrontation with the poisonous lizard in prayer rather than battle, was discussed in an article of Admiel Kossman, "Rabbi Ḥanina ben Dosa and the Snake: Daring and Courage" [Hebrew], Tractate *Gevarim* (Jerusalem: 2002), pp. 152–156. Rabbi Kook also gives a fascinating explanation of Rabbi Ḥanina ben Dosa's meeting with the poisonous lizard in *Ein Aya*. The poisonous lizard (according to Rashi) is a cross-breed between a turtle and a snake. Rabbi Kook describes Rabbi Ḥanina's personality as the paragon of honesty and simplicity, representing the natural world, as distinct from the poisonous lizard which symbolizes confusion and a distortion of nature.

In the Babylonian Talmud, however, the story is not presented in its Tosefta format, but with an entirely different thrust:

> Our rabbis taught: In a certain place there was once a lizard, which used to injure people. They came and told Rabbi Ḥanina ben Dosa. He said to them: "Show me its hole." They showed him its hole, and he put his heel over the hole, and the lizard came out and bit him, and it died. He put it on his shoulder and brought it to the study house and said to them: "See, my sons, it is not the lizard that kills, it is sin that kills!" On that occasion they said: "Woe to the man whom a lizard meets, but woe to the lizard which Rabbi Ḥanina ben Dosa meets!" (*Berakhot* 33a)

This version of the story sets out to portray Rabbi Ḥanina as a miracle worker, capable of intervening to change the course of nature. It brings the character of Ḥanina ben Dosa closer to that of Ḥoni the Circle Maker. The people identify him as capable of working miracles and as being aware of his own power. Just as Ḥoni said, "Go and bring in the ovens [on which you have roasted] the Paschal offerings," Rabbi Ḥanina says, "Show me its hole." He is aware of his ability to subjugate the lizard. This is a different version of the story, replacing the artlessness of Rabbi Ḥanina with the character of a miracle worker, conscious of his own powers. From this point on Rabbi Ḥanina develops into a person capable of reversing the natural order. Hence, when the Talmud speaks of demonic spirits which haunt our world, Rabbi Ḥanina is brought in order to "minimize" the threat:

> "And do not go out alone at night." For it was taught: One should not go out alone at night, that is, on the nights of either Wednesday or the Sabbath, because Agrat the daughter of Maḥalat goes forth, together with 180,000 angels of destruction, and each one has permission to wreak devastation. Originally they were at large all day. On one occasion Agrat met Rabbi Ḥanina ben Dosa [and] said to him, "Had they not made an announcement concerning you in heaven: 'Beware of Ḥanina and his learning,' I would have endangered you." He said to her, "If I am of account in heaven, I

> order you never to pass through inhabited regions." She replied to him, "I beg you to leave me a little room." So he left her Sabbath nights and Wednesday nights. (*Pesaḥim* 112b)

We should note that Rabbi Ḥanina does not set out to change the natural order. It is the malevolent Agrat who informs him of his influence in the celestial world, a place with which he does not concern himself. But once he becomes aware of his ability to help, he feels duty bound to be of benefit to the Jewish people.

The tannaitic portrayal of Rabbi Ḥanina is of someone who has no dealings with esoteric worlds. He seeks to serve God in innocence, from the reality of this world, and with all the natural powers given to him. The only mishna (apart from that in *Avot*) mentioning Rabbi Ḥanina is the mishna in Tractate *Berakhot*, which elaborates on the force of his prayer:

If one makes a mistake in his prayer it is a bad sign for him; if he is the leader [lit. "representative"] of the congregation it is a bad sign for those who have commissioned him, for a man's representative is equivalent to himself. It was related of Rabbi Ḥanina ben Dosa that he used to pray for the sick and say, "This one will die, this one will live." They asked him: "How do you know?" He replied: "If my prayer is fluent, I know that it is accepted; but if not, then I know that it is rejected." (*Berakhot* 5:5)

There is no flash of lightning for Ḥanina ben Dosa, nor does he witness a miraculous revelation. There is only "if my prayer is fluent..." The natural, uninterrupted flow of life signifies that all is well. The simple fluency of Rabbi Ḥanina's prayer is his inner sign that his prayer has been accepted and that the patient will live.[3]

3. See S. Na'eh, "Who Creates the Fruit of the Lips: A Phenomenological Study of Prayer" [Hebrew], *Tarbitz*, 63 (1994), 185–218, in which he explains this Mishna with reference to the precise formulation used in a manuscript version of the text: "If my prayer was fluent," and arrives at the same understanding of Rabbi Ḥanina's prayer.

THE PRAYERS OF RABBI ḤANINA: "THE ALL-MERCIFUL DESIRES THE HEART"

The Babylonian Talmud appends to the above mishna two more stories about Rabbi Ḥanina ben Dosa, whose powers of prayer made him the harbinger of the recuperation of the sons of the sages Rabban Gamliel and Rabban Yoḥanan ben Zakkai. In this rare encounter, representatives of the intellectual power of Torah confront the power of prayer of a simple righteous man. Rabban Yoḥanan ben Zakkai's words at the end of the passage illuminate the entire encounter:

> Our rabbis taught: It once happened that Rabban Gamliel's son fell ill. He sent two scholars to Rabbi Ḥanina ben Dosa to ask him to pray for him. When he saw them he went up to an upper chamber and prayed for him. When he came down he said to them: "Go, the fever has left him." They said to him: "Are you a prophet?" He replied: "I am neither a prophet nor the son of a prophet, but I learnt this from experience. If my prayer is fluent in my mouth, I know that he is accepted; if not, I know that it is rejected." They sat down and made a note of the exact moment. When they came to Rabban Gamliel, he said to them: "By the divine service! You have not been a moment too soon or too late, for it so happened that at that very moment the fever left him and he asked for water to drink."
>
> On another occasion Rabbi Ḥanina ben Dosa went to study Torah with Rabbi Yoḥanan ben Zakkai. Rabbi Yoḥanan ben Zakkai's son fell ill. He said to him: "Ḥanina, my son, pray for him that he may live." He put his head between his knees and prayed for him and he lived. Said Rabbi Yoḥanan ben Zakkai: "If Ben Zakkai had stuck his head between his knees for the whole day, no notice would have been taken of him." His wife said to him: "Is Ḥanina greater than you are?" He replied to her: "No, but he is like a servant before the king, and I am like a minister before the king." (*Berakhot* 34b)

The mishna in *Ta'anit* referred to Ḥoni the Circle Maker as "a son who importunes his father." The relationship between father and son may be particularly tense and full of anger, but when the son pleads with his father, the father is mollified and grants his wishes. This was the case with Ḥoni, who is aware of his closeness to his Father and forcefully presented the ultimatum: "He drew a circle and stood within it and exclaimed: 'I will not move from here until You have mercy on Your children.'" On the other hand, Rabban Yoḥanan ben Zakkai characterizes Ḥanina ben Dosa as a "servant" and himself as a "minister."

Rabbi Tzaddok HaKohen of Lublin (1823–1900) expounded on the distinction between a minister and a servant.

> In the entire Talmud, not a single law is cited in the name of Rabbi Ḥanina ben Dosa other than that in Mishna *Avot* [3:9]: "He whose fear of sin, etc." and "He whose deeds, etc." All the other places record his stories, his miracles, and his prayers, for this was his entire vocation. The essence of his soul in Torah is in the dictum, "He whose fear of sin, etc." for this was the striking feature of his soul, in that it teaches us that wisdom is not the ultimate goal, but rather fear of sin must take priority, and "action must be in abundance." For this reason he was always engaged in prayer, which is called service and is called fear, as the sages of blessed memory taught [*Berakhot* 9b] on the verse: "They shall fear You at sunrise" (Psalms 72:5). And this is the level of the servant who labors in service.
>
> Rabbi Yoḥanan ben Zakkai, on the other hand, is devoted to the Torah, which is continuous devotion, and he is therefore regarded as a minister to whom all the king's secrets are revealed. And because it is certain that whatever the All-Merciful does is for good, He therefore shows him the goodness that exists even without the effect of his prayer; therefore they do not respond to him. But this is not the case for the servant to whom the king's secrets cannot be disclosed, and he requests his benefit and wishes in accordance with his own level, and the king is forced to grant his wishes, for according to his understanding any other result would produce evil. And after this he is compelled to see that this too would be truly good for him. (*Tzidkat HaTzaddik*, 210)

The minister participates in all of the deliberations, and through his wisdom influences the workings of the kingdom. The servant, on the other hand, performs his duties, and in the formal sense cannot have any influence on the king's decisions, but his accessibility to the master far exceeds that of the minister. He is accustomed to being by his side, although he must always retain his awareness of his status. He is not a son – he is a servant!

Such then is the character of Rabbi Ḥanina ben Dosa. His doctrine is that fear must precede wisdom. Fear refers to the awareness of the sage, who knows his place. For a person living in the mindset of a servant, his wisdom has a clearly defined position. Where there is wisdom without fear, there is no longer any connection between the minister and the king. Ḥanina is the simple, virtuous man of deeds, by force of which he is so significant in Jewish history that the Mishna in *Sota* states: "When Ḥanina ben Dosa died, men of deeds were gone" (*Sota* 9:15). A world without Ḥanina ben Dosa loses some of its honesty, and with it some of the spontaneity that connects deeds to the upper worlds.

Chapter Six

A Contemporary Perspective: The Grandchildren of Ḥoni the Circle Maker

In one of the climactic moments of Shuli Rand's superb film *Ushpizin* (Israel, 2004), we find the couple in their home on the eve of Sukkot. Their house is empty. They have no money and no hope. The newly-religious Moshe shares some of the Torah that he learnt in the Yeshiva with his wife: "When there is lacking in the world, it's because we haven't prayed, or haven't prayed enough." Hearing this, his wife sends him away in despair: "Go pray, you haven't tried enough." The next scene is one of amazing prayer, both his and hers. The prayers are direct, as one man speaks to another, sincere, and brimming with confidence that the Heavenly Father cannot ignore His son's broken heart. Simultaneously, the miracle occurs, and the film confronts us with the miracle as it transpires. A philanthropist is drawing lots to choose the recipient of a large sum of money for the festival, and the couple's name is selected. The prayers penetrated the heavenly gates and their Father does not disappoint them.

For the duration of the film, the relationship of this Bratslaver couple with the Holy One, blessed be He, is manifested in all its directness, its spontaneity, and its innocence. It is an outpouring of exuberant talk, trust, love and frustration in view of the complex situation in which the couple finds itself. The religious person trained in the tradition of the fear of God and the sense of divine elevation, stands in awe before the raw intensity displayed on the screen. At the end of the film, I had a sense of having suddenly been transported into the world of Ḥoni the Circle Maker, a world in which the person with special powers of prayer can directly influence the Holy One, blessed be He.

In our discussion of Ḥoni, we noted elements of Elijah, the prophet who possessed the keys to rain. However, as noted, a close reading of Tractate *Ta'anit* discloses scathing criticism of Ḥoni. His famous act of engendering the miracle of rainfall during a year of drought is brought in the Mishna as an act that exemplifies the halakhic ruling of "not entreating for a plenitude of rain." On another level however, Ḥoni's act is also presented as the antithesis of Tractate *Ta'anit*. This tractate lays the framework for a long series of fasts for rain, ranging from individual fasts to fasts of the entire community. The process is a long one, consisting of a series of thirteen fasts designed to arouse the people to repentance and soul-searching for anything that may require amendment, in the hope of salvation. The process of fasting for rain is a protracted and exhausting one, engaging the people for almost the entire winter in prayer and repentance, when all the while no one has any certainty regarding of the efficacy of the prayers in the upper worlds. Until its very end, the Mishnaic treatise does not guarantee any definite reward: the fast may succeed or fail. The Talmud in Tractate *Ta'anit* (24a–25b) abounds with stories of *amora'im* who decreed fasts for rain (both in Babylonia and in *Eretz Yisrael*), but the fasts were unsuccessful and rain did not fall. It was only after "their hearts became weak" and there was some kind of personal surrender that God answered their prayers and the rain fell.

Ḥoni's presence in our world jeopardizes the entire good order of the divine service. We are all the more fortunate if one of our number is capable of bringing down rain with the confidence of a son entreating his father. We have already noted that this kind of situation exacts its price in terms of certain important qualities in the service of God: the attuned ear, the compliant heart, from where it is but a short step to arrogance and conceit. The person living in a permanent state of searching for the direct, immediate experience, devoid of prayer and labor, is liable to find himself demoralized and crushed in times when the Divine Presence is hidden. The service of God as presented by the school of Shimon ben Shetaḥ does not promise the open door and direct answer granted to Ḥoni. The world of the sages created a different order of communication between man and God. Theirs was a regime of discipline, a measured rhythm, a regular timetable of religious practice. The Bratslav world portrayed in *Ushpizin* is an attempt to pave a different path. In contrast to the "path of the just," we have "the path of the sons." This path is based on an approach of total dependence, on a father-child relationship. The relative benefits – and costs – of each of these two paths, is a question that requires deep and considered examination.

Part Two

The Period of the Pairs – Between Religion and the State

The Men of the Great Assembly	The Pairs	Shammai, Hillel and Their Students	Rabban Gamliel the Elder	The Destruction

-450	-300	-200	-50	30	60	70

Cyrus to Alexander of Macedonia	The Hasmoneans	Herod	The Governors	The War with Rome

Preface

The first part of this work introduced us to the world of the Oral Law that emerged from the confrontation with the disappearance of prophecy. The second part is different, being focused upon the political processes that affected our nation with the ascent of Greece, the edicts of Antiochus, the Hasmonean Wars, and the rise and fall of the Hasmonean state. Our concern here is with the spiritual question of the role of the sages as leaders of the people. We will deal with historical developments only insofar as they shed light on the teachings and activities of the sages of that period.

In the Oral Tradition this period is known as "The Period of the Pairs." As Greek influence increased, the institution of the priesthood declined, degenerating into an office purchased for money. With the decline of the priesthood, leadership was increasingly exercised by the Pairs, rabbinic sages whose authority derived primarily from their erudition in Torah and their prestige and popularity among the people at large. Toward the middle of this period, sectarianism found expression in the emergence of the Pharisees, the Sadducees, and the Essenes. The Sadducees attempted to maintain the *ancien régime* that preceded Ezra's revolution and the Men of the Great Assembly. Their stature and power were based on the Temple; hence they fostered the centrality of the sacred and of the Sanctuary. The Essenes segregated themselves within an isolated, separatist lifestyle, waging a spiritual battle against the "sons of darkness" from their ethereal heights. In leading the people, the Pharisees forged a new path, paying attention to questions of community, economics, foreign policy and security. The final section of this part links the declining years of the Hasmonean state to the end of the era of the Pairs.

Chapter Seven

Yose ben Yoezer

Yose ben Yoezer of Zeredah and Yose ben Yoḥanan of Jerusalem received [Torah] from them. Yose ben Yoezer used to say: Let your house be a gathering place for the sages and sit amidst the dust of their feet and drink their words with thirst.

Yose ben Yoḥanan said: Let your house be open wide to all and let the poor be members of your household and do not talk too much with women. This is said [even] of one's own wife; all the more so of another's wife. Hence the sages have said: Whoever engages in too much talk with women causes evil to himself, neglects the study of the Torah, and is ultimately condemned to perdition. (Avot 1:4–5)

HISTORICAL AND POLITICAL BACKGROUND

The period of the Pairs places us in the second century BCE, at the beginning of the Hasmonean period. This century was a crucial one for the crystallization of Jewish and national identity and the courageous defense of that identity. The century begins with the spread of Hellenism, followed by the Maccabean revolt. The second half of the century saw the establishment of the Hasmonean regime, which steadily consolidated and centralized its control over all the realms of government, culminating in the unification of the priesthood and the monarchy.

The first Pair was active during the reign of Antiochus Epiphanes, an iron-fisted ruler who sought to impose uniformity upon the entire kingdom, something one might call the "Seleucid global village."[1] First Maccabees (1:41)[2] records a letter written by Antiochus to the entire kingdom, exhorting them to become one nation. Antiochus "merited" a loyal ally from among the Jews: Jason the Priest purchased the high-priesthood from the Seleucid ruler in return for his promise to transform Jerusalem into a *polis* with all the trappings of Greek culture, including the construction of a gymnasium, as well as lectures in literature and philosophy, sport, and music. Second Maccabees attests to the success of this venture, at least among the priests, in its description of how the priests would promptly abandon their service in the Temple upon hearing the clanging of the discus being thrown in the stadium:

> To such heights did the passion for adopting Greek customs develop and the fad for imitating foreign manners advance, on account of the ever growing wickedness of the no-priest Jason, that no longer were the priests interested in the service of the altar. Despising the Temple and neglecting the sacrifices, they would hasten to participate in the unlawful exercises of the *palaestra* [boxing ring] as soon as they heard the call of the discus. (II Maccabees 4:13–15)

1. The material regarding Greek policy during the Hasmonean Period is taken from M. Stern "Eretz Yisrael during the Hellenistic Period" [Hebrew], in Israel Efal, *History of Eretz Yisrael* (Jerusalem: 5758), vol. 3, pp. 70–140.
2. The following material is based on the scientific editions of the Books of Maccabees: U. Rappaport, *The First Book of Maccabees, Introduction, Hebrew Translation and Commentary* (Jerusalem: 2004), and D. Schwartz, *The Second Book of Maccabees, Introduction, Hebrew Translation and Commentary* (Jerusalem: 2005). The English translations of the First and Second Books of Maccabees are based on the translations of Sidney Tedesche, (New York: Dropsie College Edition, Jewish Apocryphal Literature, 1954).

Similarly, I Maccabees (chapter 1) relates that the gymnasium curriculum required the men to stretch their foreskins so as not to distinguish themselves from their fellow Greek sportsmen. Hellenistic Jerusalem thus came to have a new character, and a new constitution. A compulsory education law was introduced, and became a condition for receiving citizenship of the city. And the single God of monotheism was now joined by a number of tantalizing and alluring partners, such as Hermes, Hercules and the Muses.[3]

In 171 BCE the king dismissed Jason, crowning the treasurer of the Temple, Menelaus, in his stead. The book of Maccabees even relates the price that Menelaus paid for his new job – three hundred coins more than Jason had offered.

This was the first time that a high priest had been appointed from the priestly watch of Bilgah, which had long competed with the priestly descendants of Tzaddok for seniority and leadership of the priesthood. In this struggle between the two houses, which dated back to the beginning of the Second Temple period, the descendants of Tzaddok had always had the upper hand. In priestly circles, the Bilgah watch took the lead in the Hellenizing trend,[4] as evidenced by the following Talmudic tradition:

> It happened that Miriam the daughter of Bilgah became an apostate and married an officer of the Greek kings. When the Greeks entered the Sanctuary she stamped with her sandal upon the altar crying out, "Lucas, Lucas! For how long will you consume Israel's money! And yet you do not stand by them in the time of oppression!" And when the sages heard of the incident they made her ring immovable and locked her window. (*Sukka* 56b)

Menelaus became a hostage of Antiochus, who had been responsible for the establishment and consolidation of the priest's position. The Jewish uprising against his rule began in response to Menelaus' plundering

3. M. Stern, "The Establishment of the Gymnasium, the Transformation of Jerusalem into a *Polis* and the Ascendance of Menelaus" [Hebrew], *Zion* 57, (5752), pp. 233–246.
4. M. Stern, "The Institutions of Independent Jewish Leadership" [Hebrew], in *The History of the Land of Israel*, vol. 3, p. 105, and pp. 124–125.

of the holy vessels in order to pay his debts to Antiochus. The golden altar, the Menora, the showbread table and other Sanctuary items were all taken in this wholesale plunder. This event became the watershed for the final rift between the Hellenist stratum, loyal to Menelaus, and the majority of the nation who, even if not actually identifying with the *Ḥasidim* ("pious ones"), was no longer able to bear the national and religious humiliation of the Temple's desecration.

And if these measures were not enough, Antiochus enacted a series of edicts proscribing any kind of religious practice other than the worship of the Greek gods. These edicts reached their peak in 167 BCE when, on the 25th of Kislev, an idol was erected in the Temple precincts and the daily sacrifices were offered to it.[5] The following verses in the book of Daniel (which according to many scholars relates to this period) provide the following description:

> Forces will be levied by him; they will desecrate the Temple, the fortress; they will abolish the regular offering and set up the appalling idol. He will flatter with smooth words those who act wickedly toward the covenant, but the people devoted to God will stand firm. The knowledgeable among the people will make the many understand; and for a while they shall fall by the sword and flame, suffer captivity and spoliation. (Daniel 11:31–33)

The verse concerning the smoothly flattering ones "who act wickedly toward the covenant" would seem to be a clear reference to the high priest appointed on Antiochus' behalf. Menelaus had sold out to the Seleucid policies.

So began the spread of Hellenism in Israel. As usual in processes of this kind, the movement spread from the urban centers outward to the periphery. It was during this period that the first of the Pairs, Yose ben Yoezer and Yose ben Yoḥanan, arose.

5. II Maccabees contains a detailed description of the decrees and of the surrounding events.

A ḤASID AMONG THE PRIESTS

In contrast to the dearth of information regarding Yose ben Yoḥanan of Jerusalem, a number of sources shed light on Yose ben Yoezer of Zeredah. A person's location attests to his character, and this is certainly true of Yose ben Yoezer, who lived in Zeredah, in Western Samaria (next to today's Beit Aryeh, at the Alei Zahav site, which was established by Herut veterans in memory of Aliza Begin). From his geographic location, we learn that Yose ben Yoezer was far removed from the new centers of Hellenist activity. Indeed the province of Zeredah is close to where the Hasmonean rebellion erupted.

The Mishna refers to Yose ben Yoezer as "a *ḥasid* among the priests" (*Ḥagiga* 2:7). This description points to a clear connection with the spiritual leadership that sought to preserve a distinct Jewish identity and separated by meticulous observance of the laws of purity. The Mishna in Tractate *Eduyot* (8:4) recounts three instances in which Yose ben Yoezer gave lenient rulings on matters of ritual impurity. As a result he was known as "Yose the Lenient" (further on we will compare these rulings with those of the Sadducees). The description of Yose ben Yoezer as "*Ḥasid*" ("pious") places him in the mainstream of the *Ḥasidim* of the Second Temple period who spearheaded the Hasmonean rebellion. The books of Maccabees describe the *Ḥasidim* as a group that crystallized in support of Mattathias. There is, in fact, a striking similarity between the sages who were the scribes of the Great Assembly, and the *Ḥasidim* of the Hasmonean rebellion.[6] In this context, Yose ben Yoezer played a major role. While continuing the work of the scribes, he also belonged to world of the *Ḥasidim*, making him a crucial link in the chain of tradition.

BETWEEN ISRAEL AND THE NATIONS

The first pair of sages were regarded as the spiritual leaders of the nascent rebellion. They advocated a strict and uncompromising policy of absolute separation between Jews and non-Jews. The sources record a number of their regulations and enactments as part of a policy designed to

6. V.A. Tcherikover, "The Decrees of Antiochus" in *The Jews in the Graeco-Roman World* (Jerusalem: 5721), pp. 156–180.

prevent assimilation. A *baraita* in Tractate *Shabbat* records one of their decrees:

> Yose ben Yoezer of Zeredah and Yose ben Yoḥanan of Jerusalem decreed uncleanness in respect of the lands of the heathens and glassware. (*Shabbat* 14b)

The scholar Louis Ginzberg has shed some interesting light on this decree:

> The decree on the impurity of the lands of the heathens was passed at a time when the Jews were beginning to leave the land [*Eretz Yisrael*], and going abroad in the wake of the edicts and destruction wreaked by the evil Antiochus…The second edict of the first Pair is extremely interesting and, if the first one was a political ruse, the second one was an economic one. The leading artisans in the glasswork trade were the Canaanites living in Tyre and Sidon, and all glassware in the land of Israel came from them. Importing these vessels triggered tremendous competition between local products and those produced abroad, and many preferred to use vessels that did not receive impurity rather than the clay and steel vessels produced in Israel which required particular caution because of non-cleanliness. The edict of the impurity of glassware had the effect of reducing the competition.[7]

The teachings of Yose ben Yoezer and Yose ben Yoḥanan represent a challenge to the leadership of that generation as well as to the Hellenism and edicts of the period. Yose ben Yoezer directs his energies inwards – toward the house of study: "Let your house be a gathering place for the sages." One's environment should be suffused with Torah, and one's home should be receptive to teachings of the sages. A house with a bookshelf boasting the entire works of Homer, in which the children's room features a video library of Greek mythology and which

7. "The Role of the Halakha in Jewish Studies" in L. Ginzberg, *Halakha and Aggada: Studies and Essays* [Hebrew] (Tel Aviv: Devir, 1960), p. 15.

has a fitness room in the basement, will not serve as a meeting place for the sages. The character of the house determines its affiliation. This was Yose ben Yoezer's way of confronting Hellenism: "sit amid the dust of their feet and drink in their words with thirst" – in order to elevate the standing of the Torah and the sages in the eyes of the people.

Yet alongside him, we have Yose ben Yoḥanan of Jerusalem, who stresses the imperative of tearing down the walls of the house. A house which becomes a fortress, albeit for Torah, will not be able to influence the wider community, and will remain small and elitist. In Yose ben Yoḥanan's eyes, this was not the time for raising barricades, and his teaching was therefore: "Let your house be open wide." A time of crisis requires an emphasis on the virtues of kindliness, on keeping an open house and concern for the poor. In his teaching, the core of the Jewish home is kindness, and his requirement is that it be opened wide, and that the poor be included as members of the household. Another, more literal interpretation is also worth mentioning: "Let the poor be members of your household" can be read to mean, let the poor be members of your household staff. A house which is open to all requires a large service staff; these same poor people should be employed.[8]

YOSE BEN YOEZER'S (HELLENIST) SON

The struggle between Hellenists and *Ḥasidim* was not one between two clearly defined camps. The boundaries between the rival parties were often blurred, and many families were divided between fervent supporters of the Hasmonean rebellion and Jewish sympathizers with Hellenist culture, who avidly watched the games in the stadium. Drawing the line was a formidable task, and even those who attempted to turn their homes into closed fortresses of Torah were liable to find the battle lines drawn through their own families. Such was the position of Yose ben Yoezer's

8. L. Finkelstein, *Introduction to the Treatises of Abot and Abot of Rabbi Nathan* (New York: 1950), p. 236, takes a different view of the differences between each one of the first Pair. Yose ben Yoezer was the head of the Beit Din of the more conservative party, consisting mainly of priests and the wealthy classes. His students, being primarily members of these families, were therefore educated to make their houses meeting places for the sages. A different path was adopted by Yose ben Yoḥanan, from whom Beit Hillel developed.

own family, one member of which deserted them in favor of the alien Hellenist culture. The *baraita* in Tractate *Bava Batra* records the following discussion between the sages and Rabban Shimon ben Gamliel:

> If a person bequeaths his estate in writing to strangers, and leaves out his children, his arrangements are legally valid, but the spirit of the sages finds no delight in him. Rabbi Shimon ben Gamliel said: If his children did not conduct themselves in a proper manner he will be remembered for good. (*Bava Batra* 133b)

In the context of this discussion, the Gemara relates the following story about Yose ben Yoezer:

> Yose ben Yoezer had a son who conducted himself inappropriately. He had an attic filled with *dinarim* [coins] and consecrated it [for the Temple]. He [the son] went away and married the daughter of King Yannai's wreath-maker. When his wife gave birth to a son he bought her a large fish. Upon opening it he found a pearl inside. "Don't take it to the king," she said to him, "for they'll take it away from you for a small sum of money. Instead take it to the treasurers [of the Temple], but don't offer a price, since making an offer to the Temple is regarded as no less binding than an actual delivery in ordinary transactions. Let them fix the price."
>
> The son brought the pearl to the Temple treasury where it was valued at thirteen *dinarim*. They told him: "We have seven [of them] available, [but we are] missing the remaining six. He replied: Give me the seven and I will consecrate the remaining six to heaven [the Temple]. Thereupon it was recorded. Yose ben Yoezer brought in one, but his son brought six. Others say: Yose ben Yoezer brought in one, but his son took away seven. (*Shabbat* 133b)

Yose ben Yoezer's son had gone astray and, true to his elitist tradition, Yose ben Yoezer disinherited him, dedicating all his worldly assets to the Temple. The "enlightened" son married the daughter of King Yannai's royal wreath-maker. In Talmudic literature, "King Yannai" is a code name for all hostile Jewish rulers; in this passage, it apparently refers to the Hellenistic high priest, Menelaus. The sages did not attach importance to historical precision;[9] their focus was upon moral lessons. The picture they paint of Yose ben Yoezer's son in the house of the wreath-maker of the Hellenistic high priest is heart-rending, showing just how far children can stray from their roots. In our version of the story, the son brings his wife a large fish in which they find a precious jewel. The wife, familiar with the ways of royalty and of the Temple, warns her husband not to sell the pearl to the royal circles but rather to the Temple, also advising him to let them assess its value. The jewel is valued at thirteen times the value of all the money that his father Yose had consecrated to the Temple, but the depleted Temple reserves were insufficient to cover the cost of the transaction. They had seven loaves, but needed thirteen. The son struck the deal of his life: he told the Priests: "Give me seven loaves and I will devote the rest to heaven." At this the treasurers immediately wrote, "Yose gave one and his son gave six."[10]

THE OUTBREAK OF THE HASMONEAN REBELLION; THE MURDER OF YOSE BEN YOEZER AND THE REPENTANCE OF YAKUM OF TZERUROT

In 166 BCE the officials of Antiochus IV Epiphanes went to the towns and villages of Judah, instructing them to sacrifice a pig as a gift to Zeus, the Greek god. In the village of Modi'in, about seventeen *parsot* (about sixty kilometers) from Jerusalem, all of the villagers gathered in the central square at the Greek officer's behest. The latter turned to Mattathias, the local priest, and demanded that he honor him with a sacrifice:

> You are a leader, a prominent and great man in this town, with the support of sons and brothers. Come forward first and carry out the command of the king, as all the heathen, the men of Judah, and those left in Jerusalem have done; if you do so you

9. We will expand on this in the chapter dealing with King Yannai and his character as depicted by the sages.
10. The Talmudic editors took exception at the advantage conferred upon the son, and offered a different reading: "Yose gave one and his son took seven."

> and your sons will be counted among the friends of the king and will be honored with silver and gold and many gifts. (I Maccabees 2:17–18)

Echoes of the process of Hellenization and the abandonment of Jerusalem are easily discernible in the officer's words.[11] Those desiring to keep faith with God and his Torah were compelled to live in the villages, far from the watchful eyes of the Greek officials. However, the officials also conducted searches in the villages themselves. Mattathias responded with the familiar and famous cry: "Whoever is for the Lord – come to me." So began the Maccabean revolt, with the people's flight to villages and deserts in fear of the Greek officials. The first major stage of the Hasmonean rebellion continued until the purification of the Temple (164 BCE) and the consolidation of Hasmonean control over Judea. The battle was led by Judah, who spearheaded the rebellion and managed to turn it into a full-scale war. As he went along he learned the art of guerilla warfare against a large army, taking advantage of his familiarity with the Judean terrain and of the enemy's deployment. Eventually the Greeks were left with no choice, and, with political challenges abroad, were compelled to reach a compromise with the Jews. Menelaus, the hated Hellenist high priest, was "sacrificed" by the Greeks and executed, and Judah Maccabee became the recognized leader. The Greek policy was transformed into an "official notification" by King Antiochus V:

> Since we have heard that the Jews do not agree to accept the Hellenistic customs imposed on them by my father, and prefer to maintain their own way of life, and that they have asked to be permitted to follow their own customs, we also wish that this nation shall be undisturbed. We have decided that their Sanctuary shall be returned to them, and that they shall be permitted to abide by the customs of their ancestors. (II Maccabees 11:24–26)

Antiochus V's successor, Demetrius, who ascended to the throne in 160 BCE, violated the cessation of hostilities and immediately reversed the

11. See comments of A. Rappaport in *First Book of Maccabees* (Jerusalem: 2004), p. 126.

conciliatory policy of the previous two years. He was joined by a priest named Alcimus, who bribed him and bought the office of the high priest by promising unqualified support for Demetrius' policies in return. Midrashic tradition reports that this Hellenist priest was the nephew of Yose ben Yoezer, and his midrashic appellation is "*Yakum ish Tzerurot.*" Demetrius' representative, Bacchides, coordinated his actions with the high priest and together they attempted to restore Greek-Seleucid rule throughout the kingdom. The first stage was the official execution of sixty "Hasidean priests," including Yakum's uncle, the Hasid-priest Yose ben Yoezer.

A midrashic homily relating to this story tells of the execution of Yose ben Yoezer by his nephew, Yakum-Alcimus the Priest. The midrash is based on the verse relating to Jacob when he appears before his father, dressed up as Esau: "And he smelt the smell of his clothes." The midrash tells of the point at which Isaac's sense of touch becomes confused with his sense of vision, at which point his sense of smell, the most delicate of all the senses, comes into play. The midrash depicts Isaac's sense of smell as operating in two directions: (1) the smell of the Garden of Eden; (2) an alternative reading, in which term "his betrayers" (*bogdav*) replaces the simple reading of "his clothing" (*begadav*).

> "And he smelled the smell of his garment [*begadav*] and he blessed him" [Genesis 27:27]. This refers to such as Yosef Meshita and Alcimus of Tzerurot... Alcimus of Tzerurot was the nephew of Rabbi Yose ben Yoezer of Zeredah. And he was riding on a horse on the Sabbath. Yose ben Yoezer came before the beam on which he was to be crucified. He [Alcimus] taunted Rabbi Yose: Look at the horse on which my master has let me ride, and the horse upon which your Master has made you ride." He replied to him: "If this is the end of those who anger Him, how much more with those who accomplish His will." "Has then any man accomplished His will more than you?" he jeered. "If this is the end of those who do His will, how much more with those who anger Him," he retorted.
>
> These words pierced him like the poison of a snake, and he went and subjected himself to the four modes of execution

> inflicted by the *Beit Din*: stoning, burning, decapitation, and strangulation. What did he do? He took a post and planted it in the earth, raised a wall of stones around it and tied a cord to it. He made a fire in front of it and fixed a sword in the middle [of the post]. He hanged himself on the post, the cord was burnt through and he was strangled. The sword caught him, while the wall [of stones] fell upon him and he was burnt. Yose ben Yoezer of Zeredah fell into a daze and saw his [Yakum's] bier flying in the air. "By a few moments he has preceded me into the Garden of Eden," said he. (*Bereshit Raba* 65)

This fascinating midrash links the two midrashic interpretations through a word play based on the two possible meanings of the Hebrew root *b-g-d* ("clothes" and "betrayal") in the verse, "And he smelt the smell of his garment" (from the episode when Jacob disguises himself in Esau's clothes). The midrash takes a fundamentally optimistic view of just how far a Jew can go astray. While betrayers (*bogdim*) have always been among us, the garment (*beged*) of betrayal cannot replace the original personality.

Yose ben Yoezer succeeds in "stinging" his nephew with words of reproach that induced him to return to his origins. Notably, the teaching that Yose ben Yoezer imparts to his nephew relates to precisely that problem which had troubled his own teacher, Antigonus of Sokho, as we discussed above. The students, Tzaddok and Boethus, who distorted the dictum of their teacher, taught the following generation that there was no recompense for one's acts and no World to Come. Having been raised in this kind of culture, Alcimus regarded his humiliated uncle with contempt. However, as a student with integrity, Yose ben Yoezer did not distort his teacher's doctrine, and did not act for the sake of reward, despite his confidence that it would ultimately materialize. At the moment of truth he taught his nephew a fundamental truth about reward and punishment. Above and beyond the theological question, this is a tragic story about those who turn to evil, and find themselves becoming their brothers' executioners. There is no record of Yose ben Yoezer being saved. Presumably the nephew did not have the final word in the Seleucid kingdom, being merely the executioner. There would certainly have been someone to replace him in hanging Yose ben Yoezer.

THE FIRST PAIR: BUNCHES WITHOUT BLEMISH

Of the first of the Pairs, the Mishna relates:

> When Yose ben Yoezer of Zeredah and Yose ben Yoḥanan of Jerusalem died, the bunches of grapes became spoiled, as it is said [Micah 7:1]: "There is no bunch to eat; nor first-fruit fig which my soul desires." (*Sota* 9:9)

This Tosefta adds the following:

> In all of the bunches of grapes that the Israelites grew, from the death of Moses to the rise of Yose ben Yoezer of Zeredah and Yose ben Yoḥanan of Jerusalem, there was no blemish to be found. But once Yose ben Yoezer of Zeredah and Yose ben Yoḥanan of Jerusalem died, blemishes could be found among them. (*Bava Kamma* 8:13)

The Babylonian Talmud eloquently explains the phrase, "no blemish could be found":

> Rabbi Yehuda said in the name of Shmuel: All the *eshkolot* ["bunches"] who arose from the days of Moses until Yose ben Yoezer, learned Torah like Moses our teacher. From that time onward, they did not learn Torah like Moses our teacher.
>
> But did not Rabbi Yehuda report in the name of Shmuel: Three thousand halakhot were forgotten during the period of mourning for Moses? The laws which were forgotten were forgotten, but those which were learnt, they learned like Moses our teacher. Rabbi Yosef said: The word *dofi* [blemish] refers to the dispute relating to the "laying on of hands" [i.e. placing hands on a sacrifice].
>
> But did not Yose ben Yoezer himself differ with respect to the law of laying on of hands?
>
> When he differed, it was in his later years when his mental powers had diminished. (*Temura* 15b–16a)

The Talmud contends that, until the days of Yose ben Yoezer, Torah was passed down without argument or debate, by a process of direct transmission, from one person to the next, as it had been passed down by Moses from the time of Sinai. But the era of "bunches" ended with Yose ben Yoezer, and from this point on disputes ensued. The dispute-free world still preserved something of the ancient splendor linked to Moses and Mount Sinai. But the world of dispute now contained an additional element that undermined the stability and preservation of the Torah. The dispute over the laying on of the hands began at the end of the days of Yose ben Yoezer and Yose of Jerusalem, and continued throughout the era of the Pairs, even though this constituted a new era in its own right.

Before we consider the next Pair, we need to devote some space to the Sadducees, as the first signs of the dispute between them and the sages emerged during this period. As far as we know, it was during this period of the establishment of Hasmonean rule that the sects (Sadducees and Essenes) arose. The first description of the sects appears in Josephus Flavius, who describes them when portraying the period of Jonathan. It seems reasonable to assume that the sects arose in parallel with the establishment of the independent Hasmonean state, following the initial battles, with the consolidation of the new regime of Jonathan and of Simeon after him.[12]

WHAT WAS THE ORIGIN OF THE SADDUCEES?

We will only touch briefly on the Essenes. The reason is that they defined themselves as a sect – a group that cut itself off from the broader Jewish society and withdrew into itself, exercising no influence upon the general society and endeavoring not to be influenced by it.

The Sadducees, on the other hand, were not a sect, but rather a sector – that is, a well-defined group that functioned within society and that placed great store in enhancing its position of leadership and influence. In the following chapters we shall concern ourselves with the continual struggles between the Pharisees and the Sadducees, from this point until the end of the Second Temple.

12. Josephus, *Antiquities*, 13:171–173. For the verification of this determination, see E. Regev, *The Sadducees and their Halakha* – Religion and Society in the Second Temple Period (Jerusalem: 2005), p. 247, n. 1.

The literature on these groups is prolific and in the current framework we can only touch on some of the major issues.

The name "Sadducees" indicates the group's origins in the priestly circles, presumably those of the sons of Tzaddok – the family that held the reigns of priestly leadership throughout the Second Temple until the rise of Antiochus. This group was an aristocratic one, was particularly strict about the laws of ritual purity, and exerted every effort to restore the centrality of the Temple in the national consciousness. The revolutionary innovations of Ezra the scribe and the Men of the Great Assembly had deprived the Temple of its exclusivity. Now, alongside the Temple, the sages were flourishing, as a parallel source of authority, leading the people by virtue of the Torah. Temple service was limited to ritual matters and the priests had no influence beyond that. One can imagine that the Sadducees were trying to challenge the entire tradition of innovations introduced by the Men of the Great Assembly, followed by the Pairs and the sages. Most of the laws that survive from the Sadducees' academies promote strictness in the laws relating to ritual purity and to the Temple and its vessels. This can be clearly seen in the following halakha from the *beit midrash* (study house) of the first Pair, which we discussed above: Yose ben Yoezer and Yose ben Yoḥanan.

A DISPUTE BETWEEN YOSE BEN YOEZER AND THE SADDUCEES

> Rabbi Yose ben Yoezer of Zeredah testified that the *ayil*-locust is clean and that the liquid [that flows] in the slaughterhouse [of the Temple] is not susceptible to uncleanliness, and that he who touches a corpse becomes unclean. And they called him Yose the Lenient. (*Eduyot* 8:4)

This mishna would appear to be an early and fairly ordinary halakhic testimony, describing three of the rulings of Yose ben Yoezer, among them that liquids that issue from the slaughterhouse of the Temple are considered pure. The mishna relates that he was known as "Yose the Lenient," indicating that this particular ruling did not enjoy universal approbation.

Remarkably, today we have a scroll dating from the same period, known as the Temple Scroll, which deals at length with the laws of the Temple and its vessels, which is attributed to the Qumran sect. In this early scroll we read the following:

> And you shall make a channel all around the laver along the altar... so that the water flows and runs through it and is lost in the middle of the earth and no one should touch it because it is mixed with the blood of the burnt offering.[13]

According to the Temple Scroll, the impurity of the water and the blood derives from the contact between the portions of the sacrifice and its blood, which are still considered holy, and the water which is profane.[14]

The connection between the Temple Scroll and the Sadducees becomes evident when we compare the positions adopted by the Sadducees, referred to in numerous mishnayot, and those adopted by the members of the Qumran sect, whose writings have been researched over the last fifty years. The comparison shows that, notwithstanding the similarity between the Qumran members and the Essenes in terms of their social world view, in halakhic matters they were similar (if not identical) to the Sadducees.[15] The significance of the Sadducees' dispute with Yose ben Yoezer becomes clear when viewed against the background of their desire to deepen awareness of issues of purity and impurity in the Temple. Any water coming into contact with a sacrifice becomes part of the Temple, and is prohibited to come into contact with *ḥullin*. Yose ben Yoezer rejected this position and as such "merited" the nickname "Yose the Lenient." The disparaging nickname was presumably given to him by his opponents from the priestly class of the sons of Tzaddok.[16]

13. *Temple Scroll*, 11Q19, 32:12–15; *Dead Sea Scrolls Study Edition*, F.G. Martinez and E. Tigchelaar (eds.).
14. See Regev, p. 232, n. 45.
15. See Y. Sussman's article, "The History of the Halakha and the Dead Sea Scrolls" [Hebrew], in M. Broshi et al. (eds.), *The Scrolls of the Judean Desert – Forty Years of Research* (Jerusalem: 1992), pp. 99–127.
16. See E. Regev's article on the dispute between Yose ben Yoezer and the Sadducees: E. Regev, "Yose ben Yoezer and the Qumran Sectarians on Purity Laws: Agreement and Controversy," in J.M. Baumgarten et al. (eds.), *The Damascus Document: A*

If our assumption is correct, then this text is one of the earliest pieces of evidence of the beginning of the dispute between the Sadducees and the Pharisees. As such it invites us to make conjectures regarding the origin of their dispute and its conceptual underpinnings. The Sadducees did not challenge the structure of religious, urban life. The essence of their group was bound up with the Temple, which was connected to the world of each and every Jew. Their goal was to arrest the steadily increasing trend of Torah study in the tradition of Ezra and the Men of the Great Assembly. It is unclear which group exercised a greater influence on the Temple, the Sadducees or their rivals. It has been claimed that, during this period, it was the sages who determined the proceedings in the Temple and that the Sadducees were no more than the opposition. This claim appears logical when considering the Mishnaic phrase "Yose the Lenient." Such a title would only be granted to a person with the actual authority to change and permit. Had he merely been expressing an opinion, while control of the Temple services remained in the hands of the Sadducees, no one would have been perturbed by him.

It follows that the picture of a world free of disputes that preceded the period of Yose ben Yoezer fails to take into account the gradual empowerment of the Sadducees who, alongside the consolidation of the Hasmonean state, were attempting to make their presence felt and to offer a real alternative to the world of the sages.

WHO WERE THE PHARISEES?

I have been using the terms "Sadducees" and "sages," but the sources themselves generally refer to the sages as "Pharisees." This name has been the subject of extensive debate among scholars. In view of my comments above regarding the Sadducees and their connection to the Essenes, there are grounds for accepting the claim that the name "Pharisees" derives from the Hebrew word "separate" (*p-r-sh*), and was the description of the sages in the eyes of those who separated themselves

Centennial of Discovery, Proceedings of the Third International Symposium of the Orion Center for the Study of the Dead Sea Scrolls and Associated Literature, 4–8 February, 1988 (Leiden: 2000), pp. 95–107.

from them, that is, the members of the Qumran sect. One of the important halakhic excerpts found in the Qumran writings reads as follows:

> And you know that we have segregated ourselves from the rest of the people and we have avoided mingling in these affairs and associating with them in these things.[17]

This group was "separated" from the majority of the people. Other scrolls describe how members of this sect isolated themselves by going to live in the desert. Their ideology was one of isolation and segregation from the mainstream of the Jewish people, who are referred to as "the Sons of Darkness." The people from whom they separated were referred to as *Perushim* (= Pharisees), and in the course of time, the name stuck, describing those who continued the halakhic tradition that began with the Men of the Great Assembly. The Talmud relates the following about a sage from the Temple period:

> Yehuda ben Durtai separated himself [from the sages], together with his son Durtai, and went to dwell in the South. [For he said] If Elijah should come and say to Israel, "Why did you not sacrifice the *ḥagiga* [pilgrim's festival offering] on the Sabbath?" – what will they say? I am astonished at the two greatest men of our generation, Shemaya and Avtalyon, who are great sages and interpreters [of the Torah], yet they have not told Israel that the *ḥagiga* overrides the Sabbath. (*Pesaḥim* 70b)

Yehuda ben Durtai rejects the halakhic tradition of the Pairs regarding the *ḥagiga* sacrifice, and decides to separate himself. Interestingly, in the course of the discussion of this separatists' claim in the Babylonian Talmud, Rabbi Ashi interrupts the discussion:

> Rabbi Ashi said: Need we arise and explain the reasons of separatists?

17. *Miktzat Ma'aseh HaTorah*, 4Q398, 4QMMT C 7–8, F.G. Martinez & E. Tigchelaar (eds.).

Rabbi Ashi claims that he was not a *poresh* (one who separates himself) but rather *parush* (one who is separated). The person who removes himself from the community is one who separates. Rabbi Ashi identifies himself with the community and with the world: those who leave the community separate themselves from the world.[18]

It thus transpired that, from Talmudic times onwards, the name "Pharisee" referred both to the sages in their descriptions of the disputes with the Sadducees, and to all those who sought to divide the Jewish world into different social groupings.

18. Notably, in *Seder HaDorot* (Warsaw: 1870), pt. 2, p. 83b, Rabbi Y. Halperin states that Yehuda ben Dortai "was apparently a Sadducee." This point was dealt with by Sussman in his article (see footnote 15 above), p. 18.

Chapter Eight

Yehoshua ben Peraḥia and Nittai HaArbeli

Yehoshua ben Peraḥia and Nittai HaArbeli received [the Torah] from them. Yehoshua ben Peraḥia used to say: Attain for yourself a teacher and acquire for yourself a friend, and judge every man favorably.

Nittai HaArbeli used to say: Distance yourself from a bad neighbor, do not befriend a wicked person, and do not despair of retribution. (Avot 1:6–7)

HISTORICAL AND POLITICAL BACKGROUND

We now move to the second Hasmonean period, spanning from the early days of the rebellion until the consolidation of the kingdom and political independence. Following the death of Judah the Maccabee, his brother Jonathan led the rebellion against the arrogant ruler Demetrius. After a grueling war, Jonathan succeeded in establishing himself as leader and, amazingly, the Greeks recognized his political status in Judah. With Greek consent, Jonathan took up residence in Mikhmash (about ten kilometers north of Jerusalem), from where he began to lead Israel. A few years later he allied himself with Alexander Balas who was waging a battle for power against Demetrius. The gamble was successful and Balas was victorious over Demetrius. In return for his support, Yonatan was granted the position of high priest as well as being appointed "Judean Governor." Notably, Jonathan was not a scion of the House of Tzaddok, which until the beginning of the Greek period had always held the position of high priest. The result was that from an internal Jewish perspective, he was similarly derided as being a "puppet" high priest, like his predecessors. From this time onwards the Hasmonean leaders took charge of all Temple-related matters, as well as being leaders of the rebellion, and by extension the leaders who determined foreign policy and security.

Following Jonathan's death, the third brother, Simeon, was appointed in his place (142–134 BCE), and he established and consolidated the Hasmonean state. The climax of this period was the convening of a national assembly in the Temple courtyard which established the new leader's powers and authorities. The assembly was asked to give formal recognition to the Hasmonean dynasty as the people's leader (a role equivalent to that of King of the Jews), and as a dynasty of high priests and military commanders. This was a writ of appointment that established a dynasty in which all branches of power – foreign policy, judiciary, religion and the army – were combined.

In one of his tours passing through Jericho, Simeon visited his father-in-law, Talmai ben Ḥabuv. During a banquet thrown in the visitor's honor, Talmai's cohorts attacked Simeon and murdered him in an attempted in-house coup. Talmai and his men had already tried to murder Talmai's brother-in-law Yoḥanan, who ruled in Jerusalem on his father's behalf. The attempted rebellion failed and the people of Judah and Jerusalem remained loyal to the Hasmonean dynasty, and to Yoḥanan, who was appointed to succeed Simeon, his father. Of all the Hasmonean leaders, it was Yoḥanan Hyrcanus who, more than any other, expanded the borders of the Jewish state. He embarked on wars of conquest on the east side of the Jordan, enslaving its population to his state, and from there continued south to conquer Edom. Josephus relates that he allowed the Edomites to remain in the land on condition that they would undergo circumcision and agree to convert (*Antiquities*

XIII, 257–258). During the thirty years of his rule the Jews gained control of most of the internal part of the land of Israel, from the Galilee to the Negev. This march of liberation was primarily motivated by a sense of returning to the land of the forefathers, a trend that had already begun during the time of Yoḥanan's father, Simeon. Indeed, when the Seleucid ruler Antiochus VII complained about the proliferation of Jewish settlements, Simeon responded:

> We have neither taken any other man's land, nor do we hold dominion over other people's territory, but only over the inheritance of our fathers...for a certain time it was held unjustly by our enemies. (I Maccabees 15:33)

It would seem that, by the time of the second generation after the Hasmonean rebellion, religious awareness, and hence the desire to settle all parts of the land and not just the Jerusalem area, had become more intense. Under Yoḥanan Hyrcanus' reign the country's population was once again Jewish and Hasmonean rule was consolidated, anticipating the transformation of the kingdom into an independent state.

At the beginning of his reign, Yoḥanan ruled in the spirit of the sages' teachings, and they accepted him as having been "fundamentally righteous." Halakhic tradition has preserved a number of laws that are bound up with his name. We will bring two examples:

> Who prepared them [Who burned the red heifers]? Moses prepared the first, Ezra prepared the second, and five were prepared after Ezra. Thus, in the words of Rabbi Meir. But the sages say: Seven since Ezra. And who prepared them? Simeon the Just and Yoḥanan the High Priest prepared two each, and Eliyahu Einei the son of Hakkof, Ḥanamel the Egyptian, and Yishmael the son of Piabi prepared one each. (Mishna, *Para* 3:5)

The need to replenish the ashes of the red heifer to cleanse people from impurity due to contact with the dead, may perhaps be connected to the period following the wave of Hasmonean Wars and the beginning of a period of peace and prosperity – a time suited for general reorganization and national purification.[1]

> Yoḥanan the High Priest abolished the declaration concerning the tithe. He also put an end to the "arousers" and the knockers. Until his days the hammer used to smite in Jerusalem. And during his time there was no need to inquire concerning *demai*[2] produce. (Mishna, *Ma'aser Sheni* 5:15)

This mishna describes Yoḥanan's religious activities in two areas. The first is the discontinuation of the "arousers." These were the Levites who used to sing in the Temple when bringing sacrifices: "Arise, why do You sleep O Lord?" (Psalms 44:24). Yoḥanan discontinued this song because it suggests an attitude of defiance toward Heaven. The Talmud explains the difference between the period of Yoḥanan and the period of the Levites' song:

> At a time in which Israel finds itself in trouble, while the Gentiles are in peace and comfort – of such a situation it is said: "Arise, why do You sleep O Lord?" (*Sota* 48a)

This passage sheds light on the situation of the people during Yoḥanan's reign, apparently a time of prosperity and well-being, economic stability and political tranquility. In short, a time far more suited to focusing on inner reality, and to fortifying the people's spiritual sense.

This also explains the following paragraph in the Mishna: "Until his days the hammer used to smite in Jerusalem" – that is, during Ḥol HaMoed (*Sota*, ibid.). Until Yoḥanan's time, the Intermediate Days of the festivals were not observed: for example, people were not strict

1. This tradition which connects Yoḥanan the High Priest with the burning of the heifer is also related to the tradition of the sages who attested to having witnessed Yehoshua ben Peraḥia burning the heifer, and argued over what clothing Yehoshua was wearing at the time (*Sifrei Zuta* 19, p. 302, but see also the editor's comment, rejecting any connection between Yehoshua ben Peraḥia and Hillel).
2. *Demai* refers to produce about which there is a doubt as to whether it has been duly tithed.

about restricting labor to those cases where one's livelihood would be lost. Here too, the economic situation was significant. The ability to begin to observe Ḥol HaMoed more meticulously attests to a level of general prosperity that enabled the focus to be directed on the people's spiritual condition. The Hasmonean state thus entered its "Jewish phase."

THE CONCENTRATION OF RELIGION AND STATE IN THE HANDS OF YOḤANAN, "PRIEST TO GOD MOST HIGH"

The tranquility of Yoḥanan's rule lasted for almost an entire generation, and peace reigned in the land of Israel for almost the entire duration of his rule. This was the period of the next Pair: Yehoshua ben Peraḥia and Nittai HaArbeli. In contrast to the other Pairs, we know little about the intellectual, religious, and social activities of these two sages. There is only one source which mentions an edict of Yehoshua ben Peraḥia: it recounts that he attempted to rule that wheat coming from Alexandria was impure, but that the sages would not agree. This source is instructive in terms of the limited power of this Pair and their position in the national leadership. The Hasmonean rulers arrogated themselves both religious and political leadership. Hence, on Yoḥanan's coins we find the imprint, "Yoḥanan High Priest, Head of the Jews." The title "Head of the Jews" resembles the title "Ruler of the Nation" – a status approaching the level of king. This was a declaration of the concentration of political and religious power in the same hands. After a period of extended exclusion from positions of national leadership, the priests now returned to center stage. The fighter-priest was now the contemporary political leader. The most prominent sages, on the other hand, went to the provinces in the Galilee. At this stage we hear the sages criticizing the bills issued by Yoḥanan, which boasted the heading "[High] Priest of God Most High":

> On the third of Tishrei, mention of the divine name on bills was annulled. For the Greek kingdom had decreed not to mention the name of Heaven on bills, but when the Hasmonean kingdom overcame them, they decreed that that the name of Heaven should be mentioned even on documents. And they wrote as follows: "In the year ______ of Yoḥanan, the High Priest of God Most High." And when the sages heard of this they said: Should

> a person pay his debt the next day, it would heaven forbid be thrown out in the trash. And they canceled it. And they established that day as a day of joy.

According to a number of testimonies, the name of Heaven appeared on the Hasmonean bills along with the year in the reign of the Maccabean leaders in which the bills were drawn up. *Megillat Ta'anit,* whose sole purpose was the listing of joyous days on which fasting was proscribed, mentions, rather surprisingly, the cancelation of these documents and not their establishment. We would have expected that this scroll would list as a joyous day the date on which the first Hasmonean coin was minted, and certainly not the day on which the bills were canceled. This lends credibility to Daniel Schwartz's view that the phrase "Priest of God Most High," included on the Hasmonean bills, clearly attests to the royal status of the Hasmonean priests, similar to that of Malchizedek, King of Shalem, whom the book of Genesis refers to as "Priest of God Most High."[3] Schwartz's explanation leads us directly to a substantive discussion of the sages' attitude toward the Hasmonean monarchy. Yoḥanan's defection to the side of the Sadducees further aggravated the tension, the overall result being a grave crisis, opening a chasm between the world of the sages and that of the Hasmonean kings. This crisis is reflected in the following teaching of the sage Hillel:

> Do not believe in yourself until the day of your death. (*Avot* 2:4)

And it is explained in the Talmud as follows:

> For Yoḥanan the High Priest officiated as high priest for eighty years and in the end he became a Sadducee. (*Berakhot* 29a)

In view of our discussion of the Sadducees' standing in the previous chapter, the import of this statement seems clear. Though not of Saddu-

3. D. Schwartz, "The Pharisaic Opposition to the Hasmonean Dynasty" [Hebrew], in U. Rappaport and I. Ronen (eds.), *The Hasmonean State* (Jerusalem and Tel Aviv: 1994), p. 445.

cean lineage, Yoḥanan belonged to a family of Hasmonean priests. His concentration of power in his own hands was anathema to the Pharisees, but the Sadducees accepted him warmly and sympathetically, sensing an opportunity to reestablish the Temple as the source of political and social power. The sages' claim that Yoḥanan became a Sadducee is true, albeit not in the theological sense but rather in terms of the social-political context. The schism between Yoḥanan and the sages is related to his concentration of powers, as Josephus notes in explaining the tension between the Pharisee sages and the Hasmonean leader (*Antiquities* XII, 288–299). This criticism finds similar expression in the sages' admonition to the Hasmonean leader: "Let the crown of royalty suffice you; leave the crown of priesthood to the seed of Aaron!" This critique gave him two options: either assume the role of political leadership and stay away from religious matters, or concentrate exclusively on matters of religion and give up the prerogatives of royalty. The linkage of the two was illegitimate; but for the Sadducees it was crucial.

YANNAI IS YOḤANAN

The above citation from Josephus regarding Yoḥanan the High Priest – "Let the crown of royalty suffice you" – appears in the Babylonian Talmud, albeit not in relation to Yoḥanan, but rather to King Yannai. The Talmud had no hesitation in adapting the context of stories regarding an evil king and attributing them to Yannai. The Talmud relates the following:

> It once happened that King Yannai went to Koḥalit in the wilderness and captured sixty cities there. When he returned he celebrated his victory and summoned all the sages, saying to them: "When our forefathers built the [Second] Temple they ate mallows [salty dishes]; so too should we eat salty dishes in memory of our forefathers." The King and the sages sat at golden tables and ate. An evil, worthless scoffer named Elazar ben Po'ira told Yannai: "King Yannai, the Pharisees are plotting against you." "What then shall I do?" "Test them by the golden plate [*tzitz*: sign of the high priesthood] between your eyes." So he tested them by the golden plate between his eyes. Now an elder named Yehuda son of Gedidia was present there. He said to King Yannai,

> "O King Yannai! Let the royal crown suffice thee and leave the priestly crown to the seed of Aaron" (for it was rumored that his mother had been imprisoned in Modi'im, and the charge was investigated but never sustained), and the sages of Israel departed in anger. Then Elazar ben Po'ira said to King Yannai: "O King Yannai – that is the law for even the most humble man in Israel. But you are a king and the high priest; shall that be the law for you too?" "Then what shall I do?" "If you take my advice, trample them down." "But what shall happen with the Torah?" "Behold, it is rolled up and lying in the corner; whoever wishes to study, let him go and study!" Rabbi Naḥman bar Yitzḥak said: Immediately a spirit of heresy was instilled into him, for he should have replied, "That is well for the Written Law; but what of the Oral Law?" Straightaway the evil burst forth from Elazar son of Po'ira, all the sages of Israel were massacred, and the world was desolate until Shimon ben Shetaḥ came and restored the Torah to its pristine stature. (*Kiddushin* 66a)

The Babylonian Talmud in Tractate *Berakhot* views Yannai as one who was "wicked to the core" (*Berakhot* 29b). On the other hand, there are those who have attempted "to restore the image of the greatest of the Hasmonean kings who for various reasons was not properly appreciated.... How was it that throughout the generations Yannai's character has been distorted and all his great deeds forgotten? And not only is he not remembered positively, but every evil thing is attributed to him?!"[4] This argument is justified. The sages were indeed not concerned about historical accuracy regarding Yannai's record; they were interested in establishing a model that could serve as a source for emulation or a deterrent for future generations.[5] Yannai was "chosen" as the paradigmatic "bad guy," and became identified with many flaws and failings that exacting historical research has shown were in fact attributable to kings

4. B.Z. Lurie, *From Yannai to Herod* [Hebrew], (Jerusalem: 1974), Introduction and p. 107.
5. See article of M.D. Hedd, "The Sages' Concept of History" [Hebrew], *Proceedings of the Sixth World Congress of Jewish Studies*, vol. 3.

that preceded him (such as Yoḥanan), or that followed him (such as Agrippa). The conclusion emerging from all the extant sources (*Megillat Ta'anit*, the Book of Maccabees, Josephus, and Talmudic literature) is that the criticism for concentrating the powers of religion and state in one figure should be directed first and foremost at Yoḥanan Hyrcanus.

THE SAGES' ATTITUDE TO THE ARROGATION OF ROYAL POWER BY AARON'S DESCENDANTS (THE HASMONEANS)

Let us look further at the plea mentioned above: "Let the crown of royalty suffice you; leave the crown of priesthood to the seed of Aaron!" We already find criticism in the Book of Maccabees of the attempt of the descendants of Aaron to arrogate to themselves royal privilege. Admittedly, the context (8:14) is one of praise for the Hasmonean rulers, who did not emulate the monarchic style: "Yet with all this, not even one of them put on a diadem, or donned purple, for self-aggrandizement," but scholars studying this book have noted that, while its style is essentially pro-Hasmonean, it adopts a fundamentally negative attitude to the Hasmonean usurpation of kingship.[6]

Daniel Schwartz has examined the sages' attitude toward the Hasmonean kings and suggests taking a deeper look at the *baraita* of Rabbi Yose referring to the period commencing with Yoḥanan Hyrcanus as "the evil kingdom."[7] In later periods this criticism became clearer and more pronounced. The most explicit criticism is voiced by Nahmanides in his commentary on the verse, "The scepter shall not depart from Judah":

> This was also the reason for the punishment of the Hasmoneans who reigned during the Second Temple. They were saints of the Most High, without whom the study of Torah and the observance of commandments would have been forgotten in Israel. Yet despite this, they suffered great punishment. The four sons of the old Hasmonean, Mattathias, were saintly men who ruled one

6. See *First Book of Maccabees*, ed. U. Rappaport (Jerusalem: 2004), 225, note on verse 14.
7. D. Schwartz, "The Pharisaic Opposition to the Hasmonean Dynasty" [Hebrew], in *Nation and History, Studies in the History of the Jewish People*, vol. 1 (Jerusalem: 1983), p. 46.

after another, but in spite of their bravery and prowess they fell by the sword of their enemies. Ultimately the punishment reached the stage where our rabbis, of blessed memory, stated that, "He who says, 'I come from the house of the Hasmoneans' is a slave" [*Bava Batra* 3b], as they were all destroyed on account of this sin. Now, although among the children of Simeon there was cause for the punishment imposed on account of the Sadducees, all the children of Mattathias the righteous Hasmonean were deposed; they ruled even though they were not of the seed of Judah and of the house of David, and thus they completely removed the political and legislative authority from Judah. And their punishment was measure for measure, as the Holy One, blessed be He, caused their slaves to rule over them.

It may also be that [in addition to the Hasmoneans having sinned by assuming royalty when they were not of the tribe of Judah], they sinned on account of their being priests, for they were commanded: "Be careful to perform your priestly duties in everything pertaining to the altar, and to what is behind the curtain. I make your priesthood a service of dedication" [Numbers 18:7]. Thus it was not for them to rule, but only to perform the service of God.

In Tractate *Horayot* of the Jerusalem Talmud [3b] I have seen the following text: "We do not anoint priests as kings. Rabbi Yehuda Anturya said that this is on account of the verse, "The scepter shall not depart from Judah." Rabbi Ḥiya the son of Rabbi Abba said [that Scripture states concerning the king], "To the end that he may prolong his days in his kingdom, he and his children, in the midst of Israel." Now what is written afterwards? "The priests the Levites ... shall have no portion." Thus the sages have taught here that kings are not to be anointed from among the priests, the sons of Aaron. Now at first the above text explains that this is out of respect for the tribe of Judah, as sovereignty is not to depart from that tribe. Therefore, even if Israel, out of temporary necessity, raises a king over itself from the other tribes, he is not to be anointed so that the glory of royalty

> should not be upon him. Instead, such kings are to be merely as judges or officers. The reason for mentioning "priests" [when the same stricture applies to all tribes other than Judah] is that even though the priests as such are suited for anointment, we are not to anoint them as kings; all the more so the rest of the tribes. It is as the rabbis said in the Talmud: One is only to anoint kings of the house of David. And Rabbi Ḥiya the son of Rabbi Abba, [who in the above text from the Jerusalem Talmud based the law upon a verse in the book of Deuteronomy] explained that anointing priests as kings is forbidden by a law of the Torah, which says that "the priests the Levites, even all the tribe of Levi, shall have no portion nor inheritance" in royalty. And this is fitting and appropriate. (Nahmanides on Genesis 49:10)

The Pharisaic message was clear: centralization of power was unacceptable; priesthood and kingship could not be in the hands of the same ruler.

It is during this period of expansion and consolidation that we encounter the second of the Pairs: Yehoshua ben Peraḥia and Nittai HaArbeli (the Arbelite).

THE IDENTIFICATION OF YEHOSHUA BEN PERAḤIA IN THE LOWER GALILEE

Certain ancient traditions attempted to identify Yehoshua ben Peraḥia and Nittai HaArbeli as having been active in the lower Galilee area. With respect to Nittai HaArbeli, the identification is uncertain. One of the sites in the Arbel area, adjacent to the grave of Nittai, is mentioned as a landmark for the grave of Yehoshua ben Peraḥia. However, before being identified as the burial spot of Yehoshua ben Peraḥia it was identified as that of another Yehoshua – Yehoshua bin Nun, the Joshua of the Bible. Even though the latter is recorded as having been buried "in Timnat-Seraḥ in the hill country of Ephraim" (Joshua 24:30), which has always been identified as the Ḥaras village, south of Shechem and opposite the city of Ariel, medieval travelers to *Eretz Yisrael* did not hesitate to relocate him in the Galilee. In the year 1180, a traveler from Ashkenaz, Rabbi Petaḥia from Regensburg, relates the following:

> And Mount Ga'ash is very high … and it is distant from Nittai the Arbelite, in Arbel … and the mountain consists of terraces which one ascends, and in the middle of the mountain is where Joshua bin Nun is buried, and next to him Kalev ben Yefuneh … and next to one of the tombs one discerns a footprint, like a person treading in the snow, and this is the path trodden by the angel, and the whole of the land of Israel trembled after the death of Joshua.[8]

Rabbi Petaḥia's allusion in the passage is to the midrash depicting Israel's negligence following Joshua's death:

> "Slothfulness casts into a deep sleep" [Proverbs 19:15]. [Israel was cast into a deep sleep] for being negligent in paying the appropriate honors to Joshua after his death. That is the meaning of the verse "And they buried him in the border of his inheritance … on the north of the mountain of Ga'ash" [Joshua 24:30]. Rabbi Berekhia said: We have examined the whole of Scripture and we have not found mention of a place called Ga'ash. What then is the meaning of "the mountain of Ga'ash"? [It means] that the Israelites were too preoccupied [*nitga'ashu*] to pay proper honor to Joshua after his death. The land of Israel was divided up at that time, and the Israelites valued the division overmuch and became unduly absorbed in its execution. One was occupied with his field, the other with his vineyard, yet another with his olive trees, and a fourth with quarrying stones, thus exemplifying the words, "And the idle soul shall suffer hunger" [Proverbs 19:15]. "They therefore neglected to show honor to Joshua after his death, and the Holy One, blessed be He, sought to bring an earthquake upon the inhabitants of the world, as it is said, "Then the earth did shake [*vatige'ash*] and quake" [Psalms 18:8]. "And the idle soul shall suffer hunger" – refers to those who deceived God. Who were they? They were idolators. God therefore starved them of

8. "The Travels of Rabbi Petaḥia of Regensburg in Syria and the Land of Israel" (*circa* 1180), in Avraham Yaari, *Travels in the Land of Israel* (Ramat Gan: 1976), p. 48–55 (this quotation can be found on p. 52).

> the Holy Spirit, as it is written: "And the word of the Lord was precious in those days" [1 Samuel 3:1]. (*Rut Raba*, Introduction)

Other medieval traditions also recount when the earthquake that created the Arbel valley occurred. A book known as *The Fasting Obligations According to the Months of the Year* (from the Cairo Geniza), relates:

> In Iyyar they fasted on the eighteenth because of the death of Joshua, when the earthquake occurred.[9]

It was only years later that they began to change the grave marker from Yehoshua bin Nun (which was returned to its original place, south of Shechem) to Yehoshua ben Peraḥia, next to Nittai HaArbeli.

In any event, we shall now leave the somewhat dubious geographical identification, and attempt to understand the sages' attitude to the character of Yehoshua ben Peraḥia.

In dating the activities of Rabbi Yehoshua ben Peraḥia, a contradiction emerges between the historical continuity of the Pairs and the Talmudic tradition. The chronology of the Pairs places us in the period of Yoḥanan Hyrcanus (104–134 BCE). The first Pair, Yose ben Yoezer and Yose ben Yoḥanan, were active at the outbreak of the Maccabean rebellion (167 BCE), Yose ben Yoezer being killed by Yakum of Tzerurot, otherwise known as the Hellenist priest Alcimus, in the time of Demetrius IV. Shimon ben Shetaḥ, one of the third Pair, was the brother-in-law of King Yannai – that is, he lived during the first century BCE. This compels us to fix the time of the second Pair at the end of the second century and the beginning of the first century BCE which, as stated, is the time of Yoḥanan Hyrcanus the Hasmonean, who established the Hasmonean state. On the other hand, the Talmud also identifies Yehoshua as the teacher of Jesus, who lived at the beginning of the first century CE, about a hundred years later.

9. See Fleisher's article: "Haduta-Hadutahu-Chedweta: Solving an Old Riddle" [Hebrew], *Tarbitz* 53 (1984), p. 71.

YEHOSHUA BEN PERAḤIA AND JESUS

The teaching of Nittai HaArbeli may well reflect his reaction to the persecution of the sages at the hands of the corrupt Hasmoneans. He warns against over-familiarity with bad neighbors, and forming alliances or consorting with the wicked. From the heights of his residence in the Galilee, his message is that he has nothing to seek in Jerusalem, which is in the throes of Sadducean intrigues and squabbles. He has no interest in collaborating with them or being one of them. He is not despaired by the scourges, but waits for the storm to pass.

His comrade, Yehoshua ben Peraḥia, was forced to flee to Egypt, apparently having been more involved in the opposition to the Hasmoneans. The story of his exile to Egypt appears in the Talmud (in a passage which for centuries had been censored and was only reprinted in the last generation, in the Steinsaltz edition):

> When King Yannai slew our rabbis, Rabbi Yehoshua ben Peraḥia and Jesus fled to Alexandria in Egypt. When peace was restored, Shimon ben Shetaḥ sent this message to him: "From me, Jerusalem, the holy city – to you, Alexandria in Egypt. O my sister, my husband is dwelling in your midst and I am desolate." [Rabbi Yehoshua] arose and came back and lodged in a certain inn where they paid him great respect. He said: 'How beautiful is this *akhsania* [inn, or inn hostess]. He [Jesus] said to him, "My master, her eyes are narrow!" "Wretch," he rebuked him, "Are those the thoughts that occupy you?!" He sent forth four hundred horns and excommunicated him. Later, the disciple [Jesus] came to him repeatedly, pleading, "Receive me," but he paid no heed. One day while Rabbi Yehoshua was reciting the *Shema*, he [Jesus] came before him. He intended to receive him and motioned to him with his hand, but the disciple [Jesus] thought he was rebuffing him again. So he went and set up a brick and worshiped it. Rabbi Yehoshua said to him, "Repent." But he answered him, "I have received this tradition from you: that he who sins and causes others to sin is denied the opportunity to repent." (*Sanhedrin* 107b)

The expression "when peace was restored" may allude to the transfer of power after the death of Yoḥanan, during the reign of Yannai and his wife, Shlomtziyon (Salome Alexandra), who was Shimon ben Shetaḥ's sister. The period was one of reconciliation and attempts to renew the dialogue between the sages' (i.e., Pharisaic) leadership and the Hasmonean rulers. In an apparently diplomatic initiative, "Jerusalem" turns to Alexandra ("my sister") imploring her to restore Yehoshua ben Peraḥia ("my husband") from his exile. Returning home, Yehoshua ben Peraḥia and his student Jesus rest at an inn, managed by a woman who lavishes extensive honor upon Yehoshua. Yehoshua was exuberant and praised the inn hostess, but his student, Jesus, directed his attention to her bleary eyes. Yehoshua's incensed reaction was: "Evil one, are these the wretched thoughts that occupy you?" upon which he summarily excommunicated him. The latter pleaded in vain to be reaccepted into the fold, receiving no response. Yehoshua ben Peraḥia's door remained closed.

Jesus continued coming on a daily basis requesting forgiveness, but to no avail, until the day that he came precisely when Yehoshua was saying *Shema*: "He intended to receive him and motioned to him [to wait] with his hand." His body language was ambiguous and Jesus misunderstood his gesture, thinking that he had once more been rejected. This was the last straw: Jesus became an idol worshiper and totally severed himself from the community. Yehoshua attempted to persuade him to repent, but Jesus' response was: "I have received this tradition from you: that he who sins and causes others to sin is denied the opportunity to repent." This is the Talmud's account of Jesus' banishment from the world of Judaism.

The story abounds with allusions. The issue of the bleary eyes is incisively explained in another Talmudic context:

> The House of the *Nasi* [prince, or patriarch of the Sanhedrin] decreed a fast [due to drought] but to no avail and the rains did not come. Oshaya, the youngest of the group, taught them: "And it shall be, if it be done in error 'from the eyes of the community' [Numbers 15:24]. This may be likened to a bride in the house of her father. As long as her eyes are beautiful, her body need not be examined. But if her eyes are bleary, her whole body must be examined." [...] The servants of the *Nasi*'s house heard his

> teaching and attempted to strangle him with the scarf around his neck. The other residents of the town said to them: Leave him alone. He bothers us too, but because we saw that all of his deeds are for the sake of Heaven we left him alone. So you, too, let him alone.

Rabbi Oshaya rebuked the House of the *Nasi* for decreeing a fast for rain without understanding that repentance must begin with a profound soul-searching. His basis for this is the appellation used to refer to the Sanhedrin: "eyes of the community." The health of the body is determined by the eyes: when the eyes are bleary, the entire body requires examination. Thus the fate of the nation is determined by the state of its leadership, the Sanhedrin.

Returning to the story of Yehoshua ben Peraḥia, this story may be a metaphor describing Yehoshua's return to leadership. The Sanhedrin receives him with great fanfare, but Jesus directs his attention to the bleary eyes of the inn hostess. Something here is not right; the whole body requires examination. Having received a warm welcome, Yehoshua ben Peraḥia treated the hostess graciously, politely observing her overall demeanor and accepting her cheerfully without subjecting her to meticulous examination. Jesus could not accept his teacher's well-mannered treatment of the hostess. If the eyes are faulty, the entire body needs to be examined. The student is harshly criticized and excommunicated for his comment, his teacher asking him: "Is this what concerns you?"

Any reality admits of a number of perspectives and evaluations. When the "eyes of the community" are bleary, this may indeed attest to a decrepit body, such as the aristocratic family of the *Nasi* during the period of Rabbi Yehuda HaNasi's (Judah the Prince's) grandson, when the leadership was corrupt and unstable. But Jesus' criticism had its roots in his own "evil eye" – his own disgruntlement. He was looking to find "bleary eyes," that is, tarnished and corrupt leadership. Yehoshua ben Peraḥia discerned his student's poisonous hatred, motivating him to search for flaws in the eyes that would delegitimize the entire body, and realized that he could have no place in the community.

Not content merely to recount this story, the Talmud adds its own evaluation. The story appears in the context of a passage discussing the following dictum:

> "Let the left hand reject but let the right hand draw near." Not like Elisha, who thrust Geḥazi away with both hands, and not like Rabbi Yehoshua ben Peraḥia, who rejected Jesus (the Nazirite) with both hands. (*Sanhedrin* 107b)

The Talmud openly criticizes the excommunication of Jesus, for it was Rabbi Yehoshua ben Peraḥia who taught his students that "he who sins and causes others to sin is denied the opportunity to repent."

AN ASIDE: ACCEPTANCE AND REJECTION IN LATER EXEGESIS

The last Rebbe of Chabad, Rabbi Menachem Mendel Schneerson of Lubavitch, addressed this issue in one of his talks:

> And the explanation is: the Talmud intended to warn even against the kind of rejection perpetrated by Yehoshua ben Peraḥia. For it is clear that, when dealing with Yehoshua ben Peraḥia, it is inconceivable that he was motivated by personal considerations, and the like. Furthermore, even after having rejected him he made an attempt to bring him near; nonetheless, we should be wary of this kind of rejection.
>
> After Yehoshua ben Peraḥia saw the consequences of this conduct, he stressed the teaching of: "Judge every man favorably." (*Likkutei Siḥot, Matot-Masei,* 5742)

Yehoshua ben Peraḥia understood the tragic consequences of his original teaching. His revised teaching was intended to establish a framework for transmitting the Torah while engendering an adherence to responsibility: "Attain for yourself a teacher and acquire a companion," alongside "judge every man favorably."

This was a radical departure from his earlier approach. "Judge every man favorably" is interpreted by many people as an expression of the quest for truth in a situation of doubt. Thus, for example, Maimonides explains this teaching in his *Commentary on the Mishna*:

> "And judge every man favorably," so that when you do not know whether a man is righteous or wicked, and he acts or speaks in a manner which can be interpreted in either a positive or a negative sense, consider him to be good and do not think badly of him. However, when a person who is reputed to be a righteous person who performs good deeds is seen acting in a manner that by all indications is evil and which can only be construed as a good act by the most contrived and remote manner, he should nonetheless be viewed positively, since there is a possibility of viewing the act in a positive sense and it is not permitted to suspect him, as they have said, "He who entertains a suspicion against the innocent is liable for bodily affliction" [*Shabbat* 97a].
>
> Likewise, if there is an evil person whose evil deeds are known to all, who is seen to be performing a deed which by all indications is a good deed, but there is a remote possibility of it being viewed as an evil deed, one should be wary of that person and not believe that he is good, because he has a propensity for evil. Of this it is said, "Though he be fair-spoken do not trust him" [Proverbs 25:26]. And in cases of doubt, when the act itself does not attest to either of the two extremes, one should take the path of kindness and judge him favorably. (Maimonides, *Commentary on the Mishna, Avot* 1:6)

The Lubavitcher Rebbe's interpretation, on the other hand, attempts to extract the good inherent in every person, for no person is wholly evil. A person can be restored to the correct path by finding the point of goodness within him, and through that point the person can continue to be entirely good. In that way the teaching is understood not as "Judge every man …," but rather, "Judge all of a man …," that is, the totality of each person in a positive way. Rabbi Nachman of Bratslav described this eloquently:

> Know that every person must be judged favorably; even if he is totally evil, one must search and find that bit of goodness in

> which he is not evil, and from having found that point of goodness, having judged it to his credit, it elevates him to the level of merit, and can cause him to repent. This accords with the verse: "For yet a little while, the wicked shall not be; you will look at his place and he will be gone" [Psalm 37:10]. The verse therefore warns us to judge each person favorably, and even where it is clear that he is evil we are still enjoined to search and to find that small point of goodness where evil does not exist; for this is the meaning of the words, "For yet a little while, the wicked shall not be." ... for it is impossible that he has not performed some mitzva or good deed in his life. By having found that little point of goodness where there is no evil and judging him meritoriously, you elevate him in reality from the side of debit to the side of merit, until he repents as a result. And this is the meaning of the words, "a little while, the wicked shall not be." By finding the ... good, you will merit thereby: "you will look at his place and he will be gone." This means that when you deeply search and examine his place and his level, and you ignore [the first impression] that he makes on you ... he is really moved from the side of debit to the side of merit, and then: "you will look at his place and he will be gone," as we have said – and understand this. (*Likkutei Moharan, Mahadura Kamma*, 282)

It seems the dispute between Yehoshua ben Peraḥia and Nittai HaArbeli revolved around the question of how to confront misfortune and calamity. Nittai HaArbeli's policy was understood as a guideline: In a world in which evil is rampant, one must seek fortification in a place of refuge, remote from the centers of influence. This view was countered by Yehoshua ben Peraḥia, who taught that, with the help of proper rabbinical guidance and a strong attachment to friends, as well as searching for the good in oneself and one's surroundings, one can guide each individual and the world as a whole in the correct path. This was his revised teaching, acquired in the wake of his failure with his pupil, a critical juncture in Rabbi Yehoshua's philosophy.

Chapter Nine

Yehuda ben Tabbai and Shimon ben Shetaḥ: "Justice Justice Shall You Pursue"

Yehuda ben Tabbai and Shimon ben Shetaḥ received [the Torah] from them. Yehuda ben Tabbai said: [When serving as a judge] Do not conduct yourselves like the lawyers and, when the litigants stand before you, consider them as wicked men; but when they depart consider them as innocent, as soon as they have accepted the judgment.

Shimon ben Shetaḥ said: Examine the witnesses thoroughly, and be cautious in your words lest they learn from them to deceive. (Avot 1:8–9)

POLITICAL AND HISTORICAL BACKGROUND

We shall begin with an overview of the period during which the third Pair – Yehuda ben Tabbai and Shimon ben Shetaḥ – were active.

The previous Pair – Yehoshua ben Peraḥia and Nittai HaArbeli – flourished during the period of the Hasmonean Priest Yoḥanan (Hyrcanus), who reigned until 104 BCE. He was succeeded by his first born son, Aristobulus, who killed his mother and one of his brothers (Antigonus) and imprisoned his other male siblings. Aristobulus soon went insane and died of remorse for his sins. He was succeeded by his third son, Alexander Yannai, who is generally considered the greatest of the Hasmonean kings. Yannai continued his father's territorial conquests, and during the course of his reign the expanse of the Hasmonean State reached an extent unseen since the reign of King Solomon. Yannai ruled with an iron fist until 76 BCE (for over 25 years), and in his will he bequeathed the kingdom to his wife, Shlomtziyon, who continued ruling for another ten years, until 67 BCE.

The period of Yannai and Shlomtziyon was the period during which Yehuda ben Tabbai and Shimon ben Shetaḥ were active. Unlike the paucity of references to the previous Pairs (Yose and Yose; Yehoshua and Nittai), Yehuda ben Tabbai and Shimon ben Shetaḥ feature extensively in rabbinic literature. The abundance of sources enables us to contrast the two characters and focus upon a number of significant literary phenomena. Sifting through the sources of this period, one is struck by the discrepancy between the sources of the Babylonian Talmud and those of the Jerusalem Talmud (and their respective literary offshoots). The Jerusalem Talmud treats Yannai in a measured, balanced manner, and its criticism is accompanied by tremendous admiration. Direct confrontation between Yannai and the sages is virtually absent; similarly, there is no record of Yannai's pogrom against the Pharisees. By contrast, in the Babylonian Talmud critical stories about Yannai abound or, to quote Yehoshua Efron's comment on Yannai's character: "The Babylonian Talmud depicts an image of a notorious dictator who despises the sages, murders rabbis, and is wicked and heartless."[1]

1. Based on description of Y. Efron "Shimon ben Shetaḥ and King Yannai," *Essays in Jewish History and Philology*, eds. M. Dorman, S. Safrai, and M. Stern (Jerusalem: HaKibbutz HaMe'uḥad, 1970). Efron is the most prominent of the researchers who insisted on drawing a distinction between Babylonian sources and Israel sources in the study of the period. His theory is presented in his book, *Studies of the Hasmonean Period* [Hebrew] (Tel Aviv: 1980).

SHIMON BEN SHETAḤ AND KING YANNAI IN THE BABYLONIAN TALMUD

The fascinating and tense relations between King Yannai and Shimon ben Shetaḥ are recorded in numerous sources. According to the following Babylonian tradition in Tractate *Berakhot*, Yannai's wife – Shlomtziyon – was Shimon ben Shetaḥ's sister:

> King Yannai and his queen were eating together and, since he had killed the rabbis, there was no one left to say grace for them. He said to his wife: Who can bring us someone to say grace for us? She said to him: Swear to me that if I bring you someone you will not harm him. He swore to her, and she brought Shimon ben Shetaḥ, her brother. She placed him between her husband and herself. Look at the honor I have bestowed upon you, said the king. Shimon replied: It is not you who honors me but the Torah that honors me, as it is written: "Exalt her and she will uplift you; she will honor you when you embrace her" [Proverbs 4:8]. He [Yannai] said to her: You see that he does not recognize any authority! They gave him a cup of wine over which to say grace. He said: How shall I say the grace? [Shall I say] "Blessed is He of whose sustenance Yannai and his companions have eaten"? So he drank that cup, and they gave him another and he said grace over it. (*Berakhot* 48a)

This presentation of the story lacks any historical context. Yannai and the queen sit down to dine and, with Yannai having executed the sages, there is no one left to make the blessing over the bread. Suddenly they need a religious functionary. Everything had been just fine, but the performance of rituals requires religious officiants, and King Yannai was in a predicament. The queen says to him: I will find you a sage to say grace, provided that you do him no harm. The king consents and Shlomtziyon promptly produces her brother Shimon ben Shetaḥ from his hiding place. Nonchalantly, Shimon positions himself between his sister and the very same king who murdered all of his colleagues, the sages. The ensuing conversation between them is civil, perhaps a trifle tense, but certainly not threatening. Yannai feels that Shimon should acknowledge the honor being bestowed upon him, but Shimon is quite unimpressed, clarifying to Yannai that "the Torah honors me, not you." This enigmatic story ends with the purpose for which Shimon was brought. Shimon takes the cup for the blessing, but before making the final blessing he once again embarrasses Yannai for not having honored him with food and drink.

The Babylonian tradition thus presents us with a parody about a strange king who kills all of the sages, but takes care not to eat a meal without making a blessing.

SHIMON BEN SHETAḤ AND YANNAI THE KING: THE PARALLEL ACCOUNT IN THE JERUSALEM TALMUD

The parallel story in the Jerusalem Talmud is couched in a more convincing reality.

Act One: The releasing of three hundred Nazirites

> It was taught: Three hundred poor Nazirites came up to Israel in the days of Rabbi Shimon ben Shetaḥ upon completion of their Nazirite period, and they could not afford to bring the required sacrifices. For one hundred and fifty of them he found an opening with which to release them from their vows, and for the other one hundred and fifty he did not find an opening. He came to Yannai the king and told him: there are three hundred Nazirites here, they need nine hundred offerings, but they cannot afford them. [Said Yannai:] Rather than having them not bring these offerings, you give half at your expense, and I will give half at mine. Thereupon, Yannai sent him four hundred and fifty offerings. A talebearer went to the king, and told him: Shimon ben Shetaḥ gave nothing of his own! King Yannai heard and was enraged, and Shimon ben Shetaḥ became frightened and fled for his life. (Talmud Yerushalmi, *Berakhot* 7:2 [11b])

There is considerable evidence indicating the widespread practice of Nazirite vows in the land of Israel in the time of the Second Temple. The Nazirites were not disapproved of, being regarded rather as deserving of assistance to enable them to complete their Nazirite period without prohibitive costs. The Nazirite could be freed in two ways. Either by a legal "loophole" (i.e., nullifying their vow), which requires wisdom – the domain of the sages; or by bringing three sacrifices: "One male lamb in his first year… for a burnt offering; one ewe lamb in his first year for a sin offering; and one ram… for a peace offering" (Numbers 6:14). This was a heavy expense for someone who lived off thin air and love.

Shimon ben Shetaḥ undertook to liberate the Nazirites from their vows at a minimum cost. He found loopholes for a hundred and fifty of them, but was unsuccessful regarding the rest. Hence he turned to Yannai for help, which attests to the normalcy of their relationship, perhaps even more. Yannai's proposal to Shimon was to divide the responsibility, fifty-fifty. Yannai would finance the cost of half of the nine hundred sacrifices needed, and the remainder would be financed by Shimon, ensuring that all three hundred Nazirites would be freed from their vows. Yannai discharged his part of the bargain by financing the cost of four hundred and fifty sacrifices. Since Shimon had already nullified the vows of half the Nazirites, Yannai's contribution was sufficient to complete the liberation of all the remaining Nazirites from their Nazirite oath. At this point, Yannai hears a rumor that Shimon has, in fact, not paid anything at all. This infuriates him and Shimon goes into hiding. According to the Jerusalem Talmud, this is the background to Shimon ben Shetaḥ's flight.

Act Two: The meal with the Persian scholars

> After some time, dignitaries from the Persian kingdom came to visit King Yannai. When they sat to eat they told Yannai: We remember that there was an elderly man here who would say words of wisdom before us. Yannai related to them what had transpired. But they said: Nevertheless, send for him and bring him! Yannai sent for him, and gave him a sign that he would not harm him. Shimon ben Shetaḥ came, and sat down between the king and the queen. Yannai said to him: Why did you trick me? Shimon ben Shetaḥ responded: I did not trick you, for I indeed provided for the Nazirites just as you did. You provided for half of

> the Nazirites from your money, while I provided for half of them with my Torah knowledge. As it is written: "One who sits in the shade of wisdom is as one who sits in the shade of money" [Ecclesiastes 7:12]. Yannai said to him: Why, then, did you flee? He replied to him: I heard that my master, the king, was angry with me, and I wished to fulfill the following verse: "Hide for a moment until anger passes" [Isaiah 26:20]. Yannai then recited [regarding Shimon ben Shetaḥ] the verse: "And the advantage of knowledge is that wisdom preserves the life of its possessors" [Ecclesiastes ibid.]. Yannai asked him: and why did you sit between the king and the queen? [Shimon ben Shetaḥ] responded: In the book of Ben Sira it is written: "Exalt her [Torah] and she will uplift you; between nobles she will seat you."
>
> Yannai then said to the servants: Give him a cup of wine over which to make the blessing. Shimon ben Shetaḥ took the cup and said: "Let us make a blessing for the food that Yannai and his friends have eaten!" Yannai said to him: Even now you persist in your obstinacy, mocking me in my very presence? Shimon ben Shetaḥ responded: But what, then, shall I say? "Let us make a blessing for the food that we have *not* eaten"? Yannai said to his servants: Give him food to eat. He ate and then said: "Let us make a blessing for the food we have eaten." (Ibid.)

The second act begins with a high-level diplomatic visit of aristocratic Persian leaders. Persia was ruled at that time by the Parthian dynasty that had dealt a staggering defeat to the Seleucid kingdom, changing the face of the Middle East, and enabling Yoḥanan the High Priest to transform the Hasmonean State into an empire. A vast network of foreign and security relations was thus forged between the Hasmoneans and the Parthians, as exemplified by the state visits recorded in this account.[2]

Between the courses of their festive meal, the visitors noted the absence of the distinguished sage who had participated in their previ-

2. M. Stern, "The Parthian Kingdom from the Defeat of Antiochus Sidetes until Pompey" [Hebrew], in D. Schwartz (ed.), *Hasmonean Judea in the Hellenistic World: Chapters in Political History* (Jerusalem: 1995), pt. 3, ch. 11.

ous visits, enchanting them with his wisdom. In contrast to Shimon ben Shetaḥ's exclusively religious role in the Babylonian tradition, the Jerusalem Talmud views him as part of the king's cultural entourage, whose absence makes the meal considerably less enjoyable. The visitors hear Yannai's explanation of his absence and promptly request to see him. Evidently, Shimon ben Shetaḥ's hideout was nearby because he appears immediately upon being called for. The "hideout" may in fact be a euphemism for his intentional avoidance of Yannai, in a kind of "industrial action" (though the verse, "Hide for a moment until anger passes" suggests that he actually went into hiding). Shimon enters the room and, uninvited, seats himself between the king and the queen. (It should be noted that the queen referred to here is apparently not his sister.)

At this stage the two begin a discussion of their past grievances. The visitors watch, tensely anticipating a verbal duel between the king and the sage. This is no private conversation, but rather part of a public symposium on wisdom and scholarship.

The first issue requiring clarification is the episode of the Nazirites, and Yannai is still fuming at Shimon's ruse. Feigning innocence, Shimon answers: "You provided from your wealth, I from my Torah." That is: we divided the responsibility between us, and since my assets are not financial, but intellectual, I provided for my hundred and fifty Nazirites by virtue of my Torah knowledge. In support of his position, Shimon cites the verse: "One who sits in the shade of wisdom is as one who sits in the shade of money."

Yannai, however, is relentless in his attempt to prove Shimon's wrongdoing, this time based upon the fact that he fled. Fleeing surely attests to his guilt.

For this, too, Shimon has a verse ready: "Hide for a moment, until anger passes." The problem, he suggests, is Yannai's anger and not his own conduct. Yannai is thus forced to acknowledge defeat in this encounter, and completes the verse previously cited by Shimon from Ecclesiastes: "…and the advantage of knowledge is that wisdom preserves the life of its possessors."

The second round begins with Yannai berating the sage for his impropriety in shamelessly seating himself between the king and his queen, against all rules of etiquette. Yannai attempts to show his visitors that wisdom alone is not sufficient to merit leadership. Shimon responds with another verse from Ben Sira: "Exalt her [Torah] and she will uplift you; between nobles she will seat you." With this verse, Shimon attempts to make clear to Yannai that the Torah elevates him to center stage, to the precise place where he seated himself, between the king and the queen.

Acknowledging defeat, Yannai gives Shimon the honor of making the blessing over the cup. Shimon hints to him that one cannot say grace without eating first, and Yannai again reproaches him (although this time the context suggests a more conciliatory atmosphere) and orders his servants to bring Shimon food, so that he can participate in the meal. The meal is thus a meal of appeasement, thanks to the mediation of the Parthians.

SHIMON BEN SHETAḤ AS JUDGE

Shimon ben Shetaḥ was clearly the representative of the Jewish sages in the royal court. His inclusion in Tractate *Avot* suggests that he was the head of the rabbinical court (*Av Beit Din*) and that Yehuda ben Tabbai was the patriarch, or *Nasi* (as a rule, the first of each Pair was the *Nasi*; the other, the *Av Beit Din*). However, the exceptional nature of this Pair is noted by Rabbi Yehuda in the Tosefta:

> The three authorities from the earlier Pairs who ruled not to lay on hands and the two authorities of the later Pairs who ruled to lay on hands were patriarchs. Those second to them were heads of the court – these are the words of Rabbi Meir. Rabbi Yehuda says: Shimon ben Shetaḥ was the patriarch, Yehuda ben Tabbai was head of the court. (*Ḥagiga* 2:8)

The days of Yoḥanan the High Priest were followed by a turbulent period of struggle between the sages of Israel and the Hasmonean leadership, the latter having forged an alliance with the Sadducees who held the positions of power in Jerusalem. In this period, that of Yannai and Shlomtziyon, we now seek to understand the standing and the role of Yehuda ben Tabbai and Shimon ben Shetaḥ.

In accordance with the aforementioned convention that in each Pair, the first one is the *Nasi*, we ought to have asserted that Yehuda ben

Tabbai was the *Nasi* and Shimon ben Shetaḥ was the *Av Beit Din*, which is indeed Rabbi Meir's position in the Tosefta. However, Rabbi Yehuda disputes this, and claims that Shimon was the *Nasi*. The Jerusalem Talmud provides the following explanation of this dispute:

> We have taught: Yehuda ben Tabbai was the patriarch and Shimon ben Shetaḥ was the head of the court. Some teach it vice versa.
>
> He who says Yehuda ben Tabbai was the patriarch, finds support from the incident of Alexandria.
>
> He who says Shimon ben Shetaḥ was the patriarch finds support from the incident in Ashkelon. (Talmud Yerushalmi, *Ḥagiga* 2:2 [77d])

This passage records traditions of two events, one that occurred in Jerusalem and the other in Ashkelon, each of which supports one of the opinions:

> The men of Jerusalem wanted to appoint Yehuda ben Tabbai as the patriarch in Jerusalem. He fled and went to Alexandria. The men of Jerusalem wrote: "From Jerusalem the great to Alexandria the small: How long will my betrothed dwell with you while I am miserable on his account?" (Ibid.)

The story continues in the Jerusalem Talmud as in the Babylonian Talmud, regarding Yehoshua ben Peraḥia and Jesus (see above).

Indeed, the tradition recorded in the Jerusalem Talmud regarding Yehuda ben Tabbai is almost identical to that recorded about Yehoshua ben Peraḥia, who fled to Alexandria with Jesus. In the Babylonian Talmud, Shimon ben Shetaḥ wrote: "My husband is with you," and in the present context the phrase is "my betrothed." Obviously, the same literary tradition was received by two personages from the same period and, as we observed, this tradition indicates that Yehuda ben Tabbai was the *Nasi*.

In contrast to this tradition, which does not appear in other sources, the story of Ashkelon appears as early as the Mishnaic tradition, albeit only by way of allusion. Among the sages the story was accepted as the "story of Ashkelon," in which Shimon ben Shetaḥ executed eighty witches. In Mishna *Sanhedrin* (6:4), it appears as part of Rabbi Eliezer's opposition to the tannaitic prohibition against any *Beit Din* judicially executing more than one person. The more detailed story in Tractate *Ḥagiga* of the Jerusalem Talmud relates how Shimon invokes his supernatural powers to wipe out eighty witches in Ashkelon. The story is shrouded in mystery, and adduced as proof of Shimon's patriarchal status, given that only the patriarch could have had the legal authority to perform extra-judicial executions. As we shall see presently, Shimon took up arms against social practices that violated the spirit of the Torah, and apparently, in this effort, imposed sentences that departed from ordinary criminal procedure.

INSTITUTIONALIZING THE LEGAL SYSTEM

Shimon ben Shetaḥ's role in establishing the legal system is reflected in a number of traditions. Our discussion begins with the Babylonian tradition, which relates how Yannai humiliated the Sanhedrin under the leadership of Shimon ben Shetaḥ.

> Yannai's slave killed a man. Shimon ben Shetaḥ said to the sages: "Set your eyes upon him and let us judge him." So they sent the king word, saying: "Your slave has killed a man." Thereupon he sent him to them to be tried. But they again sent him a message: "You too must come to stand trial, for the Torah says: 'If warning has been given to its owners,' teaching that the owner of the ox must come and stand by his ox." The king accordingly came and sat down. Then Shimon ben Shetaḥ said: "Stand on your feet, King Yannai, and let the witnesses testify against you; for you do not stand in our presence, but rather in the presence of He who spoke and the world came into being, as it is written: 'Then both the men between whom the controversy is, shall stand,' etc. [Deuteronomy 19:17]." Yannai replied: "I shall not act in accordance with what you say, but in accordance with what your colleagues say." [Shimon] then turned first to the right and then to the left, but they all [for fear of the King] looked down at the ground in shame. Then said Shimon ben Shetaḥ unto them:

> "Are you wrapped in thoughts? Let the Master of thoughts [God] come and call you to account!" Instantly, Gabriel came and smote them to the ground, and they died. It was there and then enacted: "A king [not of the House of David] may neither judge nor be judged; testify, nor be testified against." (*Sanhedrin* 19a)

This tradition views Shimon ben Shetaḥ as holding a crucial leadership position as early as the period of King Yannai, although a parallel tradition (*Tanḥuma, Shofetim*) omits Yannai's name, referring instead only to "one of the Hasmonean kings." Maharsha, the seventeenth-century commentator, compared the Talmudic tradition with that in the book of *Josephon,*[3] concluding that "the murderer in this case was Herod, and the king attempted to save him." Either way, Shimon ben Shetaḥ serves as the bulwark of justice, preventing governmental dictates from undermining the foundations of the law.

Other sources also attest to Shimon ben Shetaḥ's power as a judge. The Tosefta relates that Shimon's relentless pursuit of justice established him as the exclusive supreme authority in the world of the sages, even in relation to his partner Yehuda ben Tabbai:

> The witnesses are never declared to be perjurers before the trial is over. They are not flogged, nor do they pay compensation, nor are they put to death [on account of their perjury] until the trial is over.
>
> A single witness is never declared a perjurer until both witnesses are found to be perjurers, and is not flogged until both are flogged, and is not put to death until both are put to death, and is not required to pay compensation until both are required to pay.
>
> Rabbi Yehuda ben Tabbai said: May I [not] see consolation

3. From the tenth century onwards, the book *Josephon* found its way into many Jewish communities, and was widely believed to have been written by Josephus. Modern Jewish scholarship has clarified beyond all doubt that it is a late and edited translation of Josephus work *Antiquities of the Jews*. The book was republished by D. Flusser with a comprehensive introduction and notes (Jerusalem: 1979).

> if I did not put to death a single perjured witness as a demonstration against the position of the Boethusians, who stated that [a perjured witness could not be put to death] until after the accused had been executed.
>
> Shimon ben Shetaḥ said to him: May I [not] see consolation if you have not shed innocent blood, for the Torah has said: "On the testimony of two witnesses or three witnesses shall he that is to die be put to death" [Deuteronomy 17:6]. Just as the witnesses must be two, so too, the witnesses who are proved to be perjured must be two.
>
> At that moment Yehuda ben Tabbai agreed never to give a legal ruling except upon the authority of Shimon ben Shetaḥ. (Tosefta, *Sanhedrin* 6:6)

Further on in the Tosefta, the sages recount how Yehuda ben Tabbai went to seek forgiveness from the executed person:

> For the rest of his days Yehuda ben Tabbai would go and prostrate himself on the grave of the executed man, and his voice could be heard. The people believed that it was the voice of the executed man; [but] he [Yehuda ben Tabbai] said to them: "It is my voice, and you will know this by the fact that on the day after I die, the voice [of the executed person] will not be heard." (*Ḥagiga* 16b)

Shimon ben Shetaḥ's stature in the *Beit Din* led him to prescribe rigid and meticulous rules of procedure, which were neither overly "lenient" nor "rigid," but rather represented a higher and more precise judicial standard stressing the "sanctity of life." A particularly striking example of this appears in the Tosefta:

> Shimon ben Shetaḥ said: May I [not] see consolation if I did not see someone run after his fellow with a sword in his hand, and [the pursued man] went before him into a ruin, and the pursuer ran in after him, and then I came in right after him and found the victim slain, with a knife in the hand of the murderer, dripping blood, and I said to him: "Evil one! Who killed this

> person?" May I [not] see consolation if I did not see him [run in there]. Either you killed him or I did. But what can I do, for your case is not handed over to me, for the Torah has said: "On the testimony of two witnesses or on the testimony of three witnesses shall a person be put to death." However, He who knows the thoughts of man will exact punishment from that man. He did not move from that spot until a snake bit him and he died. (*Sanhedrin* 8:3)

Adjudication in capital matters requires great care and absolute certainty, and cannot be subject to conjecture and speculation. On the other hand, in combating societal dangers, such as the incident of Ashkelon, Shimon ben Shetaḥ was nevertheless prepared to accept witnesses in capital matters and to execute people on the basis of their testimony, contrary to the strict evidentiary rules of the Torah.

SHIMON BEN SHETAḤ'S SON – A "TRAMPLED THRESHOLD"

The Jerusalem Talmud describes how Shimon ben Shetaḥ's assertive confidence in judgment earned him a host of enemies:

> Shimon ben Shetaḥ's hands were heated [i.e., he was quick to execute those condemned to death]. A group of scoffers came and said: "Let us conspire against him by testifying against his son and have him executed." They testified against him, and he was tried and condemned to death. When he went forth to be executed they said to him, "My lord, we lied." His father wanted to bring him back [i.e., nullify the verdict]. His son said to him: "Father, if you sought to bring salvation by your hand, make me into the threshold." (Talmud Yerushalmi, *Sanhedrin* 6:3 [23b])

We are not told the end of the story. Was his son actually executed? The account depicts the inner tension of a person whose relentless attempt to fortify the rule of law forced him into making a sacrifice of his own son. His son offers himself as the sacrifice so as to "bring salvation by your hand." The salvation referred to is the belief in a legal system capable of dealing with all of life's exigencies, in which justice is administered equally to all, to poor and rich alike. Perhaps this personal tragedy served as the background for Shimon ben Shetaḥ's teaching:

> Examine the witnesses thoroughly, and be cautious in thy words, lest they learn from them to deceive. (*Avot* 1:9)

THE DAYS OF SHLOMTZIYON AND THE TRIUMPH OF THE PHARISEES

It was Shimon ben Shetaḥ's dedication which ultimately led to the victory of the Pharisees over the Sadducees, as recounted in *Megillat Ta'anit:*

> On the twenty-eighth of Tevet the Sanhedrin sat in session. Because the Sanhedrin was full of Sadducees, King Yannai and Queen Shlomtziyon were sitting there and no other [sages] of Israel sat with them other than Shimon ben Shetaḥ. They asked for answers and *halakhot* but were unable to substantiate their answers with verses from the Torah. Shimon ben Shetaḥ said to them: All those who are able to bring proof from the Torah are eligible to sit on the Sanhedrin.
>
> One day a case came before them and there was no one able to bring proof from the Torah other than one person who argued with him and said to him: Give me until tomorrow and I will return. [Shimon ben Shetaḥ] gave him the time. He returned home and sat and studied, but was unable to find an answer from the Torah. The next day he was ashamed to come to sit on the Sanhedrin, and Shimon ben Shetaḥ replaced him with one of his students. He said to them: A Sanhedrin cannot be less than seventy-one. And he did this every day until all of them had been removed, and the Sanhedrin of Israel sat again. On the day that the Sanhedrin was finally rid of the Sadducees they made a festive day. (*Megillat Ta'anit,* 28 Tevet)

It is apparent that this story relates to the period of Queen Shlomtziyon, described by Josephus as the period during which the Pharisees gained control of all branches of sovereign power.

> Alexandra [= Shlomtziyon]...permitted the Pharisees to do as they wished in all matters, and also commanded the people to obey them; and she reinstated all the regulations the Pharisees had introduced in accordance with the tradition of their fathers that had been annulled by Hyrcanus.... (*Antiquities* XIII, 408)

Rabbinic sources also describe this period as one in which Shimon ben Shetaḥ restored ancient practices and reinforced the institutions of government, education and the family.[4] The *Midrash Halakha* provides the following description of this period:

> "Then I will give you your rains in their seasons"...on the nights of the Sabbath. It happened in the days of Shimon ben Shetaḥ and Queen Shlomtziyon, that it would rain from Friday night to Friday night [on a weekly basis] so that the grains of wheat grew as large as beans, and the grains of barley were like olive stones, and the lentils were like golden *dinarim*. And the sages made a bundle of them, and left some behind for future generations. (*Sifra, Beḥukkotai*)

THE ENACTMENTS OF SHIMON BEN SHETAḤ

The above comments provide the historical context for the regulations enacted by Shimon ben Shetaḥ, as recorded in the Jerusalem Talmud:

> Shimon ben Shetaḥ enacted three regulations: that a man may do business with the marriage contract of his wife; that children should go to school; and that glassware is susceptible to impurity. (*Ketubot* 8:11 [32c])

In fact, as we saw above, the decree concerning glassware had already been taught by the first Pair, Yose ben Yoezer and Yose ben Yoḥanan –

4. Y.L. Levine, "The Political Struggle between the Pharisees and the Sadducees in the Hasmonean Period," *Jerusalem in the Second Temple Period, Abraham Schalit Memorial Volume* (Jerusalem: 1980), pp. 61–83.

hence the dispute among the *amora'im* of *Eretz Yisrael*. According to some, the third Pair enacted a decree regarding copper to supplement the existing decree regarding glassware, whereas another view holds that the third Pair reenacted the decree of ritual impurity of glassware because it had been forgotten during the intervening generations.

The second regulation cited is the institutionalization of schools, a regulation which we are familiar with primarily from a tradition in the Babylonian Talmud, attributed to the sage Yehoshua ben Gamla:

> Rabbi Yehuda said in the name of Rav: May the memory of Yehoshua ben Gamla be blessed, for were it not for him, Israel would have forgotten the Torah. In former times, a child who had a father was instructed by him; but one that did not, did not learn at all. The reason is that they used to explain the verse: "And you shall teach them to your children etc." [Deuteronomy 11:19] literally – that is, personally. It was therefore enacted that a school for the education of children be established in Jerusalem, on the basis of the following verse: "For out of Zion shall go forth the law; and the word of the Lord out of Jerusalem" [Isaiah 22:3]. And still the child who had a father was brought up [to Jerusalem] and instructed; but the one who did not, remained ignorant.
>
> It was therefore enacted that such schools be established in the capitals of each province; but the children were brought when they were about sixteen or seventeen years of age, and when the lads were rebuked by their teachers, they turned their faces and ran away. Then came Yehoshua ben Gamla, who enacted that schools should be established in all provinces and small towns, and that children be sent to school at the age of six or seven years… (*Bava Batra* 21b)

In the book *History of the Tanna'im and Amora'im*,[5] the author aims to show that the Babylonian and Jerusalem traditions are not in dispute. "Shimon ben Shetaḥ saw that 'the fish stinks from its head' – that is, that as long as Jewish children did not receive a proper Torah education in child-

5. A. Hyman, *History of the Tanna'im and Amora'im* [Hebrew] (Jerusalem: 5747).

hood, they would inevitably be drawn into the teachings of the Sadducees and lost forever." In other words, it was Shimon ben Shetaḥ who initiated the educational reform and Yehoshua ben Gamla who implemented it.

The institutionalization of universal education for all children was a genuine revolution, in its time and one that deserves fuller attention, though this is not the appropriate context. Suffice it to say that this initiative reflects the insight of someone who could assess the nature of his cultural surroundings, and realize that the issue could not be left to the domestic front alone, because "the child who had a father was brought up [to Jerusalem] and instructed, but one who did not, remained ignorant."

The other, most prominent edict attributed to Shimon ben Shetaḥ is that relating to the *ketuba*, the marriage contract. The sages presented the laws of the *ketuba* as having gone through three stages of development:

> Rabbi Yehuda stated: At first they used to give merely a written undertaking in respect of [the *ketuba* of] a virgin for two hundred *zuzim* and in respect of a widow for a *maneh*, and consequently they grew old and could not take any wives. Shimon ben Shetaḥ took the initiative and ordained that all the property of a husband would be pledged to the *ketuba* of his wife. So it was also taught elsewhere: At first they used to give merely a written undertaking in respect of [the *ketuba* of] a virgin for two hundred *zuzim* and in respect of a widow for a *maneh*, and consequently they grew old and could not take any wives. It was then ordained that the amount of the *ketuba* was to be deposited in the wife's father's house. At any time, however, when the husband was angry with her he used to tell her, "Go to your *ketuba*." It was therefore ordained that the amount of the *ketuba* was to be deposited in the house of her father-in-law. Wealthy women converted it into silver or gold baskets, while poor women converted it into brass tubs. Still, whenever the husband had occasion to be angry with his wife he would say to her, "Take your *ketuba* and go." It was then that Shimon ben Shetaḥ decreed that the husband must insert the pledging clause, "All my property is pledged to your *ketuba*." (*Ketubot* 72b)

The Tosefta helps us understand the various stages of the *ketuba*'s development, with which we shall deal briefly now. The economic undertaking involved in a *ketuba* deterred the men, and caused them to avoid marriage – "They grew old and did not take any wives." The background reality is succinctly described by Rabbi Saul Lieberman:

> It was difficult for them to spend two hundred *zuzim* for the sake of marrying a woman, and because they did not normally marry adult women, the money would belong to her father, and the husband would have no profit from it. They therefore amended the arrangement so that the *ketuba* would be deposited in the wife's father's house, for the wife's benefit, and were she to die thereafter, her sons would inherit from her. The problem was that when the husband was angry he would say – take your *ketuba* and leave. Hence, they enacted a third decree ordering her to leave the *ketuba* in her father-in-law's house, until [Shimon ben Shetaḥ] made a decree making the *ketuba* a source for negotiation, and he would write: "All my property is pledged to your *ketuba*. (*Tosefta KiFeshuta, Ketubot,* p. 370)

"BLESSED BE THE LORD, GOD OF SHIMON BEN SHETAḤ"

In addition to enacting these decrees, Shimon ben Shetaḥ is also credited with increasing respect for the God of Israel among the inhabitants of the land. According to the Jerusalem Talmud:

> Shimon ben Shetaḥ dealt in flax [to support himself]. His students said to him: "Rabbi, remove [this work] from yourself, and we shall buy an ass for you, and you will not have to work so much." They went and bought him an ass from a Saracen. A pearl was hanging on it. They came to him and told him: "From now on you do not have to work anymore." He asked them: "Why?" They told him: "We bought you an ass from a Saracen and hanging on it was a pearl." He said to them: "Did its master know about it?" They told him: "No." He said to them: "Go and return it. Do you think that Shimon ben Shetaḥ is a barbarian?" (*Bava Metzia* 2:5 [8c])

In another version, Shimon ben Shetaḥ said the following:

> "The blessing of God brings wealth" [Proverbs 10:22]. Shimon ben Shetaḥ replied: I purchased an ass, but I did not purchase a precious stone. So he went and returned it to the Ishmaelite, and the latter exclaimed of him, "Blessed be the Lord, God of Shimon ben Shetaḥ." (*Devarim Raba* 3)

We are witnesses here to a glorious period for the Jewish people in which God's name was sanctified on earth, and education, the family structure, and the norms of law and morality were all consolidated and fortified. In concluding this section I will mention the struggle waged by Shimon ben Shetaḥ against another trend which he viewed as jeopardizing the institutionalization of society and religion in Israel. I refer to his battle against Ḥoni the Circle Maker, whom we focused upon in the previous chapter.

In this battle, Shimon ben Shetaḥ reflects and represents the concerns of the establishment in its confrontation with miracle workers. Fearing the implications of an approach which suggested that, in times of crisis, one can draw a circle, stand in it, and proclaim, "Master of the Universe, I will not move from here until You have mercy on Your children," Shimon ben Shetaḥ tried to excommunicate Ḥoni, but was unable to do so. Here, too, Shimon was able to draw upon Solomon's wisdom: "Your mother and father will rejoice; she who bore you will exalt" (Proverbs 23:25). Ḥoni is like a son before the Almighty, whereas Shimon was analogous to a minister trying to consolidate and stabilize the kingdom. In the final analysis, Shimon the minister manages to exert his authority over everyone – except the king's favored sons.

Chapter Ten

Shemaya and Avtalyon: At the Height of the Battle between Aristobulus and Hyrcanus

Shemaya and Avtalyon received from them. Shemaya would say: Love labor, loathe mastery over others, and do not seek familiarity with the ruling authorities.

Avtalyon would say: Scholars, be careful with your words. For you may be exiled to a place inhabited by evil elements [who will distort your words to suit their negative purposes]. The disciples who come after you will then drink of these evil waters and be destroyed, and the name of Heaven will be desecrated. (Avot 1:10–11)

HISTORICAL AND POLITICAL BACKGROUND

In the previous chapter we dated the third Pair – Shimon ben Shetaḥ and Yehuda ben Tabbai – during the period of King Yannai and Queen

Shlomtziyon (67–100 BCE). Their successors in the following generation were the fourth Pair, Shemaya and Avtalyon, who were active during a particularly turbulent period for the Jews of the land of Israel. Before discussing the mishna itself, we will briefly review the events of the period.

Queen Shlomtziyon had succeeded in maintaining calm on both the internal and external fronts. Immediately after her death, Yannai's first-born, Hyrcanus II, was appointed both high priest and king. At the same time, his younger brother, Aristobulus, who was grooming himself for kingship, fomented unrest amongst his father's soldiers and stealthily organized a rebellion. After a brief battle, Aristobulus seized power. Hyrcanus surrendered but did not give up. Assisted by his friend Antipater, they enlisted the help of King Aretas of Idumea (Edom). Together they besieged the house in which Aristobulus and his soldiers had fortified themselves. It is in the context of this war that we read the shocking story of Ḥoni the Rain Maker, a story that we saw earlier in a different context, but which we will cite again due to its importance in understanding this period:

> There was a certain Ḥonio, who was a righteous man and dear to God. Once in a time of drought he prayed to God to end the drought, and God had heard his prayer and sent rain. This man hid himself when he saw that the civil war continued to rage, but he was taken to the camp of the Jews, and was asked to place a curse on Aristobulus, and his fellow rebels, just as he had by his prayers, put an end to the drought. But when, in spite of his refusals and his excuses he was forced to speak by the mob, he stood up in their midst and said, "O God, King of the Universe, since these men standing beside me are Your people and those who are besieged are Your priests, I beseech You not to hearken to them against these men nor to bring to pass what these men ask You to do to those others." And when he had prayed in this manner the villains among the Jews who stood round him stoned him to death. (*Antiquities* XIV, 22–24)

Thus began a war between brothers, a civil war which eradicated the last vestiges of sanctity that remained in the Temple since its purification by the grandfather, Mattathias, one hundred years earlier. The Talmud records a tragic story about the priests' attempts to maintain the daily ritual sacrifice, which was likewise doomed to failure:

> Our rabbis taught: When the kings of the Hasmonean house fought one another, Hyrcanus was outside and Aristobulus inside. Each day they would let down *dinarim* [coins] in a basket, and haul up [animals] for the daily offerings. An old man there, who was learned in Greek wisdom, spoke with them in Greek, saying: "As long as they carry on the Temple service, they will never surrender to you." On the morrow they sent down *dinarim* in a basket, and hauled up a pig. When it reached halfway up the wall, it stuck its claws [into the wall], and the land of Israel was shaken over a distance of four hundred parasangs. At that time they declared: "Cursed be the man who rears pigs, and cursed be the man who teaches his son Greek wisdom!" (*Sota* 49b)

Even without sifting out the particulars of the historical reality of this tragic story, the sense of the immense shame occasioned by the civil war is clear. King Pompey was at the height of a campaign of conquest in the Middle East. Having completed the conquest of Syria he entered Judah as a triumphant, unchallenged conqueror, bringing the Hasmonean kingdom to an end.

The decades after 63 BCE saw a number of rulers over the land of Israel, but it was no longer an independent state. Antipater, the Idumean governor, rose to power in 55 BCE and formed a political alliance with Hyrcanus against his brother Aristobulus. For a number of years he ruled wisely, particularly under the patronage of Julius Caesar who, as a token of his esteem, conferred upon him Roman citizenship and the title "Ruler of the Land of Israel." He appointed his sons as governors over the country: Phasael in Jerusalem and Herod in the Galilee. About ten years later Aristobulus' son, Mattathias Antigonus, became stronger and declared war against Phasael in Jerusalem. He had Hyrcanus II disqualified from the priesthood by cutting off his ears; he killed Phasael; and Herod was forced to flee, finding refuge in Rome, where the Senate proclaimed him king. In the year 40 BCE he returned to Palestine, rallied a huge military force and waged protracted wars against Mattathias Antigonus until, in 37 BCE, he finally succeeded in establishing his rule.

It was during this stormy period of internal strife that Shemaya and Avtalyon served as leaders. Josephus relates that this Pair – referred to in his writings as Samias and Polyon – was active during the Herodian era.[1] They headed the Sanhedrin and Herod treated them with respect and decorum. Their teachings in the Mishna clearly reflect the political context in which they found themselves.

SHEMAYA AND AVTALYON: SAGES "OF HEATHEN DESCENT"

The meaning of the statement "Do not seek familiarity with the ruling authorities" is clear. At the height of a civil war, non-partisanship is the best policy, as siding with either party may undermine one's stature. The Pharisees instructed their students to take a step backwards and not to become involved in the politics of government. After many years in which the Hasmonean state was characterized by a corrupt and Hellenized bureaucracy, the call "to love labor and hate mastery" was more than welcome. The call to return to a life of work and labor reflects the disenchantment with the failed Jewish state. Power had corrupted its values and undermined the foundations of society. Shemaya and Avtalyon's condemnation of political authority was sweeping, and addressed itself to all those in positions of power. The earliest record we have of them concerns their relationship to the high priest and incidentally, provides us with their biographical background.

> "And he would make a holiday for his friends." The Rabbis taught: It happened that a high priest once came forth from the Sanctuary, and all the people followed him, but when they saw Shemaya and Avtalyon they forsook him and went after Shemaya and Avtalyon. Eventually Shemaya and Avtalyon came to take leave

1. E.E. Urbach, "Class Status and Leadership in the World of the Sages of Israel" [Hebrew], in *Proceedings of the Israeli Academy of Sciences and Humanities*, vol. 2 (Jerusalem: 1968), p. 38; Y. Ben Shalom, *The School of Shammai and the Zealots Struggle Against Rome* (Jerusalem: 1991), App. II, The Pharisees, s. 1 "Polyon and Samias' Position Regarding Herod" (hereinafter, "Y. Ben Shalom, *Beit Shammai*").

> of the high priest. He said to them: May the descendants of the heathen come in peace. They answered him: May the descendants of the heathen who do the work of Aaron come in peace, but the descendant of Aaron who does not do the work of Aaron, he shall not come in peace. (*Yoma* 71b)

Shemaya and Avtalyon were held in high public esteem. Although the high priest was supposed to be accompanied by all his admirers when he emerged from the Holy of Holies, it was Shemaya and Avtalyon who attracted the following of the entire nation. This rejection of the established protocol and priority between sage and religious leader enraged the high priest and he vented his anger against them: "May the descendants of the heathen come in peace" – an allusion to their non-Jewish ancestry. Both Talmudic traditions relate that they were the children of proselytes and hence their "heathen" lineage.

> Descendants of Sisera taught children in Jerusalem; descendants of Sennacherib gave public expositions of the Torah. Who were these? Shemaya and Avtalyon. As it is written: "I have set her blood upon the bare rock that it should not be covered." (*Gittin* 57b)

Remarkably, within a generation of Shimon ben Shetaḥ "restoring the crown of Torah to its former glory," and consolidating the status of Israel and the Torah in the eyes of world, we already find two converts who rose to key positions as a Pair (*Nasi* and *Av Beit Din*). This was an unusual and complicated scenario, which would certainly have raised many eyebrows with regard to the quality of the nation's spiritual leadership. The high priest's denigration of these sages was vulgar and rude, not to mention a violation of the commandment: "You shall not oppress the convert" (Exodus 22:20). Nonetheless, we encounter criticism of the ancestry of Shemaya and Avtalyon from at least two other sources. The first is Akavia ben Mehalalel, one of the greatest sages, whose words escort us at every funeral. Without elaborating on his colorful character at this point, the account depicting his relationship with Shemaya and Avtalyon is relevant for our purposes.

> Akavia ben Mehalalel testified on four matters. They said to him: Akavia! Retract on the four matters which you have said, and we will make you Head of the Court in Israel. He said to them: It were better that I be called a fool all my days, and not to be evil for a single hour before God, that they not say of me, he retracted for the sake of public office.
>
> He used to declare unclean the left-over hair and greenish blood, but the sages declared it clean. He used to permit the hair of a first-born with a blemish which had fallen out and had been placed in a window, which afterwards was slaughtered, but the sages forbid it.
>
> He used to say, One does not give to drink [i.e., the bitter waters of the *sota*] to the female convert or the freed gentile female slave; but the sages said, One does give them to drink. They said to him, There was the case of Karkemit, a freed female slave who was in Jerusalem, and Shemaya and Avtalyon gave her to drink. He said to them: her own kind gave her to drink. And they excommunicated him, and he died whilst excommunicated, and the Court stoned his coffin. Rabbi Yehuda said: Heaven forbid that Akavia was excommunicated! For the Temple courtyard was never shut against the face of any man in Israel who was as wise and sin-fearing as Akavia ben Mehalalel. So whom did they excommunicate? Eliezer ben Ḥanokh, who questioned washing the hands. And when he died the Court sent and placed a rock on his coffin. This teaches that whoever is excommunicated and dies whilst excommunicated, they stone his coffin. (Mishna, *Eduyot* 5:6)

The story of Akavia's excommunication is a shocking one, which we shall discuss below. But here we should note that Akavia's criticism of Shemaya and Avtalyon was directed at their lineage. The context is the Talmudic dispute between the sages and Akavia about giving the *sota* waters (for a woman suspected of adultery) to a female convert. The sages attempted to substantiate their view from the actual case of a young girl who had been married as a liberated maidservant to an Israelite, who was overcome by pangs of jealousy. Shemaya and Avtalyon conducted the bitter-waters ceremony as though she were a regular Jewish woman (not a convert). Responding to their actions, Akavia said: "Her own kind gave her to drink" – that is, people like herself (i.e., descendants of converts) administered the bitter waters. While this did not constitute a direct attack on Shemaya and Avtalyon, the text clearly indicates the sages' disapproval of leaders who were the descendants of converts.

The context here, illustrating the tension between the newcomers and the establishment, may provide the background for the legend of Hillel the Elder who came from Babylonia and scorned the elders of Beteira for not properly serving the two foremost scholars of the generation, Shemaya and Avtalyon. We will consider this story in more detail below. In this context I would only point out that this is another example of the Torah having been expropriated from the elite and finding its appropriate place among those prepared to devote themselves to it, even if they come from the lower classes of the people.

THE SCHOOL OF SHEMAYA AND AVTALYON: DO NOT RAISE UP MANY STUDENTS

Shemaya and Avtalyon's most renowned disciple was Hillel (he was preceded by a lesser known student named Menaḥem, whom we shall discuss in Part Three). The Babylonian tradition relates that, upon making his first steps into the world of Torah, Hillel encountered an establishment in which only the wealthy were permitted into the study house.[2] The following story sheds light on this approach:

> Our rabbis taught: The poor man and the evil rich man will come before the [heavenly] court. They will ask the poor man: Why did you not occupy yourself with the Torah? If he says: I was

2. I use the words "Babylonian tradition" because this story has no parallel in *Eretz Yisrael* sources. Furthermore, from other sources it becomes apparent just how divorced the story is from historical reality. The subject is dealt with in Shmuel Safrai's article: "Tales of the sages in the Palestinian tradition and the Babylonian Talmud," in *Scripta Hierosolymitana*, 22 (1971), pp. 209–232.

> poor and worried about my sustenance, they will answer him: Were you poorer than Hillel?
>
> It was told of Hillel the Elder that every day he used to work and earn one *tropik*, half of which he would give to the guard at the study house, the other half being spent for his food and for that of his family. One day he found nothing to earn and the guard at the study house would not permit him to enter. He climbed up and sat upon the window, to hear the words of the living God from the mouth of Shemaya and Avtalyon. It is told that that day was the eve of Sabbath on the winter solstice and snow fell upon him from heaven. When the dawn rose, Shemaya said to Avtalyon: Brother Avtalyon, every other day this house is light and today it is dark; perhaps it is a cloudy day. They looked up and saw the figure of a man in the window. They went up and found him covered by three cubits of snow. They removed him, bathed and anointed him, and put him opposite the fire and they said: This man is worthy that the Sabbath be profaned on his behalf. (*Yoma* 35b)

The story is written in praise of Hillel, who risked his life for the love of Torah; this is also the way it is taught in our schools. But it is also a story of the tremendous tension between the worlds of Shemaya and Avtalyon, the foremost scholars of the generation, and the world outside the *Beit Midrash*. In order to enter the study house, one needed money – a lot of money.

Yonah Fraenkel has observed:

> Even without being able to make an exact calculation, it is clear that half of a day-laborer's daily wage for the guard is a prohibitive, unjustifiable sum…We must listen to the injustice in the sentence: "It happened once that he was unable to earn sufficiently, and the guard did not permit him to enter the house of study." Who was responsible for this?…We can only do justice to the story if we view it as a critique and a warning against those who

> spent all their days in the study house, engaged in "the words of the Living God."[3]

Hillel encountered a world in which the Torah was a closed, encapsulated text transmitted among members of an elite. His heroic act established a new standard, expanding the opportunity – and obligation – of Torah study to every person. From his time onward, the Torah would be open to all those wished to study it.

Shemaya and Avtalyon severed the bond between the State and the Torah. Having despaired of politicians and the government, they brought the Torah into the Yeshiva, in an attempt to have an influence on the development of the spiritual world of the people. Their students, Hillel and Shammai, would continue the tense debate over the proper place of the Torah in everyday life – as we shall discover in the next section.

3. Y. Fraenkel, *Studies in the Spiritual World of the Aggadic Story* [Hebrew] (Tel Aviv: 1981), p. 67.

Chapter Eleven

A Contemporary Perspective: Ḥanukka – Its Impact through the Generations

In Part Two of this book, we have followed the development of the Hasmonean State from the beginning of Antiochus' reign and the ensuing revolt, until the entry of Rome and the disintegration of the Hasmonean state. The festival of Ḥanukka plays a central role in this period, and we will devote a few lines to the various accounts of the festival in Jewish tradition.

In the literature of the period, the story of Ḥanukka appears in a number of versions, foremost among them in the books of Maccabees. These books, part of the Apocrypha, were written by various different authors in different places. The two most important works regarding the establishment of Ḥanukka are I and II Maccabees.

The first book of Maccabees was originally written in Hebrew, and provides a comprehensive description of the period from the edicts of Antiochus (167 BCE) until the murder of Shimon (134 BCE). The book emphasizes the military history of the Maccabees, and is written in a spirit of deep identification with the rebellion and its leaders. This is Israel's version of the Maccabees' rebellion.

Second Maccabees was written in exile by Jason of Cyrene, and its primary focus is on the religious situation of the nation during the Maccabean revolt. It was written in order to bolster the observance of the festival of the Day of Nicanor on the thirteenth of Adar. In terms of dating, it is contemporaneous with I Maccabees.[1]

The nature of Ḥanukka differs in the two books, each version reflecting its author and his culture:

First Maccabees (chapter 4) describes how Judah Maccabee and his followers conquered Jerusalem after their victory in the battle of Beit Tzur. He closed the Ḥakra fortress, purified the Temple, and renewed the Temple ritual. The celebrations of the reestablishment of the Temple ritual and of the purification of the Temple lasted eight days. Upon the completion of the celebrations, it was decided that they would be celebrated annually. The same description appears in II Maccabees, except the latter places the celebration in the context of Sukkot, the celebration of which had been cancelled during Judah's battles. The eight days of Sukkot were celebrated on the day when they triumphed over their enemies, the twenty-fifth of Kislev. The festival was thus referred to as "Sukkot in the month of Kislev" on which staffs were decorated with sprigs and dates (II Maccabees 10).

Josephus mentions Ḥanukka in *Antiquities* XII, 325, where he refers to it as the "Festival of Lights." He does not mention the lighting of candles or anything similar. He explains the name of the festival in

1. D. Schwartz wrote an article on the cultural clash between I Maccabees and II Maccabees, more than hinting at the actuality of this clash when viewed through the spectrum of the tension between Israeli religious Zionism and the Modern Orthodoxy of the Diaspora: See D. Schwartz, "What's the Difference Between I Maccabees and II Maccabees? or, The Challenging Hyphen in Such Combinations as 'State-Religious,' 'Religious-National' and 'Zionist-Religious,'" in *Jewish Tradition in a Changing Educational World* [Hebrew], ed. M. Barlev, (Jerusalem: 2005), pp. 11–20.

the context of the right granted to the Jews to return to the Temple in order to worship God without disturbance.

Megillat Ta'anit is a work that was regarded as part of the Oral Law of the Second Temple period, although for the main part it was not preserved. The *Megilla* enumerates the dates on which fasting and eulogizing were forbidden, including the twenty-fifth of Kislev. The commentary on the *Megilla*, or scholia, mentions the miracle of the cruse of oil, but it is considered to be a later source and has no bearing on the antiquity of this tradition.

As is well known, there is no tractate on Ḥanukka in the Mishna, and it only merits sparse attention in tannaitic literature. This subject has been discussed at length by scholars of Jewish history, and I shall not elaborate upon it.[2] A tannaitic reference to Ḥanukka appears in Tractate *Nezikin*, where the Mishna deals with the issue of the liability of a person who lights a fire, the flames of which burn outside his premises. A camel carrying flax passes by and the flax catches fire. Who is liable? The Mishna states that if the incident happened on Ḥanukka the owner of the camel would be liable, because he ought to have known that there would be burning lights.

From this brief reference we can deduce that at this time there was indeed a festival of Ḥanukka and that its celebration was a normative part of Jewish practice. Indeed the Mishna recognizes and justifies this, though it does not explain what the festival was. It omits all mention of the Hasmonean Wars or of the warriors' valor, nor is there any reference to political independence. There is a view that this was part of an attempt to conceal the miracle of the Hasmonean rebellion, or even

2. The standing (or more precisely – the lack of standing) of the Hasmonean tradition in tannaitic literature has been written about extensively. See J. Tabory, *Jewish Festivals in the Time of the Mishna and Talmud* [Hebrew] (Jerusalem: 5755), p. 372, n. 15. Tabory contrasts the nationalist approach with the pre-Zionist approach regarding the Hasmoneans in general, and specifically Ḥanukka. See also in the response of G. Alon to the anti-nationalist trend, in his article: "Did the Nation and Its Sages Intentionally Forget the Hasmoneans?" *Studies in Jewish History*, vol. 1, (Tel Aviv: 5738), p. 15–26. D. Schwartz wrote a response to Alon in his article cited above, "The Pharisaic Opposition to the Hasmonean Dynasty" [Hebrew], *Nation and History, Studies in the History of the Jewish People*, vol. 1 (Jerusalem: 1983), p. 39–50.

a conscious attempt to suppress the record altogether. In this context, the claim is made that during the period of the Mishna's compilation, after the Bar Kokhba revolt, there was an attempt to pacify the Roman Empire by rewriting Jewish history. They were effectively saying: "We are not a rebellious nation. We do not seek political freedom. We despise wars." Rabbi Yehuda HaNasi (Judah the Prince), the redactor of the Mishna, "concealed" the rebellion in an effort to appease. A rebellion? Us? Perish the thought!

The Babylonian Talmud, however, does refer to Ḥanukka. The Talmud asks: What is [the reason for] Ḥanukka? Why do we light eight candles? The Talmud answers: because of the miracle of the cruse of oil. It is in the Babylonian Talmud, in the profound darkness of the Babylonian exile, that the story of the vial of oil begins to flicker: "a small jug, for eight days it gave its oil." This is the most familiar of the festival's stories: the story about a cruse of pure oil that was supposed to last for only one day but which, in the absence of any other oil, provided a miracle for the Hasmoneans and burned for eight days.

Why an eight-day festival? Because the Menora remained lit for eight days. And so a new miracle story emerged, one which posed no threat to any empire, and which allowed us to remember and perpetuate the memory of Ḥanukka without any disturbance. It became a festival bearing the deep imprint of the exile, lacking any suggestion of political independence.

It was only in modern times, with the return to the land of Israel by the Zionist movement, that the story of the Hasmoneans once again became part of the national awareness. Zionists sang battle songs in praise of the Maccabees' valor: "We experienced no miracle – we found no cruse of oil." Bialik composed a number of poems about the Maccabees' bravery in comparison to that of his own generation: the last generation of slavery and first generation of redemption. The miracles and the wonders became "the miracles and wonders that were performed by the Maccabees."

The religious world continued to cultivate the story of the miracle, whereas the Zionist world cultivated the earthly valor, that of the warriors and the rebels. This underlying conflict reflects a more profound dispute over the focus of attention: Who deserves the credit? God, or the Maccabees? Should the emphasis be on the military victory, or the miracle of the oil? The roots of this dispute already appear in the conflicting accounts appearing in Maccabees I and II. In I Maccabees there is almost no mention of God's name; all of the wonders are attributed to Judah and his comrades. II Maccabees, on the other hand, is totally indifferent to the issue of the battles and acts of bravery. It tells the story of Sukkot. Had it thought of it (or known about it – depending upon whom one asks), it would have told the story of the cruse of oil.

In fact, the implications of this discussion are even more fundamental. During hundreds of years of exile, Jews were incapable of putting their military valor to the test; the right to rise up and fight was denied them in their Diasporic existence. On the other hand, the courage locked in their hearts was inviolable: this was the courage required to hold fast and continue seeing the divine image reflected in man in every time and place. Throughout the generations, the Jewish people encountered endless enslavements and harsh decrees, but interspersed among the unending stories of horror we find remarkable accounts of the bravery and valor of Jews who fought to preserve their divine image.

Since these times of darkness, with their tales of grandeur and bravery, we have been privileged to return to the land of Israel to establish the home of the Jewish people. We have now been granted the possibility of defending ourselves with courage of a physical and not purely spiritual kind. Some of the ideologues of the Zionist movement attempted to emulate the models of bravery found in the cultures of other nations, constructing a paradigm of the new Jew, who is powerful, aggressive, muscular and afraid of nothing. At times it was the kibbutz movement that promoted the image of the muscular farmer. At others, it was the military, which we likened to King David's soldiers attacking Goliath.

The Jewish calendar likewise underwent a change, adopting the trappings of the Israeli-fighter-hero. Instead of the miracle of the cruse of oil, Ḥanukka became the festival of the warrior Maccabees. From a tender age, the education system stressed the bravery of the people, without reliance upon divine intervention or heavenly miracles. The Lag BaOmer bonfire underwent a similar transformation. The bonfire at which the mystical secrets of Bar Yoḥai were revered became the assembly point at which the fighters of Bar Kokhba prepared their revolt. The new Israeli attempted to shake off the stigma of the exilic Jew, and in its place forged the image of the warrior-like Israeli. At the same time, however, Israeli society was also undergoing significant changes. With the emergence of a generation that had not personally experienced the War of Independence, the debate that divided the entire nation was whether warfare is a sign of bravery or stupidity? Is there such a thing as a just war? What, if anything, is worth dying for?

Today, from the perspective of more than sixty years of statehood, we know that there are different types of bravery.

There is bravery that relies on the "cruse of oil" tradition – the tradition of that ancient, stubborn Judaism which continues to light candles year after year, indifferent to the exigencies of time. Even in the deepest darkness the Jew can find the small jug of oil. This is the power of survival.

There is also bravery which draws on the Hasmonean tradition of fighting and the celebration of independence. This is the bravery of those who refuse to be subject to the kindness of others, and who are willing to give their lives in order to be sovereign in their land. This is an active bravery, driven by the sense of an earthly mission.

None of these levels is dispensable. Ḥanukka is a multifaceted festival and we aspire to reveal its many faces so that they may shed their radiance on the nation returning to its land and to its independence. But even in this independence, the small cruse of oil must still be found, to enable the nation to continue its national destiny in light and goodness.

Part Three

Hillel and Shammai and Their Students

The Men of the Great Assembly	The Pairs	Shammai, Hillel and Their Students	Rabban Gamliel the Elder	The Destruction
-450 -300	-200	-50	30	60 70
Cyrus to Alexander of Macedonia	The Hasmoneans	Herod	The Governors	The War with Rome

Preface

> *Any dispute that is for the sake of Heaven shall endure, but one that is not for the sake of Heaven shall not endure. Which dispute was for the sake of Heaven? That of Hillel and Shammai. And which was not for the sake of Heaven? That of Koraḥ and his company.* (Avot 5:17)

In the world of the oral tradition, Hillel is seen as the spiritual successor of Ezra the Scribe:

> When Hillel the Elder died they lamented over him: Alas, the pious man! Alas, the humble man, the disciple of Ezra! (*Sota* 48b)

This sense of continuity between Ezra the Scribe and Hillel reflects the continuing development and renewal of the Torah. In Part One, we discussed the legacy of the Men of the Great Assembly, who brought the Torah out of God's Temple and into everyday life. Hillel the Elder would have a similar impact. He would inject a spirit of humanity into the *beit midrash* and revitalize the ethical tradition. He would struggle to open the doors of the *beit midrash* to all comers, and to give equal opportunity to all. At the same time, he would develop halakhic interpretations that could successfully navigate an ever-changing reality (for example, the institution of *prozbul* during the *shemitta* year). Furthermore, he would seek to bridge the worlds of the holy and the secular in his attempt to create a model of the ideal person.

In stark opposition to this approach stand Shammai and his students, representatives of the old world, with all its spiritual security. They would strive to preserve tradition and to restrain the innovative spirit. Their elitist policy would seek to exclude from the *beit midrash* any student not born and bred in the world of Torah. In their eyes, reality should be adapted to conform to halakha, and the chasm between sanctity and secularity should be maintained.

This tension between the School of Hillel and the School of Shammai, which begins in the period discussed in this section, will continue to accompany the Jewish people in all of its incarnations until this very day.

Chapter Twelve

Hillel's Leadership and His Legacy

Hillel was born to a Babylonian family of good lineage about four centuries after the era of Simeon the Just.[1] He arrived in the land of Israel and served under Shemaya and Avtalyon in a state of abject poverty. He later achieved greatness, taking his place as the patriarch of Israel and as the link connecting the era of the Pairs with the period of the *Tanna'im*.

HISTORICAL AND POLITICAL BACKGROUND

Hillel's life spanned the Herodian era, which began in 37 BCE and lasted until the beginning of the first century CE. Herod's reign marks the final transition from the Hasmonean state to Roman sovereignty. The Jews

1. Some have claimed that Hillel did not come from Babylonia, but rather from Alexandria: a place suffused with Greek culture, the birthplace of philosophy, the cradle of mathematics and physics, and where the focus was on abstract thought and the glorification of the role of man in the world. See A. Kaminka, "Hillel the Elder and His Work" [Hebrew], *Zion* 4 (1939) p. 259.

had already begun to feel their independence slipping away during the governorship of Antipater, Herod's father, but this process accelerated during Herod's reign. Herod's rulership was founded on an extremely narrow base of domestic consensus while depending completely on the Roman Empire. His rule cemented Rome's grip over Judea, but it did not extinguish the rebellious spirit that continued smoldering in the heart of the Jews. The nation continued to harbor Hasmonean zeal in its heart. It occasionally erupted (as in the period of Aristobulus who fought Hyrcanus II), and though suppressed, it was never extinguished. One of the greatest expressions of the Hasmonean spirit is described in Josephus' account of Herod's siege against Jerusalem (*Antiquities* XIV, 468–481). This was a war fought by the Hasmoneans against all odds, but with unlimited devotion and sacrifice; the Hasmonean spirit imbued the Jewish warriors with unyielding tenacity. Ultimately, Herod only succeeded in conquering Jerusalem by virtue of his massively superior military power. The siege ended with Herod's conquest of Jerusalem and a brutal massacre of the town's inhabitants. Herod's first years in power were characterized by the repression of any opposition and the elimination of all seditious elements in Judea.[2]

At the same time, Herod sought to foster his relationship with Jews who were not associated with the Hasmonean dynasty or who had been rejected from the Hasmonean mainstream, namely, the Essenes and the Diaspora Jews. To that end, he appointed Ḥananel the Babylonian as high priest. More significantly, he married Miriam the Hasmonean, daughter of Alexandra and granddaughter of Hyrcanus II, who had been exiled to Babylonia by Aristobulus. The marriage was an attempt to preserve something of the Hasmonean dynasty within Herod's rule, but specifically from the rejected branch – the exiled family of Hyrcanus. The marriage itself triggered grave political problems;

2. Josephus (*Antiquities*, 15:3) relates that the sages tried to convince the people to surrender to Herod. Naturally, he omits mention of any particular sage, but, in principle, it stands to reason that some of the sages understood the relative desirability of surrendering to Herod and not dying. See M. Stern, "The Politics of Herod and Jewish Society toward the End of the Second Commonwealth" [Hebrew], *Tarbitz* 35, *Studies in Jewish History, The Second Temple Period* (Jerusalem: 1991), p. 181, n. 6.

Josephus relates that Herod's mother-in-law, too, had a say in the matter. Her view was that her son (Herod's brother-in-law and Hyrcanus II's grandson), Aristobulus III, deserved the office of high priest, and not Herod's Babylonian friend, Ḥananel. Left with no choice, Herod felt compelled to drown his beloved brother-in-law in the swimming pool at his Jericho palace. Next to die was the grandfather, Hyrcanus II, whose death was followed by Herod's execution of his mother-in-law in response to her attempt to exploit his illness by capturing his Jerusalem palace. Ultimately, he also killed his wife, Miriam.

Elements of this story are preserved in the Babylonian Talmud in the following narrative:

> Herod was a slave of the Hasmonean dynasty, and had set his eyes on a certain maiden [of that dynasty]. One day he heard a heavenly echo proclaim: "Every slave that rebels now will succeed [to the throne]." So he rose up and killed all of his masters but spared the maiden. When she saw that he wanted to marry her, she went up on to a roof and cried out, "Whoever comes and says, I am from the Hasmonean dynasty, is a slave," for none remained from the Hasmonean dynasty but for a maiden – who threw herself off the roof. Herod preserved her body in honey for seven years. Some say that he had relations with her, others that he did not. [...]
>
> Herod asked: "Who are those who teach, 'Set a king over yourselves from among your own people'? The sages!" He therefore rose up and killed all the rabbis, but spared Bava ben Buta, who became his advisor. (*Bava Batra* 3b)

The perspective of the history books on Herod's reign of terror is echoed by the Talmud's succinct description of his unbridled violence: he massacred the sages, wiped out the Hasmonean family, including, ultimately, his own wife (described in the Babylonian Talmud as a maiden). The saga ends with Herod's blinding of Bava ben Buta, the last surviving sage of that generation, whom we shall discuss at greater length at the end of this section.

Herod's tense domestic situation contrasts sharply with his outstanding diplomatic achievements, which included the expansion of his kingdom to include the Golan and Hauran regions. Nurturing his relations with the Romans was also an essential component of Herod's diplomacy, even to the extent of educating his children in Rome. In time the Romans viewed Herod as their most prominent representative, granting him the title "friend and ally of the Romans."

By virtue of his connections with Rome and the relative tranquility of the period, Herod was able to revolutionize the building culture of the land of Israel. During his reign dozens of immense buildings were erected. As was customary, Herod named the edifices and cities after his Roman patrons, including the two major cities – Sebastia (Samaria), on the site of the ancient capital of the Kingdom of Israel (as distinct from Judea), and the port city of Caesarea. He also built a number of private structures, such as the fortress of Masada and a palace in the upper city of Jerusalem. All of these construction projects, however, paled in comparison with his renovations in the Temple area. This was Herod's attempt to capture the people's heart. The well-known saying, "He who has not seen the Temple of Herod has never seen a beautiful building" (*Bava Batra* 4a), attests to the warmth of the people's feelings toward their renovated Temple.

This massive structure, embodying aesthetic principles and Hellenic culture, gave rise to mixed feelings among the Pharisees. Herod transformed Judea into a cosmopolitan center pervaded by Greek culture. Some of Hillel's teachings reflected the research tools and creativity of the period (we will address this in detail below, in our discussion of the rules of biblical interpretation). The sages of this period were no longer involved in politics, as the expectation of Jewish independence had all but disappeared. Discussions of the political order (such as those we encountered in our discussion of the prior generation of the Pairs) were replaced by discussions of religious matters: prayers, festivals, Shabbat, and ritual purity. It seems that, at the beginning of his reign, Herod was careful to treat the Pharisee leaders with respect, and even exempted them from the duty of swearing allegiance to the Roman emperor (*Antiquities* XV, 370). Later, however, their relations deteriorated, and again we hear about Herod executing sages (*Antiquities* XVII, 32ff.).[3] This is the historical background for the period of King Herod, who reigned in the days of Hillel and his counterpart, Shammai.

"MENAḤEM LEFT TO SERVE THE KING"

Although Hillel the Elder was the most famous student of Shemaya and Avtalyon, he was, in fact, preceded by a less well-known disciple named Menaḥem:

> Shemaya says: he may [lay his hands]; Avtalyon says: he may not lay his hands. Hillel and Menaḥem did not differ. Menaḥem left and Shammai replaced him. Shammai says: not to lay, Hillel says: to lay. The former were patriarchs and the latter were heads of the court. (Mishna, *Ḥagiga* 2:2)

The Babylonian Talmud records a dispute regarding where Menaḥem actually went to:

> Menaḥem left and Shammai replaced him etc. Where did he go? Abaye said: He left for the path of evil. Rava said: He joined the king's service. We also learned this in a *baraita*: Menaḥem left to serve the king, and eighty pairs of students, dressed in silk [official military attire], went with him. (*Ḥagiga* 16b)

The "king's service" means enlistment into the army. This period of increased affiliation with Rome had many effects, some commendable and others deplorable. The expression "Menaḥem left" places him on the outside. With the foundations of the state crumbling, there was widespread vacillation between the glistening new world of Antipatris and Rome, and the world of hard labor that characterized Judea at that time. The parallel text of the Jerusalem Talmud offers another possibility regarding Menaḥem's departure:

3. Numerous studies have been devoted to Herod's reign, the most important of which is the book by A. Schalit, *King Herod: Portrait of a Ruler* [Hebrew] (Jerusalem: 1960).

> Where did he go? There are those who say from one extreme to another. And there are those who say he left against his will, he and eighty pairs of disciples, clad in golden embroidered silk garments [official military attire], with faces blackened like the sides of a pot [i.e. shamefaced]. For they had been told, "Write on the horn of an ox that you have no part in the God of Israel." (Talmud Yerushalmi, *Ḥagiga* 2:2 [77d])

A number of scholars[4] identify Menaḥem as one of the Essene sages specifically mentioned in the writings of Josephus Flavius:

> There was a certain Essene named Menaḥem whose whole conduct of life attested to his virtue, and especially in his having received from God a foreknowledge of the future. This man once saw Herod when he was still a schoolboy and saluted him as "King of the Jews." Herod, who thought that the man either did not know who he was or was teasing him, reminded him that he was only a private citizen. Menaḥem, however, gently smiled and slapped him on the backside, saying, "Nevertheless, you will be king and you will rule the kingdom successfully, for you have been found worthy of this by God. And you will remember the slaps given by Menaḥem…" As Herod gradually rose to the throne and to good fortune and achieved the height of his power, he sent for Menaḥem…and from then on he held all Essenes in esteem. (*Antiquities* XV, 10:5)

Gedaliah Alon has suggested that Menaḥem was one of the Benei Beteira, an aristocratic clan which, upon returning to Jerusalem from Syria, rose to positions of influence in the Temple precincts. The Benei Beteira also served in Herod's army and were regarded as being closely connected to the monarchy. They took a conciliatory stance toward Rome and remained influential until the appearance of Hillel. Later, after the

4. Primarily from among the early Jewish historians such as Rabbi Abraham Zacuto, author of *Sefer HaYuḥasin* and Rabbi Azaria dei Rossi, the author of *Me'or Einayim* (ch. 3). See also G. Alon, *Studies in Jewish History*, pt. 1, p. 266.

destruction of the Temple, this group struggled with Rabban Yoḥanan ben Zakkai for control of Yavneh.

B.Z. Luria[5] cites a midrash that in his view alludes to a traumatic event, which, he suggests, is the real story of Menaḥem's departure.

> Another interpretation: "Flee, my beloved..." – When? In the days of Menaḥem and Hillel. For there was a dispute between them, and Menaḥem left, together with eight hundred students, clad in golden embroidered silk. Ḥanan ben Matron and Ba'inan ben Yehuda, Menaḥem's brothers, came and killed him. Then Elazar and his students arose and hacked him into pieces. At that same time, Orḥamo's men had besieged Jerusalem and defiled all of its women. Elazar and his students arose and killed all of the besieging soldiers. At that same time, Jerusalem was plunged into strife. Regarding that time they said: "Flee, my beloved, and become like a gazelle or a young hart...." (*Shir HaShirim Zuta* 8, Buber ed., p. 38)

The sources all indicate that Menaḥem was the leader of a large group of students who enlisted in the army. This move was challenged by Hillel, though the Midrash chooses to stress "the men of Orḥamo who besieged Jerusalem." Luria claims that the event referred to by the Midrash can be accurately reconstructed:

In the year 40 BCE, while Marcus Antonius was residing in Egypt, the Parthian kingdom allied itself with the rebel forces of Brutus and Cassius and together, they conquered Syria. In the process, they also conquered Judea. The pro-Roman Hyrcanus II was deposed and imprisoned, and his nephew, Antigonus II Mattathias, was installed in his place. Antigonus ruled for three years until he was defeated by Herod, who had him executed in 37 BCE. Luria links the enlistment of Menaḥem and his students to these events. In contrast to Yisrael ben Shalom's contention that Menaḥem enlisted in Herod's army,[6] Luria maintains that Menaḥem actually allied himself with Antigonus and fought to protect the scion

5. B.Z. Luria, *From Yannai to Herod* (Jerusalem: 1974), p. 197, n. 24.
6. See Y. Ben Shalom, *Beit Shammai*, pp. 99–100.

of the Hasmonean dynasty from Herod's Rome-endorsed takeover. At this stage, the Jewish forces were split and turned against each other in a civil war between supporters of Herod and supporters of the Hasmoneans. The Midrash further relates a story about Ḥanan and Ba'inan, members of Menaḥem's family, who conspired to assassinate him. The war itself was fought in Jerusalem, and it is clear that, for at least part of the time, it was waged within its walls. The Midrash recounts these events, based on the verse "Flee, my beloved." It was at this moment that the Jewish leadership decided to eschew all forms of political involvement. Menaḥem left and was replaced by Shammai.

SHAMMAI'S LEADERSHIP

Our information on Shammai's origins is scant,[7] and there are no explicitly biographical sources. He usually appears as Hillel's halakhic opponent, and a number of the rulings attributed to him shed light on his character and his religious stance. Shammai's halakhic approach has been characterized in two different ways: as an attempt to preserve "early" halakha, or as a conservative tendency to halakhic rigidity. The following examples will serve to highlight the different interpretations of his motivation:

1. Mishna, *Sukka* 2:8

> Women, slaves, and minors are exempt from [dwelling in] the *sukka*. A minor who is not dependent on his mother is obligated [to dwell] in the *sukka*. Shammai's daughter-in-law once had a baby. He broke away some of the roof-plaster and made a *sukka* over the bed for the sake of the child.

Commentators on this mishna have viewed it as a paradigm for Shammai's halakhic stringency. Maimonides, for example, explained the Mishnaic anecdote as being "in accordance with Shammai, who ruled stringently and mandated that males of all ages dwell in the *sukka*." Contemporary scholarly literature has taken a different approach, par-

7. This section is based on the research of Y. Ben Shalom, *Beit Shammai*, pp. 82–98.

ticularly following the study by Y.D. Gilat who views Shammai's halakha as representing the "early halakha," prior to the changes resulting from Hillel's creative innovations. Ben Shalom, for example, writes: "Shammai's approach is consistent with the early halakha."[8]

2. Tosefta, *Yom Kippurim* 5:2

> Girls should be trained [to fast] for a year or two before reaching puberty, so that they may get accustomed to the mitzvot. Rabbi Akiva would expel fathers from the study house so that they could feed their daughters. Once, Shammai did not wish to feed his son, so they decreed upon him until he fed him by hand.

Early halakha permitted children to fast, whereas later halakha forbade it, allowing parents to train their children to fast only a year or two before becoming obligated to observe mitzvot as adults. Here, as in the previous example, it can be argued that Shammai espouses a stringent reading of the halakha, mandating fasting for children (indeed, this reading of Shammai's position is adopted in the commentaries of Ran, Rashba, and Ritba). Alternatively, it could be argued that this is another example of the early halakha.[9]

Many of Shammai the Elder's rulings admit of interpretation in line with both of these characterizations: champion of early halakha and promoter of a more stringent halakhic approach. Recently, however, scholars have integrated a third element: political extremism. This is Ben Shalom's focus in his major work on the School of Shammai, in which he argues for the predominance of this aspect of Shammai's teaching and leadership. In what follows, I will demonstrate a number of these characteristic features of Shammai, as evidenced in his disputes with Hillel and the disputes between their schools.

8. Y. Ben Shalom, ibid., p. 82.
9. For additional examples, see Ben Shalom, *supra*.

HOW DID YOU RISE TO THE PATRIARCHY? THE BEGINNINGS OF HILLEL'S LEADERSHIP

Hillel's ascent to the patriarchy is described in number of parallel sources. Despite their common kernel, comparing these sources is both fascinating and revealing in terms of understanding the unique tradition that each version seeks to transmit.

The basic story is preserved in the fourth chapter of Tosefta *Pesaḥim*, but the most important contrast is between the variant versions preserved in the Babylonian and Jerusalem Talmuds (both found at the beginning of *Pesaḥim* chapter six). We will first present the text of the Tosefta, after which we will present the parallel Talmudic traditions:

Tosefta *Pesaḥim* 4:13–14

> It happened once that the fourteenth of Nisan coincided with Shabbat. They asked Hillel the Elder, "Does the Paschal offering override [the prohibitions of] Shabbat?" He replied, "Do we have only a single Paschal offering during the course of the year which overrides Shabbat? We have many more than three hundred Paschal offerings during the year, and they all override Shabbat." All the people in the courtyard ganged up on him. He said to them, "The daily burnt-offering [*korban tamid*] is a public offering and the Paschal offering is a public offering. Just as the daily offering is a public offering and overrides Shabbat, so, too, the Paschal offering is a public offering [and] overrides Shabbat.
>
> "Alternatively: Regarding the daily offering it says 'its appointed time' [Numbers 28:2], and regarding the Paschal offering it says: 'its appointed time' [Numbers 9:2]; Just as the daily offering, regarding which it states 'its appointed time,' overrides Shabbat, so, too, the Paschal offering, regarding which it says 'its appointed time,' overrides Shabbat.
>
> "Furthermore, there is an *a fortiori* [*kal vaḥomer*] argument: If the daily offering, on account of which people are not liable to extirpation [*karet*], overrides Shabbat; the Paschal offering, on account of which the people are liable to extirpation – is it not logical that it, too, should override Shabbat?

> "Moreover: I have received a tradition from my masters that the Paschal offering overrides Shabbat: not only the first Passover but the second Passover [*Pesaḥ Sheni*], and not only the communal Paschal offering, but even the Paschal offering of the individual."
>
> They asked him, "What will the people who did not bring their knives and Paschal lambs to the Temple do?"
>
> He replied, "Let them be, for the divine spirit rests on them. If they are not prophets, they are the disciples of prophets."
>
> What did the Israelites do in that hour? He whose Paschal offering was a lamb, stuck [the knife] in the wool. He whose Paschal offering was a goat, tied it between its horns. Thus, they brought their knives and Paschal offerings to the Temple and slaughtered their Paschal offerings. On that very day, they appointed Hillel as patriarch, and he instructed them on the laws of Passover.

The account in the Tosefta is informative. It describes how a problem arose and how Hillel enlisted his intellectual abilities as well as received traditions in order to solve it. It makes no reference to the questioners' identity, to Hillel's origin, or to the identity of Hillel's rabbis, and there is likewise no attempt to evaluate the validity of his proofs. It is a "dry" and succinct account of the event that precipitated Hillel's appointment to the Patriarchate.[10] The color and drama are provided by the two Talmudic traditions:

10. Y. Goldenberger, "The Sources Recording Hillel's Ascent to the Patriarchate" [Hebrew], *HaTzofeh LeḤokhmat Yisrael* 10 (5686), p. 71. Goldenberger published a table with historical calculations for dating the instances of Erev Pesaḥ falling out on Shabbat during the days of Hillel. The Open University module ("The World of the Sages," ARC, Fourth Unit), deals extensively with Hillel's character, and with this event specifically.

Talmud Yerushalmi
Pesaḥim 6:1[33a]

This halakha was forgotten by the Elders of Beteira:

It once happened that the fourteenth [of Nisan] fell on Shabbat, and they did not know whether the Paschal offering overrides Shabbat or not. They said, "There is here a certain Babylonian, Hillel is his name, who apprenticed under Shemaya and Avtalyon, who knows whether a Paschal offering overrides Shabbat or not. Perhaps something good can come from him." They sent and called him. They said to him, "Have you ever heard whether, when the fourteenth [of Nisan] falls on Shabbat, it overrides Shabbat or not?" He said to them, "Do we have only one Paschal offering each year that overrides Shabbat? Are there not many Passover offerings that override Shabbat during the year?" They said to him, "We have already said that something good can come from you."

He started to expound for them using different forms of traditional interpretation: a *hekesh* [juxtaposition], a *kal vaḥomer* [*a fortiori*], and a *gezeira shava* [analogy]…They said to him, "We have already said, 'Is there something good [that can come] from the Babylonian?'

Talmud Bavli
Pesaḥim 66a

Our rabbis taught: this halakha was forgotten by the Benei Beteira:

It once happened that the fourteenth [of Nisan] fell on Shabbat, and they had forgotten and did not know whether the Paschal offering overrides Shabbat or not. They asked: "Is there any man who knows whether the Paschal offering overrides Shabbat or not?" They were told, "There is a certain man who has arrived from Babylonia, Hillel the Babylonian is his name, and he served the two greatest men of the time, Shemaya and Avtalyon and knows whether the Paschal offering overrides Shabbat." They summoned him and said to him, "Do you know whether the Paschal offering overrides Shabbat or not?" He said to them, "Do we only have one Paschal offering during the year that overrides Shabbat?" He continued: "Surely we have many more than two hundred Paschal offerings during the year which override Shabbat!" They retorted: "How do you know this?" He answered them, "'Its appointed time' is stated in connection with the Paschal offering, and 'its appointed time' is stated in connection with the daily burnt-offering: just as 'its appointed time' said in connection with the daily offering overrides Shabbat, so, too, 'its appointed time' in connection with the Paschal offering overrides Shabbat."

Talmud Yerushalmi *Pesaḥim* 6:1[33a] *(cont.)*	Talmud Bavli *Pesaḥim* 66a *(cont.)*
"The *hekesh* that you stated has a rebuttal...the *kal vaḥomer* that you stated has a rebuttal...the *gezeira shava* that you stated has a rebuttal, for a person may not deduce a *gezeira shava* on his own..." And even though he sat and expounded to them all day, they did not accept the teaching from him until he said to them, "In Heaven's name! This is what I heard from Shemaya and Avtalyon." Immediately upon hearing this from him, they stood up and appointed him patriarch over them. As soon as they had appointed him, he began to castigate them, saying: "What caused you to need this Babylonian? Is it not because you failed to serve the two great men of the world, Shemaya and Avtalyon, who lived near you?" As soon as he castigated them, he forgot a law: They asked him, "What should we do for the people who did not bring their slaughtering knives before Shabbat?" He said to them, "I heard this law, but have forgotten it. Nevertheless, let Israel be. If they are not prophets, they are the disciples of prophets." Immediately, he whose Paschal offering was a lamb, stuck [the knife] in the wool. If it was a goat, he would tie it between its horns. Thus, their Paschal offerings brought their knives with them. As soon as he saw this happening, he remembered the law, saying, "This is what I heard from Shemaya and Avtalyon."	They immediately seated him at the head and appointed him as the patriarch over them; he sat before them for the entire day expounding the laws of Passover. Finally, he began chastising them: "What caused it for you that I should come up from Babylonia to be patriarch over you? It was your indolence, because you failed to serve the two greatest men of the time, Shemaya and Avtalyon." They said to him, "Master, what if a man forgot and did not bring a knife before Shabbat?" "I have heard this law," he answered, "but have forgotten it. However, let Israel be. If they are not prophets, they are the disciples of prophets!" The next day, he whose Paschal offering was a lamb, stuck [the knife] in the wool. If it was a goat, he would stick it between its horns. [Hillel] saw the incident and remembered the halakha, saying: "This is the tradition that I received orally from Shemaya and Avtalyon."

Both traditions rely on the same narrative kernel, but significant differences in the way each relates to the story provide for a fascinating comparison.

AN ASIDE: TORAH SCHOLARS IN ISRAEL AND IN BABYLONIA

At the beginning of this section, I presented the two narrative traditions of Hillel's ascent to the patriarchate: the traditions from Babylonia and from the land of Israel. These differing traditions reflect the profound cultural and religious divide between the two communities. In *Eretz Yisrael,* tradition and continuity were paramount, whereas Babylonian Jewry extolled the scholarship and the "thrust and parry" of Talmudic discussions, the pinnacle of Babylonian creativity. The Babylonian Talmud itself was well aware of this distinction, and on a number of occasions explains differences between the respective centers of Talmudic scholarship on this basis. For example, the Babylonian Talmud offers the following understanding of the distinctions between the sages of Israel and of Babylonia:[11]

> Rabbi Oshaya said: What is the meaning of the verse [Zechariah 11:7], "And I took the two staffs; the one I called '*No'am*' ['Pleasantness'] and the other I called '*Ḥovlim*' ['Bindings']"? – '*No'am*' refers to the scholars of *Eretz Yisrael,* who treat each other graciously [*man'imim*] when engaged in halakhic debates; '*Ḥovlim*' refers to the scholars of Babylonia, who hurt [*meḥablim*] each other's feelings when discussing halakha.
>
> [Similarly, it is written (ibid., 4:3, 14):] "Then said he: These are the two anointed ones [*yitzhar*]... and two olive

11. The first person to grace me with this insight was my relative and teacher, Dr. Yisrael Friedman-Ben Shalom, who devoted many hours to me during my first years in the world of scholarship, when we were neighbors at Kibbutz Sa'ad. Later, he gave written expression to these insights in his article "And I Took Two Staffs, One of Which I Named Pleasantness and the Other I Called Bindings" in A. Oppenheimer and A. Kasher (eds.), *Dor LeDor: A Collection of Essays in Honor of Yehoshua Ephron* (Jerusalem: 5755), pp. 235–250. I learned much of what I have written in this excursus from him.

> trees [*zeitim*] by it." Rabbi Yitzḥak said: "'*Yizhar*' refers to the scholars of *Eretz Yisrael*, who are amenable to each other when engaged in halakhic debates, like olive oil [which is soothing]; [while] and 'two olive trees' symbolize the scholars of Babylon, who in halakhic debates are as bitter to each other as olive trees. (*Sanhedrin* 24a)

In the acrimonious atmosphere of the Babylonian *beit midrash*, the students relished intellectual browbeating. Reading many of the Talmudic descriptions of the Babylonian debates, whether they are historical or literary, one is struck by the sense of tension arising from this world of creativity and innovation. The inner sancta of Babylonia abounded in polemics and disputations, rivalries, and even personal affronts. In certain cases, the Babylonian Talmud's accounts of events that occurred in the *beit midrash* of *Eretz Yisrael* actually reflect the tense reality of the Babylonian *beit midrash*. The most well-known example of this is the violent dispute between Reish Lakish and his preeminent brother-in-law, Rabbi Yoḥanan, which culminated in the death of the two sages (see *Bava Metzia* 84a). This is an exclusively Babylonian-style description of an event that in fact took place in the *beit midrash* in Tiberias. However, beyond the world of stories, we have a wealth of Talmudic examples that attest to the differences between the houses of study.

The Mishna records that Rabbi Neḥunia ben HaKaneh would recite a prayer upon entering and exiting the *beit midrash*. Each Talmud presents its specific version of the prayer, reflecting its own approach:

Talmud Yerushalmi *Berakhot* 4:2 [7d]	Talmud Bavli *Berakhot* 28b
[Upon entering] what should one say? "May it be Your will, Lord my God and the God of my fathers, that I should not get angry at my colleagues, and that my colleagues should not get angry at me; that we should not pronounce the pure contaminated, or the contaminated pure; forbid the permitted, or permit the forbidden, causing me to be humiliated both in this world and in the next world." Upon departing, what should one say? "I give thanks to You, O Lord my God and the God of my fathers, that you granted me my portion among those who dwell in the *beit midrash* and synagogues, and not in the theaters and circuses. For although I toil and they toil, I am diligent and they are diligent, I toil to inherit the Garden of Eden and they toil to descend to the pit of destruction, as it is stated: 'Because you will not abandon my soul to the grave; you will not allow your pious ones to witness destruction' [Psalms 16:10]."	Our rabbis taught: On entering what does a man say? "May it be Your will, Lord my God, that no mistake occur through me, and that I not err in a matter of halakha and cause my colleagues to rejoice at my expense: that I not pronounce the contaminated pure or the pure contaminated; all unclean clean, or clean unclean; and that my colleagues not err in a matter of halakha and cause me to rejoice at their expense." Upon departure what does he say? "I give thanks to You, O Lord my God, that You have granted me my portion among those who dwell in the *beit midrash* and You have not granted my portion with those who sit on street corners, for I rise early and they rise early: I rise early for words of Torah and they rise early for frivolous talk; I labor and they labor: I labor and receive a reward and they labor and do not receive a reward; I run and they run: I run toward eternal life and they run to the pit of destruction."

Without going into the details of the differences between the two sources, I wish only to point out the difference most relevant for our purposes: "I should not get angry at my colleagues, and that my colleagues should not get angry at me" is the text that appears in the Jerusalem Talmud, whereas the Babylonian Talmud says, "that I not err in a matter of halakha and cause my colleagues to rejoice at my expense" (I have followed the interpretation of the medieval and modern commentators who noted that rejoicing, in this context, refers to gloating at an opponent's misfortune).[12] Babylonian scholars were aware of a tendency toward *schadenfreude*, which reminds us of their characterization as sages who "hurt each other's feelings when discussing halakha."

Numerous sources also describe the sages of Israel as being more connected to the world of tradition, and even to the world of prophecy, in contrast to their Babylonian counterparts, who extolled wisdom and creativity, both of which are the products of man's intellect, as opposed to direct divine origin. The two versions of Hillel's rise to power provide but one example, but one that can serve as a key to a broad understanding of these two aspects of the world of the Torah, and the advantages and disadvantages of each approach.

THE RULES OF BIBLICAL EXEGESIS

According to the Babylonian tradition, the residents of Jerusalem had forgotten the laws which apply when Pesaḥ falls on Shabbat. The Benei Beteira, the local leadership, had heard about a certain "Hillel the Babylonian," who served the two most prominent scholars of the generation, Shemaya and Avtalyon, and reportedly knew the answer. Hillel is brought before them and, when asked about the halakhic problem, promptly responds with a barrage of proofs based on the rules of biblical exegesis: *gezeira shava* (analogy) and *kal vaḥomer* (*a fortiori*). In his answer Hillel makes no mention of his teachers, suggesting that his knowledge of the law stems exclusively from his own study of Torah. Hillel's response makes such a stunning impression on his listeners that in the face of the clarity of his logic, and his virtuoso ability to draw conclusions through the rules of biblical exegesis, they elevate him to the position of patriarch. However, at that very moment, he begins to berate them for their neglecting to study the traditions of the two Torah leaders of the previous generation. Hillel's comments make it clear that had the Benei Beteira paid more diligent attention to studying the tradition of Shemaya and Avtalyon, they would not have needed to rely on his wisdom. Hillel's hubris triggers immediate retribution: When asked

12. Maimonides, *Commentary on the Mishna, Berakhot* 4:2; and *Mishneh Torah, Hilkhot Berakhot*, 10:23. *Maharsha* on *Berakhot* 28b, s.v. "*veyismeḥu bi ḥaverai.*"

about bringing a knife for ritual slaughtering, he forgets the relevant halakha. Only after he sees the people using their designated sacrifices to transport their knives "He recollected the halakha and said, 'This is the tradition that I received orally from Shemaya and Avtalyon.'"

Thus, while extolling the virtues of innovation, the Babylonian Talmud also sounds a warning against the excessive pride that can give rise to a feeling of "My power and the strength of my hand." In this version of the incident, his forgetfullness comes to put Hillel in his proper place and to reinforce popular instincts that passively preserve the correct religious norms. The principle of "Let Israel be; if they are not prophets, they are the disciples of prophets!" is fundamental; it attempts to provide a broad basis for trusting normative conduct that does not flow from the world of sages who create new worlds in Torah, but rather from the world of everyday Jews who faithfully adhere to their ancestral tradition.[13]

The Jerusalem Talmud's approach is the antithesis of the approach of the Babylonian Talmud. It remains unimpressed by the rules of biblical exegesis, certainly does not regard them as grounds for appointing a person to the position of patriarch. These rules are fallible and any proofs based on them can be refuted. Hillel's appointment to the patriarchy could only be by virtue of the tradition that had been transmitted from one person to the next, the tradition he had received from Shemaya and Avtalyon. The Jerusalem Talmud thus teaches us that the key determining factor is the ability to preserve and not the power to create.

These differences notwithstanding, according to both the Babylonian and the Jerusalem Talmuds, Hillel introduced this hermeneutic creativity, derived from principles of logic, to his colleagues in

13. There is a similar expression: "Let Israel be; it is better that they [sin] accidentally than intentionally." Despite its apparent semblance, it is, in fact, the reverse of Hillel's statement. According to this parallel expression, the people are fundamentally untrustworthy. The author of this epithet knows that his target community is in violation of the halakha, but has despaired of affecting their religious behavior and therefore chooses to remain silent and avoid ruling, because in any case he will not be listened to. Occasionally, the abbreviated expression "Let Israel be…" is employed by halakhic adjudicators, and the reader is uncertain if it reflects the optimistic position of "if they are not prophets…" or the pessimistic position of "it is better that they sin accidentally…"

Jerusalem. The rules of scriptural exegesis are the fundamental tools for the creation and development of the Oral Law, and it was Hillel who introduced them to *Eretz Yisrael*. Until his time, halakha was practiced in accordance with the tradition transmitted from person to person. When a difficult question arose, they went to the seat of justice adjacent to the Temple, from where rulings were issued to the entire Jewish people. Indeed, this was the based on the teaching of the last of the prophets, Malachi, who identifies the priests as the teachers of Torah: "For the lips of the priest guard knowledge and they shall seek instruction from his mouth; for he is a messenger of the Lord of hosts" (2:7).

It was in the *beit midrash* of Shemaya and Avtalyon that exegesis achieved a new form. There the scholars learned how to expound verses analytically by comparing, juxtaposing, and combining texts. Apart from the *a fortiori* argument, examples of which can be found in the Torah itself, all of the other rules originate in human intellect, which can either implement or reject them. Hillel's innovation lay not in devising the rules, but in applying them to solve halakhic problems. The Babylonian tradition is enthralled by the idea of solving a halakhic problem through the power of reason – a notion that practically horrifies the Jerusalem Talmud. Babylonia idealized debate and was anchored in the tenets of logic. The Jerusalem Talmud's ideal is tradition that stems from Temple times.

Although the difference between them is fascinating, both Talmuds share the notion that Hillel introduces the practical application of the exegetical principles in the land of Israel, and that he is appointed patriarch over all of the land's inhabitants. Hillel's appointment ushers in an exciting period of creativity in developing the Oral Law, alongside the preservation of ancient traditions. Together, these two ideals serve as Hillel's guiding light: he expounds based on the rules of logic and simultaneously apprentices under the two foremost scholars of that generation. According to the Jerusalem Talmud, steeped as it is in the virtue of faithfully recorded traditions, he merits his new position precisely by virtue of that apprenticeship. According to both Talmudic traditions, his criticism of the Benei Beteira, the current leaders, for "failing to serve the two greatest men of the time, Shemaya and Avtalyon," was his stepping stone to the patriarchy. In the coming generations, his students and their students in turn, would further sharpen and intensify the tension between the importance of maintaining tradition and the primacy of human creativity in Torah. Further on, we will examine the personalities of Rabbi Eliezer ben Hyrcanus, the man of tradition who was not prepared to make any statement that he had not heard from his teachers; and of Rabbi Yehoshua, who only felt at home when in a *beit midrash* imbued with the spirit of innovation.

Apart from Hillel's superiority in learning, we should also mention another tradition in the Jerusalem Talmud, attributed to Rabbi Levi, which justified Hillel's appointment as patriarch by virtue of his lineage: "They found a scroll of lineage in Jerusalem, in which it was written: Hillel is a descendant of [King] David" (Talmud Yerushalmi, *Ta'anit*, 4:2 [68a]). In other words, Hillel was deserving of the status of patriarch according to all possible criteria – his pedigree, his familiarity with the traditions, and his intellectual legacy.

"RAISE MANY DISCIPLES" – BETWEEN HILLEL AND SHAMMAI

Since its original redaction, Mishna *Avot* has always dictated the moral heartbeat of Jewish life. Its introductory teaching establishes the framework for that role with the following teaching of the Men of the Great Assembly:

> They said three things: Be prudent in judgment, raise many students, and make a protective fence for the Torah. (*Avot*, 1:2)

This was the legacy of the Men of the Great Assembly in the chain of transmission of the Oral Law from Moses at Sinai and onwards. Their command to "raise many students" is the simplest and most succinct expression of the view that the Torah is the birthright of all Israel.

The reality, however, is that *Avot deRabbi Natan*, based on this Mishna in *Avot*, records a dispute about this very issue between the schools of Shammai and Hillel:

> "And raise many students": The School of Shammai says: One should only teach a person who is wise, humble, of distinguished ancestry and wealthy. The School of Hillel says: One should

> teach every man, for there were many sinners in Israel who were attracted to the study of Torah, and their descendants were righteous, pious, and respectable people. (*Avot deRabbi Natan*, recension A, ch. 3)

A different account of the dispute appears in *Avot deRabbi Natan*, recension B:

> "And raise many students": The School of Shammai says: Only respectable people should be taught, the sons of respectable fathers and grandfathers. The School of Hillel says: Everyone [should be taught]. To what may this be compared? To a woman who sets a hen to roost on the eggs. From a large number [of eggs] she produces a few [chickens], but from a small number she does not produce any. (*Avot deRabbi Natan*, recension B, ch. 4)

We are not concerned here with the historical background of this *baraita*, which has been discussed extensively elsewhere.[14] The important point is that this dispute reflects the elitist nature of Shammai's educational philosophy. Students entering Shammai's school were screened according to both internal criteria (wisdom, humility, respectability) and external criteria (wealth and pedigree). These criteria were alien to the school of Hillel (Beit Hillel), which sought to bequeath the Torah to all people, irrespective of their moral, social or financial standing.

Arriving in the land of Israel, Hillel found himself in a society where, for most people, the Torah was a closed, esoteric tradition, transmitted exclusively among the members of an aristocratic, elite group. Earlier, we focused on Hillel's heroic night-time vigil, studying Torah while freezing in the snow on the roof of the *beit midrash* just because he was too poor to pay the entrance fee. Hillel was prepared to almost freeze to death in order to study Torah. In the Talmud, this episode becomes a benchmark for the obligation on every person to study

14. See Y. Ben Shalom, "Torah Study for All or for the Elite Alone," *Synagogues in Antiquity* [Hebrew], eds. A. Oppenheimer, A. Kasher, U. Rappaport (Jerusalem: 1987).

Torah. Responding to a world that sought to limit the Torah's accessibility to society at large, Hillel took the approach of "raising many students," heralding a new era in which the Torah was open to all those who wished to study it.

The dispute between Beit Shammai and Beit Hillel in *Avot deRabbi Natan* actually helped many of the commentators explain the significance of the first mishna in *Avot*. Rabbeinu Yona, for example, in his commentary on *Avot* states: "And raise many students – in accordance with the view of Beit Hillel, as we have learned: Beit Shammai says...," and he cites the dispute mentioned above.[15]

This tension between elitist and universal education reflects a dilemma familiar to educational systems all over the world. In the Talmudic world, the dispute continued between the elitist patriarchy (including Hillel's progeny), and the open, inviting *beit midrash* of the disciples of Hillel and Rabban Yoḥanan ben Zakkai. We will deal with this matter at the appropriate juncture, but the dispute itself introduces us to Hillel's character: his openness, his patience, and his quality of receiving every person graciously.

"STRIVE TO BE A MAN" – HILLEL'S SOCIAL SENSITIVITY

The Mishna in *Avot* cites Hillel's teaching that explains the responsibility incumbent on both student and the teacher to attain mastery of Torah:

> A boor cannot be sin-fearing; an ignoramus cannot be pious; a bashful one cannot learn; a short-tempered person cannot teach; nor do all those who do much business grow wise. In a place where there are no men, strive to be a man. (*Avot* 2:5)

My interest here is in the concluding part of the mishna: "In a place where there are no men, strive to be a man." To begin to understand this mishna, we must look at another of Hillel's teachings, concerning

15. Rabbi Shimon ben Tzemaḥ Duran (Rashbetz) addressed this very issue in his commentary *Magen Avot*, and precisely the same explanation is given by Rabbi Yosef Alashkar, in his commentary *Merkevet HaMishna*.

the Water-Drawing Celebration (*Simḥat Beit HaSho'eva*) on the Sukkot festival:

> Hillel the Elder says: "To the place my heart loves, my feet do lead me. If you will come to my home, I shall come to yours, but if you will not come to my house, I shall not come to yours, as it is said: 'In every place where I cause My name to be remembered I will come to you and bless you' [Exodus 20:21]." (Tosefta, *Sukka* 4:3)

Who and what are the subjects of Hillel's enigmatic statement? *Avot deRabbi Natan* explains Hillel's statement in a manner implying that the Almighty Himself is speaking from Hillel's mouth:

> He used to say: If you come to my house, I will come to your house. If you do not come to my house, then I will not come to your house. What does this mean? It refers to the men who early every morning and every evening go to the synagogues and study houses; the Holy One, blessed be He, blesses them with the World to Come, as it is said "In every place where I cause My name to be mentioned I will come to you and bless you" [Exodus 20:21]. To the place my heart loves, my feet lead me. What does this mean? It refers to the men who leave their gold and silver and make the pilgrimage to pay homage to the Divine Presence in the Temple – God guards them in their camps, as it says: "No one will covet your land when you go up to appear before the Lord your God." (Ibid. 34:24)[16]

If this understanding is correct, it represents a daring innovation on Hillel's part. Hillel takes a patently colloquial saying used in every day relations between men: "If you come to my home, then I will come to yours" and "to the place I love my legs do lead me" and uses them, by alluding to the Water-Drawing Celebration, as a metaphor for the

16. This explanation was actually suggested by the *Ba'alei HaTosafot*, (*Sukka* 53a, s.v. "*sham*"), to the effect that Hillel was speaking on behalf of the Divine Presence.

intimate relationship between God and Israel. Citing the biblical phrase "I will come to you," Hillel qualifies it by the words "If you come." In other words – if You, God, come to my house as You promised, then I too will come to Your House. Hillel's declarations come at the height of the Water-Drawing Celebration, during which Hillel reminds the Holy One, blessed be He, of His duty to be present.

Another dictum of Hillel similarly raises the question of whether he is speaking in the name of the Divine Presence, or about himself.

> My humiliation is my elevation, my elevation is my humiliation; what is the reason for this? [For it says:] "...enthroned on high, and descends to look." (*Vayikra Raba* 1:5; Margaliot edition, page 16)

Obviously, the verse refers to the Holy One, blessed be He, but, in a deeper sense, Hillel is actually reflecting on himself. For Hillel, the state of personal debasement brought about his own elevation, whereas, when he was uplifted, it carried the seeds of his downfall. This dictum eloquently expresses Hillel's humility, the product not of weakness but of free choice. Acutely aware of himself and his personality, Hillel endeavors to emulate the paths of God, "enthroned on high and descends to look." It was precisely this perspective that endowed Hillel with his tremendous sensitivity to and acceptance of others, in all his aspects. This became his legacy to his students, and was the reason that the halakha follows their view.

> Why was the halakha determined in agreement with their rulings? Because they were kind and modest, and they studied their own rulings together with those of Beit Shammai, and were even humble enough to mention the teachings of Beit Shammai before their own.... This teaches you that whoever humbles himself, the Holy One, blessed be He, raises up, and he who exalts himself, the Holy One, blessed be He, humbles him. Greatness flees from those who seek it and pursues those who flee it. He who forces time is forced back by time, but he who yields to time, finds time standing at his side. (*Eruvin* 13b)

Hillel's teachings and enactments can be explained by his keen awareness of other individuals, their suffering, and their desires. Hillel, combining social sensitivity with his own doctrine, created a set of enactments that preserved the Torah's eternal relevance. The *prozbul* is the most striking example.

The background to Hillel's ruling was his recognition that "the people were avoiding giving loans to each other." Biblical law prescribes the cancellation of all debts in the seventh (*Shemitta*, Sabbatical) year (see Deuteronomy ch. 15). The Torah clearly intended to use the *Shemitta* year to redress social and economic inequality and to facilitate a fresh start for the entire society. In this context, it has been claimed that Herod's ascent and a burgeoning economy brought about extensive changes in the structure of the loan market.[17] The loan was no longer exclusively a tool for helping the poor; the entrepreneur who lacked capital utilized loans for developing investment avenues. Given this economic situation, there were inevitably those who exploited the laws of the Sabbatical year by taking loans without any intention of repaying them. As a result, those with capital refrained from giving loans to rich and poor alike. Understanding that this was not the intention of the Torah, Hillel established the institution of *prozbul* as a matter of public policy (*Gittin* 4:3). In doing so, he stimulated a sagging economy and restored thriving economic life. The *prozbul* was based on a *midrash halakha* which exempted the *Beit Din* from the requirement to remit their loans. By permitting the submission of bills of debt to the *Beit Din*, Hillel "circumvented" the Sabbatical prohibition and enabled the capital holders and creditors to collect their debts.[18]

It should be stressed, however, that *prozbul* was not Hillel's own invention, but was actually an application of an existing rule derived from biblical exegesis, whereby "He who transfers his bills to the *Beit*

17. As explained by S. Baron, *Social and Religious History of the Jews* [Hebrew] (Ramat Gan: 1960), ch. 14.
18. This is certainly one of the earliest and most striking examples of a "legal fiction," referred to in the sources as "circumvention." On the nature of "circumvention" as a legitimate method of obviating difficulties attendant to compliance with the halakha, see Zilberg, *Principia Talmudica* [Hebrew] (Jerusalem: 5724), ch. 3: "Circumventing the Law."

Din, [his debts] are not annulled" (*Shevi'it* 10:2). Hillel's "exploitation" of this halakha rescued the Torah. This is one of the greatest examples of the Torah's inherent capacity to address changing times and of the power of halakhic authorities to discover its hidden potential.

THE IMAGE OF THE OTHER – BETWEEN HILLEL AND SHAMMAI

The difference between Hillel and Shammai is most clearly demonstrated in the accounts of how each of them treated people who tried to test the limits of their patience:

> The Rabbis taught: A man should always be gentle like Hillel, and not impatient like Shammai.
>
> It happened that two men made a wager with each other, saying: "Whoever angers Hillel will receive four hundred *zuzim*." One of them said, "I will go and aggravate him."
>
> It was the Sabbath eve, and Hillel was washing his head. He went, passed by the door of his house, and called out, "'Is Hillel here? Is Hillel here?" Hillel put on a robe and went out to him, saying, "My son, what do you want?" "I have a question to ask," he said. "Ask, my son," he prompted.
>
> Whereupon he asked: Why are the heads of the Babylonians round? "My son, you have asked a great question," he replied, "it is because their midwives are not skillful."
>
> He went away, waited a while, and then returned and called out, "Is Hillel here; is Hillel here?" He donned a robe and went out to him, saying, "My son, what do you want?" "I have a question to ask," he answered. "Ask, my son," he prompted.
>
> Whereupon he asked: "Why do the Palmyrenes have bleary eyes?" "My son, you have asked a great question," he replied, "it is because they live in sandy places."
>
> He left, waited a while, returned, and called out, "Is Hillel here? Is Hillel here?" He donned a robe and went out to him, saying, "My son, what do you want? "I have a question to ask," said he. "Ask, my son," he prompted.
>
> He asked, "Why do the Phrygians have wide feet?" "My

son, you have asked a great question," said he, "it is because they live in watery marshes."

He then said: "I have many questions to ask, but I fear that you may become angry." So he donned a robe sat before him and said, "Ask all the questions you wish to ask."

"Are you the Hillel whom they call the Prince of Israel?"

"Yes," he replied.

"If it is you," he retorted, "may your kind not proliferate in Israel."

"Why, my son?" queried he.

"Because I have lost four hundred *zuzim* because of you," he complained.

"Watch your moods," he replied, "Hillel is so worthy that you may lose four hundred *zuzim* over and over again, yet Hillel will not lose his temper." (*Shabbat* 30b–31a)

This story is an emblematic description of Hillel's character, and its import is clear. The exaggerated description of Hillel as someone who simply cannot be ruffled is intentional. The questions intended to elicit Hillel's exasperation are unrelated to his spiritual-intellectual world and certainly not to its Jewish aspect. Just imagine questions of this kind being asked of your communal rabbi (or even of yourselves)! How was Hillel supposed to know why Babylonians have round heads? Indeed, later commentators were unable to accept the calm equanimity of Hillel's response to trivial questions at face value. Accordingly, they attempted to read the entire story as a parable. The Maharsha (Rabbi Shlomo Edels, sixteenth-century Poland), in his *Ḥiddushei Aggadot*, thus writes as follows:

A question arises here, for since this question did not concern matters of Torah, but only regular secular matters, even if Hillel was exceedingly modest he still should not have answered the question, for King Solomon already said: "Do not answer a fool according to his folly."

And the answer may be that, in his humility, Hillel did not imagine the person was attempting to aggravate him by

> his question, but rather that his questions hinted at matters of Torah. [Therefore,] in the three questions, he was referring to the following three evil shortcomings: pride, stinginess, and greed, which are ascribed to the students of Bilam [the Maharsha goes on to give an elaborate explanation of both the questions and the answers].[19]

The Maharsha may have been correct in understanding the entire story as alluding to more sublime matters, but it seems to me that it is precisely the literal understanding of the story that conveys the force of Hillel's personality. It is the very confrontation with the questions of the "layman," devoid of any Torah, and located more in the area of popular wisdom and the idle chatter of regular folks that places Hillel on the level of Aaron, "who loves people and brings them closer to Torah." The following incident, appearing further on in the same passage, likewise attests to Hillel's patience:

> Our rabbis taught: A certain non-Jew once came before Shammai and asked him, "How many Torahs do you have?" "Two," he replied, "the Written Torah and the Oral Torah." "I believe you with respect to the Written, but not with respect to the Oral Torah; make me a proselyte on condition that you teach me the Written Torah [only]." He scolded him and rejected him angrily. When he went before Hillel, he accepted him as a proselyte. On the first day, he taught him, *alef, beit, gimmel, dalet*; the following day he reversed the order. "But yesterday you taught me differently," he protested. Hillel replied, "Were you not relying on me? Then rely upon me with respect to the Oral [Torah] too." (*Shabbat* 31b)

In this conversation, the theological element is more promi-

19. Maharsha, *Ḥiddushei Aggadot*, Tractate *Shabbat* 31a, s.v. "Hillel." A similar idea also appears in Rabbi Nachman of Bratslav's *Likkutei Moharan* (First Edition, 58:10), where he interprets the agitator's questions as veiled criticism of a proud and alienated leadership.

nent. Shammai correctly informs the non-Jew that we also have an "Oral Torah,"[20] and appropriately refuses to countenance the possibility of distinguishing between the two Torahs. Hillel, on the other hand, does not respond to the non-Jew's demand, and summarily converts him. In the course of time, Hillel makes the non-Jew dependent on his teaching, and when Hillel reverses the orders of the letters, from *alef–beit* to *beit–alef*, the non-Jew loses his spiritual anchor and his confidence is shaken. When the convert is thus steeped in doubt, Hillel steps in, providing him with spiritual security by demonstrating the power and necessity of the Oral Law. In other words, the basis of the Oral Law is the student's belief that the Torah taught by his rabbi is true, and that he is authorized to interpret it and to reveal God's will in the world. The foundation of "rely on me" does not mean the nullification of individual interpretation, but rather the internalization of the need to interpret God's law by way of the Oral Law. Later on, the Talmud adds another incident concerning Hillel.

> On another occasion it happened that a certain non-Jew came before Shammai and said to him, "Convert me on the condition that you teach me the whole Torah while I stand on one foot." He pushed him away with the yardstick that was in his hand. He then went to Hillel, who said to him, "What is hateful to you, do not to your neighbor: that is the whole Torah. The rest is commentary: go and learn it." (Ibid.)

In this story, Hillel establishes the "great principle of the Torah" that would be expounded upon by all of the great thinkers. Its foundation is the internalization of the existence of the other.[21] From Hillel's perspective, being alert to the other is dominant and foundational to the Torah, the passport into Judaism. Hillel saw a human being before him,

20. This is the first time this expression, "*Torah shebe'al peh*," or Oral Law, appears in rabbinic literature. See E.E. Urbach, *The Sages: Their Concepts and Beliefs* [Hebrew] (Jerusalem: 1969), pp. 287–314, and particularly note 18.
21. Y. Sherlow, "And Judge Every Man Meritoriously" [Hebrew], in H. Deutch, M. Ben-Sasson (eds.), *The Other – Between Man and Himself and His Fellow-Man*, [Hebrew], (Tel Aviv: 2001), pp. 126–156.

succeeded in making him a part of his own world, and thus was able to expand and enhance the Jewish people, as the proselyte so eloquently stated:

> O humble Hillel! May you be showered with blessings for bringing me under the wings of the Divine Presence! (Ibid.)

Chapter Thirteen

Beit Hillel and Beit Shammai – Between the Sacred and the Secular

The dispute between Beit Shammai and Beit Hillel regarding the relationship between the sacred and secular domains of life is a far-reaching one, with its roots in the era of the Pairs, and with branches that continue to grow and intertwine to this very day. Almost all aspects of our lives bear some relation to the issue: human creativity in all its diversity, the world of prayer and God's presence in the world, the world of family and sexuality, the world of Shabbat and the festivals as distinct from the weekdays, and more. In the present context we will not be able to encompass the entire topic, and must be content to touch on its periphery.

ACCEPTING THE YOKE OF HEAVEN

The spiritual meaning and implications of this dispute were incisively and comprehensively presented by Dr. Israel Knohl, and the following comments are based on his study.

One of the most striking expressions of the dispute regarding the inherent sanctity of everyday life is found in Tractate *Berakhot*, in a mishna that deals with the laws of reciting the *Shema*:

> Beit Shammai says: In the evening everyone should recline and recite [the *Shema*] and in the morning they should stand erect, as it is said [Deuteronomy 6:7]: "When you lie down and when you rise up." And Beit Hillel says: Everyone may recite as it suits him since it says: "And when you walk on the way." If so, why does it state, "And when you lie down and when you rise up"? [This means] the time people lie down and the time people rise up. (*Berakhot* 1:3)

This mishna is concerned with substance and not simply form, as there is a tremendous difference between reciting the *Shema* while lying down at night and standing up in the morning (as per Beit Shammai), and reading it in whichever manner people are accustomed to read (as per Beit Hillel). Understanding this dispute requires an examination of the fundamental nature of reciting the *Shema*.[1]

When reciting the *Shema*, we "accept the yoke of heaven." Quite simply, this means recognizing God's existence and exclusive dominion over the world. Reciting the verse "Hear O Israel" is a declaration of this belief. The audible proclamation gives a concrete expression to our "acceptance of the yoke of heaven," making it less abstract. It may be likened to a classic coronation ceremony or an official welcome of a king. The public eagerly awaits the king's arrival and, as he draws near, the herald proclaims the king's glory, and the public responds in kind. The herald proclaims: "Praise the King!" and the public responds, "Long live

1. See I. Knohl, "A Parasha Concerned with Accepting the Kingdom of Heaven" [Hebrew], *Tarbitz* 53, 5744, pp. 11–33.

the King!"[2] Transposing these terms into an Israeli idiom, the following army experience aptly describes it. When the commander approaches the parade awaiting him, the cadet on duty shouts: "Platoon – Attention!" and the soldiers respond: "Attention!" As the commander's rank rises, so, too, does the importance attached to the parade and the attendant preparations. The sleepy morning parade, in which the soldiers' unit meets a low-ranking officer, is quite different from the end-of-week parade preceding the platoon's weekend furlough, attended by no less a personage than the platoon commander himself, who examines the readiness of his charges. Preparations for the platoon commander may last an entire night. At the break of dawn the soldiers change from their work clothes into full dress uniform; they polish and clean themselves in preparation for the singular moment at which the senior officer appears. And even more so when the visiting officer is of even higher rank. If this describes the way we receive a mortal king of flesh and blood, then how are we to receive the Supreme King, whose glory and awesomeness fill the world. What kind of parade should precede the proclamation "Long live the King!" when addressing the King of all Kings?

The glorification of the king or emperor in this form was well known to the Greco-Roman world. The sages were familiar with the social norms of their environment and, accordingly, they endeavored to augment the image of the Creator and to submit themselves to His yoke with at least the same ceremony as people pledged subservience to a mortal king. In Talmudic parlance, this overture was referred to as "*Perisat Shema*."[3] Talmudic sources reflect an attempt to imbue the coronation ceremony with a sense of majesty that expressed the acceptance of God's sovereignty over the entire world. The first blessing preceding the recitation of *Shema* (the blessing of the luminaries) establishes man's position among the hosts of divine servants: the celestial luminaries and the angels who serve God permanently and whose roles

2. The term "to praise" [לקלס] usually appears in the sources in the context of royalty. See S. Lieberman, "Praise of Praise," in *Studies in the Torah of the Land of Israel* [Hebrew] (Jerusalem: 5751), pp. 433–439.
3. Based on E. Fleischer, *Toward a Clarification of the Term 'Hapores al Shema,' Tarbitz* 41 (5732), pp. 133–144.

are unchanging. They are the ones who "eagerly and joyously perform their Creator's will," and so serve as an example to all those seeking to internalize the full import of "accepting the yoke of heaven." This form of service is the highest, the most absolute and eternal, independent of changing moods and conditions. The sun that shone at Auschwitz is the very same sun that shines on Israel's Independence Day: "The sun shone, the acacia blossomed, and the slaughterer slaughtered" (Bialik, "In the City of Slaughter"). This is the essence of the service of the heavenly host, for whom there is no doubt, no hesitation, no yearning and no pleading: eternal servitude.

These blessings introduce us to the recitation of the *Shema* every morning and evening. Being but flesh and blood, we are unable to automatically reach the level of accepting the yoke of heaven. Hence, we link the blessing of love to the blessing of luminaries. This blessing describes our intimacy with God: His choosing of us and our choosing to follow Him. We are not mechanical, automatic servants. We serve God out of our free choice to receive the Torah: "He who chose us of all the peoples and gave His Torah to us." Having chosen us, he gave us the Torah. Having chosen to be chosen, we received the Torah. This is the meaning of service born of love. It is only following the recitation of these two blessings that we are ready to enter the inner sanctum, the recitation of the *Shema* itself. In the blessing following the recitation of the *Shema* (the blessing of redemption), we invoke the verses from the splitting of the Red Sea, from the song in which the Jewish people crowned God for the first time with the words "God will reign forever." Positioned before and after the recitation of the *Shema*, these blessings create an atmosphere in which the sincere participant feels as though he is present at the coronation of God as King over the world, and over all worlds, throughout eternity.

Clearly, in order to crown God in this ceremony, the parade requires the participation of the public. There is a certain incongruity in the notion of single person accepting the yoke of heaven in his own private realm. This is the crux of the dispute between Beit Shammai and Beit Hillel: how to structure a divine coronation in a private domain. Conceivably, the Torah, too, did not intend the act of coronation to take place in public, in view of the specific verse: "And these words…when you stay at home and when you are away, when you lie down and when you get up." This means that, in its essence, the recitation bears no connection at all to public domain of the synagogue, but rather precisely to a person's regular, mundane world: at home, at work, or when traveling. This being the case, how does a private individual crown God as King?

This brings us back to the Mishnaic dispute between Beit Shammai and Beit Hillel about whether one must one lie down at night and stand in the morning during the recitation of the *Shema*, or if one may simply recite it during the course of his normal activities.

Based on our previous comments regarding the nature of the coronation ceremony, Beit Shammai's view is easily understood. Beit Shammai rejects the notion of accepting the yoke of heaven in the course of everyday life. One cannot stand before the King in the normal course of a working day. Accepting the yoke of heaven demands the withdrawal from ordinary life and entry into a mindset of "know before whom you stand." The different forms of reclining remove a person from his regular routine and his mundane habits, and bring him to a state of accepting the heavenly yoke; a state of sanctity that completely transcends the world of routine. Beit Hillel, on the other hand, requires a person to enlist all his powers into his service of God, and to coronate Him in each and every moment. "No place is devoid of Him"; "In all your paths – know Him." A day laborer may coronate God even at the top of a tree or at the top of a scaffold. People should learn how to encounter the King even in their work clothes. This is a far-reaching demand that leaves no room for elements of human experience or daily life which are devoid of God's presence. This may even be regarded as a particularly strict requirement of Beit Hillel, which makes no allowance for the mundane trivialities of workaday life and its secularity, and instead endeavors to sanctify all of man's actions through the recitation of the *Shema* "as you go on the way."

The Mishna continues with the following story about Rabbi Tarfon, which exemplifies the tension between the two schools:

> Rabbi Tarfon said: I was once on the road and I reclined to recite [the *Shema*] in conformity with Beit Shammai, and I thus

> endangered my life because of highwaymen. They said to him: You deserved to forfeit your life, since you did not act in accordance with Beit Hillel. (*Berakhot* 1:3)

In order to comply with the halakhic tradition of Beit Shammai, Rabbi Tarfon dismounted from his donkey and recited the *Shema* in a manner that exposed him to risk. According to Beit Hillel, he could have recited the *Shema* while continuing to ride his donkey:

> Beit Hillel says that one may recite it sitting or reclining; one may recite it walking along the road; one may recite it while working. (*Berakhot* 11a)

Here again, Beit Hillel allows the recitation of *Shema* in any situation, without disrupting one's regular life routine. According to Beit Shammai, reciting the *Shema* requires an interruption of the daily routine and a special, almost ceremonial, act of devotion. This distinction helps clarify the following dispute between Rabbi (Yehuda HaNasi) and the sages:

> The *Shema* must be recited as it appears in Scripture – thus says Rabbi. The sages, however, say: [it may be recited] in any language. What is Rabbi's reason? Scripture states: "And they [the words] shall be," implying that they shall remain as they are. What is the reason of the sages? Scripture says "*Shema*" ["hear"], implying – in any language that you understand. And according to Rabbi too, it says "hear"! He requires it [in order to derive the following law]: "Let your ear hear what your mouth utters." And the sages? They concur with the opinion that even if he did not say it audibly, he has discharged his obligation. (*Berakhot* 13a)

What precisely is the dispute between Rabbi and the sages? Technically, there are two bones of contention. According to Rabbi, a person is required to recite the *Shema* in Hebrew, even if he does not understand the words, this being the import of "'And they [the words] shall be' – they shall remain as they are." The sages allow the *Shema* to be recited in any language, because understanding it is the most important thing ("Listen – in any language you understand"). The second dispute is over the requirement of audibility. Rabbi understands the word "*Shema*" (for Rabbi, the word "*Shema*" would be better translated as "hear," not "listen") as obligating a person to hear what he says, whereas, according to the sages, there is no such obligation.

I think that our comments above regarding the dispute between Beit Hillel and Beit Shammai explain the dispute between Rabbi and the sages as well. Rabbi views the recitation of *Shema* as nothing less than a royal coronation. Even in isolation, a person is not exempt from holding his own (albeit private) coronation ceremony. The proclamation "Long live the King!" can hardly be in a hushed whisper. Moreover, is it conceivable for a congregation to proclaim "Long live the King!" in a cacophony of different languages?

The significance of a coronation ceremony goes beyond merely internalizing its meaning. The reciting of *Shema* must be an impressive and all-inclusive public act, a declaration made and heard by all in accordance with a standard format. This requires it to be said out loud, in one language, the language of the Torah.

The sages however, endorsed Hillel's approach. Reciting the *Shema* is not a public coronation. The importance of the recitation of the *Shema* lies in one's subjective, personal intention, in one's commitment to "to accept God's yoke." Accordingly, while the recitation need not be audible, it must be in a language understood by the person presuming to accept God's kingship, as explicitly noted by Rabbi Meir:

> The validity of the words depends on the heart's intention. (*Berakhot* 15a)

Our sources indicate that all of Beit Shammai's students required the reciting of *Shema* to be audible, which, needless to say, is consistent with the ceremonial approach to the *Shema*, as described.

In general however, Beit Hillel's view became the accepted view. Accordingly, purity of intention in reciting *Shema* was stressed above all else, and the ceremonial aspect was deliberately downplayed. The following midrash contrasts these two aspects in the context of comparing the honor bestowed upon a flesh-and-blood king with the honor bestowed on the Supreme King of Kings:

> Rabbi Yitzḥak said: It may be compared to a king who sent a royal proclamation to the province. What did the people of the province do? They rose to their feet, uncovered their hair, and read it with reverence, fear, awe, and trepidation. This was the way in which the Holy One, blessed be He, addressed Israel: Here is the *Shema,* My proclamation, but I did not trouble you to read the *Shema* either standing on your feet or with your heads uncovered, but "when you sit down in your house and when you walk by the way." (*Vayikra Raba* 27)

What does this mean? Normally, any decree issuing from the king sends his subjects into a state of tension and fear, and this tension increases sevenfold when the royal communiqué is addressed personally to a particular subject. Matters become even more complicated when the letter also includes the King's orders, which must be complied with.

The Midrash rather humorously depicts the manner in which royal subjects receive their King's letter: "They rose to their feet, uncovered their hair, and read it with reverence, fear, awe and trepidation." We might have anticipated that the Midrash would continue: "How much more so should we stand up and read with reverence, fear, awe and trepidation, when it is the Almighty King of all Kings who gave you the Torah, with all of its instructions and warnings, for when we accept the yoke of heaven we also accept the yoke of the commandments." But no! "I did not put you to any trouble." God has no need for us to honor Him with extravagant ceremonies – rather, "when you sit down in your house and when you walk by the way." Reciting the *Shema* and accepting the yoke of heaven must be integrated into the daily routine, as a part of everyday life.

This is the essence of Hillel's teaching.

HILLEL'S ATTITUDE TOWARD THE HUMAN BODY

> "A kindly man treats his soul well" [Proverbs 11:17] – this refers to Hillel the Elder. For when he took leave of his students, he would accompany them. His students asked him: "Where are you going, Master?" He replied to them: "I am going to fulfill a commandment." "Which commandment?" they asked. "I am going to the baths," he replied. They asked him: "But is this a commandment?" He replied: "Yes. This is demonstrated by the fact that one is given a pension to polish and buff the statues of kings that stand in the theaters and circuses, and he is even promoted to the ranks of the noblemen of the kingdom. In that case, then I who have been created in the image and likeness, as it says: 'For in the image of God He made man' [Genesis 9:6], how much more so?"
>
> It was also said: "A kindly man treats his soul well" – this refers to Hillel the Elder. For when he took leave of his students, he would accompany them. His students asked him: "Master, where are you going?" He said to them: "To bestow kindness upon a guest in the house." They asked him: "Do you have a guest every day?" He replied: "Is not the poor soul a guest in the body? The body is here today, and tomorrow it is here no longer." (*Vayikra Raba* 34)

The Midrash presents two descriptions of Hillel's attitude toward the body. The first one equates the body and soul in the sense that both are created in the "image of God." The story relates how Hillel keeps his students in suspense as he brings them with him to "perform a commandment." Hillel responds to their question "Is this [going to the bathhouse] a mitzva?" with the parable about the statues of kings. The king's statue stands in a public courtyard teeming with people, where it is guarded by an officer who continually scrubs and polishes it. This idolatrous ritual also requires him to "feed" the idol. This officer's sole and entire duty consists of guarding the idols, but he is nonetheless considered to be one of the king's most distinguished servants, with a rank equaling that of the most senior of the royal entourage. This completes the parable.

Hillel now diverts his student's attention to his own world.

Understanding the parable requires us to focus upon its three characters: the king, the idol and the guard. There is only one king: the King of the world. The idol, an image of the King, is man, who was created in God's image. The idol's guard is the very same person, charged, according to the interpretation of the sages, with taking care of his body. Hillel's "self" simultaneously includes the "self" of the image and the "self" of the guard. In the act of cleaning, he is actually nurturing the image of God inherent within him. The two domains are inseparable because all of man's components are part of a unified whole. This is a particularly refined conception of "In God's image did he make man." In the generations after Hillel, it developed into the dictum of Rabbi Akiva: "Beloved is man, for he was created in the image [of God]."

Hillel's second homily demonstrates a paternalistic concern for man's body. Though fully aware of the body's transience in contrast to the eternity of the spirit, the relationship between them is based on compassion and not contempt, for, paradoxically, it is the transient body that bestows kindness on the "eternal" soul. A slightly varied version of the story appears in *Avot deRabbi Natan,* in which Shammai's attitude toward the body appears as well.

> "And let all of your deeds be for the sake of Heaven."[4] Like Hillel. When Hillel would go somewhere, they would ask him, "Rabbi, where are you going?" [He would answer:] "I am going to perform a commandment." "Which commandment, Hillel?" "I am going to the lavatory." [They asked him:] "Is this a commandment?" He replied: "Yes, so that the body not deteriorate." "Where are you going, Hillel?" He replied to them: "I am going to fulfill a commandment." "Which commandment, Hillel?" "I am going to the baths." They asked him: "But is this a commandment?" He replied: "Yes, in order to clean the body. Know that this is so, for if the government gives an annual pension to the official in charge of polishing and shining the statues which stand in the royal plazas, and if even further he is elevated to the rank of the noblemen of the kingdom, how much more so

4. See Mishna, *Avot* 2:12.

> we, who have been created in the image and likeness of God, as it says: 'For in the image of God He made man!' [Genesis 9:6]." Shammai would not say it this way, rather [he would say]: "Let our obligations be fulfilled with this body." (*Avot deRabbi Nathan*, recension B, ch. 30)

In Hillel's understanding, the categories of "commandment" and "for the sake of heaven" apply to all aspects of life. Maintenance of the body, aesthetics, and beauty are all part of serving God, and the body cannot be separated from the image of God that inheres in man. By extension, no realm of human experience can be "outside" the service of God. The recitation of *Shema*, which expresses God's sovereignty, does not require a separate ceremony, because man is required to enthrone God at all times and in all aspects of his life.

Shammai, on the other hand, feels that the existence of the physical body has been forced upon him: "Let us fulfill our obligations with this body." Just as he sees no intrinsic holiness in washing the body in the bath-house, a person's recitation of *Shema* and his sanctification for the royal coronation must remain distinct from the mundane aspects of his life.

Shammai's conception of the body as a necessity that does not constitute part of the service of God finds expression in many of the details pertaining to man and his bodily needs. For example, Shammai's (or his disciples') attitude to sexuality can be examined from this perspective. The following incident is related by the wife of Rabbi Eliezer ben Hyrcanus, the latter known as "*Shamuti*" (i.e., from the House of Shammai),[5] when describing her conjugal encounters with her husband:

> Imma Shalom was asked: "Why are your children so exceedingly beautiful?" She replied: "Because he [my husband] 'converses' [a euphemism for sexual encounter] with me neither at the beginning, nor at the end of the night, but [only] at midnight; and when

5. This fact is broadly accepted in all of the Talmudic literature and has been extensively researched by Y.D. Gilat, in his book, *The Teaching of Rabbi Eliezer ben Hyrcanus* [Hebrew] (Tel Aviv: 5728).

> he 'converses,' he reveals a handbreadth and covers a handbreadth, and behaves as though he were compelled by a demon. And when I asked him, 'What is the reason [for choosing] midnight?' he replied: 'So that I do not think of another woman, which would render my children as bastards.'" (*Nedarim* 20a–b)

Imma Shalom's explanation for her children's exceptional beauty reflects a conception of sexuality as a lowly, shameful aspect of human existence. Bodily pleasures are not to be enjoyed; rather, a person should conduct himself as "though he were compelled by a demon." Indeed, the notion that sexual relations are permitted exclusively for reproductive purposes was familiar in the Greco-Roman world among the Stoics and similar groups. Later sages rejected this ascetic doctrine. Already in the Talmud (*Nedarim*, ad loc.), Rabbi Eliezer's view is presented as a singular view, and the accepted view is diametrically opposed to it: sexual relations are not to be performed as though one was being forced; whatever a person wishes to do – he may do.[6]

The Talmud, in Tractate *Sanhedrin*, describes a series of conversations between Yehuda HaNasi (Rabbi) and Antoninus, some of which pertain to the body's relationship to the soul. In one of them, Rabbi accepts the view of Antoninus:

> Antoninus said to Rabbi: "When is the soul instilled in man? At the moment that its identity is decreed, or from the moment that the embryo takes shape?" He replied: "From the moment it

6. D. Boyarin devoted an entire book to this subject, *The Flesh in the Spirit* [Hebrew] (Tel Aviv: 5762). He argues that Rabbi Eliezer was an exception in the rabbinical world in his attitude to sexuality (but fails to mention Rabbi Eliezer's roots in the world of Beit Shammai). See also Adiel Schremer's comprehensive study, *Male and Female He Created Them: Jewish Marriage in the Late Second Temple, the Mishnaic and Talmudic Periods* [Hebrew] (Jerusalem: 5764). In the first chapter he describes the importance ascribed by the sages to conjugal relations, as opposed to the elevation of celibacy in the various sects and primarily in the early period of the Church. Schremer also shows how Rabbi Eliezer did not represent the dominant stream in rabbinic thought, which was more attuned to the view of Beit Hillel. See also Rabbi Yehuda Brandes, *Applied Aggada: Studies on Family, Society and Worship* [Hebrew] (Jerusalem: 2005), ch. 3.

> takes shape." He objected: "Can a piece of meat be left unsalted for three days without becoming putrid? The answer must therefore be: from the moment of the decree." Rabbi said: "Antoninus taught me this, and Scripture supports him, for it is written: 'And Your command has preserved my soul' [Job 10:12]."
>
> Antoninus further asked Rabbi: "At what stage is evil instilled in man? From the moment it takes shape, or from the moment it emerges into the world?" He replied: "From the moment it takes shape." "If so," he objected, "it would kick its way out of the mother's womb and come forth. Therefore, it must be from the moment that it comes forth." Rabbi said: "Antoninus taught me this, and Scripture supports him, for it is said: 'Sin lies in wait at the door [i.e., where the baby emerges]' [Genesis 4:7]." (*Sanhedrin* 91b)

The question of when the soul is placed in the body is a fascinating one. In his initial response, Rabbi presents the rabbinic doctrine that only the fully developed body can become a receptacle for the soul. The embryo only becomes such a vessel after having developed, and, *ipso facto*, the soul would have nothing to inhere in prior to that stage. Antoninus, on the other hand, attempts to prove that the soul is bestowed at the moment of a person's conception, for otherwise, he could not develop. This brings us to one of the most riveting questions in halakhic medical ethics: the status of the embryo. Even though the Talmud states that Rabbi was persuaded by Antoninus, a plethora of sources attest to the embryo's status as "his mother's thigh" (i.e. a limb of the mother) and having no independent status outside the mother. (This is not the place to elaborate on this subject, a question of serious debate in its own right, with major halakhic implications with regard to abortion.)

Shammai, then, views the human body as merely the receptacle of the soul, and sees only the soul as being connected to the Divine. In his view, no intrinsic value attaches to bodily pleasure beyond its role to serve as the custodian of the soul. The soul is the purpose of man's existence, and everything else exists for that purpose. Hillel proposed another, radically different understanding. Above and beyond its functional role in the maintenance of soul, the body is also of intrinsic value by virtue of its being "the image of God." Man's divinity is inseparable from his lower, mortal dimension. Man's sanctity permeates his entire being, the totality of which is the image of God.

According to this understanding, Beit Shammai ascribes importance exclusively to the purpose of man's actions, whereas Beit Hillel also ascribes importance to the means of achieving them.[7] This distinction explains another dispute between Shammai and Hillel, regarding the commandment to rejoice on festivals, which we shall now consider.

THE HOLINESS OF SHABBAT AND THE HOLINESS OF THE WEEKDAYS

Tractate *Beitza* records a practical dispute between Shammai the Elder and Hillel the Elder regarding the preparation of the Shabbat meals. The dispute itself is but the tip of the iceberg, revealing the profound tension between the two dominant world views in Judaism: those who seek to sever the holy from the secular and those seeking to unite them.

> It was taught: They said of Shammai the Elder: All his days he would eat in honor of Shabbat. If he found a fine bit of meat, he would say: "This is for Shabbat." If he found another that was still better, he would set aside the second [for Shabbat] and eat the first. However, Hillel the Elder had another attitude, for all his works were for the sake of Heaven, as it is said "Blessed is the Lord day by day." [Psalms 68:20]. (*Beitza* 16a)

We have already seen how Beit Shammai's approach divides a person's daily life into distinct dimensions of the sacred and the secular. The view that a person is obliged to lie down and stand up while accepting

7. This understanding as the core of the dispute between Hillel and Shammai was identified by Rabbi S.Y. Zevin, in his study "On the Methods of Beit Shammai and Beit Hillel" in his book *Le'or HaHalakha* (Tel Aviv: 5717), pp. 302–309. He attempts to link the disputes between Hillel and Shammai with the dichotomy of "potentiality" and "actuality." Beit Shammai views things as they are in potential, whereas Beit Hillel views them in terms of their actual result. I have taken a similar, though not identical path in my attempt to sketch the contours of their dispute from the perspective of a life based on an idea (a future goal) and a life rooted in the present.

the heavenly yoke as they say the *Shema* is a natural expression of this dichotomy. Similarly, the passage above describing Shammai's eating habits, expresses his view of the tension between the realm of sanctity and the realm of the mundane. Are weekdays imbued with their own independent sanctity, or is Shabbat the spiritual font that sustains us during the mundane weekdays, from one Shabbat to the next? Shammai eats in honor of Shabbat; in themselves weekdays lack any independent value or sanctity. Essentially, one can only dine on Shabbat, and only on Shabbat can a meal constitute the fulfillment of a commandment. Clearly, there is no justification for a person enjoying his meal on a regular weekday, which only has value inasmuch as it is a preparation for Shabbat.

Hillel takes a different approach. Sanctity is to be found even within the secular, mundane dimensions of life, as per the verse: "Blessed is the Lord day by day."

Shammai's attempt to invest Shabbat with a degree of sublime sanctity finds expression in things that seem foreign to our contemporary understanding of halakha. We know, for example, that acts of personal affliction and fasting are prohibited on Shabbat, in accordance with the verse "and you shall call the Sabbath 'a delight'" (Isaiah 58:13). Various early halakhic authorities actually ruled that the prohibition on fasting on Shabbat is Pentateuchal in origin, derived from the verse: "Eat it [the manna] today, for today is God's Sabbath; you will not find it [on the ground] today" (Exodus 16:25).[8] Nonetheless, certain sources attest that sages associated with Shammai praised and even encouraged fasting on festive days:

> Our rabbis taught: It happened that Rabbi Eliezer sat and expounded on the laws of the festival throughout the entire day.
>
> The first group left [the study house] and he remarked: "Those are owners of large barrels." A second group left and he

8. See *Sefer HaYere'im* s.99, and *Ribash Responsa* s.613: "Pleasure on Shabbat is a biblical commandment." According to Maimonides too, *Laws of Vows* (*Hilkhot Shevuot*) 1:6, a vow to fast on Shabbat is made in vain because a person is foresworn from Sinai not to afflict himself on Shabbat and the Holidays. See also in the Taz, *Oraḥ Ḥayim* 278:1, and in *Biur Halakha* at the beginning of s.288.

> remarked: "Those are the owners of regular-sized barrels." A third group left. He remarked: "Those are the owners of pitchers." A fourth group left. He remarked: "Those are the owners of flasks." A fifth group left. He remarked: "Those are the owners of cups." A sixth group began to leave. He remarked: "These are people who are depressed." He gazed upon the remaining students and their faces began to pale. He said to them: "My sons, my criticism is not directed at you, but at those who left, for they forsake eternal life [study of Torah] and engage in temporal life. When they were leaving, he said to them: "Go eat rich foods and drink sweet beverages and send portions to those who did not prepare, for this day is sacred to our Lord, and do not be melancholy, for the joy of God is your strength [Nehemiah 8:10]."
>
> The master said: "They forsake eternal life [study of Torah] and engage in temporal life." But isn't rejoicing on the festival a religious duty?! Rabbi Eliezer is consistent with his [own] opinion, for he said: Rejoicing on the festival is optional. For it was taught in a *baraita*: Rabbi Eliezer says: A person has no absolute duty on the festival; he may eat and drink or he may eat and study. Rabbi Yehoshua says: Divide it up: half for the Lord [and] half for yourselves.
>
> Rabbi Yoḥanan says: They both expounded the same Scriptural proof: One verse states: "A solemn assembly to the Lord your God" [Deuteronomy 16:8] and another verse states: "You shall have a solemn assembly" [Numbers 29:35]. Rabbi Eliezer says that it may be either entirely for God or entirely for yourselves; while Rabbi Yehoshua's opinion is: Divide it: half for the Lord and half for yourselves." (*Beitza* 15a)

Rabbi Yoḥanan understands that the dispute between Rabbi Eliezer and Rabbi Yehoshua was neither motivated by external factors nor simply a question of quantity. Both are deeply rooted in Torah and are attempting to inculcate their teachers' doctrines. Rabbi Eliezer cannot accept a dualistic approach which merges bodily and spiritual pleasure: "They forsake eternal life [study of Torah] and engage in temporal life!" There is no obligation to physically indulge ourselves on the festival; accordingly each person has the freedom to decide which form of indulging suits him best: pampering the body or indulging the soul. His choice is "either-or." The festival must either be "entirely for God," or "entirely for you." He thus rejects as unworthy any attempt to live a life which mixes the sacred with the mundane.

In Rabbi Eliezer's world, striving for eternal life must dictate all aspects of temporal life, and hence his derisive contempt for all those who hurry home to the barrels of food awaiting them. Each of the departing groups is criticized until only the last group is left, torn between the desire to appease their teacher and their yearning to enjoy the festival with food and drink. Having "consideration" for them, Rabbi Eliezer sends them home with a blessing for the rest of the day.[9] Rabbi Yehoshua, on the other hand, represents the world of Hillel, and in keeping with Hillel's approach, attempts to divide the day up – half for God and half for you.

This was the worldview of Rabbi Yehoshua, and it sums up the entire teaching of Beit Hillel, in the spirit of the teachings of Hillel the Elder. Everyday secularity is not a barrier to holiness. In this world, a man must aim to uncover the holiness inherent in all times and in all places. Hillel does not deny that there are levels of holiness: there is the holy, and the holy of holies; the weekdays, and the festivals and Shabbat. Similarly, there are levels which separate physicality from spirituality, and the body from the soul. But Hillel rejects the notion that there can be anything which is totally, categorically secular, which a wholesome person must entirely abstain from. The doctrine of Beit Hillel is monistic in its assertion of the essential unity and sanctity of all reality. As such it imposes a tremendous demand on each and every individual, challenging him to live as a reflection of God's image within the world, with all his actions being directed for the sake of heaven.

9. See a literary analysis of the story in Y. Fraenkel, *The Aggadic Narrative – Harmony of Form and Content* [Hebrew] (Tel Aviv: 2001), ch. 3 ("Structures"), pp. 80–84.

Chapter Fourteen

Shammai and His Student, Bava ben Buta

Shammai would say: Make your Torah study a permanent aspect of your life; say little and do much; and greet everyone with a pleasant countenance. (Avot 1:15)

Considering Shammai the Elder's austerity, we might not have ascribed this mishna to him at first glance. In fact, certain scholars have claimed that Shammai's severity is actually the literary creation of later *amora'im*, who utilized the stories of sages as an educational tool.[1] Regardless of where the truth lies, this mishna provides the background for the following discussion relating to Shammai and one of his students.

1. This claim is a central one in Ben Shalom's book, *Beit Shammai.*

THE STRUGGLE BETWEEN THE STUDENTS OF SHAMMAI AND HILLEL: LITERATURE AND REALITY

In the previous section, we saw how, in the generation preceding Shammai and Hillel, Shemaya and Avtalyon sought to distance the sages from political involvement. The civil wars between the last scions of the Hasmonean dynasty convinced the rabbis that the wise man's lot should be within the bastions of Torah, from which the Torah's power radiates to the entire nation. Accordingly, under the leadership of Hillel and Shammai, the following generation became immersed in halakhic matters: Shabbat and festivals, the laws of prayer and blessings, the laws of purity, the laws of sanctified objects, and agricultural matters. They engaged in and debated all aspects of the halakha. Presumably, previous generations had also seen the rabbis involved in similar discussions, but certain events combined to confer the generation of Hillel and Shammai with its distinctive feature, namely, the emergence of the phenomenon of dispute. While recorded contentions between Hillel and Shammai are few, the pair nonetheless became the very symbols of dispute. Our sources indicate that their disputes were filled with tension, and at times even danger:

> When one harvests grapes for the winepress, Shammai says: "[The grapes] become susceptible [to ritual contamination]." Hillel ruled: "They do not become susceptible." Hillel said to Shammai: "Why must a person harvest grapes in purity, but not gather olives in purity?' Shammai replied: "If you continue to provoke me, I will also decree impurity for the olive gathering." They thrust a sword into the study house and declared: "Whoever wants to enter may enter, but no one may leave!" And on that day Hillel sat in submission before Shammai, like one like one of the disciples, and it was as wretched for Israel as the day on which the [golden] calf was made. (*Shabbat* 17a)

We noted above that Hillel's rulings and teachings were based on the rules of logical deduction, whereas Shammai preserved the ancient tradition, transmitted from person to person, with no innovations or upheavals. This verbal exchange between Hillel and Shammai and its violent epilogue retains something of that confrontation.

One of their disputes related to the status of grapes in the winepress. All agree that wine is one of the seven liquids that are susceptible to contamination, but the grapes from which wine derives are classified as a form of food. The point during the winemaking process at which the grapes become susceptible is a matter of dispute. Shammai maintains that grapes are capable of becoming impure as soon as they enter the winepress. Based on a logical extrapolation from the gathering of olives to the harvesting of grapes, Hillel both rejects and questions Shammai's position. For Shammai, Hillel's question is a blatant provocation: "If you provoke me I will also decree impurity for the olive gathering."

Shammai lives in a world of tradition and decrees, a world in which there is no room for intellectual argumentation and debate. The Talmudic metaphor for the gravity of their dispute is that it culminates with a sword being thrust into the *Beit Midrash,* and "that day was as wretched for Israel as the day on which the [golden] calf was made" – a statement dramatic in its severity. The day on which the golden calf was made was the day on which civil war erupted under the battle cry of "Those for the Lord – come to me" (Exodus 32:26), a day on which a man would even kill his own brother. While some have seen this passage as a dramatic metaphor which seeks to indicate the severity of the dispute, others see the description as more than simply metaphorical. Consider the following statement from the Jerusalem Talmud:

> The students of Beit Shammai stood below them and began to slaughter the students of Beit Hillel. It was taught: Six of them ascended and the others stood over them with swords and lances. (Talmud Yerushalmi, *Shabbat* 1:4 [3c])

The Jerusalem Talmud paints a picture of an all-too-real battlefield, and, as if that were not enough, a chronological fragment found in the Cairo Geniza attests to the mourning decreed in the tannaitic period and describes the very same battle:

> On the fourth of Adar a dispute erupted between the students of Shammai and Hillel and many were killed.[2]

How many students were "many"? We don't know. It is clear, though, that this tradition (corroborated in other sources) portrays the dispute between Hillel and Shammai as culminating in bloodshed and civil war. An alternative rabbinic tradition chooses to portray the relationship between Shammai and Hillel as one of reconciliation in almost idyllic tones. One such tradition is the Mishna in Tractate *Avot* (5:17), which cites the dispute between the houses of Hillel and Shammai as the model of a "dispute for the sake of heaven."

THE DISPUTE OVER "LAYING OF THE HANDS": BAVA BEN BUTA'S DECISION

In rabbinic tradition, Shammai and Hillel are the symbol of Talmudic dispute; there was, however, an earlier dispute that lasted throughout the five generations of the Pairs, and was actually resolved in the days of Shammai and Hillel: the dispute over the "laying of the hands" (*semikha*):

> Yose ben Yoezer said not to lay [the hands]. Yose ben Yoḥanan said to lay. Joshua ben Peraḥia said to not to lay, Nittai HaArbeli said to lay. Yehuda ben Tabbai said not to lay, Shimon ben Shetaḥ said to lay. Shemaya said to lay, Avtalyon said not to lay. There was no dispute between Hillel and Menaḥem. Menaḥem left and Shammai entered. Shammai said not to lay. Hillel said to lay. All of the former were patriarchs and those secondary to them were the head of the *Beit Din*.
>
> Beit Shammai says: one brings *shelamim* [peace offerings] but does not lay the hands on them; but not *olot* [burnt offerings]. But Beit Hillel says: one brings both *shelamim* and *olot* and lays the hands on them. (*Ḥagiga* 2:2)

2. Mordekhai Margalit, *Hilkhot Eretz Yisrael min HaGenizai*, [Hebrew] (Jerusalem: 1974), p. 142. See also S. Lieberman, *Yerushalmi Kepeshuto* (Jerusalem: 5795), p. 38, on parallel sources to this *baraita*.

The rule is that an individual offering a sacrifice, whether obligatory or voluntary, is obliged to place ("to lay") his hands on the head of his sacrifice. Five generations of Pairs disputed whether it is permitted to perform *semikha* on a festival. In the days of Beit Hillel and Beit Shammai, this dispute was extended to include the *Shalmei Ḥagiga* (festival peace-offering) and the *Olat Re'iya* (pilgrimage burnt-offering). According to Beit Shammai, here too there was no laying of hands, whereas, according to Beit Hillel, there was.

The literature on the essence and the unique character of this dispute is prolific. How were five generations unable to resolve this dispute? A number of strange explanations have been offered, prompting the following observation by the scholar Louis Ginzberg:

> It is clear to all, except for the particularly obtuse, that the terms "to lay" or "not to lay" are to be interpreted literally, namely: laying the hands on the head of the sacrifice – as opposed to the "head" of the elder or the "heads" of verses in the Torah for interpretive purposes... it seems clear to me that the dispute between the Pairs related to whether the festival peace-offerings required laying of the hands or not.[3]

According to Ginzberg the subject of the dispute itself was of minor significance. Its primary importance lay in its ramifications, which found expression on three levels: (a) the legitimacy of creative use of the traditional rules of interpretation. The conservative school sought to limit the institution of "laying on the hands" to its original biblical application: (voluntary offerings, sin offerings, and guilt offerings). The other, "activist," school attempted to broaden the institution of *semikha* by way of creative interpretation to include the festive *Olat Re'iya* and *Shalmei Ḥagiga* sacrifices; (b) public participation in the Temple ritual, in addition to the priests; (c) encouraging Jews to return to *Eretz Yisrael* by prohibiting the appointment of an agent for the purpose of laying on hands. (*Menaḥot* 9:8).

3. Louis Ginzberg, "The Role of Halakha in Ḥokhmat Yisrael," *Halakha and Aggada* (Tel Aviv: 1960), p. 25. See there note 14, where he brings additional explanations.

For the current purposes, we need not address all of Ginzberg's proofs and ideas; evidently, the dispute itself was finally resolved during the days of Hillel and Shammai. The following illustrates the story as presented respectively in the Jerusalem Talmud and in the Tosefta:

Talmud Yerushalmi, Ḥagiga 2:3 [78a]	*Tosefta, Ḥagiga 2:11*
Once it happened that Hillel the Elder laid his hands on a burnt offering in the Temple courtyard, and the disciples of Shammai ganged up on him. It began to wag its tail. He said to them: "Look, it is a female and I have to prepare it as a peace offering." He continued to equivocate and they dispersed. As time went on, Beit Shammai became dominant and resolved to determine the halakha in accordance with their view. One of the students at this time was Bava ben Buta, who was a student of Shammai, and he knew that the halakha was in accordance with Beit Hillel. It happened once that he came to the Temple courtyard and, finding it desolate, said: "Let desolation visit the houses of those who have desolated the House of our God." What did he do then? He went and brought three thousand lambs from the flocks of Kedar, inspected them for blemishes, placed them on the Temple Mount, and proclaimed: "Listen to me my brothers of the house of Israel: Whoever wishes to bring burnt offerings – let him bring it and lay his hands; a peace offering – let him bring it and lay his hands. At that time the halakha was fixed in accordance with Beit Hillel, and no one challenged it.	Once it happened that Hillel the Elder laid his hands on a burnt offering in the Temple courtyard, and the disciples of Shammai ganged up upon him. He said to them: "Look, it is a female and I have to prepare it as a peace offering." He continued to equivocate and they dispersed. Immediately thereafter, Beit Shammai became dominant and resolved to fix the halakha in accordance with their view. One of the students at this time was Bava ben Buta, who was a student of Shammai, and he knew that the halakha was always in accordance with Beit Hillel. He therefore went and brought all the flocks of Kedar, placed them in the Temple courtyard, and proclaimed: "Whoever wishes to bring burnt offerings and peace offerings – let him come and take one and lay his hands." They came and took the beasts and brought burnt offerings and laid their hands. On that day, the halakha was fixed in accordance with Beit Hillel, and no one challenged it.

Bava ben Buta saw the Temple in a state of desolation. To prohibit *semikha* was to grant the priests a monopoly over the Temple, and there was certainly no justification for leaving confession and sacrificial rituals in the hands of priests of questionable integrity. Bava ben Buta stepped into the breach and, in an extraordinary act by any measure, inundated the Temple courtyard with thousands of sheep, in order to galvanize the people into making the pilgrimage to the Temple.

In contrast, when confronting the zealotry of Shammai's students ganging up on him, Hillel appears as the weaker party. He can only extricate himself from the confrontation by misleading equivocation, suggesting to his opponents that he had brought a peace offering and not a burnt offering (female as opposed to male). Following Hillel's ignominious surrender to Shammai, the situation could only be changed by one of Beit Shammai's most zealous students. This was the remarkable contribution of Bava ben Buta, who embodied the precept to "say little and do much." Courageously assuming responsibility, he brought about a radical change. Beit Shammai's victory was transformed into the decision that the law would be in accordance with Beit Hillel.

Who, then, was Bava ben Buta, this unusual student of Shammai?

BAVA BEN BUTA BRINGS A GUILT OFFERING EVERY DAY

One source relates that Bava ben Buta was one of those people whose fear of God imbued all of their actions at every step of their lives:

> Rabbi Eliezer says: "A man may vow an undetermined guilt offering [*asham talui*] any day and any time he wants." It was called the "guilt offering of the righteous." They said of Bava ben Buta that he would volunteer such a guilt offering every day, except for the day after Yom Kippur. One day, he said: "[I swear by] all that is holy, if they would let me, I would offer [one, even on this day], but they told me to wait until I enter the realm of doubt." The sages, however, say: "An undetermined guilt offering is only brought for an act which, if done deliberately, is subject to the penalty of extirpation [*karet*] and, if done inadvertently, is subject to the penalty of a sin offering [*korban ḥatat*]." (Tosefta, *Keritut* 4:4)

Bava ben Buta behaves like one of the early *Ḥasidim*. Not surprisingly, Rabbi Eliezer, of the House of Shammai ("the *Shamuti*") accepts the halakhic validity of this practice. Refusing to be content with normative conduct, Bava examines himself and safeguards himself against any potential liability. In this sense, he is reminiscent of Job. It bears mentioning that a person brings an "undetermined guilt offering" when he is not sure whether he has sinned or not, or when, in biblical parlance, "his sin is not known." He has a sense of sin, but is not certain of it. Maimonides sums up the law of the undetermined guilt offering in accordance with the view of the sages:

> Wherever liability for a fixed sin would be incurred for a transgression committed through error, if committed without knowledge, liability for an undetermined guilt offering is incurred. What is meant by "without knowledge"? If a man has a doubt whether he erroneously sinned or transgressed regarding a particular matter, he is obliged to offer a guilt offering, for it is said: "And if any one sin . . . though he know it not, yet is he guilty, and shall bear his iniquity. And he shall bring a ram without blemish out of the flock, according to your evaluation, for a guilt offering" [Leviticus 5:17–18); and this is called an undetermined, or "suspensive," guilt offering since it makes atonement for what is in doubt and holds it "in suspense" for him until he knows of a certainty that he had sinned through error, in which case he must bring a sin offering. (*Mishneh Torah*, "Laws of Accidental Transgressions" [*Hilkhot Shegagot*] 8:1)

Here Maimonides explains a wonderful principle of the Torah in making provision for a person who has committed an act with a high potential for sin. The example cited by the Talmud concerns a person who sees two servings of meat and eats one of them, and is subsequently informed that one of them was not kosher, but does not know whether he ate the kosher serving or the non-kosher serving. The person is aware of his doubt, and the Torah requires him to bring a sacrifice, just to be on the safe side. By bringing the sacrifice, he ensures that, regardless, he has atoned. Should it transpire that what he ate was confirmed to be not kosher, then the guilt offering will not suffice, and he will be required to bring a sin offering. Otherwise, the guilt offering will suffice. It is stressed, however, that this option is not available in all cases of doubtful commission of a sin (established by rabbinical edict), and is limited to prohibitions which, if committed intentionally, would render the sinner liable for extirpation (*karet*) and, if unintentionally, a sin offering.

Notably, Maimonides' rendition of the halakha accords with the sages' view and not with that of Bava ben Buta. Bava ben Buta is perennially ridden with a sense of sin, but the sages refuse to accept his offering on the day after Yom Kippur, feeling that he should "wait until he enters the realm of doubt." Bava lives in a state of religious tension comparable to that of Job, who brought sacrifices on a daily basis, fearing that his sons may have sinned at one of their feasts. A person can live under a permanent cloud of fear, without any clear, objective indication of a sin, but equally unable to escape that feeling. Rabbi Moshe Ḥayim Luzzatto endorsed this model of religious tension:

> The fear of sin has two dimensions: one concerns the present and future, and the other concerns the past. As far as the present is concerned, the fear of sin consists in being apprehensive with regard to any action in which one is engaged, or is about to undertake, lest there be in it anything that is not becoming of God's glory. As far as the past is concerned, the fear of sin consists of being apprehensive lest some sin might have been committed unawares. This is why Bava ben Buta offered a daily guilt-offering at the Temple [*Keritut* 25a]. And Job, after his sons' feast, "rose up early in the morning and offered burnt offerings according to the number of them all; for Job said: 'It may be that my sons have sinned.'" Our sages relate the following concerning the anointing oil with which Moses anointed Aaron: We read in the Torah, "Upon man's flesh it shall not be poured" [Exodus 30:32]. Accordingly, when Moses was commanded to anoint Aaron with it, they both feared that they may have desecrated it in some way. (*Path of the Just*, ch. 24)

BAVA BEN BUTA'S HUMILITY (SHADES OF HILLEL THE ELDER)

The Babylonian Talmud presents Bava ben Buta's unpretentious and God-fearing nature as a model of self-effacement:

> A certain Babylonian went up to the land of Israel and took a wife [there]. One day he said to her: "Boil me two [cows'] feet." She boiled him two lentils, and he was angry with her. The next day, he said: "Boil me a *griwa* [a large measure of lentils]," so she boiled him a *griwa*. He said to her: "Go and bring me two *butzini* [denoting 'melons' or 'lamps']," so she went out and brought him two lamps. Go and break them on the head of the *bava* [gate]. Bava ben Buta was sitting at the gates, judging a lawsuit. She went up to him and broke them on his head. He said to her: "What is the meaning of what you just did?" She replied to him: "This is what my husband ordered me to do." "You have fulfilled your husband's wishes," he replied. "May the Almighty bring forth from you two sons like Bava ben Buta." (*Nedarim* 66b)

The background of the story is the problem of communication among couples from different cultures. In this consummate parody, a new immigrant from Babylonia becomes frustrated with his native-born wife for consistently misunderstanding his dialect until, in his aggravation, he causes her to break two lamps over Bava ben Buta's head. The story is told specifically about Bava ben Buta because of his name (meaning "gate"), which invites precisely that kind of confusion, but also because of his reputation as a person who could not be ruffled.

This story is clearly reminiscent of the story cited above of the man who attempted to aggravate Hillel (*Shabbat* 30b–31a). Notwithstanding his being one of the greatest of Shammai's students, Bava ben Buta conducts himself with precisely the same patience as Hillel. The very clear lesson is that one cannot draw conclusions regarding the character of the students of Hillel and Shammai based exclusively on the characters of their teachers.

BAVA BEN BUTA AND KING HEROD

The final source relating to Bava ben Buta takes us back to the historical events that we opened with. This section began with our citation of the Gemara recording Herod's massacre of the sages, leaving only Bava ben Buta. The second scene of this saga begins with a secret visit by Herod to Bava:

> One day, he [Herod] came and sat before [the now blinded Bava ben Buta] and said: "Look, master, what this wicked slave [i.e., Herod] is doing."
>
> "What do you want me to do to him?" replied Bava ben Buta.
>
> He said: "I want you to curse him."
>
> [Bava ben Buta] replied with the verse: "Even in your thoughts you should not curse a king [Ecclesiastes 10:20]."
>
> Herod said to him: "But he is no king."
>
> [Bava] replied: "Even were he only a rich man, [I could not curse him, for] it is written: 'And in your bedroom do not curse the rich' [ibid]; and were he only a prince [I could not curse him], as it is written: 'You shall not curse a prince among your people' [Exodus 22:27]."
>
> Herod replied: "This applies only to one who acts as one of 'your people,' but this man does not act as one of your people."
>
> He said: "I am afraid of [the king]."
>
> "But," said Herod, "there is no one who can go and tell him, since we two are quite alone."
>
> He replied: "For a bird of the sky shall carry the voice, and a winged creature will betray the matter [Ecclesiastes 10:20]."
>
> Herod then said: "I am Herod. Had I known that the rabbis were so cautious, I would not have killed them. Now tell me how I can make amends."
>
> He replied: "Since you have extinguished the light of the world, [i.e., the rabbis], as it is written: 'For the commandment is a light and the Torah a lamp' [Proverbs 6:23], go now and attend to the light of the world [i.e., the Temple, of which] it is written: 'And all the nations will stream to it' [Isaiah 2:2]." (*Bava Batra* 4b)

The Talmudic passage here deals with damages wrought by "visual intrusion" (*heizek re'iya*). Although Herod blinded Bava ben Buta, it transpires that Bava's vision is clearer than Herod's and that, in this particular context, Bava sees the furthest and the deepest, evoking a motif familiar from Rabbi Nachman of Bratslav's story of *The Seven Beggars*. The story seeks to provide an explanation for how the wicked Herod merited the role of restoring the Temple to its former glory. Our concern here is with the character of Bava ben Buta, the remnant of Shammai's academy who becomes the paradigm for those who continued in Hillel's path. The mishna that records Shammai's teaching, "Receive every person with a pleasant countenance," finds expression in all of Bava ben Buta's deeds. He succeeded not only in restoring the Temple to the nation, but also in elevating the Temple to such a level of prestige that it was said that one who had not seen it had never truly seen a majestic building.

Chapter Fifteen

A Contemporary Perspective: The Successors of Hillel the Elder

We have seen how it was decided that the halakha would follow Beit Hillel. But what does this mean? What characterizes the person who follows in Hillel's path?

The two schools are generally characterized in terms of their respective approaches to the halakha. The halakhic world tends to view Hillel's path as being more attuned to the demands of reality and to the imperative of finding within the halakhic framework solutions that bridge the gap between halakha and reality. I will demonstrate this with a quote from Rabbi Ovadia Yosef, in Shevat 5733, four months after his appointment as the Chief Rabbi.[1]

1. This was his response to the attacks against him in the press, which claimed that he was under the control of the ultra-orthodox.

> The Sephardic rabbis belong to Beit Hillel; they lean toward kindness and recoil from strictness. They travel on the well-worn path. The Ashkenazic rabbis, by contrast, take the stringent approach of Beit Shammai. Certain people fear that we are zealots. I wish to dispel the view that I come from the House of Shammai. Quite the opposite: I am from the House of Hillel. If only all of the Ashkenazim were like us.[2]

The prevailing view in the academic world likewise distinguishes between the halakhic creativity of Beit Hillel and the more conservative approach of Beit Shammai.[3] Beit Shammai preserved the ancient halakha while Beit Hillel, responding to the changing circumstances of his time, created a system of halakha with a mechanism for renewal and innovation.

Rabbi Ovadia's characterization of the Ashkenazic tradition as tending toward stringency and rigid interpretation of the law as distinct from kindness and leniency is largely accepted by scholars researching the sociology of the religious world in the modern period. Their studies focus on Orthodoxy as a differentiated stream in Judaism, and on the response of its representatives – the European halakhic authorities – to the changed reality that was the product of the Enlightenment and modernity.[4] Most of the articles written about the halakha in the modern era, deal with the need to take a changing reality into account and criticize the phenomenon of halakhic rigidity.[5]

There is, however, another axis along which Beit Shammai is distinguished from Beit Hillel: the religious-theological dimension.

On the religious-theological axis, Beit Shammai is characterized by its attempt to define precise and separate domains for the holy

2. Published in full in the journal *BaMa'arakha*, Adar Alef, 5733.
3. This point was elaborated on by Y.D. Gilat, in his book *The Teaching of Rabbi Eliezer ben Hyrcanus* (Tel Aviv: 5728).
4. See mainly in the studies of Yaakov Katz, in his book *Halakha in Straits* [Hebrew] (Jerusalem: 1992).
5. Examination of modern-orthodox writings clearly shows that this is a central theme, both in the context of the position of women and regarding the attitude towards secular education. This, however, is not the appropriate forum for elaboration on this issue.

and secular worlds. Beit Hillel, by contrast, seeks to infuse holiness into all aspects of earthly reality. These philosophical differences find practical expression in the halakhic world, but also go well beyond it. The different religious stances leave their imprint on the level of basic personal conduct. Beit Shammai's requirement that the *Shema* be read in a separate ceremony to isolate this act from everyday life is a statement that we live and function in a fundamentally secular world. Any aspiration to holiness is therefore limited to specifically religious daily acts: Prayer, blessings, and Torah study. Beit Hillel, on the other hand, demands that the *Shema* be read when people are in the middle of their daily affairs. Awareness of God is an imperative at all times and in any situation, and there is no real distinction between the realms of the sacred and the profane. Every person may recite the *Shema*, whether at the top of a tree or on a scaffold. In a reality where sanctity and secularity are linked, Hillel enjoys caring for his body, created in God's image. Thus, when Hillel walks to the bathhouse, it is with a sense of commandment and joy. Shammai walks to the bathhouse with a sense of despondency and awareness of his baser self. It follows naturally that all of Hillel's dealings with his body are an attempt to merge the holy and the secular, whereas Shammai's dealings with his body are in order "to fulfill our obligations."

Even though the halakhic world has accepted that "the halakha is in accordance with Beit Hillel," the position of Beit Shammai still plays a dominant role in religious life, regardless of the conflict between Orthodoxy and the demands of modernity. Hillel's doctrine, which strives to merge the holy and the secular in all realms, has proven difficult, if not impossible. This doctrine is thus one of Hillel's "stringencies," in a sense, since it demands a constant awareness of God's presence and the sanctification of everyday life. Paradoxically, the bifurcation of the sacred and the secular actually makes life easier and facilitates the individual's survival in both worlds. "There is a time for everything under the heavens": a time to worship God and a time to attend to bodily needs. The ideal person is the one who succeeds in reducing his bodily needs in order make room for religion in his life. Obviously, this does not mean total withdrawal because a person is duty bound to build a family and to establish his own posterity. Even in this area, though, moderation and limitation are preferred. This can be illustrated through the rabbinic view of one who experienced nocturnal discharge (*ba'al keri*):

> The rabbis taught: a *ba'al keri* who has washed himself in nine *kav* of water is clean.
>
> Naḥum of Gimzo whispered this to Rabbi Akiva, and Rabbi Akiva whispered it to Ben Azzai, and Ben Azzai went and repeated it to the disciples in public.
>
> Two *amora'im* in the West [i.e., the Land of Israel] disputed this matter: Rabbi Yose bar Avin and Rabbi Yose bar Zevida. One stated: "He repeated it." And one taught: "He whispered it." The one who taught "he repeated it" held that the reason [for the concession] was to prevent neglect of the Torah and of procreation. The one who taught "he whispered it" thought that the reason was in order that scholars might not always be with their wives like roosters.
>
> Rabbi Yannai said: I have heard of some who are lenient in this matter, and I have heard of some who are strict; anyone who takes the stringency upon himself, his days and years are prolonged. (*Berakhot* 22a)

According to this *baraita*, a *ba'al keri* is not required to ritually immerse himself, and a shower of nine *kav* of water is sufficient to purify him. This ruling was surreptitiously transmitted from rabbis to students until it came to the ears of Ben Azzai, who taught it to his students in public.

There are those who attempted to hide Ben Azzai's public teaching of this secret by including him in the list of those who whispered it. Yet, the style of this *baraita* does not tolerate this kind of textual "gloss." Replacing the words "he taught" with "he whispered" would not suffice, because the text relates that Ben Azzai "went and repeated it to the disciples in public." The change goes beyond the mere emendation of a single word and involves a complete revision of the *baraita* by someone who had an interest in withholding it from his own students. It would therefore seem that the *baraita* indeed tells us that Ben Azzai taught that a *ba'al keri* may study Torah (and perhaps even pray). Clearly, this halakha is grounded in a stance that regards a *ba'al keri* as being remote from sanctity and the service of God, as being unable to approach God. This outlook, with its Platonic basis, strives to separate the soul – which is man's essence – from his body, which merely covers up the soul. Philo defined the soul as being "buried in the body." In philosophical circles, the body is regarded as an enemy constantly conspiring against the soul. Holiness can only exist through dissociation from the body. Christianity took this approach to its most extreme conclusion, promising spiritual pleasures to one who succeeds in dissociating from the body.

This is the basis of the rabbinic understanding of the *ba'al keri*. The aforementioned passage in Tractate *Berakhot* begins with Rabbi Yehoshua ben Levi deriving the prohibition of a *ba'al keri* studying Torah, from the biblical description of the revelation at Sinai. Later, however, Rabbi Yehuda ben Beteira rules that the words of Torah cannot become impure, and the acceptance of this tradition concludes the discussion of the topic.

Nonetheless, it seems that this tradition was itself a source of profound dispute, and the viewpoint that allowed religious life to be compatible with seminal impurity could only be perpetuated clandestinely. Ben Azzai, however, was unwilling to be party to this secrecy, and he therefore made it public.

This is but one of many examples. Almost every aspect of our religious life demands that we struggle with the balance between the holy and the secular. Moreover, we must constantly define our relationship to the secular world and integrate it into a more comprehensive worldview. Many rabbis have preferred the worldview of Beit Shammai and bifurcated the religious and secular worlds. On the other hand, there have always been religious leaders who have attempted to apply the philosophy of Beit Hillel in the religious and halakhic spheres.

The conflict between rationalism and a life of religious intensity preoccupied Rabbi Kook. Consider, for example, the following paragraph from one of his letters:

> One must carefully distinguish between a holistic perspective, which succeeds in penetrating the roots of every opinion,

> enabling it to appreciate every opinion for its intrinsic worth, and the cold tolerance resulting from the difficulty of integrating the spiritual world into life. The latter must retreat in its confrontation with the light and energy of life. (*Letters of Rav Kook*, Jerusalem, 5745, 79)

Rabbi Kook wrote this at the beginning of the twentieth century, when there was still no religious educational network. Religious Judaism still tended to fortify itself within the yeshiva framework (in all its various forms), which focused on Torah study to the exclusion of all else; the Alliance Israelite Universelle was just starting to provide liberal Jewish education in *Eretz Yisrael*. It was only years later, with the *aliya* of German Jews educated in the spirit of "*Torah im Derekh Eretz*" and the tradition of Rabbi Samson Raphael Hirsh or other rabbinical seminaries, that the *Mizraḥi* educational system, which integrated Torah and secular studies, began to take shape. Outstanding religious academics profoundly influenced the educational system and were involved in the development of educational curricula. These frameworks dominated the religious world until the ascent of the yeshiva high schools and the dominance of their influence. The fervor of the yeshiva high schools, with their spiritual challenges and intensity, conquered *Torah im Derekh Eretz* – the cold academic spirit of German Jewry.[6] This, however, was a double-edged sword: the Yeshiva movement did not merely stoke the warm fire of Torah; it also created a mode of religious excellence that held secular, material life in contempt. The distinction between "people immersed in holiness" and "people immersed in the secular world," which was deeply rooted in the ethos of the traditional yeshiva educational system, was transferred to the world of religious Zionism.

Beit Hillel had once posed a challenge, demanding the integration of sanctity into everyday life, but the challenge wore thin. One of the tasks confronting religious Zionism today is to return Hillel's impera-

6. See Rabbi Yehuda Brandes' book review of Prof. M. Arend, *Jewish Education in an Open Society* [Hebrew] (Ramat Gan:5760), in "Whence will Come Passion," *Akdamot* 12 (Tishrei, 5760), pp. 191–197.

tive to the center of the religious educational systems and communities, and thereby to raise a generation of students of Beit Hillel, who walk before God as they fully participate in this world, and who accept the heavenly yoke in all their endeavors.

Part Four

When Disputes Proliferated in Israel

The Men of the Great Assembly	The Pairs	Shammai, Hillel and Their Students	Rabban Gamliel the Elder	The Destruction
Cyrus to Alexander of Macedonia	The Hasmoneans	Herod	The Governors	The War with Rome

-450	-300	-200	-50	30	60	70

Preface

Having completed our discussion of Shammai and Hillel and the reign of King Herod in the previous part, consistency would dictate continuing the discussion of the spiritual leaders during the first years of the Common Era. But precisely here, we encounter an awkward absence of any information regarding the Jewish leadership. Tradition mentions four patriarchs who were active during the Second Temple: Hillel, Shimon ben Hillel, Gamliel, and Shimon ben Gamliel (*Shabbat* 15a).

The first patriarch, Hillel, was discussed at length in the previous part. The latter two – Rabban Gamliel the Elder and Rabban Shimon ben Gamliel – were active during the second half of the first century CE. The Talmudic literature on both of them is extensive, and they will figure prominently in our discussion of the Destruction of the Temple. But what of the second patriarch, Shimon, the father of Rabban Gamliel the Elder and the son and successor of Hillel (according to Rashi, ad loc.)? Here, the sources are virtually silent. In fact, the entire period following Hillel is anonymously labeled as the era of "the students of Shammai and Hillel," apparently due to the absence of any prominent leader of the community. The Tosefta relates that this was the time when disputes began to proliferate:

> When there was an increase in students of Shammai and Hillel who did not properly apprentice their teachers, the disputes in Israel multiplied, and two Torahs emerged. (Tosefta, *Ḥagiga* 2:9)

Rabbi Sherira Gaon provides us with following background and reasons for the phenomenon of "the students who did not properly apprentice their teachers":

> Due to the upheavals, and persecutions, and disturbances that prevailed at that time, the students were unable to properly serve their teachers and there was a proliferation of disputes. (*Epistle of Rabbi Sherira Gaon*, p. 10)

Rashi concurred with this explanation:

> There were numerous students of Shammai and Hillel during the three generations that preceded [Rabbi Yehuda HaNasi], and there was a proliferation of disputes and the Torah became as two Torahs as a result of the subjugation to the nations and the decrees enacted against them, so that they were unable to clarify the views of the disputants. (Rashi, *Bava Metzia* 33b)[1]

1. As is well known, Maimonides preferred to explain the Tosefta from an academic, analytical perspective, as opposed to a historic perspective, and he writes the following in his "Introduction to the Mishna" (emphasis is mine):

> Their statement that "when there was a proliferation of students of Shammai and Hillel who had not adequately served their rabbis, disputes proliferated," is explained as follows: Where two people are of equal intellect, study, and knowledge of the principles and their reasons, they will have no arguments, and should there be disputes they will be in the minority of cases, just as there were no disputes between Hillel and Shammai except in relation to isolated halakhot. This is because their positions were almost identical in all matters that were based on reasons and principles, and they both based themselves on the same principles. **However, when the students became less diligent** in

The following focuses primarily on the streams and sects that comprised Jewish society during this period and less on the characters of the sages, who, as mentioned, are largely anonymous. In a fragmented Jewish society, the central problem was the leadership vacuum, resulting in a national agenda that was determined by all manner of marginal groups. The lessons of this period are almost self-evident from the descriptions of the groups themselves: men of religion cloistered up in the Temple; ideological extremists collaborating with criminal elements; and sages who failed to respond.

their acquisition of wisdom, their powers of reason weakened in comparison to those of Shammai and Hillel and they began to dispute many matters, for each one of them gave reasons in accordance with his level of intellect and whatever he had received from among the principles.

Chapter Sixteen

An Idol in the Temple

HISTORICAL AND POLITICAL BACKGROUND

The post-Herodian period (4 BCE–6 CE) was a turbulent period of Jewish revolts and Roman attempts at repression, and is known as the period of the War of Varus, after the Syrian governor Publius Quinctilius Varus, who ruthlessly ensured Judea's continued subjugation to Rome.

Herod's son, Archelaus, reigned over Judea and succeeded in raising the ire of the Jews, the Samaritans, and ultimately even the Romans, who exiled him to Gaul. It was in in this period that the land of Israel became just another one of Rome's provinces, headed by governors appointed by the emperor directly and whose term in office was dependent upon a number of factors. The first governor was Coponius, who promoted a more conciliatory policy toward the Jews, and who merited having one of the gates of the Temple Mount named after him (*Middot* 1:3). The ensuing years witnessed the coming and going of many governors, the most famous of whom was Pontius Pilate, who ruled from 26–36 CE. His reign, following two relatively peaceful decades, ushered in a bloody and violent period that ended when he was finally deposed by his superior, Vitalius, the governor of Syria. The latter assumed control of the political and religious powers (including the appointment of the high priest), and, in his efforts to establish Roman religious-political hegemony, attempted to force the Jewish people to swear loyalty to Emperor Gaius Caligula.[1]

CALIGULA AND THE STOPPING OF THE IDOL ON ITS WAY TO THE TEMPLE

Emperor Gaius Caligula ushered in a reign of terror, ultimately deciding to renew the ritual worship of the emperor, a form of state religion practiced by the first emperors, but discontinued by his predecessor, Tiberius.[2] The background of this drastic measure was an attempt by Caligula's subjects to set up his statue in the center of the city of Yavneh. The Jews of Yavneh responded by furiously smashing it to pieces, viewing its placement as blatant idol worship. Perceiving a challenge to Roman hegemony, Caligula retaliated by declaring his intention to set up an idol in the Temple.

In reality, the Jews' shattering of the idol was typical of fervently religious Jews who yearned to expunge any trace of paganism from the Holy Land; it was not intended as a challenge to the Roman Empire. For the emperor, however, any religious challenge to the political agenda of the State was unacceptable. As such, the desecration of the Jewish holy sites was not Caligula's original intention, for he strove to promote religious pluralism, whereby each religious group, including the Jews, was free to worship its own god in accordance in its own rite – the only demand being that each group also accept the divinity of the Roman emperor. The Jews of Yavneh had violated a foundational principle of the empire and purportedly attempted to subject the Roman state to the authority of their own religion. Caligula therefore responded in kind, commanding that the bust of a Roman god, the emperor himself, be erected in the Temple courtyard.[3] Petronius, the Syrian prefect,

1. For a complete description of the rule of governors in Judea, see M. Stern, "The Status of the Province of Judea and Its Governors" [Hebrew], *Eretz Yisrael* 10, (5731/1971) pp. 282–274.
2. Regarding this ritual see Y. Geiger, "Emperor Worship as the Ideology of the Roman Empire" [Hebrew], *Priesthood and Monarchy – Studies in the Historical Relationship of Religion and State*, eds. I. Gafni, G. Motzkin (Jerusalem: 1987), pp. 51–60.
3. This was the explanation given by D. Schwartz, *Agrippa I: The Last King of Judea* [Hebrew] (Jerusalem: Zalman Shazar Center, 1987), pp. 93–94.

was ordered to carry out the emperor's behest, and in the summer of 40 CE, began planning its execution. He was accompanied to Judea by two legions, in order to preempt any chance that the expected uprising would succeed. It is clear that both Caligula and Petronius knew that this measure was a drastic one, and that their decision to carry it out was, in fact, a declaration of war against the Jews and Judaism.

The Jewish people, despite their divisions and differences, reacted vigorously in one of those rare moments of grace in which national unity, courage, and willingness to die sanctifying God's name peaked. Both Philo[4] and Josephus (in *Antiquities* and *The Jewish War*) provide wonderful descriptions of the event. Philo relates how he received the news of the emperor's decree while staying in Rome as a member of a delegation of Alexandrian Jews who came to Rome to complain about the deterioration in the treatment of the Jews:

> While we were anxiously considering the statement of our case, since we were expecting to be summoned [to Gaius] at any moment, a man came to us with a panicky look in his bloodshot eyes and gasping convulsively. He drew us aside, since there were other people standing near, and said, "Have you heard the tidings?" And, just as he was about to tell us, he stopped, as a flood of tears burst forth from his eyes. He began again and for the second time stopped short and so, too, a third time. Observing all of this we were aghast and we bade him to tell us the matter which he said had brought him there. "For," we said, "you have not come just to have your weeping witnessed. If the facts are worth tears do not be the only one to feel sorrow. We have become inured to misfortunes by now." He managed with difficulty while sobbing and breathing spasmodically to say, "Our temple is lost; Gaius has ordered a colossal statue to be set up in the inner sanctuary dedicated to himself in the name of Zeus." As we were astonished at his words and petrified by consternation, we froze in our steps, standing there speechless and powerless in a state of collapse as

4. Philo the Alexandrian, *On the Embassy to Gaius*, from *Philo*, trans. F.H. Colson (Cambridge/London: Loeb Classical Library, 1943).

> our hearts turned to water, and others appeared too, bearing the same woeful tale. Then we all gathered together in seclusion and bewailed the tragedy that was personal for each and common to all of us, and each of us poured his heart out being so shaken by the news, for no person is so ready to talk as the man in misfortune…

Later, Philo relates what happened when Petronius came to Tiberias with his armies, on his way to Jerusalem:

> Some of Petronius' people, seeing a vast crowd moving closer, thought that war had broken out and immediately ran to inform him so that he would place people on guard. They had not finished their story and Petronius still remained unguarded, when the multitude of the Jews suddenly descended like a cloud and occupied the whole of Phoenicia, causing panic among all those who did not know [until then] how populous our nation was. The first thing to be observed was the great shouting which arose mingled with weeping and smiting of breasts, so great that it was more than the ears of those present could contain. For even when they stopped shouting there was no pause in the sound, which continued to echo even amid their silence…
>
> They were divided into six groups: old men, young men, and boys on the one side, and old women, maidens, and girls on the other side. When Petronius first appeared in the distance, all the companies, as though in response to a command, fell before him to the ground uttering a dirge-like wail and bitter tears of supplication…
>
> "We have not come to fight, for who is it that will oppose the more powerful nation, the emperor himself? Yet, there are only two possibilities: either refrain from placing the idol in the sanctuary, or destroy the entire nation in Judea, to the very last one. And if you have decided to install an idol in the sanctuary, first kill all of us and then do what your heart bids. For as long as we have even one remaining breath we cannot permit this violation of our Torah. We are not so mad as to raise our hands

> against our master who is stronger than us. We gladly place our throats at your disposal. Let them slaughter, butcher, carve our flesh. Indeed, what need have you of soldiers? We, the priests, whose hands have been charged with making these sacrifices of justice, first we will bring our wives to our holy altars and will become wife slayers, and then our brothers and sisters, and we will become fratricides, and then our boys and girls and we will become child-murderers. And then we will mingle our own blood with the blood of our relatives that we spilt. Then, when not one of us is left, you can fulfill Gaius' decree." (*On the Embassy to Gaius*, 230–238)

This was a spontaneous outburst of civil disobedience, and there is no evidence to suggest that it was orchestrated from above. According to Joseph Klausner, "There were people conducting an energetic propaganda campaign in the cities and villages of the land of Israel, extending from the end of the winter to the beginning of the harvest, attempting to inspire and galvanize the people into preventing Petronius from carrying out Gaius' edict at any cost!"[5] Under the circumstances, a civil rebellion was the most effective tool, and, presumably, had Petronius not backed down, the movement would have turned into an open, military rebellion. However, even though the willingness of the people to sacrifice themselves to prevent the placement of the idol in the Temple foreshadows the events at Masada, it is clear that they had no intention of committing suicide out of despair.

In any event, it is significant, and nothing short of amazing, that the entire nation – Pharisees, Sadducees, Essenes, and sympathizers with Hellenism – participated in the protest and all rose up in unified opposition to the decree. The unification of the people was even greater than it had been in the times of Antiochus, when there were Hellenists and those who practiced epispasm, who could not be relied upon at the decisive moment.

Petronius understood the futility of battle against this determined

5. J. Klausner, *The Second Temple Period* [Hebrew] (Jerusalem: 5714/1954), p. 59. Also published in A. Kasher (ed.), *The Great Revolt* (Jerusalem: 5743/1983).

and unified opposition, and wrote to the emperor informing him of the reason for the decree's delay in fulfillment. Josephus relates that this did not dissuade Caligula from enforcing his order or even threatening Petronius with execution if he was lax in carrying it out. A letter to this effect was sent, and the insurrection in Judea would have been triggered anew had it not been for a miracle, as recorded by Josephus:

> However, it so happened that the bearers of this message [from the emperor] were weather-bound for three months at sea, while others, who brought news of the death of Gaius, had a fortunate passage. Thus, Petronius received this message twenty-seven days earlier than the emperor's ultimatum. (*The Jewish War*, II.10:5)

Gaius Caligula was murdered on his way to the theatre by a revolutionary student in an underground tunnel, on January 24th, 41 CE (he was then aged twenty-eight). The edict to place the idol in the Temple was annulled, and the rebellion subsided. This is one of the most glorious stories in the annals of Jewish history to merit historical verification by all historians of the period. There can be no doubt that the impact of the event engraved itself deeply in Jewish consciousness during the days of the Great Revolt in the following generation, at Masada, and finally during the period of Bar Kokhba.

Surprisingly, memory of these events faded and even disappeared from national memory. How many people remember the wonderful uprising that united all factions of the nation into a cohesive, resilient, and tenacious body? What now remains of that amazing story?

Examination of the Jewish sources shows that the period of Caligula is almost entirely omitted, along with his failed attempt to install an idol in the Temple. There are, however, a handful of allusions in rabbinic narratives about King Agrippa, and in *Megillat Ta'anit*. In what follows, I will attempt to collate these allusions, using them to shed light on this intermediate period, the eve of the Destruction. As mentioned earlier, during this time, there was a dearth of charismatic spiritual leadership; thus, it was also a time in which the seeds of zealotry began to strike root.

KING AGRIPPA AGAINST THE BACKGROUND OF CALIGULA'S REIGN

Agrippa I (10 BCE–44 CE) was the son of Aristobulus IV and Berenice, and grandson of King Herod and Queen Miriam the Hasmonean. Agrippa's maternal grandfather was Costobarus, and his maternal grandmother was Salome I, Herod's sister (his parents were thus first cousins). Agrippa spent his childhood and youth in Rome under his mother's watchful tutelage. She preferred emigration to Rome over living in Judea amongst her husband's heirs. Agrippa grew up in the emperor's court, initially behaving as a licentious, frivolous prince. At a certain stage, however, he assumed certain administrative roles in the area, which he fulfilled until the death of Emperor Tiberias (37 CE). With the ascent of his close friend Gaius Caligula to the imperial throne, Agrippa's star began to rise. He was crowned ruler of the entire area of northern Israel. This coincided with the period in which Caligula attempted to install the idol in the Temple, and Agrippa attempted to persuade his close friend Caligula to annul the order. Their friendship remained intact despite Caligula's disregard of Agrippa's advice. In the interim, Caligula died and was replaced by Claudius.

In the year 41, Agrippa became the king over the whole of Judea, Samaria and Idumea (Edom), and effectively became the king of the Jews on behalf of the Roman rulers. This was just after the Caligula episode was brought to an end. In this context, the following mishna in Tractate *Bikkurim* has been viewed by some as reflecting the general sense of tension that took hold of the Jewish people upon the resolution of a struggle during which they were prepared to forfeit life itself in the sanctification of God's name.

> The flute was played before them until they reached the Temple Mount. When they reached the Temple Mount, even King Agrippa would take his basket on his shoulder and enter as far as the Temple Court. When they reached the Temple Court, the Levites sang the song: "I will exalt You, O Lord, for You have raised me up and prevented my enemies from rejoicing over me [Psalms 30:2]." (Mishna, *Bikkurim* 3:4)

The contents of the psalm cited in the Mishna are appropriate for the atmosphere of a period during which "weeping may tarry for the night, but joy comes in the morning" (Psalms 30:6). The reign of Caligula was a night – during which there was crying – and the subsequent reign of Agrippa was the morning, when happiness burst forth.[6] There was a release of accumulated tension during which the nation was intimately and intensely aware of the thin line dividing life from death.

The sages' attitude toward Agrippa is complex, and the present framework only allows us to scratch the surface. The Mishna attests to a *Hak-hel* ceremony (a ceremony that took place at the Temple during the Sukkot holiday following each *Shemitta* year, and in which the king would publicly read large sections of the Torah) in which Agrippa was sitting and publicly reading the Torah:

> How did they read the king's chapter? At the conclusion of the first day of the festival of Sukkot, at the conclusion of the seventh year, they would erect a wooden platform in the Temple Court and the king would sit thereon, as it says: "At the end of seven years, at the appointed time" [Deuteronomy 31:11]. The attendant of the assemblage would take the Torah scroll and hand it to the head of the assemblage, who would hand it to the deputy high priest, who would hand it to the high priest, who would hand it to the king, who would stand up to receive it and then sit down and read it. King Agrippa stood and received it, and then read it while standing, and the sages praised him. When he came to the verse, "You shall not place a foreigner over you" [Deuteronomy 17:15], his eyes filled with tears. They appeased him saying: "Fear not Agrippa, you are our brother; you are our brother." (Mishna, *Sota* 7:8)

The Mishna stresses the nation's love and sympathy toward Agrippa, who

6. This suggestion is made by Graetz, but rejected by D. Schwartz (in *King Agrippa*, p. 177), as being "pure conjecture" with little to rely on. However, Schwartz also mentions Albeck's observation that "this theory need not be rejected" (ibid., n. 71), and I see value in an interesting speculation.

notwithstanding his being a "foreigner," still won them over. Scholarly literature has discussed the issue of his lineage in depth, and I will present the main conclusions here.[7] Both of his mother's parents and his grandfather were of Idumean descent. His Jewish descent was exclusively by virtue of his father's mother, Miriam the Hasmonean. Agrippa's tears, along with the sages' words of comfort, may attest to the dispute over the validity of his conversion. However, it is more likely that it reflects the demand for the king to be of impeccable lineage, as mandated by the accepted exegesis of the verse in Deuteronomy:

> "From one of your own people shall you appoint a king" – any person appointed over you shall only be from the pedigreed of your people. "You shall not set a foreigner over you" – this excludes a convert. (*Midrash Tanna'im* to Deuteronomy 17:15)

The proclamation of "you are our brother" is the nation's attempt to allay Agrippa's fears and to include him among those who are halakhically eligible for the Jewish monarchy. At a later stage, however, this position was castigated as being contemptibly obsequious:

> It was taught in the name of Rabbi Natan: At that moment, the despicable ones of Israel were condemned to destruction for having flattered Agrippa. (*Sota* 41b)

Notably, rabbinic leaders do not feature in any of the sources dealing with Agrippa. He may have been popular and received the people's sympathy and even excessive flattery, but he was not a real leader.

THE TESTIMONY OF MEGILLAT TA'ANIT

Preserving the spirit of the Revolt

A second source that explicitly refers to the events of this period is *Megillat Ta'anit*, the earliest rabbinic document. The main purpose of this scroll was to record all the festive dates that had been established by the Jewish people at that time, primarily in the context of the Hasmonean

7. According to Schwartz, ibid., Appendix 11, pp. 228–231.

Dynasty. The scroll contains thirty-five dates, set out according to the calendar (from Nisan to Adar), on which it was prohibited to fast, and on some of them even to eulogize.[8] Regarding the 22nd day of Shevat, it states:

> On the twenty-second of it, the [pagan] abomination [*avidata*] that the hated one wished to bring to the Temple was annulled – it is forbidden to eulogize.[9]

This is elaborated in the scholia (an additional commentary to the ancient Scroll, appended to each entry therein some time during the tannaitic era, after the Destruction):

> Caligula sent a statue to be erected in the Temple, and the tidings reached Jerusalem on the eve of Sukkot. Simeon the Just said to them: "Rejoice on your festival. There is no substance in anything that you have heard; He who caused His honor to be present in this House just as He wrought miracles for our forefathers in every generation, so will He wreak miracles for us in these times." When he saw that they were drawing nearer, he said: "Go out and greet them." Emissaries went out and they greeted them: one emissary to Acre, and the second to Tyre, the third to Sidon, and the fourth to Keziv. When the matter became known, all of the dignitaries of Jerusalem came out to him, and they said: "We will die and not let such a thing be." They cried and pleaded with the emissary. The emissary said to them: "Before you all shout and plead with me, you should shout and plead to your God in heaven." When he arrived at each village, he saw people from every village coming out to meet him. When he saw them, he

8. See introduction of Vered Noam, *The Fast Scroll* [Hebrew] (Jerusalem: 2004).
9. See Lieberman, *Tosefta KiFeshuta*, on Tractate *Sota*, p. 740, who interprets the word *avidata* (ritual) as "an abomination," and hence its annulment as referring to a halakhic act of annulment; in this case, dragging it on the ground as a form of degradation and thus permitting it (Mishna, *Avoda Zara* 4:6; also Tosafot on *Avoda Zara* 53a, s.v. "*aval*").

> was astonished and said: "Are they so numerous?" They informed him: "These are the Jews who go out and meet you as you arrive in each village." He entered the village and he saw people lying in the market in sackcloth and ash. Before he arrived at Antipatris he received the tidings that Caligula had died. He immediately removed the statues and delivered them to the Jews, and they dragged them away. Simeon heard a voice issuing from the Holy of Holies: "the abomination which the enemy ordered to bring to the Temple is revoked. Caligula has been killed and his edicts are revoked." They named that day as a festival.

In addition to *Megillat Ta'anit*, this date also appears in the Tosefta (*Sota* 13:6) and in the Babylonian Talmud (*Sota* 33a). The similarity between the rabbinic sources and the external sources is striking.[10] Rabbinic tradition tells us of Simeon, who heard a voice issuing forth from the Holy of Holies in Aramaic. The scroll's tradition relies on the original traditions with which the sages were likewise familiar (as stated in the Talmud: "It was taught in Aramaic"), and in the words of Vered Noam: "The commentary on the date under discussion preserves a dramatically authentic example of this phenomenon [i.e., the scroll's reliance on external sources]. Jews were ready to die in the sanctification of God's name in order to foil the idolatrous edict. This readiness, which is also stressed in the external testimony about the event, is conveyed in precisely the same lingual format in the scholia."[11]

Who wrote *Megillat Ta'anit*?

Rabbinic tradition ascribes the writing (or redaction) of *Megillat Ta'anit* to Ḥanania ben Ḥizkia ben HaGaron:

10. See in the study of Vered Noam, "Commentary on the Dates," in *Megillat Ta'anit*, pp. 283–290, 386–391. She demonstrates that some of the versions of this date were "supplemented" with details ascribed to another date, including the issue of dragging: "This was not anchored in historical reality, being rather a literary device of an early compiler" (thus rejecting Lieberman's suggestions in footnote 9 above).
11. V. Noam, ibid., p. 284.

> Our rabbis taught: Who wrote Megillat Ta'anit? They answered: Ḥanania ben Ḥizkia and his companions, who cherished troubles. Rabban Shimon ben Gamliel observed: We too cherish troubles, but what can we do? For if we began to write [them down], we would never finish. (*Shabbat* 13b)

The Talmud cites this *baraita* in relation to the Mishnaic reference to Ḥanania ben Ḥizkia:

> These are amongst the halakhot which they stated in the attic of Ḥanania ben Ḥizkia ben HaGaron; when they went up to visit him, they took a count, and Beit Shammai outnumbered Beit Hillel. On that day, they enacted eighteen matters. (Mishna, *Shabbat* 1:4)

Further on in that passage we read:

> Rabbi Yehuda said: This man should be fondly remembered and his name was Ḥanania ben Ḥizkia. For if not for him, the book of Ezekiel would have been hidden away, for it contradicts the Torah itself. What did he do? Three hundred barrels of oil were taken up to him, and he sat in an attic and reconciled them. (*Shabbat* 13b; *Ḥagiga* 13a)

The sources present us with a portrait of a disciple of Shammai, in whose attic it was decided that the halakha would be in accordance with Shammai. He bears the credit for upholding the canonicity of the book of Ezekiel, and because he was one of those who "cherished troubles," *Megillat Ta'anit* remains extant today.

The *baraita* of "Eighteen Matters"

The scholarly literature surrounding the eighteen matters disputed between Shammai and Hillel is prolific, and a number of theories have been offered. Some have discerned the traces of a struggle between a "peace faction" and a "war faction" on the eve of the revolt, and there is no doubt that it reflects a halakhic attempt to establish barriers between

Jews and non-Jews.[12] The Talmud presents several versions of the list of eighteen disputes between Beit Shammai and Beit Hillel regarding which the law accords with Beit Shammai, and the *Rishonim*, too, debated the question extensively. The core passage appears in Tractate *Shabbat* (13b–17b), but the Talmudic discussion does not help us take the pulse of the history of the period. Y. Ben Shalom devoted extensive attention to the sources of the "eighteen matters" *baraita*, and concluded that its main thrust was the attempt to anchor Shammai's policy at the beginning of the Great Revolt, stressing the rigid distinction between Jews and non-Jews.[13]

Elazar ben Ḥanania ben Ḥizkia

There are other sources in which the traditions relating to the father, Ḥanania ben Ḥizkia, are replaced by traditions referring to his son, Elazar ben Ḥanania. For example, there is a halakhic midrash that recounts a homily of the son that manages to "solve" a difficult question posed by the book of Ezekiel:

> Elazar ben Ḥanania ben Ḥizkia ben HaGaron says: Scripture says, "An ephah for each bull, an ephah for each ram, and an ephah for the lamb" [Ezekiel 46:11]. Is the same amount designated for bulls, rams, and lambs? Does it not state elsewhere: "Three tenths for each bull, two tenths for each ram, and one tenth for each lamb" [Numbers 29:3–4]? Rather, this teaches you that both the large ephah and the small ephah are called "ephah." (*Sifrei Devarim* 294)

Similarly, regarding the authorship of *Megillat Ta'anit*, there are traditions[14] that ascribe its redaction to Elazar ben Ḥanania, instead of to

12. This view was taken by Graetz, see *History of the Jews*, vol. 2, p. 269–272.
13. Ben Shalom, *Beit Shammai and the Zealots' Struggle Against Rome* [Hebrew] (Jerusalem: 1994), ch. 7, pp. 252–272: "They Decreed Eighteen Matters on That Day." After discussing the entire subject, Ben Shalom concludes that "the passage in the Babylonian Talmud does not help us reconstruct the historical events that led to the enactment of eighteen matters."
14. See V. Noam, ibid., p. 334.

Ḥanania himself. Another tradition replaces the words of Elazar ben Ḥanania with those of Shammai the Elder himself.

> Elazar ben Ḥanania ben Ḥizkia ben Garon says: "Remember the day of the Sabbath to keep it holy" [Exodus 20:7]: Keep it in mind from the first day of the week, so that if something good happens to come your way, set it aside for the Sabbath. (*Mekhilta deRabbi Yishmael, Yitro* 7, p. 253; also Tractate *Beitza* 16a in the name of Shammai the Elder; *Mekhilta deRashbi*, p. 148)

What is clear is that the Garon (or Gurion) family was connected to Beit Shammai, and that, throughout that century, there was a tradition passed from Shammai to Ḥanania, to Elazar. Another passage tells about Elazar ben Ḥanania during Temple times:

> When a person has lost an object, they say to him: "May He who dwells in this house put it into the finder's heart to immediately return it to you." It once happened that Elazar ben Ḥanania ben Garon lost a Torah scroll that he had purchased for one hundred maneh, and he went up to the Temple Mount, went round it, and did not move from there until they came and told him, "The scroll of the Torah has been found." (*Semaḥot* 6:11)

Some historians have identified Elazar ben Ḥanania as one of the leaders of the Great Revolt who, upon the outbreak of the revolt, discontinued the offering of a sacrifice for the welfare of the emperor. According to this view, the writing of *Megillat Ta'anit* was an attempt to enlist the Hasmonean spirit of rebellion and the cherished memory of glorious events as a source of inspiration in the war against the Romans, a war in which Beit Shammai and his students, including Elazar ben Ḥanania and his father (to whom *Megillat Ta'anit* is attributed), belonged to the war camp.[15] The events recounted in *Megillat Ta'anit* provide a wealth of information about the Hasmonean days of glory: 25 Kislev – Dedication of the Temple (*Ḥanukka*); 13 Adar – the day of Nicanor; 28 Shevat –

15. On this theory, its supporters and opponents, see V. Noam, p. 335, nn. 21–22.

Antiochus' departure from Jerusalem; 24 Iyar – the conquering of the Ḥakra fortress in Jerusalem, and others. The exile of the Jewish people from their land, however, consigned *Megillat Ta'anit* to the dustbin of history, with Ḥanukka the only holiday that has been preserved from that era. The impetus for writing a detailed history of the Hasmoneans gave expression to the tension between the two principal rival parties in Jerusalem at that time: the party of rebellion, intent upon reigniting the holy fire of the Hasmoneans, and in doing so, rebelling against the Romans; and the conciliatory party, that was attempting to adapt to life under Roman rule. The revolutionary party originated in the school of Shammai which, in time, would become the breeding ground of the leaders of the Great Revolt. As mentioned, one of those leaders was Elazar ben Ḥanania ben Garon, the possible author or co-author of *Megillat Ta'anit*.

Against this background, we can return to our point of departure: the students of Shammai and Hillel who failed to apprentice under their teachers. These were the days of "the upheavals, and persecutions, and disturbances" in which there was no significant spiritual authority, days of doubt in which they attempted to prevent the Torah from being divided into a number of Torahs. With this in mind, we now proceed to our discussion of Rabban Gamliel the Elder.

Chapter Seventeen

Rabban Gamliel the Elder: Providing Stability for a Life of Torah

Rabban Gamliel would say: Acquire a teacher for yourself; remove yourself from doubt; and do not accustom yourself to tithe by estimation. (Avot 1:16)

This brings us to the final decades that preceded the destruction of the Second Temple, the years of Rabban Gamliel the Elder, Hillel's grandson. A study of his life's work and his teachings paints a portrait of life in a sovereign Jewish state. This was a life unfettered by external problems of security and foreign relations, and internal problems like "the students of Hillel and Shammai killing each other," or Roman soldiers who ruthlessly undermined normal economic life and a functioning tax regime. Rabban Gamliel's legacy is an impressive list of legislative initiatives and achievements, and the overall picture emerging from tannaitic sources is of a leader accepted by all sectors of the nation and whose rulings permeated every aspect of life. A full appreciation of the magnitude of his responsibility is only possible when it is viewed against the historical backdrop of the period, which we addressed earlier. Working within the framework of the Jewish leadership, with no apparent political intervention, he formulated a canon of daily practice that has survived throughout the nation's history, until this very day. The image that develops from the relevant sources is that of a leader involved in every aspect of life, who takes full responsibility for everything in his capability.

THE CHAMBER OF HEWN STONE

The Sanhedrin was the most important institution of this time, and has been extensively addressed in writing from a variety of perspectives.[1] Traditional scholarship identifies the Sanhedrin with the *Beit Din HaGadol*, the Torah's supreme court, which convened in the Chamber of Hewn Stone (*Lishkat HaGazit*), located in the Temple precincts, adjacent to the altar (see Mishna, *Middot* 5:4). The sources depict Rabban Gamliel as a sage who both utilized the service provided by the *Beit Din HaGadol* and also functioned there in his rabbinic capacity:

> It once happened that Rabbi Shimon of Mitzpa sowed in the presence of Rabban Gamliel and they both went to inquire at the Chamber of Hewn Stone. Naḥum the Scribe answered: "I received [a tradition] from Rabbi Meyasha, who received it from his father, who received it from the Pairs, who received from the Prophets – a law given to Moses at Sinai – regarding one person who sows his field with two types of wheat. If he threshed them on a single floor, he leaves one *pe'ah* [i.e., one corner of the field unharvested for the poor]; two threshing floors – he gives two *pe'ot*." (Mishna, *Pe'ah* 2:6)

A basic halakhic question was thus presented in the chamber, and the

1. A partial bibliography appears in E.E. Urbach's article, "Class Status and Leadership in the World of the Sages of Israel" [Hebrew], *Proceedings of the Israeli Academy of Sciences and Humanities* (1968), p. 38, nn. 28–31.

question's impersonal nature enables us to assess the manner in which halakha was transmitted in that period.

A person sowing two kinds of wheat in his field, harvesting each one separately – is he liable for one *pe'ah* or two? This is a classical question for a tax consultant, given that setting aside *pe'ah* is a tax imposed on every farmer. The Mishna describes the process by which the query was clarified. Rabban Gamliel accompanied the questioner, Rabbi Shimon of Mitzpa, to the *Beit Din*. Rabbi Shimon is one of the sages of that period, appearing in other sources (*Yoma* 14b) as the teacher and redactor of the mishnayot of *Tamid*, a tractate distinguished by the fact that it was not edited by Rabbi Yehuda HaNasi. The halakhot of *Tamid* are all transmitted anonymously, no mention being made of those who taught them or their disputants.[2] According to the Tosefta of Tractate *Yoma* (1:13), Rabbi Shimon was also responsible for instituting the lottery that determined the schedules of the priests for serving in the Temple during festivals.

The Mishna in Tractate *Pe'ah* relates that Rabbi Shimon arrived at the *Beit Din* together with Rabban Gamliel. There, the judges of the Chamber of Hewn Stone gave Rabbi Shimon an answer that drew its authority from the transmission of halakha that was traced to Moses at Mount Sinai. The Mishna emphasizes this continuous transmission of halakha and its roots in the legacy of the prophets, making it the mirror image of the first mishna in *Avot*, which begins at Sinai and concludes with the sages. The tradition is attributed to the father of Naḥum the Scribe, whereas Rabban Gamliel has no family tradition on this issue. The mishna thus contrasts two models of authority: Rabban Gamliel the Elder represents the sage who studies and innovates in Torah in accordance with the rules for its interpretation, though he is unable to formulate an answer in this case. Naḥum the Scribe, on the other hand, finds his answer in a tradition transmitted to him from Sinai, via the prophets. When tradition derives its authority from Moses at Sinai,

2. See in the study of L. Ginzberg on Tractate *Tamid*, in his book, *Halakha and Aggada* [Hebrew] (Tel Aviv: 1960), pp. 41–65. As to his claim that reference is made to the second Rabban Gamliel, see the refutation of Y.N. Epstein, *Introduction to Tannaitic Literature* (Jerusalem: 1957), p. 31.

Rabban Gamliel does not function in his authoritative capacity, and is no greater than the other wise men of the generation in this regard. Furthermore, as indicated in the following question that was asked of Rabban Gamliel, it is apparent that he lacked the halakhic tradition that Naḥum the Scribe had, being the grandson of Hillel, who stressed innovation at the expense of tradition. In our comments above, we mentioned the transmission of Torah that preceded the proliferation of dispute, and this example provides a good demonstration thereof.[3]

In a mishna in Tractate *Orla*, Rabban Gamliel is asked a question by one of the students of Beit Shammai regarding the laws of mixtures of forbidden and permitted foods (a common topic for discussion among those studying for the rabbinate). In this case Rabban Gamliel functions in his capacity as a member of the *Beit Din* on the Temple Mount:

> Yoezer Ish HaBira was one of the students of Beit Shammai and he said: I asked Rabban Gamliel the Elder, while he was standing at the Eastern Gate [about the rule of leaven of common produce], and he said: "It does not render [the dough] prohibited unless there is enough of it to leaven [by itself]." (Mishna, *Orla* 2:12)

A third source finds Rabban Gamliel on a stairway leading up to the Temple Mount:

> Rabbi Yose said: It happened that Rabbi Ḥalafta went to Rabban Gamliel in Tiberias, and found him seated at the table of Yoḥanan ben Nezif. He was holding and reading the *targum* [Aramaic translation] of the book of Job. Rabbi Ḥalafta said to him: "Let me tell you what I saw." He replied: "Tell me." He said to him: "I recall seeing Rabban Gamliel the Elder, your grandfather, when he was sitting on the steps going to the Temple Mount. They brought him a copy of the translation of the book of Job, and he instructed his sons to bury it under a pile of stones." (Tosefta, *Shabbat* 13:2)

This passage deals with the ritual sanctity of translated books. Rabban

3. I refer to the Tosefta in *Sanhedrin* which describes the development of dispute.

Gamliel was sitting on the steps leading to the Temple Mount, suggesting he was presiding as judge in the *Beit Din*, although parallel sources indicate that he was standing on the steps leading up to the Temple Mount (*Shabbat* 115a). A more interesting version of this story, however, appears in Tractate *Soferim*:

> It is related of Rabbi Ḥalafta that, when he visited Rabban Gamliel, he found him sitting at his table and reading the translation of Job. He said to him: "Master, will you permit me to tell you what my eyes saw?" "Tell me," he replied. "I saw Rabban Gamliel the Elder, your grandfather, as he sat atop the building on the Temple Mount when a translation of Job was brought to him, and he instructed the builders to remove a row of stones and bury it underneath." (*Soferim* 5:15)

Rabbi Saul Lieberman contends that "according to the text of the Jerusalem Talmud and of Tractate *Soferim*, it appears that Rabban Gamliel was supervising construction on the Temple Mount, enabling us to conclude that, in the days of Rabban Gamliel the Elder, Temple construction was always supervised by the Nasi" (*Tosefta KiFeshuta*, p. 204). The fact that Rabban Gamliel, the leader of the sages, was supervising construction work in the priestly domain of the Temple, raises the more general question of the relations between the sages and the priests, a question that will not be discussed here.

As mentioned above, the priests' absence from the mishna in Avot, was not coincidental, but rather a reflection of the sages' appropriation of the priestly duty to teach the people. It is not by chance that Hillel taught "be as the students of Aharon" and not "be as the sons of Aharon"; the continuity of Torah is via the transmission of learning and not via pedigree or birthright. This interaction of sage and priest in the nation's spiritual instruction and political leadership was a source of constant tension. Thus, for example, when Hillel came up from Babylonia, he was asked about the deferral of Shabbat by dint of the Paschal offering. Though definitely a "priestly" question, it was resolved by a sage. There are grounds for claiming that the high priesthood was, at that time, entirely under Sadducee control, whereas the Sanhedrin (from the time of Shlomtziyon onwards) was controlled by the Pharisees. Indeed, this division of power suffices to explain the ongoing friction. It also explains the sages' desire to minimize priestly power and to relegate them from being servants of God to being no more than clerks charged with executing technical ritual matters. For now, suffice it to note that Rabban Gamliel totally ignored the priests. Notwithstanding his physical proximity to them on the Temple Mount and in the Chamber of Hewn Stone, they played no part in his world. He governed the Jewish world from within the community of sages.

SANCTIFICATION AND INTERCALATION OF MONTHS

Determining the annual calendar, including declaring the beginning of new months and the addition of a thirteenth month to a leap year, was one of Rabban Gamliel's most important duties, for everyone was dependent on it. Managing the calendar required extensive administration, which apparently was within the authority of the Sanhedrin's *Nasi*. A *baraita* in Tractate *Sanhedrin* explains that both the king and the high priest were prohibited from sitting on the Sanhedrin to set the annual calendar: "The king – because of the upkeep of the army; the high priest – because of [the autumnal] cold" (*Sanhedrin* 18b). Apparently, the king was an unreliable "interested party" in the determination of the calendar. If he paid salaries on a monthly basis and collected taxes on an annual basis (according to *Sefer HaArukh*[4]), he had an interest in making sure that the years remained twelve months. Alternatively, if he collected monthly taxes but paid annual salaries, then he would have an interest in prolonging the year as much as possible (in accordance with Rashi's interpretation of the passage). Either way, his objectivity was compromised, disqualifying him from sitting in the forum charged with deciding these matters.

The Talmud explains the high priest's ineligibility to serve on the calendrical court as being the result of the "cold." Rashi and the Tosafot, disagree over the meaning of this explanation: Rashi is concerned that the high priest, who must perform the Yom Kippur service in the Temple,

4. *Sefer HaArukh*: a Talmudical lexicon compiled by Rabbi Natan bar Yeḥiel of Rome, 1030–1106, a student of Rabbeinu Ḥananel, and a contemporary of Rashi.

would try and prevent the intercalation of an extra month so that the month of Tishrei would remain in the warm season, and he would not have to perform the frequent Yom Kippur immersions and ablutions in the rainy chills of autumn. The Tosafot reject this explanation, pointing out that the water could have been warmed for the high priest. They contend instead that the floor would have remained cold under his bare feet.

On the one hand, it is interesting to note the law's awareness and concern for the physical comfort of the individual.[5] In this sense, we have a picture of an exemplary and morally sensitive legal system. Nonetheless, I suspect that this passage discloses the sages' cynicism regarding the integrity of the high priests of that time: while the court deliberated weighty matters such as the national calendar, the high priest's primary concern was to avoid treading on a cold floor. Our discussion below about the standing of the high priesthood at the end of Temple period will illuminate our comments here.

Returning to Rabban Gamliel the Elder, his responsibility for the calendar actually invested him with extensive power over the Jewish Diaspora. His status as the leader of the generation finds clear expression in letters that he sent to various locations:[6]

> It was taught: It once happened that Rabban Gamliel was sitting on a step on the Temple Mount, and Yoḥanan, the known scribe, was standing before him with three pieces of letter paper. "Take a sheet," he said, "and write an epistle to our brothers in Upper Galilee and to those in Lower Galilee, saying: 'Peace unto you! We wish to inform you that the time of *bi'ur* [removal of all

5. As part of his Yom Kippur prayers for the entire nation's welfare for the coming year, the high priest would include a plea that God not heed those travelers who would pray that their journeys not be made in wet discomfort. The high priest had to put the needs of the people as a whole (plentiful rain in its season) ahead of individual self-interest. Interestingly, the communal prayer for rain was deliberately instituted to take place at a time after which pilgrims to the Temple during Sukkot were expected to have arrived back home, out of consideration for their comfort.
6. The Talmud refers to him as Rabban Gamliel of Yavneh (Gamliel the Elder's grandson) but the geographical context and the event itself lend credence to Rabbi Zacharias Frankel's view (*Darkhei HaMishna*, [Hebrew] [Tel Aviv: 1959], p. 79) that these were letters written by Rabban Gamliel the Elder.

> undonated tithes from the home] has arrived for setting aside the tithe from the olive heaps.'
>
> "Take another sheet and write to our brethren in the south: 'Peace unto you! We wish to inform you that the time of *bi'ur* has arrived for setting aside the tithe from the corn sheaves.'
>
> "And take the third and write to our brethren, the exiles in Babylon and Media, and to all the other exiled Israelites, saying: 'Enduring peace unto you! We hereby inform you that the doves are still tender, the lambs still too young, and the crops are not yet ripe. It seems advisable to me and to my colleagues to add thirty days to this year.'" (*Sanhedrin* 11b)

The first two letters, concerning the *bi'ur* of tithes, are addressed to the residents of the north (the Upper and Lower Galilee), and those of the south (the Lod region). The two letters differ regarding the type of produce requiring *bi'ur*. In the Galilee, olives were the primary cash crop whereas, along the coastal plain and the Shephelah (lowlands) region, it was wheat. In *Eretz Yisrael*, as opposed to the Diaspora, letters containing information about the leap year were unnecessary because local avenues of communication would certainly bring it to the people's attention before Pesaḥ.

The third letter was addressed to the Jews of the Diaspora: Babylonia, Greece, and other Jewish communities. The *Nasi* spoke in the name of "myself and my colleagues" as the forum authorized to make such decisions. In that capacity, they were qualified to assess the economic status of the livestock and agriculture during the winter months, and to identify whether Nisan, "the Spring Month" (see Deuteronomy 16:1), should be deferred. As the head of this body, the *Nasi* – Rabban Gamliel – bore ultimate responsibility for the decision to add an extra month to the year.

The sanctification of the month was another duty that conferred extensive power on the supreme *Beit Din*: "This month shall be the head of the months for you" (Exodus 12:2) – that you shall sanctify the months. Roman rule meant that there was no Jewish state or government, no Jewish army, and no sense of Jewish sovereignty. Nonetheless, the Jews retained their religious autonomy, and were at liberty to establish their own national life and religious life cycle without interference of others.

An essential component of this religious autonomy was the *Beit Din*'s determination of whether each month was "complete" (thirty days), or "incomplete" (twenty-nine days; a lunar cycle is approximately twenty-nine and a half days). Accordingly, the beginning of each new month, based on the first sighting of the new moon, would have been either on the thirtieth or thirty-first day after the previous new moon). The Mishna provides the following description of how the witnesses testifying to the new moon were received.

> There was a large courtyard in Jerusalem called Beit Ya'azek, to which all of the witnesses came before being interrogated by the *Beit Din*. Lavish meals were prepared for them [the witnesses], so that they would grow accustomed to coming. At first [if they arrived on Shabbat], they would remain [in the courtyard] the whole day. Rabban Gamliel the Elder enacted that they be able to move two thousand cubits in every direction. (Mishna, *Rosh HaShana* 2:5)

The significance of this enactment cannot be overstated. Having observed the new moon on the eve of Shabbat, a witness would hurriedly travel to Jerusalem, to be able to testify the next morning. However, after giving his testimony and being cross-examined, he was not able to travel outside that courtyard, as he had already traveled beyond the permitted "Shabbat boundary" (albeit for a permitted and valid reason, that is, to testify regarding the new moon), when he came to Jerusalem in the first place.[7] Being forced to remain in the courtyard, away from home, for the entire Shabbat would certainly have deterred potential witnesses from coming to testify. Rabban Gamliel's amendment was a courageous one insofar as he permitted that which had previously been forbidden by allowing these potential witnesses to travel two thousand amot in each direction, so as not to discourage them from coming to Jerusalem. This element of Rabban Gamliel's creativity is highly reminiscent of that of his grandfather, Hillel (as we saw regarding, for example, the *prozbul*).

7. A full understanding of this paragraph requires an in depth discussion of the laws of Shabbat and *Eruvin*, and is not possible in this framework.

PERMITTING A WOMAN TO MARRY BASED ON SINGLE TESTIMONY: THE POWER OF THE NASI

The strength and power of Rabban Gamliel the Elder's authority also finds expression in another one of his enactments:

> Rabbi Akiva said: When I went down to Nehardea to declare a leap year, I met Neḥemia of Beit Deli. He said to me: "I heard that, in Israel, only Rabbi Yehuda ben Bava permits a woman to remarry based on the evidence of a single witness [to her husband's death]." I said to him: "Correct." He said to me: "Tell them in my name – you know that the country is ruined by ravaging troops. I have a tradition from Rabban Gamliel the Elder that they permitted a wife to remarry based on the testimony of a single witness." When I came and presented the matter to Rabban Gamliel, he rejoiced at my report, saying: "We have now found a counterpart to Rabbi Yehuda ben Bava." As a result, Rabban Gamliel remembered that certain men were slain at Tel Arza, and Rabban Gamliel the Elder had permitted their wives to remarry based on the testimony of one witness. The rule was thus established, permitting a woman to remarry based on hearsay or on the testimony of a slave, of a woman, or of a maidservant (Mishna, *Yevamot* 16:7).

This enactment can only be understood as the *Nasi*'s intervention for the betterment of society, and in violation of Torah law, which states unequivocally: "Upon the testimony of two witnesses or three witnesses" (Deuteronomy 7:16). Rabban Gamliel was nevertheless prepared to permit a woman to remarry based on the testimony of one witness.

What is the background and the analytical basis for this bold amendment? When a woman's husband has disappeared, there must be clear proof of his death if she is to be permitted to remarry. Cases of this kind are an unfortunate part of reality, and Agnon's story "And the Crooked Shall Be Made Straight" ("*VeHaya HeAkov LeMishor*"), about trapped women (*agunot*) whose husbands had disappeared, rendering them unable to remarry, was not just the product of the author's imagination. Rather, it reflected his direct confrontation with the world of

Jewish law. There were, in fact, heartbreaking cases in which a woman was erroneously informed by the army that her husband had died in battle, on the basis of which she remarried, after which her soldier husband returned.

This tragic reality, with its terrible consequences, provides the background for Rabban Gamliel's audacious enactment. It must first be clarified, however, that his ruling did not presume to define death. Rather, its objective was to promote quality of life, specifically, that of the woman trapped in such a situation. In other words, the testimony of one witness does not confirm the husband's death, but rather, creates a presumption that allows the woman to remarry. Rabban Gamliel created a halakhic mechanism for accepting the testimony of one person in order to release an aguna. As a halakhic innovation, this enactment became the symbol for halakhic sensitivity toward the tribulations of individual people.

Some have viewed this enactment as an example of the rabbinic license to actively abrogate biblical law (i.e., the evidentiary requirement of no fewer than two witnesses) out of fear of leaving a woman unable to remarry. The Talmudic discussion of this rabbinic license appears in Tractate *Yevamot* (89a–90a), and concludes that "uprooting a commandment from the Torah" may only be done passively, by omission, and not by commission. The *Rishonim* (ad loc.) note that this conclusion is inconsistent with Rabban Gamliel's acceptance of the testimony of a solitary witness as grounds to permit an *aguna* to remarry. The Ritva (Rabbi Yom Tov ibn Ashvili, thirteenth-century Spain) presents the question, and gives the following answer:

> The rabbis were certain that the ultimate severity of the matter ensures that he would give truthful testimony. Therefore, if she married on the strength of his testimony, she would be considered to have lawfully remarried, for it is as though we bear witness to the matter, and this kind of testimony is always considered to be complete testimony, even according to Torah law. Indeed, for the Torah invests the sages with the authority to determine which matters are considered to be so well known, and the truth of which is so obvious, that it can be regarded as evidence. (Ritva on *Yevamot* 88a)

In other words, the halakhic authorities are authorized to determine when one witness will suffice and when to insist upon compliance with the Torah's demand for two witnesses. The innovative nature of the enactment lies in the conferral of broad discretionary power to the rabbis to determine whether or not to comply with the scriptural commandment. If the *Beit Din* is persuaded that "the truth of the matter is evident," one witness can indeed suffice. This principle relies more on the subjective intuitions of the rabbinic authorities and less on rigid halakhic definitions.[8]

8. See comments of Rabbi Eliezer Berkovitz, *The Nature and Function of Halakha* [Hebrew] (Jerusalem: 1981), pp. 200–202. Maimonides provides a slightly more nuanced, moderate version of the enactment to accept the testimony of one witness:

> Let it not seem perplexing to you that the sages have permitted a woman of hitherto strictly forbidden degree, on the strength of the testimony of a woman, a slave, a bondswoman, a heathen speaking in his innocence, a witness who offers hearsay evidence taken from another witness, or a written document without subjecting the witness to inquiry and examination as we have just explained. For the Torah insists upon the testimony of two witnesses and upon the other rules concerning testimony, only in matters of truth which cannot be ascertained except out of the mouths of the witnesses and by their testimony, as for instance when they testify that A has slain B, or has made a loan to B. In matters that can be ascertained through means other than the testimony of the particular witnesses, where he cannot clear himself if he is exposed as a false witness, as when he has testified that So-and-So is dead, the Torah does not so insist, because in such cases it is uncommon for a witness to testify to a falsehood. The sages have therefore been lenient in this matter, and have given credence even to the testimony of a single witness, of a bondswoman, or of a written document, without the requirement of inquiry and examination, in order that the daughters of Israel should not remain in a trapped state. (*Mishneh Torah, Hilkhot Gerushin,* 13:29)

Maimonides admits that the motivation for waiving the requirement of two witnesses is a social one so that the women "should not remain … *agunot*." Nonetheless, he claims that the testimony of one witness is not the category of testimony prescribed by the Torah, because the Torah only required two witnesses for cases in which without the witnesses the truth would not come to the fore (due to a dispute). Where the truth can be objectively verified from another source there is no need for two witnesses.

PUBLIC POLICY AND THE BETTERMENT OF SOCIETY

The fourth chapter of Tractate *Gittin* records examples of Rabban Gamliel's responsibility for public policy:

> Originally, a man could convene a *Beit Din* anywhere to cancel a bill of divorce. Rabban Gamliel the Elder, however, enacted as a matter of public policy that this should not be done [thus preventing abuse].
>
> Originally, a man could change his name and her name and the name of his town and the name of her town. Rabbi Gamliel ordained, as a matter of public policy, that it be written [in the bill of divorce]: "Mr. So-and-So and whatever alias he has"; "Mrs. So-and-So and whatever alias she has." (Mishna, *Gittin* 4:2)

A brief explanation of the essence of these important enactments: The mishna deals with the case of a husband who sends his wife a *get* (bill of divorce) by way of an agent. Prior to Rabban Gamliel's enactment, the husband was at liberty to convene a *Beit Din* (without the wife's attendance) wherever he happened to be, and cancel the *get* before it reached her. The danger was that a woman who was unaware of the husband's annulment of the *get,* might remarry and the children from that marriage would be *mamzerim.*[9] In addition, enabling the husband to cancel a *get* in this manner empowered him to make his wife an *aguna*. Rabban Gamliel's enactment provided a solution to the problem, by prohibiting the annulment of the *get* unless it was done in the woman's presence. In discussing the enactment, the Talmud questions the status of a *get* annulled without the wife's presence. The annulment would definitely be valid under Torah law and the woman's married status would remain unchanged. Nonetheless, based on the rationale of "how great is the power of the *Beit Din*" (Rabban Shimon ben Gamliel, *Gittin* 33b), the Talmud concluded that the enactment supersedes the law of the Torah.

This is the broadest possible interpretation of Rabban Gamliel's enactment (and rabbinical enactments in general); a more restrictive

9. A *mamzer* is defined as a person born of a forbidden relationship, or the descendant of such a person.

approach would undermine the basic purpose of the amendment. The argument of "how great is the power of the *Beit Din*" augments rabbinic authority, because the Torah law would not require the wife's presence as a condition for the validity of the annulment, and should she remarry, her children would be *mamzerim*. On the other hand, following Rabban Gamliel's enactment, the husband's annulment would have no effect and the children from the second marriage would not be *mamzerim*. In other words, giving full force to this rabbinic enactment meant uprooting the law of the Torah.[10]

The second enactment concerns a person who changed his name or moved to another town, and is now known exclusively by his new name and address. Rabban Gamliel made an enactment to prevent people from "disappearing," and the Talmud explains its background:

> The Jews from overseas sent the following inquiry to Rabban Gamliel: If a man comes here from *Eretz Yisrael* whose name is Yosef but who is known here as Yoḥanan, or whose name is Yoḥanan but who is known here as Yosef, how can he divorce his wife? Rabban Gamliel thereupon enacted that they should write in the *get*: "the man So-and-So and any other name he is known by; the woman So-and-So and any other name she is known by," as a precaution for the general good. (*Gittin* 34b)

10. I have explained the Talmudic passage according the approach adopted by R.A. Weiss, *Research of the Talmud* (New York: 1955), p. 389, and n. 366. My explanation is consistent with the position taken by the Jerusalem Talmud to the effect that Rabban Gamliel's enactment could actually uproot a biblically anchored commandment. On the other hand, the Babylonian Talmud offers a more toned down explanation, based on the concept of "anyone who marries [a woman], does so subject to the conditions laid down by the rabbis, and [therefore] the rabbis have the power to annul [the betrothal]." That is to say, if the laws of marriage are determined by rabbinic authority, it follows that the annulment of marriage is also in the rabbis' jurisdiction, and therefore, no Torah law has been uprooted. See also M. Elon, *Jewish Law* [Hebrew] (1988), p. 463 who concurs with this explanation. On the other hand, D. Halivni (*Sources and Traditions* [Hebrew] [Tel Aviv:1969], p. 631) challenges this version of the Talmud.

This enactment was enacted exclusively in order to assist in verifying and ascertaining people's identity, but nowadays, when people are identified by numbers and not just according to various names that they may have assumed at various times in their lives, this requirement has become somewhat cumbersome. Rabban Gamliel's enactment, motivated exclusively by his concern for the public good, constituted a crucial stage in the sages' religious perception as such, and of their role as leaders. They were not passive partners to the divine word. Rather, they were active legislators, and their formulation of the halakha created new social realities.

The sages' active involvement in the formulation of the halakha was not accepted with equanimity. Hillel created a storm when he enlisted the rules of logic and human intellect in order to create a new law concerning the Paschal offering on Shabbat. This kind of halakhic innovation was alien to the Benei Beteira, the veteran leadership in Temple circles. In this context, an interesting observation was made by Rabbi Tzaddok HaKohen (nineteenth-century Lublin), who describes the creativity of the early *tanna'im* as their entry into a dialogue that began with the receiving of the Torah at Sinai. Basing himself on the tradition that God forced the people to accept the Torah by holding a mountain over the people's heads, Rabbi Tzaddok argues that this entitles us to enforce our own innovations of Torah upon God. The following is the essence of his words:

> For although the Torah had already been given, its full virtues were not manifested until the Second Temple – even though the Divine Presence was not present. For they did not leave any stone unturned, until they forced the Holy One, blessed be He, and He revealed to them the deeper secrets in every matter. Their act of forcing was a response to God's act of forcing when He held the mountain over them at Mount Sinai. And this is true of the Second Temple in the time of the Mishnaic sages. And in respect of this they said that, then, there was a greater manifestation of all the virtues of the Torah. And so it was really a greater period. And this accords with what the sages have said: "The sage is preferable to the prophet" [*Bava Batra* 12a]. (*Tzidkat HaTzaddik* § 93)

REMOVE YOURSELF FROM DOUBT

Rabban Gamliel sought to unify the people under the authority of the sages. His rule heralds the beginning of the tannaitic period. The era of the Pairs has ended and we have entered a period of wide ranging disputes and continued conflict. Someone was needed to unite the powers-that-be in order to prevent the bifurcation of the Torah (from becoming "two Torahs") and of Jewish society. Rabban Gamliel (incidentally, the first to be known by the title of *Rabban*) assumed this responsibility. Two missions confronted him: Firstly, he had to maintain and perpetuate the tradition of creativity instituted by his grandfather, enabling the renewal of the Torah in a manner that addressed the dynamic needs of the generation. Secondly, he had to ensure the universal Jewish acceptance of the Torah in its entirety. For example, an annual calendar not universally adhered to was worthless. Had nobody complied with his enactment prohibiting a husband from cancelling a *get*, what power would he have had? The secret to the sages' power lay in their ability to combine these two factors: creativity and authority.

"Acquire a teacher for yourself and remove yourself from doubt" – The failure of the students of Shammai and Hillel to "properly serve their teachers" resulted in the proliferation of disputes which stifled progress, brought confusion and a general lack of direction. Addressing this problem, Rabban Gamliel centralized and stressed rabbinic authority, preventing its development along multiple tracks, streamlining the entire system, and channeling it toward defined horizons devoid of doubt.

Nonetheless, it was Rabban Gamliel who said, "Do not accustom yourself to tithing by estimate." Tithing by estimate inevitably produces mistakes. When a person tithed too little produce, the tithes would be valid but the remaining fruit would remain in the category of *tevel* (i.e., untithed), and hence prohibited. Tithing too much produce meant that while the fruit is ritually acceptable it contains an element of *ḥullin* (that which is not sanctified). Rabban Gamliel presented a solution to the problem of doubt and of mistakes, not by adopting the path of stringency, but rather by "acquiring a teacher for yourself."

Our description of Rabban Gamliel's activities illuminates the mishna at the end of Tractate *Sota*: "When Rabban Gamliel the Elder died, the honor of Torah died with him." We will presently see that his death ushered in a period in which honor for the Torah was a rare sight.

Chapter Eighteen

The Priests at the End of the Second Temple Period

The previous chapter focused upon the character of Rabban Gamliel the Elder as he presided over the *Beit Din* on the Temple Mount, enacting regulations and coordinating the social-religious practices of the people. He was the source of teaching and instruction that sustained the entire Jewish people. As outlined above, the priests were not partners to Rabban Gamliel's spiritual enterprise, nor did he require them in order to bequeath his Torah to Israel. Nonetheless, as a significant social force during the Second Temple they exercised a profound influence on everyday life. The following section explores the world of the priests, who in fact had already forfeited their spiritual status in the times of the Men of the Great Assembly.

The religious public confronted the Temple in all its splendor, suffused by the majesty of the priests and all-pervasive holiness, during the focal days of remembrance: Tisha B'Av and Yom Kippur. The song, "*Emet Ma Nehedar*" ("True! How Glorious"), of the Yom Kippur liturgy, portrays the moment that the sublimely pure high priest emerges from the Holy of Holies unscathed.

In reality, the situation in the Temple in the generation preceding its destruction was complex. The high priesthood, and the entire priesthood in its wake, had become an office of power and authority closely intertwined with the sovereign political power. From the times of Herod onward, high priests were not chosen based on pedigree and virtues, but rather in accordance with their political connections and economic stature. The oligarchic form of government enabled a minority of well-born and wealthy families to rule over everything. The high priests were at the pinnacle of state leadership and were responsible for foreign relations (see Josephus, Antiquities XX, 251). The office of high priest was not one of "permanent priesthood," being determined rather according to the needs of the foreign government. During the times of Herod, the Boethus family held the office of the high priest. This family originated in Alexandria, and was "imported" by Herod in order to help him gain control of the country. In the days of the first governors, the priestly offices were held by the House of Ḥanan (Ananias), and also mentioned in our sources is the House of Piabi (Fabus). In the twenty years that preceded the revolt, the office of the high priest was held by the Kathros family. Tractate *Avot* only cites one priest: Ḥanina (or Ḥanania), the deputy high priest.

I now propose to outline the characters of some of the priests of that period, and in so doing, attain an understanding of the relations between the priestly class and the rest of the people.

THE PRIESTS ACCORDING TO THE MISHNA, TRACTATE YOMA

Tractate *Yoma* describes the ritual performed by the high priest, and portrays the routines associated with the priesthood and the Temple. Combining these Talmudic sources with external historical sources clarifies the nature of the problems that plagued the priesthood of that time. The picture of the high priesthood presented by these sources is rather remote from the idyllic form that we encounter in the liturgy.

1. Ineligible priests on Yom Kippur (*Yoma* 1:1)

In its opening mishna, Tractate *Yoma* describes the high priest's removal from his home prior to Yom Kippur:

> Seven days before Yom Kippur, they removed the high priest from his home to the councilor's chamber, and another priest was appointed as his deputy in case something happened to render him ineligible. Rabbi Yehuda says: "They would also appoint another woman as a substitute for his wife, in case she died, since it says 'And he shall make atonement for himself and for his house' [Leviticus 16:6] – 'his house' refers to his wife." They said to him: "If so, there would be no end to the matter."

This mishna is supplemented by the following description from the Tosefta:

> Rabbi Ḥanania, deputy high priest, says: "For that reason the deputy was appointed." (Tosefta, *Yoma* 1:4)

The Babylonian Talmud phrases it somewhat differently:

> Rabbi Ḥanania, deputy high priest, says: "Why was a deputy appointed? If something happened to render the high priest ineligible, he [the deputy] would enter and serve in his stead." (*Sota* 42a)

The Tosefta then tells us about a priest who was found ineligible, forcing them to enlist the services of his deputy:

> "When a priest was rendered ineligible, the other one will take his place, and when the high priest is restored to his position in priesthood, the one who served in his place remains bound by all of the religious requirements of the high priesthood" – so said Rabbi Meir. Rabbi Yosa says: "Even though they said 'All the religious requirements of the high priesthood apply to him,' he is not eligible to serve as a high priest or even as an ordinary priest."
>
> Rabbi Yosa said: "It once happened that Yosef ben Eilim of Tzippori served as the high priest for one hour, and from that time on he was not eligible as a high priest or as an ordinary priest. When he went forth [from his hour-long high priesthood]

> he said to the king: 'The bull and the ram that were offered today, to whom do they belong? Are they mine or are they the high priest's?' The king knew what to answer him. He said to him: 'What's going on, Son of Eilim? Is it not enough for you that you served in the place of high priest for one hour before He-Who-Spoke-And-The-World-Came-Into-Being? Do you also wish to take over the high priesthood for yourself?' At that moment, Ben Eilim realized that he had been removed from the high priesthood." (Tosefta, *Yoma* 1:4)

Here we have an interesting description of how they prepared the deputy to replace the high priest, placing him on alert in case the high priest became ineligible. He retained his status as "deputy" for as long as the high priest was eligible to serve. If the latter became ineligible, the deputy would replace him until his return. The *tanna'im* (of the Usha generation) disputed the question of the deputy's status after the reinstatement of the high priest. Does he resume his position as a regular priest, with the title of deputy, or perhaps he no longer serves in any position (because one ascends in matters of holiness and does not descend)? In support of his view that he does not return to his old position, Rabbi Yosa relates the case of Yosef ben Eilim, who filled the position of high priest for one hour only, after which he never returned to his regular position. This dialogue appears in the Tosefta, which is more allusive than explicit: Yosef ben Eilim had terminated his (only) day of service and enigmatically asked the king: "The bull and the ram that were offered today, to whom do they belong? Are they mine or are they the high priest's?" Immediately understanding his intention, the king promptly shows him the door. The king appears to have been a righteous person capable of properly admonishing the acquisitive deputy.

Fortunately, Josephus provides a description of the same incident, in his description of the priesthood under Mattathias (Matityahu):

> Now it happened that during Mattathias' term as high priest that another priest was appointed for a single day – a day on which the Jews observe a fast – for the following reason. While serving as a priest during the night preceding the day on which the

> fast occurred, Mattathias dreamed that he had relations with a woman, and as a result was unable to serve as a priest, and a relative of his, Yosef ben Elim, served as a priest in his place…and on that same night there was an eclipse of the moon. (*Antiquities* XVII, 164–170)

Let us acquaint ourselves with the characters:

One of Herod's wives, Miriam (Mariamne), was the daughter of Shimon from the House of Boethus. As a wedding gift, Herod appointed her father as high priest (23 BCE). A few years later, his two brothers and brother-in-law were also appointed to the high priesthood, each one for a few years. These three priests – Yoezer, Elazar and Mattathias – served as priests until 6 BCE. Evidently, Herod intentionally nurtured the Boethus family as an alternative to the Hasmonean priestly family that belonged to the Yehoyariv clan. A number of interesting events are linked to the transition of the priestly office among the members of this "distinguished" family and serve to illustrate their moral deterioration.

In the year 4 BCE, Herod became gravely ill and a number of young men exploited his absence to remove the golden eagle (the symbol of Roman sovereignty) that hung over one of the Temple gates. These men were caught and executed. As part of the punishment, Herod also dismissed Mattathias the high priest (whom he held accountable) and appointed Yoezer, his wife's brother, as the priest.

At an earlier stage of Mattathias' priesthood, he became ineligible on the eve of Yom Kippur (apparently due to a nocturnal discharge), and was compelled to abdicate his position in favor of his deputy, Yosef ben Eilim. Based on his own tradition, Josephus relates that there was a lunar eclipse on the very same night, in addition to the priest's disqualification. In a fascinating and meticulous research project utilizing astronomic tables of the ancient period, it has been verified that the eve of Yom Kippur, in the middle of September in the year 5 BCE, indeed coincided with a lunar eclipse.[1] This was Yosef ben Eilim's Yom Kippur

1. D. Schwartz, "Yosef ben Eilim and the Death of Herod" [Hebrew], in A. Oppenheimer (ed.), *Jews and Judaism in the Second Temple and Talmudic Periods* (Jerusalem: 5753), pp. 65–74.

as high priest. The confluence of the lunar eclipse with the high priest's *ba'al keri* status on the eve of Yom Kippur was an ominous sign. In the words of the Talmud:

> A lunar eclipse is an evil omen for the "enemies of Israel" [euphemism for Israel], for they [Israel] count according to the moon. (*Sukka* 29a)

For a high priest to become a *ba'al keri* on the eve of Yom Kippur was likewise considered a cataclysmic event, so much so that the Mishna in *Avot* counts as one of ten miracles of the Temple era that "no physical impurity ever befell the high priest on Yom Kippur."

Accordingly, the case of Mattathias the Boethusian high priest was the exception. There are also rabbinic sources that attribute the same occurrence to the high priest Shimon ben Kimḥit:

> It happened that Shimon ben Kimḥit went to speak with an Arab king, and spit came out of his [the king's] mouth and fell on his [Shimon's] clothes [rendering him ineligible]. His brother went in and served as high priest in his stead. The mother of these [brothers] witnessed two [officiating] high priests on the same day. (Tosefta, *Yoma* 1:3)[2]

2. Ignorant high priests (*Yoma* 1:3)

Recalling the majestic, almost angelic image of a high priest such as Simeon the Just, we are jarred by the reality of the Mishnaic description of the elders' attempts to keep the high priest awake on the eve of Yom Kippur, prior to his Temple service:

> Elders were sent to him from among the elders of the *Beit Din*,

2. This is the well-known story about a woman named Kimḥit who was careful that "the walls of her house should not see the hairs of her head." She was rewarded with seven sons who served as high priest. Most likely, the number seven is exaggerated, but as we also saw in the story of the Boethus family, there was no problem in having three sons serving consecutively as high priest.

> and they would read him the order of the day; they said to him: "My lord High Priest, read it yourself, lest you have forgotten or never [even] learnt it to begin with. (Mishna, *Yoma* 1:3)

As we see in the Jerusalem Talmud, the inevitable question bursts forth:

> But was it not taught: "The priest who is chief among his brothers" – his greatness should come from his brothers. "Upon whose head the anointing oil is poured" – Rabbi says: in beauty, in strength, in wealth, in wisdom, and in appearance?
>
> Rabbi Yose the son of Rabbi Bun said: These [cited passages] refer to [the learned high priests of] the first Temple, while these [mentioned in the mishna] refer to [the ignorant high priests of] the second Temple. (Talmud Yerushalmi, *Yoma* 1:3 [39a])

Only during the first Temple was there was an ideal priest, one who rose above his brothers. In the time of the second Temple, priests of this nature no longer existed. The Babylonian Talmud, too, was aware of this answer, adding the following real life example to illustrate it:

> As Rabbi Asi said: Marta bat Boethus gave a basket of *denarii* to King Yannai in return for his appointment of Yehoshua ben Gamla as the high priest. (*Yoma* 18a)

This Talmudic tradition is mentioned amongst the stories of the high priesthood being purchased, at the twilight of the Second Temple period, a practice attested to in external sources as being widespread in the Hellenistic world and throughout the Roman Empire.[3] Thus, Marta donated a huge sum of money to King Yannai to secure the appointment of Yehoshua ben Gamla as high priest. We have already noted that in Babylonian tradition, King Yannai became the symbolic codename for the wicked Hasmonean rule, and that on a number of occasions, events are attributed to Yannai when they really occurred to another of the

3. G. Alon, *Studies in Jewish History* [Hebrew], vol. 1, p. 60 ff.

Hasmonean kings. Furthermore, during the Hasmonean period it was not yet possible to purchase the high priesthood, which was still held by the Hasmoneans themselves. In fact, the Hasmoneans were criticized for combining the high priesthood and the monarchy. This reality changed from the days of Herod onward, when the high priesthood became an official appointment of the ruler, and began to change hands frequently. Accordingly, any of these rulers with the power to appoint the high priest could theoretically be the "Yannai" that the Talmud refers to.

Returning now to Marta and her beloved Yehoshua ben Gamla, there is a Mishnaic tradition that preserves some interesting details of their wedding:

> A high priest should not marry a widow, regardless of whether she was widowed from a betrothal or a marriage.
>
> Furthermore, he should not marry a woman who has reached adulthood. Rabbi Elazar and Rabbi Shimon teach that he may marry an adult. He should not marry a girl who was "injured by wood" [i.e., who lost her virginity through some non-sexual encounter or accident].
>
> [If] he betrothed a widow and was then appointed high priest, he may consummate the marriage. And it happened with Rabbi Yehoshua ben Gamla that he married Marta bat Boethus, and the king then appointed him high priest, and he consummated her [in marriage]. (Mishna, *Yevamot* 6:4)

The Mishna thus teaches us that Marta was a widow and Yehoshua ben Gamla married her prior to his appointment as high priest.

Marta was the paradigmatic rich matron in the sages' world. The power, dignity, and beauty of her station is reflected in the following description of her son, who appears in the Talmudic account of the procession led by the priests' children, who carried the jugs of oil at the *Simḥat Beit HaSho'eva* (Water-Drawing Celebration):

> It was taught: And they were more praiseworthy [in their prowess] than the son of Marta bat Boethus. It was said of the son of Marta bat Boethus that he could take two thighs of a large ox

> purchased for one thousand *zuzim*, and walk heel-to-toe up the ramp to the altar. But his fellow priests would not allow him to do so, for it says: "In the multitude of the people is the glory of the King" [Proverbs 14:28]. (*Sukka* 52b)

Marta is similarly the archetypal wealthy woman in descriptions of the clothing of the rich:

> "And you shall not pawn the garment of a widow" – whether she is poor or rich, and even if she is [as rich as] Marta bat Boethus. (*Sifrei Devarim* 281)

The rabbinic traditions regarding the destruction of the Second Temple preserve Marta's character in all its delicate elegance:

> It is related of Marta bat Boethus, that Yehoshua ben Gamla married her and the king then appointed him to be high priest, after which he consummated the marriage. One day she said: "I will go and see how he reads the Torah in the Temple on Yom Kippur." They laid out carpets for her from the door of her house to the entrance to the Temple so that her feet might not be exposed; nevertheless, they were exposed. When her husband Yehoshua died, the rabbis gave her an allowance of two *se'ah* of wine daily. (*Eikha Raba* 1)

These traditions demonstrate how the high priesthood had become a purchasable office during the period of the Roman governors of Judea. The decision to appoint or dismiss a high priest was no longer related to family or even to political considerations, and had become nothing other than a favor to be bestowed by the ruler. Toward the middle of the first century, after the days of Agrippa, the high priesthood had become devoid of any substance, having degenerated into an office that changed hands from year to year, as described in the Tosefta:

> When there was a proliferation of [unworthy or unacceptable] kings, they enacted the practice of appointing the high priests on a yearly basis. (Tosefta, *Yoma* 1:6)

A *baraita* in the Babylonian Talmud rather cynically describes the reasons for the high priest's office in the Temple becoming known as the "Chamber of *Parhedrin*" (councilors, or appointees):

> Was the chamber [in which the high priest was sequestered] indeed that of the *parhedrin* [councilors]? Was it not rather the chamber of the *balvatei* [senators/aristocrats]? Originally, it was called the Chamber of *Balvatei* [because the high priests were honorable men]. Later on, when money was being paid to the king in order to obtain the high priesthood, and the position of high priest was changed every twelve months, similar to the councilors who are changed every twelve months, it was henceforth referred to as the Chamber of *Parhedrin*. (*Yoma* 8b)

G. Alon wrote an article analyzing this Talmudic passage,[4] concluding that the Chamber of *Parhedrin* was in fact a chamber of "deputies," no longer manned by authentic high priests, but by a group of stand-in replacements. Accordingly, Marta bat Boethus could use her connections to arrange the appointment of Yehoshua ben Gamla as the high priest. We will return to him as we approach the period of the Great Revolt.

3. Sadducee high priests (*Yoma* 1:5)

The Mishna in Tractate *Yoma* provides an idyllic description of the night preceding the high priest's Yom Kippur service, smoothing over the well-known tension between the Pharisees and the Sadducees over how the high priest should enter into the Holy of Holies. There was no dispute regarding the Torah's command of the high priest to enter the holy sanctum holding a pan of burning coals in one hand, and a pan of incense in the other. The aim was to ensure the rising of a cloud of incense in the Holy of Holies to conceal the covering of the Holy Ark. Their dispute related to the place at which the priest was commanded to pour the incense into the burning coals. The Pharisees argued that the ritual must be performed inside the Holy of Holies, to fulfill the verse, "He shall put the incense on the fire before the Lord" (Leviticus

4. G. Alon, "Parhedrin" [Hebrew], *Studies in Jewish History*, vol. 1, pp. 48–76.

16:3). The incense was only to be kindled when the priest was "before the Lord" and no earlier. The Sadducees argued that the incense must be poured on the fire while the priest was still outside. This ensured that he would enter the holy sanctum enveloped in the cloud, in fulfillment of the verse, "For I appear in the cloud" (Leviticus 16:2).

Taking place in the Holy of Holies, entry to which was otherwise prohibited to all men, the Yom Kippur ritual was actually an intimate meeting of the high priest and the Holy One, blessed be He, for "No person shall be in the Tent of Meeting when he goes in to make atonement in the Sanctum" (Leviticus 16:17). According to the tannaitic tradition, the priests did not abuse this trust and did not defect to Sadduceeism:

> The elders of the *Beit Din* delivered him to the elders of the priesthood and they brought him up to the upper chamber of Beit Avtinas, and they adjured him, and when they took their leave and departed they said to him, "My lord, High Priest, we are delegates of the *Beit Din*, and you are our delegate and the delegate of the *Beit Din*. We adjure you by the One who made His name to dwell in this house, not to change anything of all that we have said to you. He would turn aside and weep and they would turn aside and weep. (Mishna, *Yoma* 1:5)

The Talmud subsequently explains the colorful description of mutual weeping: "He would turn aside and weep and they would turn aside and weep"

> "He would turn aside and weep" – because they suspected him of being a Sadducee. "And they turned aside and wept" – for Rabbi Yehoshua ben Levi said: Whoever suspects innocent people of misdeeds is punished by being stricken in his body. And why then was it necessary? To ensure that he did not prepare it [the incense] outside and then enter [the Holy of Holies] as the Sadducees did. (*Yoma* 19b)

The Talmud's interpretation of the Mishna reflects the trust referred to above; it was inconceivable that the high priest would wantonly deviate from the Pharisaic interpretation of how the ritual should be performed.

Nonetheless, the *baraita* cites a tradition indicating that the suspicion did have a historical context:

> There was a Sadducee who prepared the incense outside [of the Holy of Holies] and then brought it inside. As he left he was exceedingly happy. When coming out he met his father who said to him, "My son, although we are Sadducees we are afraid of the Pharisees." The son replied: "All my life I was troubled by the verse, 'For I appear in a cloud upon the Ark's cover' [Leviticus 16:2]. When will I have the opportunity of fulfilling this verse? Now that this opportunity has come to, me, should I not have fulfilled it?" It was reported that it took only a few days until he died and his body was thrown on the dung heap and worms came out of his nose. Others said that he was struck as he came out [from the Holy of Holies], for Rabbi Ḥiya taught: A noise was heard in the Temple Court, for an angel had come and struck him down on his face and his brethren the priests entered and they found the imprint of a calf's foot between his shoulders, as it is written: "And their feet were straight feet and the sole of their feet was like the sole of a calf's foot" [Ezekiel 1:7]. (*Yoma* 19b)

This passage merges two traditions: the first relates a dialogue between the high priest and his father upon the completion of the Yom Kippur ritual. Having survived the ritual, the high priest emerges from the Holy of Holies in a state of exaltation: "As he left he was exceedingly happy." At this stage, according to the second tradition cited by Rabbi Ḥiya, noises started issuing from Temple court – the priest who had digressed from the Pharisaic protocols was struck dead.

The first tradition places the Sadducee priest in a position of seniority, on the level of Rabbi Akiva who said: *When will I be able to fulfill that obligation?* This is an idealistic priest with only the purest of motives. According to his father the Sadducees complied with the Pharisees' directive only in order not to aggravate them. Eventually, along comes a young and courageous priest who has no fear and performs the ritual guided by his own understanding. Indeed, as the following passage from the Tosefta indicates, there was a clear distinction between the generation of Sadducees who were prepared to compromise and the priest who exemplified the idealistic Sadducee:

> For there had already been a case concerning a Boethusian who offered incense while he was still on the outside and the cloud of incense came forth and frightened the entire house. Because the Boethusian argued that…he should burn the incense while still on the outside, as it states: "For in a cloud." But the rabbis said to them: Has it not also been stated, "And put the incense on the fire before the Lord?" From this it follows that whoever offers up incense must only do so inside. If so, why does it say: "the cloud of the incense may cover." This teaches that he places something which causes smoke to rise. Therefore, if he omitted placing that which makes smoke rise, he is liable for the death penalty. When the Boethusian went forth he said to his father: "All your lives you have been expounding the Scriptures but you never did the deed properly, until I came and did it correctly." They said to him: "Even though we expounded the matter as you do, we do not perform in accordance with the manner in which we expound them. We obey the words of the sages. I will be exceedingly surprised if you live very long." Not three days had passed and they put him into his grave. (Tosefta, *Yoma* 1:8)

This tradition discloses the murky reality beneath the Mishna's idyllic depiction of the priesthood. We are introduced to a number of Sadducee families who served as priests during the twilight period of the Second Temple. These families maintained a façade of obedience to the Pharisees. The Boethus family was one of the most powerful and wealthy families in Jerusalem, with a particular affinity to the Sadducees, though posing as Pharisees. It was families of this kind that King Yannai referred to in his testament to his wife Queen Shlomtziyon:

> King Yannai said to his wife: "Do not fear the Pharisees or those who are not Pharisees, rather fear the hypocrites who are like Pharisees, whose actions are those of Zimri but who ask for the reward of Pinehas. (*Sota* 22b)

THE HIGH PRIESTS AND THE RED HEIFER

In the Mishna of Tractate *Para* (3:5), Rabbi Ḥanina, the deputy high priest, recalls how they used to prepare the ashes of the heifer. Just as the priest was separated from his house on Yom Kippur, they would also separate him from his house in anticipation of the heifer's burning. Rabbi Ḥanina relates two distinct traditions regarding the number of days on which they would sprinkle the blood on the high priest. The blood was sprinkled for seven consecutive days on the priest burning the heifer, whereas before Yom Kippur it was only on the third and seventh day. The Mishna describes how the priests' children would grow up in special quarantined neighborhoods, immune to the penetration of any form of impurity. In this state of purity they were able to draw the water that had been sprinkled on the priest. Mishnaic tradition relates that during the Second Temple period, seven red heifers were burnt:

> ... and five [were prepared] since Ezra, so says Rabbi Meir. But the sages say: seven since Ezra. And who prepared them? Simeon the Just and Yoḥanan the High Priest each prepared two, and Eliyahu Eini the son of Hakkof, and Ḥanamel the Egyptian and Yishmael the son of Piabi prepared one each.

A closer examination of the Mishna discloses some important details regarding the period. For the duration of the Second Temple there was a quantity of cow ashes ready for use, gathered over a period over four hundred years from just seven heifers. The political-security situation dictated the periodic renewal of the supply of ashes. Naturally, times of war required larger quantities of ashes to purify those who had become unclean, and in days of peace, there was the regular, standard supply. The Mishna relates that the last three gatherers of ashes all lived during the first century CE, which was a time of peace. Why did the consumption of ashes during that period exceed their consumption over the entire four hundred year period that preceded it? This question requires us to take a closer look at these three characters.

1. Eliyahu Eini ben Hakkof

Josephus (*Antiquities* XIX, 342) tells us of a high priest named "Elioneus, the son of Cantheras," who can almost certainly be identified as the priest referred to by the Mishna, as "ben Hakkof." The spelling is apparently defective and almost all of the more accurate manuscripts read "*Hakeef.*" The name refers to the livelihood of its bearer, and its accepted meaning is "the burden carrier."[5] One of the senior priests during the period of Agrippa was Simeon Cantheras, who was the son of Yoezer or Elazar from the Boethus family. Evidently, Elioneus and Simeon were brothers, belonging to the Cantheras family; their mother was from the prestigious Boethus family, and their father from the Cantheras family.

2. Ḥanamel the Egyptian

The reference here is apparently to a member of the Beit Ḥanan family, a distinguished priestly family (who apparently replaced the Boethus family). The family patriarch served at the time of the procurators, and his five sons served alternately as the high priests until shortly before the Great Revolt. The identification with the Hasmonean family is indicated by the sons' names: Elazar, Yonatan, Theopolis, Mattathias, and Ḥanan. In our comments on the revolt itself we will deal with the relations between this family, the other priests and the zealots.

3. Yishmael the son of Piabi

The Piabi (Phiabi/Fabus) family was the third family in administration of the priesthood in Israel, from whom three high priests originated: Yehoshua ben Piabi (who served from 35 BCE), Yishmael ben Piabi (in the days of Gratus), and another Yishmael ben Piabi (59 BCE).

During the days of the second Yishmael ben Piabi, there was a dispute between him and Agrippa II, regarding the independent status of the Temple. Agrippa ordered the building of a room adjacent to his house in Jerusalem, enabling him to supervise the priests' fulfillment of their duties. Yishmael responded to this request by building a barrier on the west side of the inner Temple courtyard, precisely in order to

5. On the name and its meaning, see R. Brody, "Caiphas and Cantheras," in D. Schwartz, *Agrippa* I, appendix 4, pp. 203–208.

conceal the priestly ritual from royal supervision. Agrippa countered with a command to demolish the wall. Yishmael and the Temple treasury promptly filed a complaint with Agrippa's superior, the Emperor Nero himself, requesting his annulment of Agrippa's order to demolish the wall. In classically imperial style, Nero accepted their request to leave the wall intact, but simultaneously arrested both the priest and the treasurer in Rome, enabling Agrippa II to appoint another, more conciliatory and accommodating high priest. Referring to Yishmael ben Piabi the Mishna in *Sota* states: "When Yishmael ben Piabi died, the glory of the priesthood died with him" (*Sota* 9:15). In our discussion of the closing scene of the revolt we will see what happened to Yishmael ben Piabi.

We can now return to the Mishna in Tractate *Para*. The three priests mentioned by the Mishna represent the three priestly families who shared the priesthood between them for the duration of the first century. The question is why they needed to burn three red heifers – a requirement of ashes that was far in excess of what had sufficed in the hundreds of years that preceded.

MURDER ON THE ALTAR

The following story, found in a number of versions in the sources, may provide at least a partial insight into the obsession with impurity and purity that pervaded the Temple environs. This is the version of the story as it appears in the Babylonian Talmud:

> The rabbis taught: It once happened that two were even as they ran up the ramp. And when one of them came first within four cubits of the altar, the other took a knife and thrust it into his [the other priest's] heart.
>
> Rabbi Tzaddok stood on the steps of the Hall and said: Hear me, our brothers of the house of Israel! Behold it says: "If one be found slain... the elders and judges shall come forth and measure" [Deuteronomy 21:1–2]. On whose behalf shall we offer the heifer whose neck is to be broken, on behalf of the town or on behalf of the Temple Courts? All the people burst out weeping. Afterwards, the father of the young man came and found him still in convulsions. He said: Our brothers, may he be your

> atonement for you. My son is still in convulsions and the knife has not become unclean. [His remark] comes to teach you that the impurity of the knife was of greater concern to them than the shedding of blood. (*Yoma* 23a)

Any elaboration is superfluous. This is a religious society that is meticulous on matters of ritual purity but indifferent to bloodshed. The result was that the priests were continually replenishing the storerooms of red heifer's ashes. A boy might be bleeding to death, but so long as the knife had not become impure everything was fine.

The years preceding the revolt witnessed a Temple functioning in accordance with its regular routine, but devoid of the divine spirit that was supposed to hover over it; the House was bereft of sanctity. The garments of priesthood were external fixtures beneath which there was no inner content or substance. This is the context of the tradition usually attributed to Rabbi Yose, but cited in the *Avot deRabbi Natan* in the name of Ḥanina the deputy high priest:

> During the last forty years before the Destruction, the lottery did not come up in the right hand; nor did the crimson colored strap become white; nor did the westernmost light shine; and the doors of the *Heikhal* [Sanctuary] would open by themselves, until Rabban Yoḥanan ben Zakkai rebuked them saying, "*Heikhal, Heikhal,* why do you terrify yourself? I already know that you are destined to be destroyed, for Zekharia ben Ido has already prophesied concerning you: "Open the doors, O Lebanon, and let the fire consume your cedars" [Zech. 11:1]. (*Yoma* 39b; *Avot deRabbi Natan,* recension B, ch. 7)

This phenomenon sowed the seeds of zealotry, which as we will see in the following chapter, had particularly fertile ground on which to spread.

Chapter Nineteen

Zealots and Zealotry toward the End of the Second Temple

> *Pray for the welfare of the kingdom; for without fear of governmental authorities, people would swallow each other alive.* (Avot 3:2)

THE SAGES AS FISH IN THE SEA

The previous chapter introduced us to the problematic position of the priests in the social fabric of the twilight period of the Second Temple. Our discussion of Rabban Gamliel the Elder demonstrated the sages' success in creating a fortress of Torah, and the severing of his connections with the priesthood and the rotting political leadership. The sages' leadership had its own specific agenda, one which did not include political matters regarding which it remained silent. Rabban Gamliel the Elder compared the world of Torah scholarship to that of fish in the sea, and his choice of metaphor was intentional:

> On the subject of disciples, Rabban Gamliel the Elder expounded

> on four kinds: An unclean fish [ritually inedible], a clean fish, a fish from the Jordan river, and a fish from the Great Sea [Mediterranean]. Who is the unclean fish? A son of poor parents who studies Scripture and Mishna, Halakha and Aggada and is without understanding. Who is the clean fish? This is the son of rich parents who studies Scripture and Mishna, Halakha and Aggada and has acquired understanding. Who is the fish from the Jordan? This is the leaned scholar who studies Scripture and Mishna, Halakha and Aggada and does not know what to reply. Who is the fish from the Great Sea? This is the scholar who studies Scripture and Mishna, Halakha and Aggada and who knows what to reply. (*Avot deRabbi Natan*, recension A, ch. 40)

The comparison to fish is complex. First of all it stresses the natural habitat of the fish, the very same idea that would be repeated one generation later by Rabbi Akiva, in the period of Hadrian's decrees:

> Our rabbis taught: It happened that the wicked government issued a decree forbidding the Jews to study and practice the Torah. Pappus ben Yehuda came and found Rabbi Akiva convening the public and teaching Torah. He said to him: "Akiva, are you not afraid of the Government?" He replied: "I will explain the matter to you with a parable. A fox was once walking alongside of a river and saw fish going in shoals from one place to another. He said to them: 'From what are you fleeing?' They replied: 'From the nets cast for us by men.' He said to them: 'Would you like to come up on to the dry land so that you and I can live together in the way that my ancestors lived with your ancestors?' They replied: 'Are you the one that they call the cleverest of animals? You are not clever but foolish. If we are afraid in our natural element, in which we live, how much more in the element in which we would die!' So it is with us. If this is our condition when we sit and study the Torah, of which it is written, 'For that is your life and the length of your days' [Deuteronomy 30:20], then if we go and neglect it how much worse off we shall be!" (*Berakhot* 61a)

But the comparison also has a flip side; even in their natural habitat, the fish in the sea are eternally engaged in a struggle for survival. They require protection. Accordingly, when the Talmud expounds on the verse from Habakkuk, "You have made mankind like the fish of the sea" (1:14), it invokes the teaching of Rabbi Ḥanina the deputy high priest:

> As it is with the fish in the sea – the larger ones swallow up the smaller ones – so it is with men, were it not for the fear of government, men would swallow each other alive. This is what is taught: Rabbi Ḥanina the deputy high priest, said, "Pray for the welfare of the government; for were it not for the fear thereof, men would swallow each other alive. (*Avoda Zara* 4a)

This teaching originated in fear; there are whales in the sea who threaten to devour the smaller fish, and by dint of the "fishermen's nets" (that is, fear of the authorities that both entrap and simultaneously protect us from the dangers of the outside world), we are saved. The times were such that the protection provided by the natural habitat of study and commitment to Torah was no longer sufficient. The sages therefore recommended that we avoid separating the world of Torah from external governance by which law and order are upheld.

All of these sources evoke a feeling of imminent strife characteristic of the period. In what follows we shall meet some of those who were responsible for that sense of fear.

ELAZAR BEN DINAI

The Midrash expounds upon the verse aforementioned in connection with the *egla arufa* (a heifer's neck was broken as an atonement for an unsolved murder): "If a slain person be found… and the identity of the killer is not known" (Deuteronomy 21:1).

> "If one happens to be found" – but not when it is a frequent occurrence. Hence the sages said: From the time when murderers proliferated, the breaking of the heifer's neck was discontinued. When Elazar ben Dinai and Teḥina ben Perisha appeared,

> he [Teḥina the son of Perisha] was subsequently renamed "the son of the murderer." (*Sifrei Devarim*, 205)

According to the *tanna* the law of the *egla arufa* only applied in an ideal society, one in which murder was not commonplace. In times in which "murderers abound," there is no legitimacy in implementing a law that enabled the declaration, "Our hands did not shed this blood" (Deuteronomy 21:7). The *tanna*'s naming of notorious murderers, including one whose infamy even attached to his name, is indicative of the scourge of bloodshed at that time.

This teaching appears in the Mishna at the end of Tractate *Sota* (9:9), which depicts the decline of morally based rituals that were intended to preserve an ideal Jewish society. Ben Dinai also figures in additional sources which warrant closer attention.

One of these sources (Mishna *Kelim*) refers to a particular kind of oven made by Ben Dinai. This is the same oven as the "Oven of Akhnai," known to many as it features in the famous dispute between Rabbi Eliezer and Rabbi Yehoshua. The Mishna describes the oven as being of a type over which there is controversy as to whether or not it contracts impurity. Immediately after that section the Mishna states:

> As for the cauldrons of Arabs which are hollows dug in the ground and plastered with clay, if the plastering can stand of itself – it is susceptible to impurity; otherwise it is not susceptible. Such was the [kind of] oven made by Ben Dinai. (*Kelim* 5:10)

This oven is a kind of outdoor stove, sunk into a pit whose walls are coated with cement. The sages question whether this type of oven can be categorized as one that contracts impurity. The determining criterion is the independent durability of the oven. In other words, will it remain intact even if one digs another hole just behind it, or will it cave in? This kind of oven was named after Ben Dinai, the murderer described in other sources as being a mountain dweller, living in isolation from civilized places. The oven described by the Mishna was admirably suited to Ben Dinai's nomadic, on-the-run lifestyle.

The Mishna in Tractate *Ketubot* (2:9) discusses the status of a

Jewess captured by non-Jews, distinguishing between a person captured for purposes of negotiations and one who was imprisoned as a punishment for an offense punishable by death. In the name of Levi (Rabbi Yoḥanan's student), the Talmud (27a) cites the case of Ben Dinai's wife as an example of imprisonment for purposes of imposing the death sentence. The Roman authorities were all too familiar with the Ben Dinai family, and were determined to bring them to justice. In the words of Rashba in his commentary on the passage:

> This means that he was a bandit and had been sentenced to death, thus the king had no compunctions concerning his wife. (Rashba, *Ketubot* 27a)

This family's questionable heritage was preserved among the *amora'im* of Babylonia, as attested by Rava:

> Rava proclaimed in Meḥoza: "Balai, Dinai, Talai, Melai, Zagai – are all disqualified." (*Kiddushin* 70b)

Josephus too tells us about this "distinguished" family, though like other historians, he provides a number of rather more colorful particulars. Josephus relates that Elazar ben Dinai met a group of Galilean Jews at the height of their struggle with the Samaritans. This meeting took place during the reign of the Procurator Cumanus (circa 50 CE) when the Roman administration was adopting an increasingly tyrannical attitude toward the Jews, which triggered the first Jewish revolt against Roman hegemony. Predictably, the revolt erupted on Pesaḥ, and fearing that the Pesaḥ pilgrimage to Jerusalem would further stoke the fires of rebellion, Cumanus summoned reinforcements for the soldiers guarding the walls of the Temple mount. Josephus gives the following description of what ensued:

> On the fourth day of the festival, one of the soldiers uncovered his genitals and exhibited them to the multitude – an action which provoked anger and rage among the onlookers, who said that it was not they who had been insulted but that it was a blasphemy

> against God. Some of the bolder ones also reviled Cumanus, asserting that the soldier had been prompted by him. Cumanus, when informed, was himself not a little provoked at the insulting remarks, but still merely admonished them to put an end to this lust for revolution and not to set disorders ablaze during the festival. However, he failed to persuade them, for they only attacked him with more scurrility, and he therefore ordered the whole army to don full armor and come to Antonia; this was, as I have said before, a fortress overlooking the Temple. The crowd, seeing the arrival of the soldiers, was frightened and started to flee. But since the exits were narrow, they, supposing that they were being pursued by the enemy, pushed together in their flight and crushed to death many of their number who were caught in the narrow passages. Indeed, the number of those who perished in that disturbance was figured at twenty thousand. (*Antiquities* XX, 105–124)

This massacre heralded the beginning of a national uprising that began in Jerusalem from where it spread to the plain. Josephus recounts acts of Jewish banditry against Roman soldiers in the villages and on the highways, and usually the soldiers concerned were not trained combat soldiers, having been brought over for purposes of administrative duties and policing.

The second confrontation erupted in the north. A group of Galileans on their festival pilgrimage to Jerusalem had been attacked and slaughtered in the Jenin area by a group of local Samaritans. Josephus records the following Jewish response:

> The leaders of the Galileans, hearing of the occurrence, came to Cumanus and besought him to avenge the murder of those who had been slain. He however, having been bribed by the Samaritans, neglected to avenge them. The Galileans, indignant at this, urged the Jewish masses to take up arms and to assert their liberty, for they said that slavery itself was bitter, but when it involved insolent treatment it was intolerable. Those in authority tried to mollify them and to reduce the disorder, and offered to induce Cumanus to punish the murderers, but the masses paid no heed

> to them and rather took up their arms and enlisted the assistance of Elazar son of Deinaeus [= ben Dinai] – he was a brigand who for many years had had his home in the mountains, and they fired and sacked certain villages of the Samaritans… From that time onwards the whole of Judea was infested with bands of brigands. (Josephus, ibid.)

Josephus describes the meeting between Elazar ben Dinai, the notorious bandit and murderer, and a group of Jews motivated by their zeal for God and the besmirched national honor. This alliance of idealists with criminal elements made it difficult to distinguish between the "good" and the "bad," to discern whether a particular act was the product of zealotry in divine service or nothing more than violence for its own sake. For example, the midrash on the verse, "I adjure you the daughters of Jerusalem" (Song of Songs 2:7):

> Rabbi Onia said: They were adjured for four oaths corresponding to four generations who tried to hasten the end and came to grief, namely one in the days of Amram, once in the days of Dinai, once in the days of Ben Koziva and once in the days of Shutelaḥ the son of Ephraim. (*Shir HaShirim Raba* 2)

In this source Ben Dinai is counted among a distinguished gallery of individuals. He is no longer the murderer whose actions fomented anarchy, culminating in the abolition of the law of the *egla arufa*. Instead, he has become one of those who "hasten the end" – a visionary whose passionate sense of redemption renders him incapable of witnessing national humiliation, and prompts him to attempt to accelerate the messianic process. The midrashic references to Amram and to Shutelaḥ ben Ephraim are obscure. The latter may be an allusion to the famous tradition of the tribe of Ephraim that attempted to hasten the Jewish people's redemption by prematurely escaping from Egypt. This source already appears in the *Mekhilta*:

> Another interpretation: "For God said" – this refers to the war of the sons of Ephraim, as it is said: "And the sons of Ephraim:

> Shutelaḥ, and Bered his son ... were killed by the men of Gath" [1 Chronicles 7:20–21], and as it is said: "The children of Ephraim, though armed with bows, turned back on the day of battle" [Psalms 78:9]. Why? Because "they kept not the Covenant of God and refused to walk in His Law" [ibid. 78:10], that is, because they violated the oath. (*Mekhilta, Beshalaḥ*)[1]

The Midrash similarly refers to Ben Koziva (also identified as Bar Kokhba) as the classic case of a rebel attempting to hasten the redemption. Ben Dinai the brigand is thus commemorated in the pantheon of Jewish freedom fighters. From here it was just small step to his incorporation into the prayer book in the heart of the Tisha B'Av lamentations:

> My opponent's troops ambushed me on the mountain;
> they flooded the heads of Zion as a raging river.
> The murderous sin of Nob was held fast against me;
> You set the snare, inciting my enemies.
> My people shrieked in the days of the rebel Ben Dinai:
> "God is the Righteous One!"
>
> (Rabbi Elazar HaKalir, "*Shavat Suru Meni*")

The simple import of the poem is that, in the nation's later historical memory, Ben Dinai was remembered as having spearheaded a national and spiritual rejuvenation. The entire period bears his name as "the days of Ben Dinai" evoking precisely the same connotation as the "Days of Mattathias" or the "Days of Mordekhai and Esther."[2]

1. The translations of Exodus compiled in Israel retained an explicit description of the departure of the sons of Ephraim as an act of "hastening the end." See Joseph Heinemann, *Aggada and Its Development* [Hebrew] (Jerusalem: 1974).
2. Rabbi Yehuda Assad, a nineteenth-century Hungarian rabbi (and student of the Ḥatam Sofer) offered the following explanation of this poem:

> The poet's words: "My people cried in the days of Ben Dinai," in the poem "*Shavat Suru Meni,*" refer to whom? The illustrious Rabbi, Asher son of Rabbi Yehuda, of blessed memory, gave the following explanation: "It has been said that this is the name of a great man, for the Jewish people in his era sought to rebel by force and they failed, as recorded in *Shir HaShirim Raba*, and there are

In summary, religious Judaism has always been ambivalent toward zealots. While the distinction between the murderer and the zealot is frequently tenuous, zealots in the name of God will certainly not be execrated as were the murderers who lead to the annulment of the *egla arufa* law. We acknowledge the zealot's role in precipitating the Destruction, but from a historical-religious perspective we take pride in their religious and spiritual fortitude and resilience, and ultimately they merit entrance into the pantheon of national heroes.

THE SICARII

A social and political agenda

Things were no calmer during the days of Felix, the next governor. His failed attempts to quell the incendiary spirit by wholesale execution of "bandits," were paralleled by the steadily increasing power of the zealots. In the general atmosphere of conflagration and revolution a new group emerged, the Sicarii, a group of zealots who armed themselves with small daggers (*sicarii*) concealed under their garments. Aiming to eliminate all who were suspected of collaboration with the Roman government, their first victim was Jonathan the High Priest, whom they suspected of having allied with the Governor Felix. The background of these suspicions may have been Jonathan's trip to Rome in 52 CE in order to resolve the dispute with the Governor Cumanus. Indeed, during that visit he secured the appointment of the Governor Felix. However, apart from being an insurgent nationalist force, the Sicarii's emergence also had ramifications in other directions as well. As mentioned above, the elite ruling class of priests had joined forces with the Jerusalem

those who say that this is a hint to [King] Josiah who revoked all of his decisions until his eighteenth year and he was killed because of his generation's sins, and at the time of his soul's departure he proclaimed, "God is righteous ... etc." And there are those who have said that it refers to Elazar ben Dinai, who was a bandit who robbed and killed people, and all of the Jewish people pleaded before God, "You are a righteous God who sees this person's deeds and remains silent." And see in the Mishna in the final chapter of *Sota*, "Elazar ben Dinai came ... they began to call him 'the son of the murderer.'" See also in the Tosafot *Yom Tov* [ad loc.], and in Tractate *Kilayim*, 5:10 and 8:9." (*Responsa Yehuda Ya'aleh*, pt. 1, *Yoreh De'ah*, 1:359) oligarchy, operating to oppress the rural classes, who found an ally in the Sicarii. The Jewish society in the twilight period of the Second Temple was thus divided, and polarized, a phenomenon that was aggravated by the deterioration of relations with Rome which worked to the detriment of the rival groups. The high priests seeking to retain Judea's status as a Roman vassal-state met with the opposition of priests from the periphery villages who aligned with the zealots and stepped up the struggle against Roman rule over the Roman satellites. Both rabbinic and external literature abound with testimony regarding the period in general, providing us with descriptions of aristocratic priests from the ruling classes stealing produce from the threshing floors of periphery priests in order to appropriate their tithes.

In the war between rival sectors of Jewish society the sages played a peacemaker role, attempting to douse the flames of rebellion. Contemporaneous testimonies depict the sages' opposition to the aggressive zealotry that originated with the Sicarii. Josephus informs us of the "dignitaries of Jerusalem" who attempted to restore a semblance of normalcy and calm by advocating conciliation with the Romans. Unfortunately, the rivalry between the two groups played right into the hands of the zealots. The high priests, whose spiritual and moral shortcomings were recounted above, nonetheless merited the support of the wealthy local Jerusalem leadership with whom they joined forces in oppressing the lower-level village priests. Not surprisingly the socio-economic gaps were compounded by the political rivalry. The Sicarii already had a political agenda of national freedom, and waving the card of social justice broadened their appeal to additional classes of society. The *baraita* in *Avot deRabbi Natan* (recension B, ch. 13) describes the "burning of food reserves" by Sicarii. Along with the burning of bills of debt, this was part of a policy intended to undermine debt collection from the poor by the wealthy classes of Jerusalem (see Josephus, *The Jewish War* II.17:6). They capitalized on the convergence of ideology with economic hardship and as the economic crisis deepened, the zealots' movement increased in strength. The fires of zeal spread throughout the country until they reached the streets of Jerusalem.

Hatred of Rome

The various insurgent movements roaming the country during this period were united by their hatred of Rome and all that was associated with it. Resentment seethed at the Promised Land being trampled under the boots of an alien, hostile ruler. This resentment fueled the flames of a rebellion that had never been totally extinguished and only temporarily doused during the century following the loss of Hasmonean independence.

This was a period in which the sages were wary not to openly challenge the Roman rulers, and avoided direct pronouncements concerning their attitude to the Romans. Their silence enables the conclusion that *de facto* at least, they agreed to tax evasion even if it meant swearing falsely, as indicated in the Mishna:

> Men may vow to murderers, robbers and tax collectors that what they have is a heave-offering [priest's-due] even if it is not a heave-offering, or that they belong to the king's household even though they do not belong to the king's household. (Mishna, *Nedarim* 3:4)

Based on a number of other tannaitic sources Rabbi Saul Lieberman demonstrates (*Tosefta KiFeshuta, Nedarim,* p. 419) that the term "murderers" (*haragin*) should actually read *ḥaragin*[3] which he interprets as referring to official inspectors with powers of expropriation, and hence the connection to the term "*ḥerem*" in the sense of dedicated or sanctified property. The Mishna teaches that it is permitted to create a fiction of produce having been "dedicated to heaven" so as to exempt it from government taxes. A variation on this view appears in the early Geonim, for whom the *ḥaram* was a non-Jew charged with collecting customs for the king, that is, another bureaucrat filling the royal coffers with subjects' money. Regardless of its precise meaning, the Mishna's overall intention is clear: it is permitted to intentionally lie to the tax collector coming

3. Lieberman published a detailed discussion of this question, (together with Y. Kutcher): "Murderers, Confiscators and Tax collectors" [Hebrew], *Studies in the Torah of Eretz Yisrael* (Jerusalem: 5751), pp. 456–462.

to levy taxes on produce by telling him that the produce is sanctified (*teruma*). This was a form of tax evasion, arising from Roman deference to the tithes and sanctified donations which had been designated by their owners for the Temple.[4] The Mishna thus permits the exploitation of the Roman law in order to evade taxes.

For the Babylonian Talmud (*Nedarim* 28a), it was inconceivable that the halakha permitted this kind of tax evasion, inasmuch as the Babylonian tradition accepted the position of Shmuel, a first generation Babylonian *amora*, who established the rule *dina demalkhuta dina* (the law of the Kingdom is law).[5] In its response, the Talmud distinguishes between "unlimited tax" (that which is collected capriciously and arbitrarily) or a tax collector who acts of his own initiative (without any higher authorization), and an organized legal system which satisfies the condition of *dina demalkhuta dina*. It almost goes without saying that the Talmud's answer does not relate to the problem of taxes under the Roman regime, because the tax collectors were legally authorized and under the law were entitled to an allowance. The problem was that this allowance imposed an inhumane burden on the citizen.[6]

The sages' confrontation with the Zealots

Naturally, the zealot forces were not all of the same mettle, consisting of different and often antithetical factions. Any idealistic group inevitably also absorbs a number of free-riding hooligans who discredit the group as a whole. The Galilee zealots such as Elazar and Yehuda were

4. On this Roman law, see Ben Shalom, *Beit Shammai*, p. 190, n. 86.
5. On this subject, see S. Shilo, *Dina DeMalkhuta Dina* (Jerusalem: 1974).
6. In this passage, the *Rishonim* differentiate the laws of the land of Israel and the Diaspora, explaining that the rule of *dina demalkhuta dina* only applies in the Diaspora (as per Tosafot and the Ran). This geographical distinction is actually rooted in the difference between non-Jewish government which can enforce its own laws contrary to Torah law by which it is not bound, and Jewish government, which cannot enforce its own laws contrary to Torah law, "because all of Israel have a partnership in the land of Israel" (Ran, s.v. "*bemokhes ha'omed me'elav*"). Maimonides, in his *Commentary on the Mishna,* ruled that there was no difference between a non-Jewish king and a Jewish king (see *Hilkhot Melakhim* ["Laws of Kings"] 4:1). This Talmudic passage is the basis of the question of the halakhic status of the Israeli legal system, but this is not the place for elaboration.

thus a class above the Sicarii or Ben Dinai. In the next part of this book we will deal independently with the Sicarii Zealots of Masada, their suicide and their legacy. However, despite our awareness of the salient differences between the groups, we cannot ignore that which they had in common: the creation of a volatile climate that is hostile to the authorities and everything related to them. In this context the rabbinic perspective of zealotry, as seen through the spectrum of Pinehas, bore no trace of caprice:

> Whereupon Pinehas immediately stood up from his Sanhedrin seat and took a spear in his hand and put the iron head of it into his belt. He leaned on the wood [of the spear, concealing its purpose] until he reached the door. When he came to the door, the occupant said, "Where are you headed to Pinehas?" He said to them, "Do you not agree with me that the tribe of Levi is near the tribe of Shimon under all circumstances?" They said to him, "Leave him alone. Maybe the separatists have permitted this matter after all. (Talmud Yerushalmi, *Sanhedrin* 10:2 [28d])

It is interesting that the Midrash describes Pinehas as one of the Sicarii. His zealotry along with the blessing conferred upon him (a covenant for eternal service) is deeply rooted in our culture and is utilized when necessary. It belongs to a system of unwritten laws: "This is the law, but not to be instructed." For example, according to one of the mishnayot from the Temple times:

> If a man stole a sacred vessel, or was cursed by a sorcerer, or had relations with an Aramean woman, the zealots may fall upon him. If a priest served [at the altar] in a state of uncleanliness, his brothers the priests would not bring him to the court but the young men among the priests took him outside the Temple Court and would split his brain open with clubs. (Mishna, *Sanhedrin* 9:6)

The Mishna prescribes a norm of willful disregard. The subject is a complex one for any society that finds itself in a twilight zone between the imperative to uphold the law, and an awareness of a reality that circumvents the law and is in need of a normative response to zealotry. The attitude toward zealotry in the sources is not uniform; there are those who seek to repress the phenomenon and those who seek to elevate it.

The disputes between Beit Shammai and Beit Hillel are generally viewed as also reflecting a tension between the zealots and the moderates: Beit Shammai as the zealots and Beit Hillel as the moderates.[7] In this section I have endeavored to show a somewhat more complex picture. On the one hand, zealotry and the nationalist spirit have deep roots in Judaism and would certainly not have been totally rejected by the various streams of the Jewish people. On the other hand, the sages were paralyzed by their fear of the zealots taking control, creating a void in which other forces could thrive. It is this aspect which underlies Rabbi Ḥanina's prayer for the welfare of the government, when he confronted the corruption that had penetrated the priesthood, and the bloodshed: "For without fear of governmental authorities, people would swallow each other alive."

7. This distinction is the topic of Ben Shalom's study, *Beit Shammai*, and in a broad sense, he adopts and develops the view of Graetz.

Chapter Twenty

A Contemporary Perspective: Leadership in the Face of Extremism

The fourth part of this book has shone a light on the signposts of a society in the process of disintegration, in which violence has assumed control of all of life's crossroads, threatening to destroy all those who stand in its way. It began with the dearth of an activist leadership capable of restraining and effectively channeling the strife that was erupting among the various sectors of the population. It continued with a glimpse into the Temple, only to flee from its harsh scenario of godless priests of religion, and men of ritual devoid of holiness – technicians of the Temple who focused exclusively on themselves and their own survival. This would not be the source of salvation. As the economic crisis grew more profound the periphery groups steadily increased their influence over the mainstream. Admittedly, the desire to be liberated from under the yoke of Rome and to reestablish Jewish independence in the Holy

Land is an integral element of serving God. The actions of the zealots of Beit Shammai, who compiled *Megillat Ta'anit* and refused to bring sacrifices to the emperor, displayed their conviction that reality is not determined by fate, and that mortal men have the capacity to change it. The zealot tradition goes back to the Hasmonean period and is certainly well anchored in the Pharisee tradition.[1] The trouble was that this form of zealotry merged with an entirely different kind of zealotry, motivated by criminality and aggression, and totally devoid of any holiness or service of God. There was a convergence of four factors: a society in disintegration, a corrupt priesthood, silence from the sages, and Roman tyranny. The combination of these factors released the Jewish society from the need to conduct its struggle based on the foundations of morality and Torah. The society degenerated into a situation of "might is right."

Modern Jewish nationalism made a similar attempt to revolt against the yoke of foreign government, to return to the patriarchal heritage and to settle in the Promised Land. The zealotry motivating the return to Zion and Jewish sovereignty contains an inner kernel of sacred fire. Even when Israeli society tired of bearing the torch of holy revolt, there were still those who persisted in replenishing the fire and continued to hold the torch up high. Zealotry of this kind became a symbol of devotion and of sanctification of God's name.

But in our times as in theirs, the combination of certain forces creates alliances that undermine the legitimacy of any struggle and of any revolt. This happens when negative, criminal elements infiltrate those of pure and holy motivation, thus defiling the legitimacy of the struggle. Evidently, history repeats itself, except that unlike our forefathers, we can learn from our history.

Our lesson from this section is that everything depends on the leadership that is capable – or incapable – of assuming responsibility. There is never a vacuum in any generation or in any movement. Leadership that stands up and takes responsibility can also lead the turbulent, idealistic and zealous forces, diverting them toward the direction of repair and growth. Leadership that withdraws from the public arena inevitably finds that those very same forces motivated by an idea, endan-

1. Ben Shalom, *Beit Shammai*, ch. 4, pp. 157–171.

ger the entire building by the fire of zealotry. In this section we saw how leadership reached a stage where it was too late and it could not jettison those forces. The fires of zealotry had extinguished the spirit.

Part Five

Destruction

The Men of the Great Assembly	The Pairs	Shammai, Hillel and Their Students	Rabban Gamliel the Elder	The Destruction
-450 -300	-200	-50	30	60 70
Cyrus to Alexander of Macedonia	The Hasmoneans	Herod	The Governors	The War with Rome

Preface

The Temple's destruction was not a sudden event, having been preceded by a gradual internal disintegration and the increasingly oppressive Roman rule. The Romans did their utmost to intensify the tyranny of their rule, particularly against the Jewish population. However, the later procurators failed to navigate between the conflicting tendencies and aspirations of the Jews and other subjected populations – thereby fomenting insurgency and ultimately outright rebellion among the Jewish population. The leading sage of that time, Rabban Yoḥanan ben Zakkai, decided to abandon the city of Jerusalem when he realized that the Destruction was inevitable. Other leaders such as Rabban Shimon ben Gamliel and the High Priest Ḥanan ben Ḥanan established a provisional emergency government and attempted to influence matters from within. The Sicarii sought allegiances with non-Jewish elements and chose Masada as their fortress in which to consolidate their forces and to isolate themselves. Confronted by a nationalistic zealotry infiltrated by criminal elements, the nation's moderate leadership was powerless to stop the rebellion or even to quell its intensity. The Romans responded with the full fury of the forces at their disposal. Under these circumstances, the Destruction was a foregone conclusion.

Our concern in this section is not with the Destruction and the war that led to it but rather with its social and political context, including its effect on the sages themselves, and naturally, the sages' response. From the perspective of the Jewish leadership, the enchanting figure of Rabbi Tzaddok encapsulates the essence of this period. It was he who stood at the steps of the altar, remonstrating with the people over the moral degeneracy of their punctilious concern for ritual purity while showing total indifference to blood shed on the altar's steps. It was he who wandered the streets of Jerusalem, witnessing the economic crisis that preceded the Destruction, and it was he who wept and lamented over the ruins.

Chapter Twenty-One

Historical and Political Background: Jerusalem on the Eve of the Destruction

ANARCHY AND THE RISE OF THE ZEALOTS

The previous section concluded with a discussion of the emergence of the Zealot camp – an amalgam of ideologically motivated Galileans and blatantly criminal elements such as Ben Dinai. We also dwelt upon the character of the Sicarii, who combined nationalistic fervor with hatred of Rome and aggressive, socially oriented activities. The discussion now focuses on the final years before the Destruction and the Destruction itself. As in Parts 1–4, here too we begin with an introduction to the period for a better understanding of the sages' role and their intellectual and spiritual response to the *zeitgeist*.[1]

1. The description is taken from Josephus, *Antiquities of the Jews*, XX, 189–196. The discussion in the following chapter is based on a series of articles in A. Kasher (ed.), *The Great Revolt* [Hebrew] (Jerusalem: 5743).

THE DAYS OF THE PROCURATOR FELIX: DETERIORATION OF RELATIONS WITH THE PROCURATORS

The fifth decade of the first century CE (the days of the Procurator Felix) was characterized by stiffening opposition to Rome on religious and economic levels. Both the Jewish and the non-Jewish historians of the period tell us about the corruption that riddled Felix's administration. Everything was legitimate for the satiating of his desires, and his governance exemplified the "slave who becomes king."[2] In addition to all of this, he also did his utmost to subdue the nascent nationalist elements among the Jewish people. In the previous section, we touched on the Galileans who adopted Ben Dinai as their leader. Felix succeeded in arresting Ben Dinai and sending him to stand trial in Rome. Nonetheless, the Roman attempts to crush the rebellion only gave rise to leadership that was even more extreme and more ideological, championing the cause of struggle for religious freedom. For the rebels, the worship of God precluded the service of any other authority and legitimized all means of attaining national-religious freedom. Anyone joining forces with the alien government was considered a "pursuer," liable for death. Josephus gives the following description of the growing power of the Zealots:

> Now when these were quieted, it happened, as it does in a diseased body, that another part was subject to an inflammation; for a company of deceivers and robbers got together, and persuaded the Jews to revolt, and exhorted them to assert their liberty, inflicting death on those that continued in obedience to the Roman government and saying that those who willingly chose slavery ought to be forcibly removed. They divided themselves into different groups and spread out all over the country; they plundered the homes of the powerful, and killed them, and set the villages ablaze so that the whole land was filled with their violence. This war spread and intensified every day. (*The Jewish War* II.13:6–7)

2. Aryeh Kasher, "Factors and Circumstances Leading to the War of the Jews against the Romans," in *The Great Revolt* (see footnote 1 above), pp. 74–75.

THE DISPUTE BETWEEN THE JEWS AND GREEKS IN CAESAREA

One of the events that sparked off the struggle against the Romans was Emperor Nero's verdict in a dispute between the Jews and Greeks of Caesarea.[3] The dispute was a protracted one, having its origins in the days of Herod. The two populations of Caesarea – the Jews and the Greeks – were divided over the status and control of the city: Would it be a Greek *polis* or a Jewish city? During the late fifties CE, this dispute degenerated into open violence. The procurator Felix attempted to restore law and order by ordering a ceasefire, but was far from impartial, and sided openly with the Greeks. When local Jews defied his orders he responded by ordering his soldiers to attack, resulting in the death of many of Caesarea's Jews. Josephus relates that the Caesarean Jews would sooner have died than have their demands for privileged status in the city rejected. The situation continued to deteriorate until the matter was brought before Emperor Nero (in 60 CE) who had asked to hear both sides. For six years Nero withheld judgment, until in the spring of 66 CE, he ruled in favor of the Greeks. Josephus (*The Jewish War* II.14:4) establishes this event as the beginning of the war.

THE RULE OF PROCURATOR ALBINUS AND THE STRUGGLE AGAINST THE "BANDITS"

In 62 CE, Albinus was appointed Roman procurator. His rule signified the most significant deterioration prior to the actual rebellion. In addition to the struggle against Roman rule, Jewish society was ridden by internecine strife. Assisted by the Jerusalem oligarchy, the high priesthood extorted the property of the weaker classes, further aggravating their hatred for anything associated with the forces of authority and further stimulating anarchy. Albinus, for his part, stiffened the already unbearable tax burden and pushed the farmers into an intolerable situation in which they had nothing to lose. Paradoxically, it was precisely during that period that Herod's building and renovation of Jerusalem

3. This dispute is superbly documented in Israel Levin's article, "The Jewish-Greek Conflict in First Century Caesarea," *JJS* 25 (1974), pp. 381–397 (reprinted in Kasher, *The Great Revolt*, pp. 173–195).

and the Temple was completed, but the completion of the building resulted in increased unemployment and attendant social unrest. Until 64 CE, tens of thousands of people had been involved in the construction and renovation of the Temple, but with the completion of the project they all found themselves without work. Evidently, instead of alleviating the tax burden and taking measures to diffuse the social time-bomb, Albinus acted in a manner that merely exacerbated the situation. Josephus observes that "nor was there any sort of wickedness that could be named but he had a hand in it" (*The Jewish War* II.14:1).

THE DAYS OF THE PROCURATOR FLORUS – SPARKING THE REBELLION

Gessius Florus came to power in 64 CE and continued the policy of economic oppression, which culminated in the pillaging of entire cities. It was during Florus' reign that Emperor Nero issued his judgment granting the Greeks political and cultural seniority in Caesarea, at the expense of the Jewish population. According to various accounts, the Greeks attempted to test their newly acquired seniority, intentionally blocking the entrance to a synagogue by the construction of a factory. The Jewish attempt to circumvent crisis by purchasing the site was rejected by the Greeks. Instead, deliberately attempting to aggravate matters, the Greeks sacrificed birds on Shabbat in a cynical effort to mock the Jewish ritual of bringing a sacrifice for the purification of the leper (Leviticus 14:1–7). This humiliation proved too much for the Jews, and fist fights broke out between Jewish youths and the Greek provocateurs. The event was etched into the national Jewish consciousness by naming the synagogue "The Synagogue of the Rebels" (Talmud Yerushalmi, *Bikkurim*, 3:3 [65d], and parallel sources), and in its wake masses of Jews deserted the city, taking the scrolls of the Torah with them.

This period was also witness to a massacre of the Jews in Caesarea. Josephus relates (*The Jewish War* II.18:1) that over twenty thousand Jews were killed, and that the massacre released the pent-up hatred between the Jews and non-Jews in the border cities, too. The entire country soon became consumed by the flames of slaughter and banditry. As if to further stoke the flames, the Procurator Florus embezzled the Temple funds on the pretext of having to pay for the damages caused by the

Jews to government officials. The Jewish response was spontaneous and immediate. First, the Zealots isolated the fortress of Antonia, the symbol of Roman hegemony over the Temple Mount and the Temple itself. They subsequently disrupted the daily sacrifice for the wellbeing of the emperor and the Roman people. This move was initiated by one of the younger deputy priests, Elazar ben Ḥanania (according to Josephus' account). Actually, his family is already familiar to us from previous chapters. His father was Ḥanania ben Ḥizkia ben Garon one of Shammai's outstanding pupils, who authored *Megillat Ta'anit* in an attempt to revive the Hasmonean legacy in the national consciousness.[4] The nationalistic trend of this family was clear, and they had succeeded in transmitting their fanatic nationalism from one generation to the next, from the days of Shammai until the Destruction.

4. This subject was dealt with in the chapters on the students of Shammai and Hillel.

Chapter Twenty-Two

Zekharia ben Avkulos

THE EMPEROR'S SACRIFICE AND THE EXCESSIVE HUMILITY OF ZEKHARIA BEN AVKULOS

The clarion call of Elazar ben Ḥanania to discontinue the sacrifice for the emperor's welfare touches on the famous Talmudic story of Kamtza and Bar Kamtza, the most famous of the legends of the Destruction. A careful reading of the story illuminates the nature of the social structure of Jerusalem at the outbreak of the Great Revolt, from the perspective of the Babylonian Talmud:[1]

1. I have cited the version of the story as it appears in the Babylonian Talmud, as distinct from its parallel in the Israel sources: *Eikha Rabati*, 4:2 (Buber edition, pp. 142–143). P. Mandel wrote a comparative study in which he claims that the Israel version of the story omits any mention of Zekharia ben Avkulos' "humility," focusing rather on exemplifying the internal-social reasons for the Destruction. The Babylonian version focuses on the bankruptcy of the rabbinic leadership and the collapse of the halakhic system that it established. See P. Mandel, "Tales of the Destruction of the Temple: Between the Land of Israel and Babylonia," in I. Gafni (ed.), *Center and Diaspora: The Land of Israel and the Diaspora in the Second Temple, Mishnaic and Talmudic Periods* [Hebrew] (Jerusalem: 1994), pp. 141–158.

> It was because of Kamtza and Bar Kamtza that Jerusalem was destroyed.
>
> There was a man who was a friend of Kamtza, and an enemy of Bar Kamtza. He made a feast and said to his servant, "Go and bring Kamtza to my feast," but the servant brought Bar Kamtza instead. Looking at his guests, the host saw that Bar Kamtza was seated there.
>
> He said to him, "Since you are my enemy, what are you doing here? Get up and get out!"
>
> Bar Kamtza said, "Since I'm here already, let me stay and I will pay you for what I eat and drink."
>
> The host responded, "No!"
>
> "I will pay for half the cost of the feast."
>
> "No!"
>
> "I will pay the entire cost of the feast!"
>
> "No!" And he seized Bar Kamtza, stood him up, and threw him out!
>
> Bar Kamtza thought, "Since the rabbis were there, saw the whole thing, and did not protest, obviously they had no objection to my embarrassment! I will go and inform on them to the emperor." (*Gittin* 55b–56a)

This is an uncensored picture of the alliance between the Jerusalem aristocracy and the sages. The same story appears in number of sources, and its message is unequivocal: the sages were supported by the aristocracy and as such were incapable of challenging their actions. With the generation's spiritual leadership economically subordinate to the wealthy classes and the politicians, money reigned supreme over all walks of life. We have already seen how the high priesthood was purchased for money, creating an alliance of priesthood and government. We pondered the sages' passivity and silence in confronting the events of the period. It transpires that this plight was the inevitable consequence of a system in which Torah scholars relied on the benevolence of the wealthy. We need only recall one of the dinners at which Rabban Yoḥanan ben Zakkai hosted the Jerusalem aristocracy, in the course of which he discovered his brilliant pupil, Eliezer ben Hyrcanus:

> On that day, Rabban Yoḥanan ben Zakkai sat expounding in Jerusalem and all of the leadership of Israel sat before him. Rabban Yoḥanan heard that Hyrcanus (the father of Rabbi Eliezer) was coming and he appointed guards and said to them: "If Hyrcanus comes, do not let him sit down." Hyrcanus arrived and they would not let him sit down. He weaved through the crowd until he reached Ben Tzitzit Hakeset, Nakdimon ben Gurion, and Ben Kalba Savua. He sat among them trembling. (*Avot deRabbi Natan*, recension A, ch. 5)

Our concern here is not with the character of Eliezer ben Hyrcanus, but rather with the background images: a banquet for the wealthy upper classes; the hosts are the prominent Torah sages of Jerusalem. Rabban Yoḥanan is holding court, expounding the Torah, and all of the Jerusalem dignitaries are sitting before him. Who exactly are these leaders? Further on, we learn that it was an assembly of the foremost personae of Jerusalem, some of whom we are already familiar with: Ben Tzitzit Hakeset, Nakdimon ben Gurion, and Ben Kalba Savua, the three foremost tycoons of Jerusalem. *Avot deRabbi Natan* (recension A, ch. 6) reports that Tzitzit Hakeset merited his name by virtue of his silver-coated bed (*keset* = coating). The daughter of Nakdimon ben Gurion was reputed to have a bed lined with twelve thousand golden *dinarim*. Ben Kalba Savua was so called because one would go into his house hungry as a dog (*kelev*) and come out satiated (*savea*). Hyrcanus was Rabbi Eliezer's father, an estate owner in one of the neighboring villages, apparently from the upper classes, though not part of the Jerusalem aristocracy. Pushing his way in, he found himself seated with the financial magnates of Jerusalem. However, there was also a "bouncer" at the entrance, receiving precise instructions as to whom to allow in and whom to kick out. The emerging picture of the Jerusalem *beit midrash* is that of a carefully screened club house, closed to the public at large. It was precisely in this *beit midrash* that an alliance was forged between the Torah scholars and the moneyed classes.

The particular importance of this picture lies in its being an incidental and hence authentic description. The author certainly had no advance intention of depicting Jerusalem's social structure on the eve of the Destruction, other than to tell us about Rabbi Eliezer's status in making the transition from his father's house to the *beit midrash*. We can easily imagine the handsome contributions made by the city's rich to the prosperity of the house of study. But there are no free lunches. The wealthy influential people needed to be connected to the wellsprings of wisdom and Torah in Jerusalem, and they acquired this connection through their coffers.

Was Rabban Yoḥanan ben Zakkai's yeshiva involved in local politics? Did it blow with the turbulent winds of war and national spirit of zealotry? It is difficult to assume that the students of the yeshiva were oblivious to the agitation that spread throughout Jerusalem during the years preceding the Destruction. Jerusalem was the arena for so many power struggles and intrigues between the various streams of Zealots during those years that it seems inconceivable that the winds of war failed to leave their mark on the yeshiva. Unless, we find that the yeshiva consciously decided to fortify itself against all of the Zealots' tendencies and to become an "ivory tower," intent on surviving, come what may.

The sages also partook in the meal to which Bar Kamtza was mistakenly invited. The visitor's identity is unknown to us, but evidently he was one of the wealthy patrons who supported the yeshiva or was affiliated with it. The sages were perhaps not overjoyed with the conduct of the rich, but they reconciled themselves to it, and hence they failed to respond to Bar Kamtza's humiliation. Parallel to the Talmudic story, mention is made of another prominent sage who was there and who failed to respond.

> Zekharia ben Avkulos was there and he had the opportunity to protest but remained silent. (*Eikha Rabati* 4)[2]

2. This particular line is central to Mandel's entire thesis (see footnote 1 above). He claims (Mandel, ibid., p. 148) that it was actually a later addition to the original story: "Its language attests to this because the story in its entirety was written in Aramaic apart from its preface and this sentence." He further adds (note 29) that this linguistic phenomenon only applies to the Geniza manuscripts and that the other manuscripts contain additional sentences in Hebrew, although "it appears that the Aramaic version is the original one." I think that he forces the text somewhat in order to make it conform to his theory of a discrepancy between the Israel version

Who was Zekharia ben Avkulos? In Talmudic sources, he is mentioned on one other occasion apart from our story, in connection with a dispute between Beit Shammai and Beit Hillel regarding the laws of Shabbat.

> Beit Hillel said: One may take bones and peels off the table. Beit Shammai said: One moves the entire table and shakes it. Zekharia ben Avkulos did not comply with either Beit Shammai or Beit Hillel – rather, he would take [the refuse] as he ate and throw it behind the couch. (Tosefta, *Shabbat*, 16:7)

This is one of the regular disputes between Beit Shammai and Beit Hillel, dealing with the laws of *muktzeh*. Beit Hillel permits taking refuse (bones and peels) off the table to discard them. Beit Shammai prohibits taking it off the table, but permits shaking out the entire tabletop. The dispute admits of extensive commentary, though not in the current context.[3] Our interest is in the fact that Zekharia ben Avkulos avoided siding with either Beit Shammai or Beit Hillel and instead, in the course of eating, would throw away the food, thus avoiding leaving anything on the table. Regarding this conduct, Rabbi Saul Lieberman says that, "Rabbi Zekharia ben Avkulos avoided deciding in favor of either school, and hence did not lift up the bones, nor shake the table. In doing so he circumvented any kind of leaving bones on the table to avoid having to decide. This timidity was chronic and reflected his conduct in other cases too" (*Tosefta KiFeshuta*, p. 269). Indeed it was in respect of this timidity that Rabbi Yosa said:

> The humility of Rabbi Zekharia ben Avkulos led to the burning of the Temple. (Ibid.)

The simple interpretation of Rabbi Yosa's observation is that Rabbi

and the Babylonian version, whereas the manuscripts of the version unequivocally attest to the integrity of the sentence.

3. In the Mishna of Tractate *Shabbat* (in early manuscripts), the views of Beit Shammai and Beit Hillel are reversed so that Beit Shammai rules leniently. See Y.N. Epstein, *Introduction to the Mishnaic Text* [Hebrew] (Tel Aviv: 1941), pp. 357–358, who claims that the Mishnaic version is the principle one, and the Tosefta version secondary.

Zekharia's self-effacement in matters pertaining to the law ultimately led to the Destruction. At first glance, the dispute over *muktzeh* seems unrelated to the destruction of the Temple. A number of commentators and scholars have noted that this passage is actually a relic of the principal tradition pertaining to Rabbi Zekharia, located in the story of Kamtza and Bar Kamtza in the legends of the Destruction, and incidentally appended to the dispute about *muktzeh*.[4]

The obvious connection, however, is that in a world in which the humility of Hillel was considered a virtue ("self-effacing like Hillel and not insistent like Shammai" – *Shabbat* 30a), excessive humility can be disastrous when it renders the leadership incapable of making a decision when required.

Returning to the story of the Destruction, which continues from Bar Kamtza's response to the insult, the story indicates that his ire was not directed at his host's behavior as much as at the deafening silence of the sages (or at least at Zekharia ben Avkulos) who failed to respond:

> Bar Kamtza went to the emperor and declared, "The Jews have rebelled against you!"
>
> The emperor responded, "Who said so?"
>
> Bar Kamtza said, "Send them a sacrifice, and see if they will offer it."
>
> The emperor sent [with Bar Kamtza] a healthy, unblemished ram. While going, Bar Kamtza caused a disfigurement in the animal. Some say that it was a blemish on the upper lip; others say that it was a blemish in the eye [perhaps symbolizing the silence of the rabbis or their witnessing of the event of his disgrace without protest]; in any case, it was a place where for us it is a disqualifying blemish while for the Romans, it is not.
>
> The rabbis had in mind to sacrifice it anyway to maintain

4. This is Lieberman's understanding; see *Tosefta KiFeshuta*, p. 269. Mandel (ibid. [see footnotes 1 and 2 above] note 5), on the other hand, challenges this position, in line with his hypothesis that omits Rabbi Zekharia from the Bar Kamtza legend, and relegates him to the Babylonian sources only. However, he fails to provide any significant reasons for his position.

> peaceful relations with the government. But Rabbi Zekharia ben Avkulos objected, "People will say, 'Animals with blemishes may be sacrificed on the altar!'"
>
> The rabbis had in mind to kill Bar Kamtza so that he would not report back to the emperor what had happened. But Rabbi Zekharia ben Avkulos objected: "People will say, 'One who makes blemishes in sacrifices is killed!'" (*Gittin* 56a)

The passage concludes with the ironic observation of Rabbi Yoḥanan:

> The humility of Rabbi Zekharia ben Avkulos destroyed our Temple, burned our Palace, and exiled us from our land.

According to the Talmudic narrative, Bar Kamtza reported to the emperor that the Jews were rebelling against him. He proves this by claiming that they would refuse to bring the sacrifice for the emperor's welfare. The account of the blemish he made in the animal is actually an indictment of the Torah leadership for its inability to make difficult halakhic decisions.

This story links the abolition of the sacrifice for the emperor's welfare to the silence of the sages, thus placing the sages at the forefront of political involvement and decisions on the eve of the Destruction. Josephus relates that the abolition of the sacrifice was related to the activities of the rebelling Zealots, and was, in fact, the act that sparked the revolt. Rabbi Yoḥanan's response, "The humility of Rabbi Zekharia ben Avkulos destroyed our Temple," reflects a rabbinic understanding, in which historical fates are determined by the internal spiritual positions of the wise men of each generation. Zekharia ben Avkulos may have been aware of the ramifications of the annulling the sacrifice, but was personally and politically incapable of giving expression to his view. The most plausible reading would thus be as follows: Elazar ben Ḥanania (the deputy high priest) physically prevented the bringing of the sacrifice for the emperor's welfare. The hypocritical priests found themselves in a quandary; a position of dual loyalty was hardly novel for them, but this time a confrontation was inevitable. The elders too were paralyzed by the fear of deciding, leaving the decision of whether or not to bring the sacrifice in the hands of Zekharia ben Avkulos. He, however, was concerned with purely halakhic considerations: "People will say, 'Animals with blemishes may be sacrificed on the altar.'"

Evidently he was one of the most prominent leaders of the generation, one to whom people looked for guidance. The leaders of the generation, "the eyes of the community," were apparently afflicted by the defect that disqualified the sacrifice, for they too had "blemishes" in their eyes, meaning that their vision was blurred and lacked perspicuity. This kind of hesitation generates the desire to satisfy all opinions. Indeed, there are cases in which the desire to discharge one's duty according to all opinions is a catalyst for increased activity, but in this case it led to paralysis. Even when the danger could still be averted by doing away with the courier who had brought the sacrifice, Zekharia ben Avkulos insisted: "People will say, 'One who makes blemishes in sacrifices is killed!'" The ineluctable conclusion is he was afraid of issuing judgment, or afraid of the Zealots, or perhaps both.[5] The result however was clear: the silence of the leadership meant abandoning the arena to the influence of other forces.

5. D. Rokeaḥ, "Zekharia ben Avkulos – Humility or Zealotry" [Hebrew] in *Tziyon* 53 (1988), pp. 53–56, views the expression "the humility of Rabbi Zekharia ben Avkulos" as a euphemism for "his zealotry" and thereby places him (based on a comparison with Josephus) with the Zealots. In my view this is an extremely irresponsible reading of the Talmudic literature, making it totally subservient to Josephus. See Daniel Schwartz's response, "More on Zekharia ben Avkulos: Humility or Zealotry?" [Hebrew], *Tziyon* 53 (1988), pp. 313–316.

Chapter Twenty-Three

Rabban Yoḥanan ben Zakkai: Fortifying the World of Torah during the Rebellion

The rebellion having begun, we proceed to the character of one of the greatest Jewish leaders, whose leadership of the nation in turbulent times raises a slew of difficult questions. Rabban Yoḥanan ben Zakkai made his mark not as one who paved a new path of halakha, but rather for having saved the people from absolute decimation in a time of national crisis.[1] The Talmud portrays his departure from Jerusalem at the height

1. We refer to his image in the national consciousness over the course of Jewish history, as distinct from an assessment of his various enactments or his overall halakhic activity. A search for his name in the databases shows a huge number of articles analyzing his political activities pertaining to the rebellion and the Romans, but relatively scant mention of his halakhic output.

of the siege of the Zealots, and his meeting with Vespasian, soon to be appointed emperor. A heated conversation between them culminated in Rabban Yoḥanan being granted his requests concerning the rehabilitation of the people in the post-Destruction period:

> He [Rabban Yoḥanan] said to him [Vespasian]: Grant me Yavneh and its sages, the dynasty of Rabban Gamliel, and a physician to heal Rabbi Tzaddok. (*Gittin* 56b)

Rabban Yoḥanan's requests were primarily directed at the preservation of the spiritual life after the termination of the "Jerusalem Era." He sought a new spiritual center in the form of "Yavneh and its sages," symbols of sovereignty in the form of the patriarchal family from the line of Rabban Gamliel, and, in a personal request, the recuperation of Rabbi Tzaddok, who was still languishing inside the besieged city. This was Rabban Yoḥanan's way of securing a national palliative for the scourge of the destruction and creating a structure for continued Jewish existence in the absence of the Temple. Further on in the same passage, the Talmud records the words of Rabbi Yosef (which have also been ascribed to Rabbi Akiva) severely criticizing Rabban Yoḥanan for having surrendered and deserted Jerusalem:

> Rabbi Yosef, or as some say, Rabbi Akiva, applied to him the verse: "[God] turns wise men backward and makes their knowledge foolish" [Isaiah 44:25]. He should have used the opportunity to ask the emperor to leave Jerusalem alone. But he thought that such a request might be rejected and he would thus forfeit an even smaller salvation. (Ibid.)

Even after the passage of many centuries of Jewish history, the debate over this singular act and over Rabban Yoḥanan in general, still rages between the advocates of proud nationalism and those who tend toward pragmatism and survival.[2]

2. For example, an article was written by (Knesset Member) Aryeh Eldad continuing the criticism of the Jewish tradition represented by Rabban Yoḥanan, and praising

Our comments on Rabban Yoḥanan ben Zakkai are divided into two parts. We will begin with his character up to his departure from Jerusalem, including his struggle against the priestly leadership and primarily against the Sadducees. We will also discuss his decision to abandon the city in favor of the reestablishment of the world of Torah and its preservation. Following this, in the second volume of this work, we will deal with the Jewish sages of Yavneh until the Bar Kokhba rebellion, and, in that framework, with Rabban Yoḥanan ben Zakkai as the national leader in Yavneh after the Destruction.

THE EARLY YEARS OF RABBAN YOḤANAN BEN ZAKKAI

Our knowledge of Rabban Yoḥanan ben Zakkai is patchy. He was not a scion of the patriarchal dynasty, notwithstanding that he served in the capacity of patriarch, operated under the title of "Rabban," enacted regulations, and issued decrees that touched on all matters in the period following the Destruction. It seems that he emerged as a national leader from within the world of Torah at that time, and began to lead upon the eve of the rebellion in Jerusalem.

Talmudic tradition tells us that Hillel the Elder had eighty students, the most minor of them being Rabban Yoḥanan ben Zakkai:

> They said of Rabban Yoḥanan ben Zakkai that he did not leave [unstudied] Scripture, Mishna, Gemara, Halakha, Aggada, details of the Torah, details of the scribes, *a fortiori* inferences, analogies, astronomy, mathematics, the speech of the ministering angels, the speech of the spirits, the speech of the palm trees, launderer's parables, fox fables, great matters, and small matters. (*Sukka* 28a)

For the sages of Rabban Yoḥanan's time, their whole world consisted of the study of Torah. They were ensconced in the ivory tower of the *Beit Midrash* and unaffected by the tempestuous winds of the time. This is certainly the picture emerging from the banquet hosted by Rabban Yoḥanan in his yeshiva for the rich of Jerusalem, and its disturbing

the tradition personified by Rabbi Akiva (the article appears on the internet site of the *Moledet* movement).

questions about the connection between the men of money and the Torah scholars.

The same source also sheds light on Rabban Yoḥanan's connection to the *Beit Midrash*:

> They said of Rabban Yoḥanan ben Zakkai that during his whole life he never engaged in trivial conversation, nor walked four cubits without [studying] Torah, or without *tefillin*, nor did any man precede him to the *beit midrash*, nor did he ever fall asleep or doze in the *beit midrash*, nor did he meditate in filthy alleyways, nor did he ever find himself sitting idly, but only sitting and studying, and no one but himself ever opened the door to his students. He never said anything that he had not heard from his teacher, and other than on the eve of Pesaḥ and the eve of Yom Kippur he never said: it is time to leave the *beit midrash*. His disciple, Rabbi Eliezer, conducted himself in the same manner. (Ibid.)

This is a superb description of a person entirely immersed in Torah, a person who responsibly and faithfully served as a conduit for the transmission of Torah from one generation to the next. A gallery of leading sages of the following generations imparted traditions which they had received from Rabban Yoḥanan ben Zakkai, "who received it from his teacher, and his teacher from his teacher, back to the law received from Moses at Sinai" (Mishna, *Eduyot* 8:3; *Yadayim* 4:3). Rabban Yoḥanan's entire world can only be understood in the context of his involvement with and connection to the Torah.

The Talmud tells the story of a Jerusalem family whose sons all died young. The parents desperately searched for a panacea that would release them from the curse that had plagued them. It transpired that the family was apparently a family of priests, perhaps even affiliated with the Sadducees. The solution they searched for was in the esoteric realm, but Rabban Yoḥanan's comments to them disclose his radically different perception of their predicament:

> Perhaps you are from the House of Eli, as it says: "All of the increase of your house shall die in their prime" [I Samuel 2:33].

> Go and occupy yourselves in Torah and live. And they went and engaged in Torah and they lived. They were called "the family of Rabban Yoḥanan" in his honor. (*Rosh HaShana* 18a)

This is his character and this is his message: don't look for external, esoteric solutions. The world finds its rationale in and through the Torah. This understanding may also shed light on the episode of the non-Jew who came to Rabban Yoḥanan to be converted, and questioned the rationale behind the purification properties of the ashes of the red heifer:

> A certain heathen asked Rabban Yoḥanan ben Zakkai: "The rites you perform in connection with the red heifer reek of witchcraft! You bring a heifer, burn it, grind it and take its ashes. You sprinkle two or three drops on one of you who is contaminated with corpse defilement and say to him, 'You are clean.'"
>
> Rabban Yoḥanan ben Zakkai said to him: "Have you ever been possessed by a demon?"
>
> "No," he replied.
>
> "Have you never seen a man possessed by a demon?"
>
> He answered, "Yes."
>
> "And what do you do for him?"
>
> "We bring herbs and make them smoke beneath him, then throw water on him, and the demon is exorcised."
>
> He answered: "Let your ears hear what your mouth has spoken. The spirit of defilement is the same as your demon, as it is written: 'And I will also make the prophets and the unclean spirit vanish from the land' [Zechariah 13:2]. We sprinkle on it the waters of purification and it is exorcised."
>
> After the heathen had left, Rabban Yoḥanan's disciples said to him: "You dismissed him with a superficial answer, but what answer can you give us?"
>
> He replied to them. "By your life, the dead does not defile nor does the water purify, but the Holy One, blessed be He, said: 'It is a statute I have laid down, a decree that I have decreed, and you are not authorized to violate My decree.'" (*Midrash Tanḥuma, Ḥukkat* 8)

This perspective of the red heifer's purity characterizes Rabban Yoḥanan's overall approach to the Torah and its commandments. He is always able to provide a rationale for the reasons behind the commandments; the specific rationale will change in accordance with the target audience. When explaining the purification ceremony for the non-Jew, his answer leaves the non-Jew in his familiar pagan magic-ritualistic environment. He guides his students, however, away from that realm, back toward the attitude of "this is the statute of the Torah." Nonetheless, there is also a more radical, subversive reading of his words: "By your life, the dead does not defile nor does the water purify." The religious act does not involve any intrinsic independent religious essence; it is just another one of the commandments to be complied with, and its essence consists of the act of compliance. The paradoxical nature of the ritual indeed provokes questions, but these do not detract from its status and hence "you are not authorized to violate My decree."

THE STRUGGLE AGAINST THE SADDUCEES

Rabban Yoḥanan's interpretation of the red heifer brings us to one of the foci of his religious activities outside the yeshiva: his struggle against the Sadducees.

Our discussion of the Sadducees began with their dispute with Yose ben Yoezer in the period of the Pairs. Power struggles between the Pharisees and the Sadducees characterized the entire Second Temple period, and the two groups never reached any kind of understanding. The Sadducees fortified themselves in the Temple and in their specific perception of holiness, and fought with all their might for their beliefs and their interpretation of the halakha. Rabban Yoḥanan ben Zakkai was the most prominent of the first-century leaders to struggle against them.[3] He is described as having had the upper hand against them in a

3. See Eyal Regev, *The Sadducees and Their Halakha: Religion and Society in the Second Temple Period* [Hebrew] (Jerusalem: Yad ben Zvi, 2005), p. 361. Regev questions the reliability of the Talmudic account of Rabban Yoḥanan's role in the controversy with the Sadducees. "There is no certainty that the author of this tradition was accurate in ascribing the victory over the Sadducees to Rabban Yoḥanan ben Zakkai. Conceivably his name was inserted into this tradition. In the eyes of various sages after his time, Rabban Yoḥanan had a reputation for his involvement in the struggle

number of halakhic disputes. The most famous of these traditions attests to his involvement in the burning of the heifer by one of the priests:

> It happened that there was a Sadducee for whom the sun had set [terminating the period of impurity], and he came to burn [the red heifer] and the matter became known to Rabban Yoḥanan ben Zakkai. He came and placed both hands upon him [to make him impure] and said to him: "My lord, High Priest, how fitting are you to be high priest! Now go down and immerse one time." He went down and immersed and emerged. After he came up, he tore his ear [rendering him unfit to serve]. He said to him: "Ben Zakkai – when I have time for you..." He said to him: "When you have time." Not three days had passed before they buried him. His father came to Rabban Yoḥanan ben Zakkai and said to him: "Ben Zakkai, my son did not have time." (Tosefta, *Para* 3:8)

According to this tradition, Rabban Yoḥanan perpetrated two acts against the high priest: He "placed" his hands upon him, thereby contaminating him, and compelling him to once again burn the red heifer before being purified, and he also injured his ear, rendering him unfit to serve. Notwithstanding the clearly Aggadic nature of this passage from the Tosefta, especially the concluding act in which divine justice is meted out,[4] its halakhic significance cannot be ignored. The Mishna in Tractate *Para* (3:8) presents the contamination of the high priest as standard procedure, intended as a refutation of the Sadducees. The aim was to compel the supplicant to acknowledge Pharisee superiority by requiring the high priest to have immersed on the day itself and not wait until the purification takes effect after sunset. The purification process consisted of two stages: one of them dependent on a human act (immersion in the ritual bath), and the other on the setting of the sun.

against the Sadducees, and hence, these victories were attributed to him." I accept the identification presented in the sources, in accordance with my methodology throughout this volume, which is to accept the authenticity of the Talmudic sources for as long as there are no empirical considerations that preclude reliance on the rabbinic sources.

4. As per Regev, ibid., pp. 179–180.

The dispute between the Sadducees and the Pharisees regarding the burning of the heifer can be explained from a broad perspective of the human role in purity and impurity. Is man an active agent in his purification, or is impurity (and purity) the result of a cosmic effect? In keeping with their doctrine, the Sadducees maintained that the setting of the sun is what induces the priest's purity. The Pharisees required only immersion in the ritual bath, thus giving expression to the active role played by the human being in his purification.

The Mishna records another famous dispute between Rabban Yoḥanan ben Zakkai and the Sadducees:

> The Sadducees say: "We cry out against you, Pharisees, for you say, 'the holy Scriptures render the hands unclean, but the books of Homer do not render the hands unclean.'" Rabban Yoḥanan ben Zakkai said: "And is this our only complaint against the Pharisees? For they say, 'The bones of an ass are clean but the bones of Yoḥanan the high priest are unclean!'" They said to him: "Their uncleanliness corresponds to our love for them, so that no man will make the bones of his father or mother into spoons." He said to them: "So it is with the holy Scriptures, their uncleanliness corresponds to our love for them. But the writings of Homer, which are not beloved, do not render the hands unclean. (Mishna, *Yadayim* 4:6)

At the heart of the Pharisee argument is the conception that the contamination of the hands need not render the entire body impure. The subject of "impurity of the hands" belongs to the category of "scribal amendments" (rabbinic laws) and originated in an amendment from the days of Shammai and Hillel. Rabban Yoḥanan's comments are apparently directed at the Sadducee claims against Pharisee leniency in matters of purity and impurity.[5]

5. This subject has been discussed in a number of places. See Regev, ibid., pp. 192–194 and his footnotes.

THE STRUGGLE AGAINST THE PRIESTS

In addition to his struggle against the Sadducees, Rabban Yoḥanan also waged a battle against the priests, although it may have been the same battle:

> Rabbi Yehuda said: Ben Bukhri testified at Yavneh: "Any priest who pays the annual contribution of a shekel does not sin." Rabban Yoḥanan ben Zakkai responded: "Not so! Rather, any priest who does not pay the shekel sins. However, the priests expounded this verse for their own benefit: 'And every gift of the priest shall be wholly burnt; it shall not be eaten' [Leviticus 6:16] – if the *Omer*, the Two Loaves, and the Show Bread are ours [purchased with our contributions], how can they be eaten? (Mishna, *Shekalim* 1:4)

This mishna refers to a fierce dispute about the post-Destruction status of the priests. The biblical commandment of the half-shekel (Exodus 30:11–16) was a permanent commandment, even though in context it served as a means of conducting a census of the Jewish people in the desert. It was a uniform, per capita poll tax ("the rich shall not pay more and the poor shall not pay less" – ibid. 15), obligatory upon every male of twenty years or older. Nonetheless, on a practical level the commandment had always related to donations to the Temple for general needs such as public sacrifices (*tamid, musaf, omer*, etc.). The Mishna in Tractate *Shekalim* describes the collection process, including the securing of a pledge from those who could not afford the payment. At the end of the third mishna we read that "the pledge was not taken from the priests because of ways of peace." The implication is that the priests were also obligated in the giving of the half-shekel, and that it was only out of deference to their status that they were not pledged like the other citizens (this is the plain meaning of the Jerusalem Talmud).

The mishna cited above reports the conflicting testimonies of Ben Bukhri and Rabban Yoḥanan regarding the priestly participation in the half-shekel. Ben Bukhri attests to the priests having been exempt from paying the half-shekel, but permitted to donate any sum without undermining the character of the mandatory donations. This is the meaning of "every priest who pays the shekel does not sin." Rabban Yoḥanan, on the other hand, challenges this testimony, claiming that the opposite was the case, namely that any priest who failed to contribute his half-shekel committed the sin of "separating oneself from the community." He intimates however that the priests "expounded this verse for their own benefit." In other words, by way of a contrived explanation of the laws of *menaḥot*, they attempted to prove that they were exempt from this standard, fixed tax. This was part of Rabban Yoḥanan's struggle against the prevalent priestly policy that placed them outside the financial obligations that bound the people as a whole, and his attempt to equate their standing with that of all other citizens. In the absence of the Temple, this dispute is no longer of any practical significance. Nevertheless, it highlights the tension between Rabban Yoḥanan and the priests, who attempted to retain their unique, separate status. Notably, and again indicating the gap between Rabban Yoḥanan and the priestly class, during the time of the revolt most of the leaders and commanders came from the ranks of the priesthood, as indicated by Josephus (*The Jewish War* II.2:3–4). Yet, despite their leadership position in the revolt against the Romans, the priests made every effort to maintain their separatist status vis-à-vis the rest of the nation. The testimony of the following mishna indicates the brazen manner in which the priests maintained their privilege and status over the rest of the people:

> A priestly *beit din* would collect four hundred *ma'ot* [as a dowry] for a virgin, and the sages did not oppose them. (Mishna, *Ketubot* 1:5)

The regular sum for a woman's *ketuba* was two hundred *zuzim*. The priests doubled this sum for the *ketuba* of one of their own daughters in order to stress her special status. The sages did not oppose them, regarding it as a tolerable custom for preserving the separatism of the priests.

Another source clearly attesting to Rabban Yoḥanan's conscious disaffiliation from the priests is the *baraita* that depicts Rabban Yoḥanan's departure from Jerusalem together with his foremost pupil, Rabbi Yehoshua:

> Once, Rabban Yoḥanan ben Zakkai was leaving Jerusalem with Rabbi Yehoshua following him, and he saw the Temple in ruins. Rabbi Yehoshua cried out: "Woe to us, for it lies in ruins, the place where atonement was made for Israel's sins!" Rabban Yoḥanan responded: "My son, do not grieve for we have another form of atonement that is similar. And what is it? Acts of loving-kindness, as it is written [Hosea 6:6]: 'I desire loving-kindness and not sacrifice.'" (*Avot deRabbi Natan,* recension A, ch. 4)

Rabban Yoḥanan thus heralded a radical innovation in the religious life of Jews, affirming the equivalent value of religious life without sacrifices: "We have another form of atonement that is similar." According to Rabban Yoḥanan, the absence of the Temple, a place to atone for their sins, was not cause for national despair. The people were now confronted by a new and alternate challenge: the challenge of creating a society founded on kindness. For Rabban Yoḥanan, the absence of the Temple would not sever the Jewish people's connection with their Father in heaven. In the absence of the atoning sacrifices, loving-kindness had become the connecting link.

THE STRUGGLE AGAINST THE ZEALOTS

For the most part, the Zealots, who came from younger elements of the population,[6] controlled all the critical junctures of political life and thus led the people into the war of the Destruction. They unleashed a reign of terror against the residents of Jerusalem that finds its tragic expression in the following conversation between Rabban Yoḥanan ben Zakkai and his nephew, Abba Sikra:

> Abba Sikra was the leader of the *Biryonim* [one of the anti-Rome factions] and was the nephew of Rabbi Yoḥanan ben Zakkai. Rabban Yoḥanan sent him a message: "Come to me in secret."

6. Regarding the zealots' ages and the impact as such on relations with Rome, see I. Levin, "The Zealots at the End of the Second Temple Period as a Historiographical Problem" [Hebrew], *Cathedra* 1 (1976), p. 39.

> He came to him. He said to him: "How long will you carry on this way and kill all the people with starvation?" Abba Sikra replied: "What can I do? If I say anything, the *Biryonim* will kill me." (*Gittin* 56a)

The Sicarii and the other connected groups had imposed a reign of terror over the city, attested to by a number of sources depicting the burning of food reserves by the Zealots or the Sicarii,[7] a step that led the revolt past a point of no return. This was still at the initial stage of the revolt, but already at this point, when the leadership had fallen into the hands of the violent and factionalized rebel forces, Rabban Yoḥanan decided to abandon Jerusalem and to surrender to the Romans. There are several versions of this story, and the version below is the one appearing in *Avot deRabbi Natan*:[8]

> When Vespasian came and besieged Jerusalem, he set up camp opposite the wall of Jerusalem and said to the citizens of Jerusalem: "Send one bow and one arrow from Jerusalem and I will leave you in peace." He said this to them once, and then a second time, but they did not accept. Rabban Yoḥanan ben Zakkai said to the men of Jerusalem: "You are causing the destruction of this city and the burning of this Temple." They said to him: "Just as we rallied forth and prevailed against the first command-

7. Historians have labored hard to distinguish between the Zealots and the Sicarii. See the collection of articles in A. Kasher's book on the *Great Jewish Revolt*. Rabbinic tradition on the other hand was not concerned with these distinctions. In my view they grouped all of the factions fighting the Romans into the same category. The burning of the food supplies of Jerusalem, for example, is cited in numerous sources, and is alternately ascribed to the Zealots and the Sicarii. See *Avot deRabbi Natan*, recension A (p. 32): "The Zealots sought to burn all of that wealth in fire"; and recension B (p.31): "The Sicarii burned all the provisions that were in Jerusalem" (see also p. 20). In *Kohelet Raba* we read, "There was also Ben Batiaḥ, the nephew of Rabban Yoḥanan ben Zakkai, who was appointed in charge of the Sicarii in Jerusalem, and he arose and burnt the storehouses."
8. For a comparison of the sources and a discussion of the differences between them, see G. Alon, *Studies in Jewish History* [Hebrew], vol. 1 pp. 219–250.

ers so too we will rally forth and prevail against this one and we will kill him."[9]

When Rabban Yoḥanan ben Zakkai saw that the people were not willing to listen to him, he said to his disciples: "Comrades, get me out of here at once." They placed him in a wooden coffin. Rabbi Eliezer carried him at his head, and Rabbi Joshua was at his feet. They weaved their way through until they reached the city's gates. When they reached the gates, they said to them [the guards]: "Open up for us at once so that we can go out and bury him." The guards replied: "We will not open the gates without first stabbing the body with a sword." The disciples replied: "You will be responsible for the spreading of an evil report about your regime. Tomorrow they will say: 'They even stabbed Rabban Yoḥanan.'" Finally the guards stood up and opened the gates for them. (*Avot deRabbi Natan*, recension B, ch. 6)

And so Rabban Yoḥanan left Jerusalem, from which his path of leadership would continue after the Destruction. He would never again be active inside the walls of the city, which he relinquished to the priests, the Zealots and the rest of the people. His task was now to forge a new path and prepare the ground for the absorption of the exiles from Jerusalem who would survive the war.

9. This may be an allusion to the rebels' first victory in the battle at Beit Ḥoron, which inspired the rebels with tremendous hopes. See next chapter.

Chapter Twenty-Four

The Beginnings of the Revolt in Jerusalem

Before our diversion to the early history of Rabban Yoḥanan, we focused on the annulment of the sacrifice for the emperor's welfare. This event, recorded in both internal and external literature and dated at 66 CE, signifies the end of Jewish readiness to tolerate the cruelty and oppression of the Roman procurators. The oppression found expression primarily in economic matters, but also in the degradation and humiliation of the Jews in the national-religious sphere, and it was precisely the national-religious oppression that may ultimately have pushed the Jews over the edge, onto the path of rebellion. Before proceeding, we will briefly describe the Jewish leadership of Jerusalem.

AGRIPPA II BETRAYS HIS PEOPLE

Agrippa II was born in 27 CE, the son of Agrippa I, and his wife Cypros. Agrippa I was Herod's grandson from his wife Mariamne (Miriam) the Hasmonean, meaning that both Herodian and Hasmonean blood coursed through his veins.[1] As mentioned in the previous section, his father had connections to the Roman emperor (primarily Caligula).[2] He was seventeen years old at the time of his father's death, and the Roman emperor Claudius was not prepared to install such a young man in his father's place as King of Judea. A few years after completing his royal education in Rome, Agrippa II was appointed procurator of the small principality of Chalcis (in the northern part of the country, near the Lebanese mountains).[3] He also retained several of his father's entitlements, including the power to appoint high priests. However, his use of power was generally corrupt, and his appointments guided by bribery and intrigue.[4]

When the revolt erupted in 66 CE, Agrippa initially implored the people to desist from the battle and lay down their arms. Josephus records Agrippa's particularly moving speech to the people, in which he tried to convince them that challenging Roman rule would be an exercise in futility and indeed, God Himself would not help them, because He favors the Romans.[5]

Josephus relates that Agrippa's efforts to bring the people back from the brink of revolt almost succeeded, but when he urged the people to tolerate the heavy-handed rule of Florus until he (Agrippa) replaced him, they lost their patience with him. The very mention of the hated procurator sufficed to provoke the people's rancor and reignite their passions.

Having failed to prevent the onset of the revolt, Agrippa sent three thousand horsemen from his kingdom in the north in order to quash the rebellion. Upon reaching Jerusalem, they were astonished

1. For a description and discussion of Agrippa's genealogy according to the halakha, see Appendix 11 of D. Schwartz's book, *Agrippa the King* [Hebrew], pp. 228–231.
2. On his tight connection with Caligula, see Schwartz, ibid., ch. 3, pp. 78–100.
3. According to Josephus, *The Jewish War* II, 220 and *Antiquities of the Jews*, XIX, 363.
4. According to G. Alon, *Studies in Jewish History* [Hebrew], pt.1, pp. 59–80.
5. According to Josephus, *The Jewish War* II, 388–399. But see A. Kasher, "The Great Jewish Revolt: Factors and Circumstances Leading to its Outbreak," in A. Kasher (ed.), *The Great Revolt*, p. 89, n. 263. Kasher notes that "it is not inconceivable that Josephus, having the benefit of hindsight, simply put these words into his mouth."

to discover that, for the most part, it had been conquered by the rebels. In the ensuing battle, the palaces of Agrippa and his sister Bernice were razed, together with the houses of the aristocracy, the wealthy classes, and the high priest, as well as repositories for keeping promissory notes. Agrippa's soldiers took refuge in the Antonia fortress and, following a short siege, were permitted to leave the city.

By this stage, Agrippa was clearly identified as being in cahoots with the enemy forces. He led the soldiers of the Syrian procurator to Jerusalem, but was ambushed on the way by the rebels, who routed his army. Following this failure and before the subsequently laying siege to the city, Agrippa made another attempt to negotiate with the leaders of the revolt, sending them two emissaries: Borceus and Phebus. However, both of them were killed by the rebels before they could even present their case. Following this, Gallus, the Syrian procurator, attempted to conquer the city with the remaining soldiers, but after five days of siege concluded that he lacked the power to conquer the city and retreated to the coastal plain. In the course of the retreat, his army was entrapped in a valley between two mountains in Beit Ḥoron, and most of his army, numbering six thousand troops, was routed. The rebels appeared to have gained the upper hand. It was then that Agrippa totally severed his connection with the Jews of Jerusalem and aligned himself unreservedly with the Roman army.[6]

THE SICARII ABANDON JERUSALEM

The Sicarii initially waved the flag of rebellion. Their ideology was based on three central tenets, as formulated by the founder of their movement, Yehuda the Galilean:

1. God is the only Ruler and King of the Jewish people.
2. The land of Israel should be ruled exclusively by the Jewish people and not by any alien nation.
3. The rural and village population should be empowered economically by breaking the yoke of the oligarchy.

6. I. Levin, "The Great Revolt," in M. Stern (ed.), *The History of the Jewish People* [Hebrew], vol. 4 (Jerusalem: 1984), p. 255.

Following Agrippa's speech and the ensuing unrest, the Sicarii made their move and left for Masada, then controlled by a Roman legion and serving as an ammunition depot for the Roman army. Under the leadership of Yehuda the Galilean's grandson, Menaḥem, the Sicarii conquered the Roman military outpost, murdered the soldiers, and looted their ammunition caches. With renewed ammunition supplies and the prestige of a military hero, Menaḥem could return to Jerusalem to resume his leadership of the revolt, which now seemed increasingly viable. He aligned himself with Elazar ben Ḥanania the priest (who took control of the Temple and initiated the cancellation of the offering for the emperor's welfare). Menaḥem arrived in Jerusalem as a powerful war general, and according to Josephus, at a certain stage he even began wearing royal attire, suggesting that he had messianic pretensions.

The Sicarii's wresting of control of the Temple culminated with the burning of the house of the high priest (who controlled Temple affairs as the representative of the much despised Agrippa), as well as the palace of Agrippa and Bernice. Nonetheless, Elazar retained a lowly opinion of Menaḥem. Menaḥem and Elazar divided control of Jerusalem, with Elazar assuming control of the Lower City and the accesses to the Temple, and Menaḥem assuming control of the upper city with its fine houses and priestly mansions. Elazar's soldiers could not tolerate Menaḥem's pretentious, arrogant conduct and assassinated him. This induced a violent struggle between the two groups, in the course of which Elazar ben Yair and the remaining Sicarii fled to Masada, where they remained until the end of the rebellion and the Roman conquest of Masada. The Sicarii flight to Masada signified the end of their role as a meaningful factor in Jerusalem, and they now began to spread their reign of terror over the residents of Ein Gedi and its environs. Numbering about one thousand people, they lived communally at Masada until 74 CE. The story of their mass suicide lies beyond the scope of this work.

Another central figure during the same period was Yoḥanan of Gush Ḥalav (John of Gischala), a wealthy Galilean. He made his fortune primarily from the sale of Galilean oil to the Jews of Caesarea who refused to use non-Jewish oil (one of the eighteen edicts of Beit Shammai). Yoḥanan of Gush Ḥalav had numerous connections in the Galilee and was generally regarded as an authentic local leader. When the manner in which Yosef ben Matityahu (later known as the historian Josephus Flavius) defended the Galilee met with Yoḥanan's disapproval, he summarily dismissed him from his post. Josephus himself mentions Yoḥanan's close relationship with Rabban Shimon ben Gamliel, the son of the patriarch, whom we will deal with below. Following the fall of the Galilee, Yoḥanan appeared in Jerusalem at the head of the Galilean regiments and quickly became one of the leaders in the city. He was a kind of "Supreme Commander," until a new character entered the scene – Shimon bar Giora.

Shimon bar Giora came from an entirely different background and therefore had a different status. He was the recognized leader of the lower classes all over the country, and his successful military campaigns against the Romans vested him with a reputation of a hallowed commander. By virtue of the internal struggles in Jerusalem he became one of the rulers of the city, being based primarily in the Upper City.

A REVOLUTIONARY GOVERNMENT OR A REVOLUTION-QUELLING GOVERNMENT?

After the rebels' military victory at Beit Ḥoron, their conquest of both Upper and Lower Jerusalem, their torching of palaces and their discontinuation of the offering for the emperor's welfare, there was no turning back. The revolt had begun.

At this stage we hear about the establishment of a government that was supposed to lead the rebellion but which did not include the leaders of the rebellion itself. From what we know, this government was established in 66 CE and was overthrown by other Zealots in the winter of 68 CE. The members of the government whose names are known are: High Priest Ḥanan ben Ḥanan (Ananus ben Ananus), Yosef ben Gurion, Yehoshua ben Gamla, and Shimon ben Gamliel. These four were apparently chosen by virtue of their public standing and prestige.

Following the victory in Beit Ḥoron, a public assembly was convened and a government elected. From the list of its members, it appears that the Jerusalem aristocracy determined the government's composition. Accordingly, the Zealots were not represented. It seems reasonable to conclude that the Jerusalem nobility found itself unwillingly in the throes of the rebellion, and attempted to establish a leadership that would hold the reins of the rebellion with the aim of stopping it in its tracks in the near future. The leadership saw no reason or point in enabling the situation to degenerate into a full scale war.[7] Its members were afraid of the Zealots usurping control of the government and thus losing control of the situation. This is indeed the way it is recorded by Josephus:

> So when Cestius had been beaten, as we have related, the principal men of Jerusalem, seeing that the bandits and revolutionaries had arms in great plenty, and fearing lest they, being unprovided of arms, should be in subjection to their enemies. (*The Life of Josephus* 7)

It was then that Josephus was appointed commander of the Galilee, under the assumption that he would be able to calm things down (the revolt had yet to break out in the Galilee). This was also the first time in which there was a unified, non-extremist, non-Zealot leadership at the helm of the state, and so began an interesting period of cooperation between the respective leaderships of the Pharisees and the Sadducees. One of the government members was Ḥanan ben Ḥanan, whom we have identified as a Sadducee high priest. Serving together with him in this government was the patriarch, Rabban Shimon ben Gamliel.

7. This leadership was written about by A. Rappaport, "The Jewish Leadership in Jerusalem during the First Half of the Great Revolt" [Hebrew], in I. Malkin and Z. Tzahor (eds.), *Leaders and Leadership in Jewish and World History – Collected Essays* (Jerusalem: 1992), pp. 133–142.

Chapter Twenty-Five

Rabban Shimon ben Gamliel

His son Shimon used to say: All my life I have grown up amongst sages and have found nothing better for man's welfare than silence; study is not the most important thing, rather practice; and too much talk brings sin. (Avot 1:17)

AN ALLIANCE BETWEEN THE SADDUCEES AND THE PHARISEES: ḤANAN BEN ḤANAN AND RABBAN SHIMON BEN GAMLIEL

Josephus gives the following description of Ḥanan ben Ḥanan:

> But this younger Ananus [Ḥanan] . . . , who took up the high priesthood, was an insolent man of bold temper; he was also of the sect of the Sadducees who are very rigid in judging offenders, above all the rest of the Jews. (*Antiquities* XX, 9:1)[1]

1. Josephus' description of Ḥanan's character in *The Jewish War* contradicts the

A number of testimonies record Rabban Shimon ben Gamliel's replacement of his father in the spiritual leadership of the city until his death in the course of the revolt. Unfortunately, rabbinic literature has not preserved many of his teachings. Sources that mention Rabban Shimon ben Gamliel usually refer to the patriarch during the Usha generation (following the Bar Kokhba rebellion), with only a few referring to his grandfather, Rabbi Shimon ben Gamliel of the Temple times. There is one mishna that reports an enactment made by Rabban Shimon ben Gamliel with the aim of stabilizing the dire economic situation that prevailed just before the Destruction:

> Once, in Jerusalem, a pair of birds cost a golden *dinar*. Rabban Shimon ben Gamliel said: "By this Temple [a mild oath], I will not suffer a night to pass before they cost but a [silver] *dinar*!" He went into the *Beit Din* and taught: "If a woman suffered five certain miscarriages or five certain discharges, she need bring only one offering before she may partake of them, and she is not obligated to bring the other offerings." On that same day, the price of a pair of doves stood at a quarter of a *dinar*. (Mishna, *Keritot* 1:7)

A woman was obligated to bring a sacrifice after giving birth. According to the Torah (Leviticus 12:6–8), the sacrifice should be a sheep, but "if her means did not suffice for a sheep, she shall take two turtle doves or two pigeons," meaning that the impoverished woman can substitute this offering with a sacrifice of birds.

The mishna cited describes a grave economic situation. The sums being charged for a sacrifice of fowl ("two turtle doves or two pigeons") were immense, certainly for women belonging to the poorer classes. According to the mishna, Rabban Shimon understood that his responsibilities in public policy and the stabilization of religious life also extended to the economic sphere. It was his duty to establish a normative economic framework that would make the Temple ritual accessible to the public at large. The indigent woman charged a golden *dinar* in order

description given in *Antiquities*. See Rappaport's article (as cited in footnote 7 of ch. 24 above), pp. 136–138.

to bring a bird sacrifice has no possibility of fulfilling her obligation, and finds herself excluded from Temple ritual. Rabban Shimon was sensitive to the limits of public tolerance and its willingness to sacrifice prohibitive sums of money for the purposes of Temple worship. His enactment defied biblical law but was justified by the rabbinic understanding of "in a time to act for God, the teaching may be violated" (based on a common rabbinic understanding of Psalms 119:126). Such a daring act could only have been carried out by a sage of prominent standing among the rabbinic elite of that time. Josephus too, though he could never be confused with one of Rabbi Shimon's ardent admirers, wrote that he was "a man of great wisdom and reason, and capable of restoring public affairs by his prudence in times of strife" (*The Life of Josephus* 38).

Apart from the aforementioned mishna, the *Midrash HaGadol* (*Devarim* pp. 697–698) relates that Rabban Shimon ben Gamliel wrote letters concerning the declaration of the leap year, following the tradition established by his father, Rabban Gamliel the Elder.[2]

It is widely accepted that Rabbi Shimon replaced his father as head of the supreme *Beit Din* or Sanhedrin, enacting regulations and providing the people with religious and halakhic leadership. What, however, do we know about his socio-political status during these turbulent times?

According to Josephus' autobiographical *Life of Josephus*, Rabbi Shimon switched his loyalties to the rebels' camp, and was apparently killed in the course of the revolt. In rabbinic literature, however, apart from the mishna at the end of Chapter One of *Avot* and the two aforementioned sources, Rabbi Shimon's personality and world are basically unknown, certainly in the political-social context. The beginnings of an answer to this riddle may be found in his statement in the mishna: "All my life I have grown up amongst sages and have found nothing better for man's welfare than silence." What silence was he referring to?

The classical Mishnaic commentators understood Rabbi Shimon to be expressing an eternal truth that was not particularly reflective of rabbinic sentiment during that time. The mishna extols inwardness and berates extroversion.

2. The authenticity of such letters is disputed. See Ben Shalom, *Beit Shammai*, p. 247, n. 83.

Rabbi Ovadia of Bertinoro channels Rabbi Shimon's teaching toward the chasm between the theoretical expounding of the Torah and its application in the real world:

> You should know that silence is commendable. For though one may speak and expound on the Torah, and indeed, there is no higher virtue, the reward is essentially given for the action, whereas he who expounds and fails to fulfill – it would be better for him to have kept his silence and not spoken.[3]

The sagacity of these words do credit to any sage, irrespective of his time and place, but I wish to add another explanation, echoing the voice (or the silence) of the period. We commented at length on the state of the society during the Temple's twilight days; the corruption of the priests, the Zealots' usurpation of the reins of power, and the debasement of the wealthy all demanded the clear voice of the Torah sages. Against this background, Rabbi Shimon's words evoke a wistful sadness. He had grown up and lived among sages and saw their inability to stop the impending Destruction. All that remained for them was to be silent and perhaps to retreat and establish an alternative focus for Jewish life after the Destruction. The status quo in which the sages became part and parcel of the governing system, compelled them to remain silent, and thereby rendered them irrelevant.

TORAH, WEALTH, AND POLITICAL POWER

The perennial phenomenon of the men of law aligning themselves with the wealthy and politically interested circles of society has always portended grave dangers for any society. As pointed out above, this was certainly true for the Jewish society of the Second Temple in which the connections between those identified with Torah leadership and the moneyed classes were inappropriately close. Already during the First Temple period, the prophet railed against relationships of this kind:

> And He will make boys their rulers, and babes will govern them.

3. This subject is elaborated upon in *The Ways of the Righteous*, ch. 21, "Silence."

> So the people shall oppress one another, each oppressing his fellow: The young shall bully the old; and the despised [shall bully] the honored. For a man will seize his brother, in his father's house saying: "You have a cloak. Come be a chief over us, and let this ruin be under your care." (Isaiah 3:4–6)

This is the stage at which the fiery, hotheaded youth lacking the cautious, moderating perspective of national responsibility and holding their elders in contempt, took charge. They search for the powerful strongman, telling him: "You have a cloak. Come be a chief over us." This is a not-so-subtle reference to the elders' words to Jephthah: "Come be our chief so that we can fight the Ammonites" (Judges 11:6). Instead of searching for the idealistic, morally motivated leader, they search for one who brandishes his weapon without a trembling hand. In this context, the prophet promises:

> The Lord will bring this charge against the elders and rulers of his people: "It is you who have ravaged the vineyard; that which was robbed from the poor is in your houses." (Isaiah 3:14)

The prophet foresaw a judgment in which the elders and the officers of the people were to be tried and punished. This judgment is the focus of the first chapter of Isaiah, which is the *haftara* of *Shabbat Ḥazon*:

> Alas, she has become a harlot, the faithful city that was filled with justice, where righteousness dwelt – but now murderers. Your silver has turned to dross; your wine is cut with water; your rulers are rogues and cronies of thieves, every one avid for bribes and greedy for gifts; they do not judge the case of the orphan; and the widow's case never reaches them. (Isaiah 1:21–23)

In chapter three, however, Isaiah demands judgment for the elders in addition to the rulers. The Talmud thus asks: "If the rulers sinned, what was the sin of the elders?" (*Shabbat* 55a). The Talmud's response is short and sharp: "We say: the elders – because they failed to rebuke the rulers" (ibid.).

God judges the elders who collaborated with the rulers. Protest is the antithesis of silence. The biblical precept of "you shall reprove your kinsman and incur no guilt because of him" is a demand for perspicuity, alertness and involvement. The meekness of silence may be commendable in one context and a tool of destruction in another context. The elders were indicted for their failure to distinguish between the two contexts.

Chapter Twenty-Six

Rabbi Tzaddok: A Mirror of the Period

The outbreak of the rebellion found Jerusalem in the clutches of the uncompromising leadership of the Zealots. They purged their ranks of any conciliatory elements, usually by force of the sword. According to Josephus (*The Life of Josephus*), some of the moderate leaders also joined the Zealots, among them Rabban Shimon ben Gamliel, the patriarch, who formed an alliance with Yoḥanan of Gush Ḥalav. According to *Avot deRabbi Natan*, Rabbi Shimon was ultimately executed by the Romans. The midrashic liturgical poem recited on Yom Kippur – "*Eleh Ezkera*" ("These I will remember") – mournfully describes the execution of Rabban Shimon ben Gamliel together with Rabbi Yishmael, the high priest.

The foremost rabbinic personality among those who refused to toe the rebel party line was Rabban Yoḥanan ben Zakkai. After escaping from the besieged Jerusalem, Rabban Yoḥanan came under the protection of Vespasian, and the Midrash (*Eikha Raba*) relates that Vespasian also permitted him to evacuate his disciples from the doomed city. We will discuss the overall historical significance of Rabban Yoḥanan ben Zakkai's legacy below. Here, we begin with this midrashic description of Rabban Yoḥanan at the hour of the Destruction:

> Rabban Yoḥanan ben Zakkai was sitting opposite the wall of Jerusalem, watching to see what would happen, as Scripture says of Eli: "Eli was sitting upon his seat watching" [I Samuel 4:13]. When Rabban Yoḥanan ben Zakkai saw the Temple destroyed and the Sanctuary burned, he rose and tore his clothes, removed his phylacteries, and sat down to mourn with his disciples. (*Avot deRabbi Natan*, recension B, ch. 7)

Rabban Yoḥanan ben Zakkai is compared to Eli the priest. He was not party to the rot that directly precipitated the Destruction and was painfully aware of its inevitability. Like Eli the priest, he "sat and waited," understanding that reconstruction could not begin until the roots of decay were removed and the holy Temple destroyed. The Destruction threw Rabban Yoḥanan into a period of mourning until it became possible to recover and start building a new life for the Jewish people without the Temple. At this juncture we will focus on the character of the *tanna* and priest Rabbi Tzaddok, whom Rabban Yoḥanan sought to evacuate from the besieged city. Before citing the midrash describing his evacuation, we will depict Rabbi Tzaddok's role immediately prior to and during the Temple's destruction.

RABBI TZADDOK: THE PREACHER AT THE GATE

We have already come across Rabbi Tzaddok in the previous section. Following the murder of the priest who overtook his friend running up to the altar, it was Rabbi Tzaddok who stood on the stairs of the Temple courtyard, crying out:

> Hear me, our brothers of the house of Israel! Behold it says: "If one be found slain ... etc., the elders and judges shall come and measure" [Deuteronomy 21:2]. Let us measure to see who must offer the calf: the sanctuary or the courtyard? (Tosefta, *Yoma* 1:12)

Our knowledge of Rabbi Tzaddok is scant,[1] but we know that he was a person of integrity and eminence who could stand in the Temple courtyard and decry the moral depravity of his brothers, the priests. The image of Rabbi Tzaddok standing on steps of the courtyard highlights the stark contrast between what should have been and what was. These were the steps on which the priests were supposed to stand with their hands spread out as they blessed the people in a prayer terminating with the words, "and He shall give you peace." The priestly blessing of divine peace was replaced by Rabbi Tzaddok crying out, "On whose behalf shall we offer the calf?" The calf offering was the responsibility of the spiritual leadership (see Mishna, *Sota* 9:5). Rabbi Tzaddok turned to all of those present, including himself, and challenged them with the terrifying question: "Can any of us say today, 'Absolve your people and do not let guilt for the blood of the innocent remain among your people Israel'?" (ibid.). He shoulders the responsibility that should have been borne by the community elders who saw that blood was shed, knew very well who shed the blood, yet could not say "our hands did not shed this blood."

RABBI TZADDOK AS A SOCIAL REFORMER

The event on the altar was a formative moment in Rabbi Tzaddok's life. He withdrew from a life of involvement in communal affairs and from his position as a leader and halakhic authority (in pre-Destruction years), into a life of ascetic solitude. His son, Rabbi Elazar, relates a number of stories about Rabbi Tzaddok at the peak of his career. He remembers being a little boy riding on his father's shoulders at the Temple Mount, and watching his father rule on halakhic matters related to the Temple.

One of the *aggadot* on the Destruction period also informs us of Rabbi Tzaddok's standing:

> It happened that Miriam the daughter of Nakdimon was awaiting *yibum* [levirate marriage]. She came before Rabbi Tzaddok, who awarded her an allowance of twenty five silver litrae for perfumes

1. On the attempts at identifying him, see Rabbi S. Lieberman, *Tosefta KiFeshuta*, on *Yoma*, pp. 735–736.

> and for food, plus two *se'ah* of wine for meals, on a weekly basis. She said to him: "Award that sum to your own daughters!" When the famine came, starvation caused her hair to fall out, and Rabbi Tzaddok saw her wandering with her father in the market. Her father said: "This is the same Miriam for whom you awarded that amount per week and she cursed you." Rabbi Tzaddok said: "May it befall me if I did not behold her as she was picking barley grains from the dung of cattle, and on seeing her I expounded this Scriptural text as relating to her: 'If you do not know, O fairest of women, go follow the tracks of the sheep' [*Song of Songs*, 1:8]." (*Pesikta Rabati*, 28)

It was Rabbi Tzaddok who fixed the sum of the *ketuba* for a woman awaiting *yibum*. The response of the daughter of one of the richest men in Jerusalem, was one of outrage: "Rule that sum for your own daughters!" meaning, "That's all?!" Rabbi Tzaddok remained silent. Many years passed, and during the Destruction they met again, "when the famine came." The Zealots had already burned all of the storehouses, and the erstwhile wealthy of Jerusalem (those who had not fled in time) were now impoverished; their fate was no different from that of all their starving brothers, if not worse. Rabbi Tzaddok met the same woman, and seeing her in rags greeted her with a withering homily on the verses of Song of Songs, relating them to her current standing: "If you do not know, O fairest of women…" The irony in his response is palpable. The verse relates to the lover giving directions to his beloved: "If your path is unclear, follow the footsteps of the flock." Rabbi Tzaddok is telling her: "Look how disconnected you were from us. When you received prodigious amounts of gold and silver, you abused us. You had no inkling of the economic and mental chasm between yourself and the rest of the nation. For us, the *ketuba* that you regarded as a disgrace was something that we could only conceive of in our dreams. But you could not understand. Now, after all these years of estrangement and aloofness, years in which you had no notion of the people's poverty, "follow in the footsteps of the flock."

It bears note that in the parallel version of the story, the person witnessing the ignominy of Nakdimon's daughter is Rabban Yoḥanan ben Zakkai, who left Jerusalem with his pupils:

> He saw a girl picking barley grains from the dung of Arab cattle. As soon as she saw him, she wrapped herself with her hair and stood before him. "Master," she said to him, "feed me." "My daughter," he asked her, "who are you?" She replied, "I am the daughter of Nakdimon ben Gorion." [...]
>
> She said to him: "Do you remember, Master, when you signed my *ketuba*?" He said to his disciples: "I remember that when I signed her *ketuba* I read therein: 'A million gold *dinarim* from her father's house, besides [the amount] from her father-in-law's house.'" Thereupon Rabban Yoḥanan ben Zakkai wept and said: "How fortunate are Israel; when they do the will of the Omnipresent, no nation nor any language has any power over them, but when they do not do the will of the Omnipresent, he delivers them into the hands of a low people, and not only in the hands of a low people but into the power of the beasts of a low people." [...]
>
> Rabbi Elazar the son of Rabbi Tzaddok said: "May I [not] behold the consolation [of Zion] if I did not see her picking barley grains from the horses' hooves at Acre. [On seeing her plight] I applied to her this Scriptural text: 'If you do not know, O fairest of women, go follow the tracks of the sheep and graze your kids.' Do not read this as 'your kids' [*gediyotayikh*], rather as 'your corpses' [*geviyotayikh*]." (*Ketubot* 66b–67a)

Rabban Yoḥanan saw her gathering grain as one of the most wretched of Jerusalem's poor. Rabbi Tzaddok's son saw her in Acre, where the Jews of Jerusalem were being sold into Roman slavery. Josephus relates that about one hundred thousand Jews were sold from the Judean markets into slavery in Rome, and a slave was one of cheapest commodities. Rabbi Elazar saw her in the slave market, scavenging around for food by the horses' hooves. It triggers his memories of his father's ironic homily on the verse: "If you do not know...," only this time he concludes the homily: "Do not read this as 'your kids,' rather as 'your corpses.'"

The Jerusalem Talmud reports a very similar story about Marta the daughter of Boethus:

> Marta bat Boethus was one of the richest women in Jerusalem. When the sages awarded her two *se'ah* of wine on a daily basis, she cursed and said to them, "award that sum to your own daughters!" Rav Aḥa said: "And we answered *Amen* after her [i.e., we echoed her sentiments]."
>
> Rabbi Elazar ben Tzaddok said: "May I [not] behold the consolation [of Zion] if I did not see her picking barley grains from the horses' hooves at Acre. [On seeing her plight] I applied this Scriptural text to her: 'And she who is the most tender and dainty among you…' [Deuteronomy 28:56], and 'If you do not know, O fairest of women, go follow the tracks of the sheep.'" (Talmud Yerushalmi, *Ketubot* 5:11 [30c])

The verse that Rabbi Elazar ben Tzaddok uses to portray this scene conjures up the memory of how Marta purchased the high priesthood for her husband, Yehoshua ben Gamla, and her request to see him perform the Yom Kippur ritual:

> It is related of Marta bat Boethus, that Yehoshua ben Gamla married her and the king then appointed him to be high priest, after which he consummated [the marriage]. One day she said: "I will go and see how he reads the Torah in the Temple on Yom Kippur." They laid out carpets for her from the door of her house to the entrance to the Temple so that her feet might not be exposed; nevertheless, they were exposed. (*Eikha Raba* 1)

In the Babylonian Talmud's collection of stories about the Destruction, we find the following account of the meeting between Marta bat Boethus and Rabbi Tzaddok:

> Marta bat Boethus was one of the richest women in Jerusalem. She sent her man-servant out saying, "Go and bring me some fine flour." By the time he went it was sold out. He came and told her,

"There is no fine flour, but there is white [flour]." She then said to him, "Go and bring me some." By the time he went he found the white flour sold out. He came and told her, "There is no white flour but there is dark flour." She said to him, "Go and bring me some." By the time he went it was sold out. He returned and said to her, "There is no dark flour, but there is barley flour." She said, "Go and bring me some." By the time he went this was also sold out. She had taken off her shoes, but she said, "I will go out and see if I can find anything to eat." Some dung stuck to her foot and she died. Rabban Yoḥanan ben Zakkai applied to her the verse: "And she who is the most tender and dainty among you, whose foot has never deigned…"

Some say that she ate of Rabbi Tzaddok's dried figs and became sick and died due to her delicacy. For Rabbi Tzaddok observed fasts for forty years in order that Jerusalem might not be destroyed, [and he became so thin that] when he ate anything the food could be seen [as it passed through his throat]. When he wanted to restore himself, they used to bring him a fig, and he used to suck the juice and throw the rest away. When Marta was about to die, she brought out all her gold and silver and threw it in the street, saying, "What is the good of this to me," thus giving effect to the verse, "They shall cast their silver in the streets" [Ezekiel 7:19]. (*Gittin* 56a)

Numerous sources depict the decline of the rich aristocracy into the humiliating depths of abject poverty. These stories also contain reflections on life's wheel of fortune that elevates people on one day and brings them down the next. You were so debased and corrupt that you were incapable of seeing the poverty and indigence that struck every home – until it was your turn to dirty your feet and to grovel in the sewage and the filth.

RABBI TZADDOK LEAVES THE CITY

We noted above how, just before the Destruction, Rabban Yoḥanan ben Zakkai requested to evacuate Rabbi Tzaddok from the city. The following story highlights Rabbi Tzaddok's amazing fortitude:

> [Vespasian] asked [Rabban Yoḥanan]: "Do you have any friend or relative there? Send away and bring him out." He sent and they brought out all of the sages. They looked for Rabbi Tzaddok and could not find him. He sent Rabbi Eliezer and Rabbi Yehoshua to bring out Rabbi Tzaddok. They searched for three days and did not succeed in finding him until they saw him at the city gate. When he arrived, Rabban Yoḥanan stood up in his honor. Vespasian asked him: "You stand up before this emaciated old man?" He answered: "By your life, if there had been just one more like him in Jerusalem, you would never have been able to conquer it." He asked him: "What is the secret of his power?" Rabban Yoḥanan answered: "He eats one fig, and on the strength of it teaches one hundred lessons at the academy." He asked him: "Why is he so emaciated?" Rabban Yoḥanan answered: "Because of his numerous abstinences and fasts." Vespasian sent for physicians who came and fed him small portions of food and drink until he recuperated. (*Eikha Raba* 1:3)

According to this midrash, Rabban Yoḥanan made an unsuccessful attempt to locate Rabbi Tzaddok. Rabbi Tzaddok, however, wanted no part in any of the factions – not Rabban Yoḥanan's group that departed early, and not in a city in which bloodshed is a trivial, routine matter. He chose to sit at the city gates, living in his own tormented world, and attempting to maintain his connection with the Almighty.[2]

Finally, Rabban Yoḥanan's pupils found Rabbi Tzaddok at the city

2. Various historians have attempted to show that Rabbi Tzaddok already appears in connection with the ascendance of the Zealots in the Galilee and their call for a war of liberation. In other words, the claim is that he was closer to the world of the Zealots than to the world of Rabbi Yoḥanan. Josephus (*Antiquities*, XVIII, 3) tells us of Judah of the Golan, from the town of Gamla, who together with Tzaddok the Pharisee incited a rebellion against the procurator's order to conduct a census for taxation purposes. They claimed that the census was a blatant expression of Jewish slavery and exhorted the people to fight for its freedom. According to Josephus, this is an example of the "Fourth Philosophy" which stimulated all of the uprisings at the time, and which terminated in the Temple's destruction. Graetz identified this Tzaddok with Rabbi Tzaddok, but the identification has been challenged by many. See Ben Shalom, *Beit Shammai*, p. 126, n. 5.

gates. The unrelenting leader who conducted the Temple services and castigated the people at the Temple gates had taken a fast upon himself and apparently looked very sick; years of fasting had made him deathly ill. And so Rabbi Tzaddok finds himself between Rabban Yoḥanan and the puzzled gaze of Vespasian. Remarkably, Rabban Yoḥanan had the temerity to claim in the presence of the Roman general that had Jerusalem been blessed with one more person of Rabbi Tzaddok's stature, it would have decided the battle in Jerusalem's favor. Rabbi Tzaddok was a heroic figure, sitting at the city gate with the world upon his shoulders. The tragic reality, though, was that he was alone. There were no others like him, so Jerusalem's fate was sealed, and with a heavy heart Rabbi Tzaddok threw his lot in with Rabban Yoḥanan's group that had set its sights on Yavneh. There is a tendency to forget that Yavneh was a city under Roman rule, and while religious freedom was granted, its residents were still subjects of the Roman emperor. Their status as protected dignitaries did not transform them into free men. Rabbi Tzaddok was evidently sensitive to the fragility of such a situation. Living at the grace and mercy of the Roman authorities was fraught with danger, and he therefore warned his friends not to exploit their scholarly status in order to attain positions and power:

> Rabbi Tzaddok taught: Make it not into a crown with which to aggrandize yourself, nor an axe with which to strike. And thus said Hillel: He who makes use of the crown [of Torah] shall pass away. This is to teach you that he who derives selfish gain from the words of Torah takes his own life away from this world. (*Avot* 4:5)

THE TRAGIC END OF RABBI TZADDOK'S CHILDREN

Rabbi Tzaddok's power also finds expression in his enemies' recognition of his singular stature. *Avot deRabbi Natan* relates that the Romans were deeply aware of Rabbi Tzaddok's standing among the people, and this prompted their attempt to assimilate him into their culture and norms:

> Rabbi Tzaddok was the leader of his generation. When taken captive to Rome, a certain matron took him into her patronage and she sent a beautiful maidservant to him. As soon as he saw

> her he averted his eyes to the wall to avoid looking at her. All night he sat studying. In the morning the maidservant went and complained to her mistress: "I would rather die than be given to this man." The mistress sent for him and asked him: "Why didn't you conduct yourself with this woman as men normally do?" He replied: "What could I do? I am from a family of high priests, a most distinguished family. I thought that if I consummate with her I would proliferate bastards in Israel." When she heard this, she gave orders that he be freed in great honor. (*Avot deRabbi Natan*, recension A, 16)

In other circumstances, this episode might have been regarded as an interesting anecdote. It is clear that Rabbi Tzaddok was no ordinary slave, and even in Roman eyes he was a most venerable personality. In deference to his status, the Romans sought to shower him with the best of lavish treatment. The expression, "a certain matron took him into her patronage," can be interpreted as referring to a rich Roman matron adopting him as her protégé. As a token of respect she grants him a maidservant, but he glues his eyes to the wall. The offended maidservant complains to her mistress and the latter quickly realizes the real greatness of her ward – Rabbi Tzaddok. This wonderful story emphasizes his uniqueness, but its grandeur is eclipsed by the tragedy that befell his two children:

> It is related that the two children of Tzaddok the priest, a boy and a girl, were each taken captive by a different officer. One officer went to a harlot and paid her by giving her the boy [as a slave]. The other went to a storekeeper and paid for wine with the girl, thus fulfilling the verse: "And they have given a boy for a harlot and sold a girl for wine, and they drank" [Joel 4:3]. Some time passed and the harlot brought the boy to the shopkeeper and said to him: "Since I have a boy who is suitable for that girl, will you agree that they should marry and we will divide the offspring between us?" He accepted the offer. They immediately took the two of them and placed them in the same room. The girl began to weep and the boy asked her why she was crying. She responded: "Should I not weep when the daughter of the high priest is given

> in marriage to a slave?" He then asked her: "Whose daughter are you?" She replied, "I am the daughter of Tzaddok the priest." [He continued:] "And where did you live?" She answered: "In the upper market place." He then inquired: "What was the sign above your house?" She told him. He said: "Do you have a brother or sister?" She answered: "I had a brother with a mole upon his shoulder, and whenever he came back from school I would uncover it and kiss it." He asked her: "If you were to see it, would you know it?" She answered that she would. He bared his shoulder and they recognized one another. They embraced and kissed until they expired. Then the Holy Spirit cried out: "For these things I weep." (*Eikha Raba* 1:46)

We are familiar with this tradition from the *kinot* of *Tisha B'Av*, where it is told about the son and daughter of the High Priest Yishmael. In the midrash cited above, it relates to the children of Rabbi Tzaddok. Either way, the Destruction of Jerusalem exposed us to the depravities of an evil nation.

RABBI TZADDOK RECONCILES HIMSELF TO THE DESTRUCTION OF THE TEMPLE

The Sicarii fortified themselves for another four years in the Masada fortress until the Romans besieged them and brought about their collective suicide. The sages, on the other hand, had fortified themselves in their newly established world of Torah in Yavneh, where they blueprinted the foundations of a religious world without a Temple. Rabban Yoḥanan ben Zakkai, who apparently needed Rabbi Tzaddok as a moral compass with the authority to rebuke, asked the emperor to provide medical care for Rabbi Tzaddok. This is how Rabbi Tzaddok joined the Yavneh generation, even as his heart still yearned for Jerusalem. As indicated by the following story of his days in Yavneh, he had yet to come to terms with the Destruction:

> It once happened that Rabbi Eliezer, Rabbi Yehoshua, and Rabbi Tzaddok were reclining at a banquet in honor of Rabban Gamliel's son while Rabban Gamliel was standing over them

> and serving drink. He offered a cup to Rabbi Eliezer who did not accept it. He offered a cup to Rabbi Yehoshua who accepted it. Rabbi Eliezer said to him: "What is this, Yehoshua? We are sitting while Rabban Gamliel is standing over us and serving us drink!" He replied: "We find that even greater than he acted as a waiter; Abraham was the greatest man of his age, as it is written: 'And he stood over them' [Genesis 18:8]. And should you say that they appeared to him as ministering angels – they appeared to him only as Canaanites. So is it not proper for Rabban Gamliel to serve us, and give us drink?"
>
> Rabbi Tzaddok said to them: "For how long will you continue to disregard the honor of the Omnipresent and occupy yourselves with the honor of men?! The Holy One, blessed be He, causes the winds to blow, He causes the clouds to rise, the rain to fall, the earth to yield and He sets a table before every one, and we should not allow Rabban Gamliel to wait upon us and serve drink?" (*Kiddushin* 32b)

The debate between Rabbi Eliezer and Rabbi Yehoshua touches a raw nerve with Rabbi Tzaddok. The sense of routine that emerges from their discussion angers him because, as it were, they "disregard the honor of the Omnipresent and occupy yourselves with the honor of men." Rabbi Tzaddok had not yet settled accounts or resolved his issues with God. He was in pain, and he sought refuge from that pain.

According to another midrash, Rabbi Tzaddok visited the Temple ruins, where a unique corrective experience allayed his doubts:

> Once Rabbi Tzaddok entered the Temple site and saw it in ruins. He exclaimed: "My Father in heaven: You have destroyed Your House and burned Your Temple and then You sat in peace and tranquility!"
>
> Whereupon Rabbi Tzaddok fell asleep and he saw the Holy One, blessed be He, standing and eulogizing, and the ministering angels together with him, exclaiming: "Lo, the faithful and Jerusalem." (*Tanna devei Eliyahu Raba*, 28)

Rabbi Tzaddok becomes aware of the awesome secret that the Destruction is not only his personal loss, or even the national loss of his people. Its dimensions are metaphysical, for God, too, has lost His home in this world. There can be no place for God in a house of bloodshed and groundless hatred. "Lo, the faithful and Jerusalem" – no longer are there men of faith in Jerusalem. The Mishna in *Sota* teaches us that the cessation of prophecy was accompanied by the disappearance of men of faith from Jerusalem, as it says: "The faithful have vanished from among men" (Psalms 12:2).

This *baraita* imparts a similar lesson:

> Jerusalem was not destroyed until the faithful were no longer there, as it says [Jeremiah 5:1]: "Roam the streets of Jerusalem, search its squares, look and take note: you will not find a man; there is none who acts justly, who seeks integrity." (*Ḥagiga* 14a)

GOD MAKES PEACE WITH HIS SONS

The Tosefta (*Berakhot* 3:7) cites a number of prayers said in times of danger. It cites the prayer of Rabbi Eliezer, who says to the Almighty: "May Your will in heaven be done, and do that which is good in Your eyes" (complete acceptance of divine justice). Rabbi Yose's prayer is also included, in which he asks God to listen to the requests of Israel. In the same passage, we then read the prayers of Rabbi Elazar ben Tzaddok and Rabbi Tzaddok himself:

> Rabbi Elazar ben Rabbi Tzaddok said: "Listen to the shouting voice of Your nation Israel and speedily answer their requests. Blessed is He who answers prayer."
>
> Rabbi Elazar ben Rabbi Tzaddok said: "Father would pray briefly on the Sabbath Eve – 'And in Your love, our God, with which You loved Your nation Israel and in Your compassion, our King, with which You had mercy on the members of Your covenant, You have granted us, our God, this awesome and holy seventh day in love.'"

Rabbi Tzaddok's prayer is out of place in the classical format of prayers.

The short prayer is classically recited when confronting danger, in anticipation of salvation, but Rabbi Tzaddok offers a short prayer for the acceptance of Shabbat. Apparently, Rabbi Tzaddok's innovation was that God who is prayed to for salvation from danger is also God who has compassionately conferred His blessing of Shabbat on His people, a blessing that is of equal if not greater relevance in the midst of danger. Tragedy had struck him, his children, Jerusalem, and the entire Jewish people. Yet, despite all these upheavals, he had finally arrived at his day of rest, his Shabbat, and succeeded in reaffirming his life of belief infused with love. The lamentations he had heard in the ruins of Jerusalem restored him to a world of hope. For as long as God continued to weep, there was hope.

Epilogue

Rejuvenation after the Destruction

"THE WATCH"

Rabbinic language contains numerous layers of meaning. The Talmud frequently attempts to uncover the hidden meaning of a word in the Mishna, thereby revealing new understandings of the tannaitic teaching or ruling. This method was utilized in the beginning of Tractate *Berakhot*, in clarifying the meaning of the word "watch." The opening mishna of *Berakhot* cites the view of Rabbi Eliezer, which limits the time for reciting the *Shema* "until the end of the first watch." The Talmud then asks:

> What was Rabbi Eliezer's view? If he contends that the night has three watches, let him say: until the end of the fourth hour. And if he contends that the night has four watches, let him say: until the end of the third hour. (*Berakhot* 3a)

The question seems to be purely technical. In the world of the *tanna'im* and *amora'im,* each period of daylight or darkness was divided into twelve equal hours. Hence the Talmud's question: Why does Rabbi Eliezer burden us with a different definition of time units ("a watch")?

The use of the more familiar hour would have been perfectly adequate. Instead of offering a simple and direct response to the question, the Talmud projects us into heavenly realms: "Indeed, he contends that the night has three watches, but he wants to teach us that there are watches in heaven and there are watches on earth" (ibid.).

The Talmud's understanding is that Rabbi Eliezer did not intend to simply define the end of the time for reciting the *Shema* at night. He wanted to teach us something about the spiritual quality of nighttime. His use of the word "watch" directs the attentive ear to the meeting point of the heavenly and earthly worlds: one watch confronting another watch. Every earthly watch has its corresponding heavenly watch.

How are we to understand the essence of these watches? In the following *baraita*, the Talmud provides the beginnings of an answer, also originating in the teachings of Rabbi Eliezer:

> For it was taught, Rabbi Eliezer says: The night has three watches, and at each watch the Holy One, blessed be He, sits and roars like a lion. For it is written: "The Lord roars from on high, He makes His voice heard from His holy dwelling; He roars aloud over His [earthly] abode." (Jeremiah 25:30)
>
> And the sign of the thing is: In the first watch, the ass brays; in the second, the dogs bark; in the third, the child sucks from the breast of his mother, and the woman talks with her husband.

This is Rabbi Eliezer's description of the heavenly watch and its correspondence to the earthly watch.

Three heavenly watches: all of identical duration. No significance attaches to the transition from one watch to the next and there is no changing of the guard. Divine nighttime progresses at a uniform pace – there are no ups and downs. In the silence of night, the roar of a lion is heard, continuing uninterruptedly for the duration of the watches: "He roars aloud over His [earthly] abode." The *baraita* describes God as one who has lost His home. Though still Master of His "holy dwelling," it cannot replace His earthly abode. The Temple is the home of the entire world, the home of God's revelation on earth. In its absence, God's nights are an anguished roar, piercing the skies on its way to this world.

In contrast to the unending roar echoing in heaven for the length of the each and every night, the nights of this world are divided into three distinct watches. A number of homiletic and Kabbalistic interpretations have been given to the symbolism of the nightly watches of the donkey, the dog, the baby, and the woman. In my view, the nightly watches can be interpreted not as symbols, but as natural descriptions of everyday life.

People work from morning until night. The end of a day's toil is described by a man returning home, tying up his donkey (his vehicle of transport and beast of burden) in its stall and quietly entering his house. The donkey's bray is the final sound, ending the day and heralding the night. This is the transition from the man's daily labor to the tranquility of his home – the routine of the first watch: nightfall and dinner, clearing the room and preparing for sleep; all this occurs against the background of the braying donkey.

In the natural human world (without artificial lighting), nights are for sleeping. When the house is sleeping, the dog's bark, the sound of that universal sentinel, is the only sound to be heard.

At the end of the night, when the members of the house are still sleeping, man and wife wake up and (euphemistically) "talk to one another." The woman talking to her husband and the nursing baby are two wonderful descriptions telling man to awaken himself to a life of love, of birth, and of nurturing.

During the human watches there is no destruction and no anguished roaring over the lost homestead. There is only the transition from the everyday bustle to the sleep of the innocent and to a love-filled awakening.

Rabbi Eliezer creates a sharp contrast between God's roar and man's peace in this world. At the beginning of Tractate *Berakhot,* he reminds us that reading *Shema* at night places us in the realm of the watches. Even as we settle down to sleep at night after a day of work, without considering the lost Temple, the heavens too are settling down for another night of restless roaring and lamenting for the House that was destroyed. Rabbi Eliezer's grasp of the lion's roars during the night watch, introduces us to the conversation between Rabbi Yose and the prophet Eliyahu, cited in the continuation of this Talmudic passage.

RABBI YOSE MEETS ELIYAHU AT THE ENTRANCE OF A RUIN IN JERUSALEM

Rabbi Eliezer's contrast between the divine roar and earthly tranquility can be viewed as a harsh critique. In the post-Destruction world, in which God is unable to sleep, is it possible for us to sleep? Perhaps our daily routine is nothing more than vulgarity and callous insensitivity. This indeed was the conclusion drawn by certain sages who did not wish to let life move on in the aftermath of the Destruction. The Talmud provides the following description of this group:

> Our rabbis taught: When the Temple was destroyed for the second time, there were many in Israel who became ascetics, resolving neither to eat meat nor to drink wine.
>
> Rabbi Yehoshua engaged them and said: "My sons, why do you abstain from meat and wine?" They replied: "Can we eat flesh that used to be brought as an offering on the altar, now that this altar is in abeyance? Can we drink wine which used to be poured as a libation on the altar, but now no longer?"
>
> He said to them: "If that is so, then neither should we eat bread, because the meal offerings have ceased." They said: "[That is so, and] we can manage with fruit."
>
> "Neither should we eat fruit, because there is no longer an offering of first fruits."
>
> "Then we can manage with other fruit."
>
> "But we should not drink water, because there is no longer any ceremony of the pouring of water."
>
> For this they had no answer.
>
> So he said to them: "My sons, listen to me. Not to mourn at all is impossible, because the blow has fallen. To mourn overmuch is also impossible, because we do not impose on the community a hardship which the majority cannot endure..."
>
> The sages therefore ordained the following: A man may plaster his home, but should leave a little bare. How much? Rabbi Yosef says: One square cubit. Rabbi Ḥisda added: it must be opposite the door. A man can prepare a full-course banquet, but he should leave out an item or two... A woman can put on all her

> ornaments, but leave out one or two... for it says [Psalms 137:5–6]: "If I forget you, O Jerusalem, let my right hand forget [its skill]; let my tongue cleave to my palette if I do not remember you, if I do not think of Jerusalem during my chief joy." (*Bava Batra* 60a)

Second Temple scholars have already noted that the conversation between Rabbi Yehoshua and this group of ascetics reflects the tension between the students of Beit Shammai and the students of Rabban Yoḥanan ben Zakkai, founder of the Yavneh academy. With the destruction of the Temple, Beit Shammai's students confronted an ideological crisis that resulted in their exit from the stage of history. The fanatical faith in hastening the messianic process had led them into a terrible crisis. The greater their faith in the Temple, the more difficulty they had in recovering from the disaster of its destruction. They had placed all of their hopes in the success of the revolt, encouraged by their vision of national and religious freedom and the glory of the Temple intact. They were crushed by the rebellion's failure and the reality of humble servitude.[1]

Against the background of the exceptional ascetic group that refused to come to terms with the Destruction of Jerusalem, I wish to study the following story from Tractate *Berakhot*:

> It has been taught, Rabbi Yose said: I was once traveling on the road, and I entered one of the ruins of Jerusalem in order to pray. Eliyahu the prophet appeared and stood guard at the door until I finished my prayer.
>
> After I finished my prayer, he said to me: "Peace unto you, my master!" and I replied: "Peace unto you, my master and teacher!"
>
> And he said to me: "My son, why did you go into this ruin?" I replied: "To pray."
>
> And he said to me: "You ought to have prayed on the road." I replied: "I feared lest passers-by might interrupt me."
>
> He said to me: "You ought to have said a short prayer."

1. See at length in Ben Shalom, *Beit Shammai*, ch. 7, "Beit Shammai after the Destruction."

> Thus I then learned from him three things: One must not go into a ruin; one may say the prayer on the road; and if one does say his prayer on the road, he recites a short prayer.
>
> He further said to me: "My son, what sound did you hear in this ruin?" I replied: "I heard a divine voice, cooing like a dove, and saying, 'Woe to the children, on account of whose sins I destroyed My House and burnt My Temple and exiled them among the nations of the world!'"
>
> He said to me: "By your life and by your head! It does not only make this exclamation now, but three times every day! Moreover, whenever the Jews go into synagogues and study houses and respond, 'May His great name be blessed!' the Holy One, blessed be He, nods His head and says: 'Happy is the King who is thus praised in His house! Woe to the Father who had to banish His children, and woe to the children who had to be banished from the table of their Father.'" (*Berakhot* 3a)

The first part contrasts prayer in a ruin to prayer on the main road. Rabbi Yose was walking along the main road. Fearing interruption from passers-by, he entered a ruin in order to pray. The ruins are the ruins of Jerusalem,[2] which transported Rabbi Yose to a world that was, and to the memories of Temple times.

Rabbi Yose's departure from the main road symbolizes his departure from the dynamic flow of life, the transience and immediacy of which may preoccupy him. He enters a ruin, the antithesis of a road. A person enters a ruin to barricade himself in a closed-off reality that is connected only to the distant past. His world is his memories and his nostalgia, oblivious to the future and present.

In halakhic parlance, the road is the public domain. In the laws of domain on Shabbat, the surface area of a public domain is unlimited,

2. I was told by Yehuda Etzion (in the name of Rabbi Yaakov Medan) that this was not just any demolished building, but rather the "One Demolished Building" – referring to the ruins of the Temple itself. This supports my interpretation of the Aggada, and heightens the tension between Rabbi Yose and Eliyahu.

but only extends to a height of ten *tefaḥim*. Prayer in a public domain is all-inclusive, but its ability to rise to greatness is stunted.

A ruin is defined as a private domain. As the term indicates – it is intended for the private individual. According to its halakhic definition, the private domain extends up to the heavens themselves. There are no limits to the heights a person can reach with the assistance of seclusion and prayer poured out before his Creator. Immersed in his own world, especially in the ruins, which belong to the world of memory and yearnings, the individual can rise to the sublime worlds of spiritual perfection. It induces the desire to bury oneself deep in the ruins, in a sea of memories.

In her anthology of poems *Be Not Far,* Zelda writes:

> Did my longings create the black rose that you gave me in the
> dream
> Or did your longings pierce my dream
> in the form of a flower from the hidden world?
> And why did I suddenly ask you for earrings
> Something I never did when you were in the land of the living?[3]

In Zelda's poem, the rose represents a wholeness created when the source of a person's soul touches the cosmos. It gives expression to a spiritual fullness attainable in this world. Longings may give birth to a rose (even if black). The world of longings elevates a person to spiritual peaks at which he feels things that he would never have dared to feel on the road, in the world of the living. This was the rose that Rabbi Yose was searching for.

Eliyahu teaches him that he should pray on the road, and not for the practical reason that the ruins may collapse. The danger of collapse is a spiritual-psychological one. God forbid a person may wind up living in his yearnings. There are times for cherishing memories in the ruins, but prayer must empower us for the present and the future. As such, it

3. Translation of "Black Rose" by Marcia Falk, in her book of selected translations of Zelda's poems, *The Spectacular Difference* (Cincinnati: Hebrew Union College Press, 2004).

must be linked to the road, to the passers-by and to the public domain. This kind of prayer may lose its spiritual intensity, but it is preferable to pray a short prayer and not to forfeit the public domain.

This was Eliyahu's lesson in halakha to Rabbi Yose, but it invites another question: If yours is the correct path, he asks Eliyahu, then why was I rewarded for my prayer in the ruins? Why did I merit a heavenly voice?

And so follows Eliyahu's second lesson:

> "What exactly did you hear?" he asked him.
>
> "I heard a divine voice, cooing like a dove, and saying, 'Woe to the children, on account of whose sins I destroyed My House and burnt My Temple and exiled them among the nations of the world!'"

All that Rabbi Yose heard was the heavenly response to the rose of his longings: "Or did your longings pierce my dream in the form of a flower from the hidden world?" Listen well, Rabbi Yose, to the yearnings of the heavenly voice. It joins you in lamenting the past. You hear the heavenly voice during the nightly watches. You hear the weeping of the Divine Presence that has lost Her home. This is the heavenly voice that cries "Woe!"

But there is another heavenly voice, making its proclamation three times a day and whenever the Jewish people stand united in the synagogue. When the community of fellow travelers on the road proclaim "May His great name be blessed!" the Holy One, blessed be He, nods His head and says: "Happy is the King."

Pain, too, belongs to the synagogue experience, but the power of prayer does not derive from addiction to the world of nostalgia, rather from proclaiming God's name while walking on the road. This road is far more meaningful, even if no higher than ten *tefaḥim*. Eliyahu's message is that human beings can elevate life. We can sanctify God's name in the land of the living and inspire God Himself to sing "Happy is the King."

About the Author

Rabbi Dr. Binyamin Lau is an Israeli community leader and social activist. He founded Beit Morasha's Moshe Green Beit Midrash for Women, and directs the Beit Morasha Beit Midrash for Social Justice. Rabbi Lau lectures on halakha and social justice at Bar-Ilan University, and serves as Rabbi of the Ramban Synagogue in Jerusalem. He studied at both Har Etzion Yeshiva and Kibbutz HaDati Yeshiva, and received a PhD in Talmud from Bar-Ilan University.

The fonts used in this book are from the Arno family

Other books in *The Sages* series
by Rabbi Dr. Binyamin Lau

Volume II: From Yavneh to the Bar Kokhba Revolt

Volume III: The Galilean Period

Maggid Books
The best of contemporary Jewish thought from
Koren Publishers Jerusalem Ltd.